CONTEMPORARY WALES

Volume 19

Editors

Paul Chaney (Cardiff University)
Jonathan Scourfield (Cardiff University)
Andrew Thompson (University of Glamorgan)

Published on behalf of the Board of Celtic Studies
of the University of Wales

Cardiff
University of Wales Press
2007

www.wales.ac.uk/press

British Library Cataloguing in Publication Data
A catalogue record for this book is available from the British Library.

ISBN 978-0-7083-2110-2
ISSN 0951-4937

Original cover design by Marian Delyth
Cover photograph: © Top Foto
Printed in Great Britain by Cambridge Printing, Cambridge

Contemporary Wales

Volume 19

CONTENTS

THE LIFE COURSE

OTHER ARTICLES

CONTRIBUTORS

Jane Aaron is Professor in Literature in the Department of Humanities and Social Sciences, University of Glamorgan.

Jonathan Bradbury is Lecturer in British Politics at University of Wales Swansea.

Steve Bruce is Professor of Sociology at the University of Aberdeen.

Jane Bryan is Research Associate at the Welsh Economy Research Unit, Cardiff Business School.

Vanessa Burholt is Head of the Centre for Social Policy Research and Development and Co-director of Post-graduate Gerontology at University of Wales, Bangor.

Douglas Caulkins is Wilson Professor of Enterprise and Leadership at Grinnell College, Grinnell, Ia.

Deborah Cook is currently a social researcher working for the Scottish Executive. She was formerly a Ph.D. student at the University of Glamorgan.

Anne Crowley is a policy officer with Save the Children Cymru.

David Dunkerley is Professor of Sociology and Head of the Policy Centre at the University of Glamorgan.

Rebecca Edwards is a currently a Ph.D. candidate in the History Department, University of Wales Swansea

Shane Fudge has recently completed a Ph.D. at the University of Glamorgan.

William Housley is Lecturer at Cardiff School of Social Sciences.

Kerry E. Howell holds the Chair in Governance and Leadership in the Business School at the University of Glamorgan.

Professor Max Munday is Director of the Welsh Economy Research Unit, Cardiff Business School.

Judith Phillips is Professor of Social Work and Gerontology at University of Wales Swansea.

Dr Neil Roche is a member of the Welsh Economy Research Unit, Cardiff Business School.

Molly Scott Cato is Lecturer at the Business School, University of Wales Institute, Cardiff.

Dai Smith holds the Raymond Williams Chair in the Cultural History of Wales at University of Wales Swansea.

Nigel Thomas is Senior Lecturer in Childhood Studies at University of Wales Swansea.

Andrew Thompson is Principal Lecturer and Head of the Field of Society and Culture in the Department of Humanities and Social Sciences, University of Glamorgan.

Jennifer Thornton is an archaeologist with the New Mexico Forest Service.

Carol Trosset is Director of Institutional Research at Hampshire College, Amherst, Mass.

Christopher Williams is Professor of Welsh History at University of Wales Swansea.

Colin H. Williams is Professor in the School of Welsh, Cardiff University.

Glyn Williams is Research Professor at Facultat de Ciencias de la Communicacio, Universidad Ramon Llull, Barcelona.

Howard Williamson is Professor of European Youth Policy at the University of Glamorgan.

Mark Leslie Woods is currently completing his Ph.D. in Film Studies at the University of Glamorgan.

1. OBJECTIVE 1 AND COMMUNITY DEVELOPMENT: DEMOCRATIZING THE ECONOMIC AND POLITICAL LANDSCAPE IN SOUTH WALES?

Shane Fudge

ABSTRACT

This article collates data gained from interviews undertaken during the period 2003–5 with representatives from the European Commission, the National Assembly for Wales, third sector organizations and local government officials involved in the 2000–6 Objective 1 programme in south Wales and the Valleys. While the idea of 'partnership working' has been seen as a particularly innovative development in trying to link regeneration issues into mainstream policy, this article explores some of the qualitative experiences of third sector groups in the community development measures of the programme. The main findings suggest that while there is general consensus that a more 'joined up' approach is the way forward as a democratic forum through which to achieve this, the concept of 'partnership' has not as yet been fully realized for many community groups working at the sharp end of regeneration. In this way, individuals from community organizations based in the south Wales area of the programme talk about their experiences with local authorities on partnership boards and why the dynamics of this relationship are very often perceived as a barrier to the effective input of 'local knowledge' and in addressing many of the issues involved in social exclusion.

INTRODUCTION

The background to this article revolves around the claim that in more recent times, European integration has changed from a top-down endeavour and has moved to recognition of the need for wider consultation and more direct citizen involvement, particularly in market regulation initiatives such as the structural funds. Data drawn from interviews with the European Commission, for example, confirmed that the new multi-level governance agenda seems to be better enabling the EU to adapt to local conditions in regard to improving efficiency and the decision-making procedures that constitute the 'how to' practicalities of regional development. Here it is argued that in programmes such as Objective 1, the incorporation of 'local knowledge' into formal structures of governance is the most effective way through which to aid regeneration in socially and economically marginalized communities. Commenting on rhetoric from both the European Commission and the Welsh Assembly Government on some of the principal aims behind the 2000–6 Objective 1 programme, Royles points out that:

> More than any other sector perhaps, it was civil society organisations that were to be the main beneficiaries of this new dawn. Given the immense practical and symbolic importance of the Objective 1 programme for West Wales and the Valleys, the extent of civil society involvement in the programme provides a good test of the degree to which the rhetoric is reflected in reality. (Royles, 2004, p. 101)

This article examines these claims through interviews drawn principally from the third sector and with those groups and organizations that have engaged in some way with the community development measures – Priority 3 and Priority 4 – of the Objective 1 programme.

While many of the groups directly involved in community regeneration have been successful in obtaining funding and providing projects in the relevant areas of the 2000–6 programme, as the Wales Council for Voluntary Action have pointed out, 'despite millions of pounds worth of Objective 1 funding reaching voluntary organizations in Wales, research has revealed that there are still barriers preventing the scheme from being a complete success' (WCVA, 2003). Problems that have been identified as hindering effective engagement from the community level have included the levels of the bureaucracy involved in the process and, relatedly, the problems that are involved in building capacity in socially and economically marginalized communities.

AIM OF THE ANALYSIS

The particular aim of the following discussion is to compare policy discourse on the benefits of the greater emphasis that has been placed on partnership working in the 2000–6 Objective 1 programme in Wales with the experiences of community organizations who have engaged in the process. Some of the issues explored include:

- how community groups and organizations have experienced 'partnership working' in the new programme;
- what new channels of engagement have been opened up for third sector community groups within the new emphasis on partnership;
- the extent to which 'partnership working' has provided more of a democratic platform through which to facilitate the needs of third sector groups participating in the community regeneration measures of the programme;
- whether 'local knowledge' – by way of what community organizations deem to be the salient social issues in regeneration targeted communities – are being assimilated by the new political structures.

BACKGROUND TO THE 2000–6 WALES OBJECTIVE 1 PROGRAMME

The European structural funds are designed to tackle regional disparities in social and economic development across the EU. In line with the aims of what has become known as the 'European social model', the primary aim of the structural funds is to provide funding in order to facilitate GDP convergence between the richer and the poorer regions in the EU 25. The funds themselves consist of the following three policy instruments:

- *Objective 1.* To promote the development and structural adjustment of regions whose development is lagging behind. Regions covered by Objective 1 are those where per capita GDP is less than 75 per cent of the EU average. A total of 69.7 per cent of the structural funds is allocated to Objective 1;
- *Objective 2.* To support the economic and social conversion of areas facing structural difficulties. Among areas covered are those undergoing socio-economic change in the industrial and service sectors, declining urban and rural areas, and depressed areas dependent on fisheries. A total of 11.5 per cent of the structural funds is allocated to this objective;
- *Objective 3.* To support the adaptation and modernization of policies and systems of education, training and employment. This objective provides for formal assistance outside the areas covered by Objectives 1 and 2. A total of 12.3 per cent of the structural funds is allocated to the Objective. (Nugent, 2003, pp. 312–13)

While Wales has been the beneficiary of different forms of European funding provision from as far back as the late 1970s, it has been argued that the opportunities presented by the arrival of Objective 1 in Wales are somewhat unique. Criticisms of the previous 1994–9 Objective 2 programme concerned accusations that funding and decision-making tended to converge around the 'usual suspects' – notably the Welsh Development Agency and the local authorities – with the Welsh Office being complicit in an economic strategy that was inherently inefficient and unaccountable. However, as Bachtler points out, prior to the arrival of Objective 1, 'there was much more extensive consultation with partners and wider groups and organizations during the preparation of the Single Programming Document' (2003, p. 35). Aligned to complement the National Assembly for Wales's own subsequent economic blueprint *A Winning Wales* (NAW, 2001), the 2000–6 Objective 1 programme has been based principally upon strategic collaboration between ten thematically based *regional* partnerships and fifteen geographically based *local* partnerships. These are augmented by a further four *strategy* partnerships. This more joined-up approach has been regarded as holding the potential to be particularly innovative to the newly introduced community regeneration measures whereby a more direct involvement of the groups and organizations who hold 'local knowledge' on issues such as poverty and social exclusion is thought to hold the potential for a more effective problem solving strategy than previous 'top-down' policy approaches.

The thirty-four interviews that formed the basis for this research were conducted on a semi-structured basis and were designed to facilitate an inductive approach to exploring the form and dynamics of the partnership structure that has evolved subsequent to the final form that was decided for the Single Programming Document (SPD). While partnership working has sometimes been adopted as a 'catch-all' approach and has very often been seen as something of a panacea to the problems involved in social and economic regeneration, the aim here was to obtain a perspective from third sector community organizations: groups who were intended to be some of the principal beneficiaries of this new way of working. As argued above, the partnership structure has been a new and, not unexpectedly, a fairly amorphous political process. While the three-thirds arrangement agreed upon in the preliminary negotiations for the SPD is intended to be a reflection of the public/private/voluntary composition, many of the roles and duties of the 'partners' have changed and adjusted as the process of tailoring procedures to the requirements of the programme has been adapted over time. Benfield (2003) argues that this has been a particular concern for community and voluntary organizations however, where participants have very often been confused over partnership roles and responsibilities and, subsequently, their place in the administrative structure.

The qualitative research design was also intended to provide a counter argument to the predominantly output driven impetus behind Objective 1 as an example of the turn towards 'evidence-based policy-making' (Bristow, 2005:

p. 14). Thus, while successful projects for Priority 3 are systematically catalogued on the Wales European Funding Office (WEFO) website alongside continuous updates on the financial figures for the programme measures, there is a case for arguing that this does not tell the whole story. As Boland (2005) has argued, there needs to be a greater acknowledgement of the 'civic' as opposed to the 'political' interpretation of the way in which Objective 1 has been implemented where policy-makers must be more prepared to listen to criticisms of the programme, much of which, as Boland points out, has come from the 'civic' voice of the third sector. Simply interpreting the 'political narrative' by way of outputs and targets gathered by official sources may well be misleading in regard to judging the effectiveness of the 'grassroots' reach of the programme, as Boland's (2000) research into the local implementation of the 1994–9 Merseyside Objective 1 programme flags up.

PARTNERSHIP AND OBJECTIVE 1: 'NEW GOVERNANCE' FOR REGENERATION IN WEST WALES AND THE VALLEYS?

As Benfield argues: 'the Objective 1 partnerships are the cornerstones of the process and are quite clearly the way forward, not just for Objective 1, but also for other initiatives and schemes in Wales also' (2003, p. 49). He adds a cautionary note, however, pointing out that, although based upon the three-thirds principle – where the public/private/voluntary split must be present at all levels of the partnership structure – 'these partnerships must be *true* partnerships where everyone has an equal say and is able to make a valid contribution' (2003, p. 49). The true test as to whether this way of working is 'happening' for the community development measures for example, would quite clearly seem to be how much involvement and input can be discerned from the third sector alongside the views and issues that they correspond to. This interviewee from the Objective 1 Monitoring Committee pointed to the importance of 'partnership' in enabling these aims:

What we wanted to achieve was a sustained commitment, growth and culture change in terms of partnership. And that was greatly influenced by *how* we used the money; not just what we used it for. Objective 1 finishes soon and hopefully the change in culture and in the way we work will be a little more 'bottom up' and a little less of the 'top down' and far, far more partnership working in Wales. (Objective 1 Monitoring Committee interview, 17 October 2003)

Changing the dynamics of the existing political culture was as important as the money involved in the programme itself he argued. In particular, he pointed to the role of local authorities – organizations that had been criticized for playing a part in monopolizing EU funds in previous programmes – who had developed in part through a very strong culture of central control and delivery. One of the aims of the Objective 1 partnership strategy was that they now needed to be made aware that they no longer had a monopoly over public service delivery, particularly in areas such as community development where relevant groups and organizations often provide greater expertise and know-how as to what is needed in the way of service provision.

Some local authorities had themselves taken the lead in pushing a more inclusive, partnership approach to service delivery prior to Objective 1. Changes in geographical boundaries and activities initiated by the Local Government (Wales) Act in 1994 had begun a breakdown in the traditional dichotomy that had 'insulated' the roles of local councils from other potential service providers. Evidence of a closer working relationship between the local authority and third sector organizations has now become evident in some Objective 1 areas where there have been changes such as the growth of 'community resource teams'. This interviewee from one such team saw this as a significant change, particularly in regard to facilitating effective community development:

> From my perspective, the management of the parts of the programme that relate to community regeneration have really been led by community organizations. I think the current programme period really has made a difference and I don't know how much you can put that down to EU level policy, it's difficult to say; but I think that certainly for us it was very helpful. (Community resources manager interview, 3 March 2004)

Other interviewees pointed to the higher profiles and partnership roles that were now being adopted by the County Voluntary Councils (CVCs) in providing a more effective channel for community groups to access funding:

> There was always a problem with community development and how you stop the top-down approach. They do it differently according to how each authority has evolved. It's certainly not like it used to be which was a bunch of councillors doing it . . . the idea is that it now comes from the community. (CVC interview, 15 July 2004)

Clearly, the new Objective 1 partnership structure has helped to facilitate a variety of ways through which the third sector is able to engage more effectively in community development. Organizations such as the WCVA, as an umbrella representative for the third sector, have also gained a higher profile and a more active political role in this situation. The WCVA plays a central role in providing a bridge between civil society and formal political structures.

OBJECTIVE 1, PARTNERSHIP AND COMMUNITY DEVELOPMENT: REACHING THE 'GRASSROOTS'?

This section looks at some of the first-hand experiences of community groups within the new partnership arrangement. It will consider whether partners that have been involved from community organizations feel that they have been heard and have been able to make a contribution to the programme by way of issues they address and consider to be important to community development in their areas. While there are undoubtedly greater points of contact and a rhetorical awareness of the importance of local knowledge and grassroots community input, do these groups and organizations feel that they are able to provide adequate input to the programme?

This interviewee, employed by an organization working closely with socially excluded individuals and groups in that area, was ideally placed to compare differences and similarities between Objective 1 and older programmes as her organization had accessed money and delivered projects in both. She argued that the new way of working had been invaluable in helping her organization to be more effective in accessing money under both the Priority 3 and Priority 4 measures:

Objective 1 has come in, what has happened is it has broadened the way we can access funds if you like. We have topics that we can access funds under and there is a community priority now which means we can go in on that. (Community group interview, 2 February 2004)

The new programme had also been important in enabling this group to becoming more established and more influential in addressing social exclusion in that particular community:

When we started as a small group we didn't have the capacity to deliver or monitor an Objective 1 bid but over the course of a three year period we were in a good position to be able to do so. It was important for us to do that so that then we could be in a position to be able to control and deliver to the community. (Community group interview, 2 February 2004)

The advantages of this new way of working are apparent from these interviews where the potential benefits for the community regeneration parts of the programme were summed up by this CVC official:

There are lots of community projects that have got very, very good ideas. They've got the commitment and it's projects that will make a difference in the community. But a lot of community groups haven't got sufficient capacity really to deal with all of the administration. If we can assist in this way and to access European funding, then groups become more confident in the way that their organization is set up with things like advice on policies and procedures. That will build their capacities sufficiently. (CVC interview, 15 July 2004)

This was not a view that was shared by all. This interviewee representing one of the more successful community organizations in terms of accessing European money and influencing partnership boards had this to say when asked about the impacts that grassroots, community projects had been able to achieve in general and what he felt had been the overall contribution of the third sector to the regeneration parts of the programme:

What I would be wary of is that you are going to say 'here it is, Objective 1 worked'; but it hasn't necessarily. Like I said, all this could fall down if they don't get their heads right and say 'hang on a minute, we can't just do little bits of funding here and there'. (Community group interview, 20 October 2004)

The next section looks at what some of the problems have been for community organizations in influencing the partnership structures and accessing money for regeneration projects. It looks in particular at criticisms that have been made of some of the local authorities on the partnerships, considering the observation of Geddes and Benington (2001, p. 12) and their argument that: 'at the local level, the emergence of horizontal partnership between different actors depends on the structures of power and the way in which it is exercised'.

MANAGING THE AGENDA? LOCAL AUTHORITIES AND PARTNERSHIP WORKING

Some interviewees were less than impressed with the 'new' way of working and remained sceptical as to any great changes that could be discerned, particularly for community groups. Some interviewees felt that the greater emphasis on partnership collaboration had simply meant that newer exclusionary measures were restricting access for many groups. One interviewee observed that there was now a noticeable level of rivalry within the new partnerships reflecting, he felt, the increased emphasis on competition that is now apparent in contemporary public service delivery. He pointed out that, very often, partnerships seemed to be marked by antagonism rather than trust, mutuality and cooperation:

It's the local authorities that are the level of bureaucracy and I can't understand why the National Assembly are still feeding through to the local authorities – why can't they meet and deal with the communities directly and engage with the necessary dialogue at this level? (Community group interview, 3 June 2004)

The interviewee felt that, in many cases, local authorities noticeably had their own political agenda and could not always be counted on to take a supportive role in encouraging the activities of community groups. The next interviewee illustrated this point in regard to their own community written action plan which, according to the recommendations in this part of the programme, must be drawn up in consultation with relevant community organizations:

We had a draft of the local authority community plan through the post and they said 'give us your thoughts'. And I sent it back and said 'you've already developed . . . you already know your thoughts. You haven't asked us as a community'. There were no questions for us to ask, it had already been formulated. I think that it was just so that they could say that they had consulted us. And we are like 'that's not consultation, that's not participation'. (Community group interview, 17 March 2004)

This organization had done their own research into the particular regeneration issues in their community with the intention of consulting with the local authority on an *equal basis* to deliver a joint action plan. However, the local authority had already drafted its own action plan for the area. Democratic consultation with the community did not happen. As she argued: 'it's like them trying to impose their vision on the people here and it doesn't meet our needs'

(Community group interview, 17 March 2004). This interviewee felt that there had merely been a 'tokenistic' consultation with their organization. 'Partnership' had quite clearly been driven by the agenda of the local authority and consultation had in effect taken place *after* the real decisions – the ones that would ultimately impact on funding decisions – had already been made.

This community regeneration worker who was interviewed also pointed to the significance of the undue influence of local authorities in some areas of the programme, a process that invariably tended to occur in tandem with a lack of influence from grassroots community organizations:

> It's been very top-down so far in its implementation. It still means that those old prejudices and ideas which exist within the insider mentality of the local authorities are passed down into those partnerships. And it just gives that kind of double prejudice that people in communities have to work against. Idealistically, the idea of partnership does increase participation but in reality, and the pragmatic sense, it doesn't always manage to do that. There are examples where it does, but those are few and far between at the moment. (Community regeneration worker interview, 15 December 2003)

She pointed out that it was quite clear in many areas that local authority dominance was driving the Objective 1 programme and, in many cases, excluding effective input from community organizations:

> There is no validation process to looking at how these partnership boards are constructed and how they actually operate. Building a good partnership takes about ten years. Very often, I think these partnerships are hijacked by people who have professional backgrounds and also local authority members. I think community people need empowering to be able to join in on these committees and to get their voices heard. (Community regeneration worker interview, 15 December 2003)

This interviewee from the Objective 1 Monitoring Committee pointed out that it is useful to look at the changing role of the local authority in more recent years in order to see how the local political culture can shape the way in which regeneration initiatives play out in reality. The use of 'political strategies' in the face of increased 'competition' for services has now become more of an issue than that of cooperation he argues. In the face of the delivery and the increased validation of services, some local authorities are trying to control the agenda and the extent to which community involvement may ultimately pose a threat to the way in which services have been traditionally delivered:

They say 'we are best placed to do this because we are the democratically elected representatives of the people. Who are you to come in and do this? Who are you accountable to?' It is a strong argument and that creates a culture that is a block to real grassroots community development and capacity building. (Objective 1 Monitoring Committee interview, 17 October 2003)

The issue of who drives the agenda, and in what context that agenda takes place, was flagged up as a very important issue. Rather than being equal partners with community groups in a more *equal* approach to revitalizing marginalized communities, many local authorities are seen by these groups as constituting a direct hindrance in being able to access funding and a barrier to the development of effective grassroots, community projects. A few interviewees actually felt, for instance, that many of the projects that had come out of the Priority 3 measures, where the lead body has been the local authority, were simply developed as an alternative funding stream. The issues involved in these projects were pointed out very clearly by this community volunteer when asked whether he thought that there were any differences in Priority 3 projects that were led principally by local authorities and those that were led by community organizations:

No, it's just an alternative funding stream for them. I honestly know this. They just use that as an avenue to underpin a lot of their services. They will say 'well this project is coming through and it's gonna be this . . . and this' . . . well I know that 'that, and that' already exists but that that funding stream is due to run out. So what they do is change the names of the officers and just apply for that money. (Voluntary sector interview, 20 October 2004)

This CVC interviewee had this to say about the difficulties faced by community organizations, many of whom were now working in a more direct way with local authorities in the new partnership arrangement:

I think it's a double edged sword really because it's obvious that the voluntary sector is not benefiting as much as it should be doing and the local authorities are because they've got the resources etc . . . well they've got a European department haven't they, most of the local authorities? (CVC interview, 15 July 2004)

As the above interviewee stressed, this new relationship has brought its own double bind for community organizations in scenarios where they are very often reliant upon the 'expertise' of local authorities to keep them 'in the loop' of the funding process. This can mean that a strong presence from the local authority on the partnership board may mean there is very often a 'tokenistic' consultation and that input from community groups – by way of dialogue and grassroots projects – is ultimately 'cosmetic' in real terms. As this interviewee argued:

> It's about whether it is a lip service thing really isn't it? The community have been consulted to death and if they don't see any results of that consultation then it's just going to alienate them even more. That was the idea with some of the European money, to have some quick wins so that people could see a difference, see what difference Europe is making. Because that is the way that you get communities energized and you can only get regeneration if communities are energized. (Community group interview, 17 May 2004)

As Misztal (2000, p. 9) points out, while the emphasis on partnership, particularly in addressing issues of regeneration and social exclusion, assumes a degree of 'trust' 'we need to look beyond blind faith in trust and check the accountability, transparency and goals of reciprocal networks'. This has been an argument put forward by Taylor (2003, p. 56) who argues that networks, such as those characteristic of partnership working, are almost always invariably 'private and opaque rather than public and transparent'. In this way she argues that these networks of association can be implicit in creating a particular set of norms where the more 'informal' processes that lubricate the internal dynamics of partnership working may promote 'activities which take on an aura of normality and members come to be protected from external sanctions' (2003, p. 56). Thus, in this case, some local authorities are able to exert greater influence on proceedings even within a supposedly democratic partnership structure. This influence can serve to exclude the supposedly 'weaker' members of these arrangements. Thus, as Blaug argues:

> It is often assumed that representative democracy will be strengthened by participatory democracy, yet time and again we are unable to locate and motivate the active citizens required by our designs and often these political reforms fail to impact upon entrenched inequalities; merely offering easier access to carefully controlled spaces in which to sanction elites. (Blaug, 2002, p. 103)

THE ROLE OF COMMUNITY DEVELOPMENT PROGRAMMES IN 'RAISING CONSCIOUSNESS'

Despite these criticisms, almost all interviewees suggested that the emphasis on partnership driven by the programme is still the best way forward to widening participation and in trying to address the social and economic problems that brought the Objective 1 programme to Wales in the first place. Another community regeneration worker who was interviewed argued, for instance, that one of the *informal* effects of the 2000–6 programme has been to 'raise consciousness' and to increase awareness of the kinds of local political issues that have been pointed out in this article:

> I always say that it's gonna take five years to unstitch the old municipal model and come down to the community centred model. By municipal model I mean that communities get things done to them by a range of statutory agencies within a legislative framework determined by the central state. There is a sense in which things like Communities First and New Deal for Communities have opened a kind of a Pandora's box of community activity that you can't put the lid back on but will run through to its logical conclusion, which is much more control for local communities. (Community regeneration worker interview, 3 February 2004)

He suggested that the programming aspect of the Objective 1 programme has played a part in informing a process whereby community groups will get to play an increasing role in changing the local political culture as part of an informal process of capacity building:

> I mean, obviously there is a formal process where, you know, community members can now sit on regeneration partnerships. What many communities lack of course are the informed and confident members to sit on those partnerships as equals and feel strong enough to exert their role and that . . . there is a consciousness raising process there and it's a capacity development process as well: it's getting people to that position as quickly as you can. And, you know, loads have. (Community regeneration worker interview, 3 February 2004)

To a certain extent, the need to promote 'indirect' or 'softer' measures, which may aid these kinds of developments in future programmes, has been acknowledged in the Mid-term Evaluations. Recommendations on future community development measures in 2005's Final Evaluation Report for instance have included: the need to recognize more of a balance between economic and social goals; a greater awareness of the need to identify and quantify softer as opposed to direct outcomes; and a much greater alignment between Objective 1 and the local Communities First programme, with its more realistic, longer term capacity building element (pp. 191–6). As with previous evaluations, however, there remains no mention of the kinds of political issues addressed in this article.

CONCLUSION

While rhetoric from the European Commission and from the Welsh Assembly Government has stressed the importance of involving 'local knowledge' and expertise from the third sector in the West Wales and the Valleys Objective 1 programme, this has not been a process without difficulties. The bureaucratic design of the programme and an awareness of the time-span involved in building capacity in economically and socially marginalized communities have both been acknowledged as being problematic to the successful incorporation of 'local knowledge' to the community development measures of the programme. However, this article suggests that while the development of the new partnership structure has been able to stimulate greater points of access and a greater voice for many third sector organizations, local political cultures remain entrenched in some areas, mitigating against the full participation of these groups, alongside the 'grassroots' regeneration expertise which they may hold.

While some of the partnership process may be currently influenced by these kinds of local politics, it was pointed out however that there is a 'consciousness raising' process occurring whereby more *informal* processes have now been set in motion. In this way, the 'partnership strategy' of Objective 1 is starting to bring previously embedded political cultures into wider awareness; opening up and challenging the previously 'zero-sum' approach of decision-making hierarchies and public service delivery mechanisms.

REFERENCES

Bachtler, J. (2003). 'Objective 1: a comparative assessment', *Contemporary Wales*, 15, 30–40.
Benfield, G. (2003). 'A voluntary sector perspective on European programmes 2000–2006', *Contemporary Wales*, 15, 45–50.
Blaug, R. (2002). 'Engineering democracy', *Political Studies*, 50, 1, 102–16.
Boland, P. (2000). 'Urban governance and economic development: a critique of Merseyside and Objective 1 Status', *European Urban and Regional Studies*, 7, 3, 211–22.
Boland, P. (2005). 'An assessment of the Objective 1 Programme in Wales, 1999–2003', *Contemporary Wales*, 18, 66–78.
Bristow, G. (2005). 'Everyone's a "winner": problematising the discourse of regional competitiveness', *Journal of Economic Geography*, 5, 3, 285–304.
Geddes, M. and Benington, J. (eds) (2001). *Local Partnerships and Social Exclusion in the European Union: New Forms of Local Social Governance?* London: Routledge.
Mid-term Evaluation Update for the 2000–2006 Objective 1 Programme Final Report (2005), *www.wefo.wales.gov.uk/resource/2005-12-23-01-MTEU-Final-Report6568.pdf.*
Misztal, B. (2000). *Informality: Social Theory and Contemporary Practice*, London: Routledge.

National Assembly for Wales (NAW) (2001). *A Winning Wales: The National Economic Development Strategy of the Welsh Assembly Government*, Cardiff: NAW. *www.wales. gov.uk/themesbudgetandstrategic/content/neds/index.html.*

Nugent, N. (2003). *The Government and Politics of the European Union (5th Edition)*, London: Palgrave.

Royles, E. (2004). 'Civil society and Objective 1', *Contemporary Wales*, 16, 101–21.

Taylor, M. (2003). *Public Policy in the Community*, New York: Palgrave MacMillan.

Wales Council for Voluntary Action (2003). Press release: research reveals barriers to complete Objective 1 success (7 July 2003). *www.wcva.org.uk/content/all/ dsp_text. cfm?0=0&display_sitetextid=1005.*

2. WALES AND THE EUROPEAN CONVENTION: ANY SCOPE FOR CIVIL SOCIETY?

Deborah Cook

ABSTRACT

This article draws on empirical research on civil society groups and policy-makers in Wales to explore the involvement/non-involvement of these civil society groups in the Convention on the Future of Europe.[1] It is argued that an exploration of civil society involvement in the Convention firstly provides an opportunity to assess the extent to which inclusive politics occurs in the arena of high politics. Secondly, this investigation further helps in gauging the Convention's success in reconnecting citizens with the European Union on the ground. Overall, the nature of the studied groups' participation tended to be one-off, indirect and concentrated among a few group members, with groups mainly acting as an audience to the Convention rather than full participants. Factors explaining this limited involvement include the power/autonomy of the different institutional actors in the process, the lack of formal opportunities, the European institutional conception of civil society and the presence of other issues and media coverage. However, disparities of involvement among the groups seem to rely on actor specific concerns such as levels of awareness, resources, communication and internal devolution structures. Inclusive politics in this instance was limited by a lack of Welsh autonomy due to the limited formal opportunities for the Assembly, together with 'supply side' civil society concerns. Finally, limited civil society involvement means that the Convention failed to link with citizens on the ground.

INTRODUCTION

Wales' involvement with Europe does not begin and end with the Assembly.

(Clifford, 2002, p. 44)

One of the arguments cited for devolution was that it would give Wales a stronger and more active voice in Europe (Bulmer et al., 2002, p. 146). Whilst there is some analysis of the devolved administration's European Union (EU) affairs[2], the EU activities of devolution's beneficiaries – civil society in Wales – remain largely unknown (for exception, see Royles, 2004). Exploring the involvement in EU policy issues by civil society in Wales is important because of the onus placed on civil society participation both by the Assembly and more recently by some of the EU's institutions (for example in the European Commission's European Governance White Paper, 2001). This article seeks to give insight into civil society–EU dynamics by looking at their interaction in the context of the Convention.

In light of the failure of the Nice Inter-governmental Conference (IGC) to reform a cumbersome EU structure in the face of EU enlargement, the 2001 Laeken Council decided to convene a Convention. Over the course of a year the Convention would consider the EU's future role, reforms to the EU and offer some reform options. In the process of its deliberations, it was hoped that the Convention could help tackle the EU's 'democratic deficit' and reconnect the EU with its citizens. Civil society provides one such 'communications interface' connecting the citizen and the EU (Editorial Team, 2002, p. 3). It should be noted the Laeken Declaration did not view an EU constitution as a given Convention output, but rather saw the Convention as a vehicle to investigate the possibility (Regan et al., 2003, p. 15). In the end, the Convention drafted a Constitution, a large part of which made its way into the final constitutional treaty agreed at the Brussels European Council in 2004. Civil society participation in the Convention was also important to help legitimize the constitutional treaty because some positive constitutional perspectives believe a constitution must come from the people: 'A proper constitution should not, according to democratic criteria, be made unless it has been mandated by the people and been subjected to public debate and ratified through proper legitimate processes subjected to judicial review' (Eriksen, 2004, p. 35).

To explore this phenomenon the article will draw upon semi-structured interviews with civil society organizations and policy-makers, documents, news-papers and academic literature. In order to analyse EU–civil society dynamics, the concept of civil society and the background on civil society in Wales and EU policy-making must first be detailed. Secondly, general Convention–civil society relations shall be discussed to highlight the constraints and oppor-tunities presented to civil society by the Convention. This is supplemented by a review of Convention activity in Wales to explore how the Welsh context may have shaped civil society involvement. In relation to this context, the empirical findings on the participation in the Convention by the studied civil society groups in Wales will be outlined. This will demonstrate that the role of civil society in Wales in the Convention was limited due to a number of structural and actor specific factors. This suggests that the Convention failed to reconnect with its citizens through civil society at the regional level. Moreover, it appears that inclusive politics with the Assembly may have been a little wanting due to power and formal constraints and an uncertain role in the Convention process.

CIVIL SOCIETY, WALES AND EUROPEAN UNION POLICY-MAKING

Defining 'civil society' is by no means a settled matter. Currently there is a consensus of sorts, particularly in empirical studies, which Anheier (2004, p. 20) evokes: that civil society is not state, nor economic and usually not familial. Instead, civil society is the space of independent self-organizing citizens (Beetham et al., 2002: 208). This article shall use this conception of civil society, whilst admitting that in practice the boundaries of the state, economy and family overlap with civil society. Specifically, civil society will be explored through civil society organizations (CSOs) as sites of possible interaction. The EU has its own conception of civil society, which is similarly focused largely on organizational components (see ECOSOC, 1999), however the ECOSOC initially employs a very broad definition: 'Civil society is a collective term for all types of collective actions, by individuals and groups that do not emanate from the state and are not run by it' (ECOSOC, 1999, p. 5).

As argued elsewhere (Goehring, 2002; Cook, 2006), the definition of civil society by political institutions in turn helps to shape civil society's role in the policy-making process by setting the parameters of who in civil society can legitimately and practically participate in the process. Significantly for this discussion both of the key institutions in shaping the EU's understanding of civil society – the European Economic and Social Committee (ECOSOC) and the European Commission – elevate *European* civil society (or Euro-groups) (see European Commission, 2001, p. 15), which is defined as groups having a presence in at least three Member States at the European level.

Prior to devolution, civil society in Wales was said to be weak and lacking the political institutions arguably needed to sustain it (Drakeford, 2006). It was hoped that devolution would help to cultivate a civic culture and buoy civil society (Day, Dunkerley and Thompson, 2000, p. 25). Indeed, Osmond (2003, p. xxvii) claims that post-devolution a *Welsh* civil society is emerging. Moreover, civil society is viewed as an essential component for a democracy (see discussion of this in Pietrzyk, 2003). The Assembly needed to engage with civil society in its work to foster its legitimacy. However, Chaney and Fevre (2001) perceived inclusiveness at the Assembly's start as mixed.

The matter of civil society engagement is even more precarious in the field of EU policy-making, as EU matters are reserved powers to the UK government, and at the same time affects many of the Assembly's competencies. The Assembly has very little legal power, being extremely dependent on the UK government to involve it in EU discussions[3]. As Meyer (2003, pp. 23–4) points out, a strong degree of nesting (i.e. high integration in other institutional contexts) not only decreases the Assembly's potential for innovation, but also reduces civil society's ability to press competing claims to the Assembly as it will be less open to alternative views.

Despite this limited role, the Assembly has evoked the 'one-thirds' principle of partnership, as it includes the public, private and voluntary/community sectors in EU structural funds programmes and monitoring committees (Royles, 2003). Thus, civil society in Wales is heavily involved in this area of EU policy-making. The importance of structural funding is indicated by the Wales European Forum (WEF – where public, private and voluntary sector representatives meet), being specially reconvened to prepare for the European Structural Funding post-2006 as part of the 'all-Wales' or 'team Wales' approach to EU policy issues. Moreover, the Assembly has also made efforts to include some of civil society in crosscutting European issues through forums, such as a preparation committee for the Euro and an enlargement-working group. A further emphasis on partnership working was notable via the Wales European Centre (WEC) in Brussels, looking after the European interests of a collection of mainly Assembly sponsored bodies (many of which are to be burnt in the quango bonfire), universities and some large voluntary groups.[4] Thus, the Assembly has made efforts to include civil society organizations, albeit a small section of largely Wales-wide and profes-sionalized groups in EU policy issues and in EU policy-making (although the type of groups involved may also reflect that they are the only groups able/willing to engage on these issues). The importance of the Assembly in facilitating civil society in Wales' involvement in EU policy-making is further warranted by research that suggests the Assembly is the key political institution by which civil society groups in Wales participate in EU policy-making (Cook, 2006) Thus, the role of the Assembly in the Convention must be examined to see what scope it had as conduit for and generator of CSOs' Convention participation. However, much of the Assembly's role depends on the nature and procedures of the EU policy at hand, and is constrained by the legal and formal parameters. Therefore, we must turn to the Convention's procedures and structures to see the opportunities it presented to civil society and for Welsh political institutions.

THE CONVENTION

The Convention was different from both IGCs and ordinary EU policy-making in terms of its broad mandate, long duration, composition and process. It brought together the usual cast of government ministers but also European Parliamentarians, national parliamentarians and two Commission officials. There were observers from the social partners, Committee of the Regions, ECOSOC and the European Ombudsman. It was led by a presidency of three, who were part of a praesidium that gave impetus to the Convention.

The presidency set the agenda by implicitly calling on the Convention to try to produce a final constitutional text. The Convention was to work on the method of consensus[5] (The European Convention, 2002a, p. 4), to encourage conventioneers to transcend their sectional interests, and to reason and deliberate with each other rather than bargain. President d'Estaing also stipulated that there would be three phases to the Convention's work: the listening phase, which ended in June 2002; the study phase, which finished in December 2002; and the reflection phase, which ran from January 2003 until June 2003 (The European Convention, 2002a, p. 20; Miller, 2003, p. 7).

In the listening stage, the Convention explored people's future expectations of the EU through publicly broadcast plenaries (the Praesidium set the agenda for these beforehand). During the study phase, the Praesidium created six working groups (expanding into eleven) which allowed in-depth exploration into the Laeken declaration's topics by the conventioneers. The final reflection/proposing stage concentrated more fully on institutional concerns. At this stage the Praesidium suggested draft texts, which the conventioneers debated and then proposed amendments. In the decision-making stage, traditional EU cleavages opened up on certain issues along the fault lines of pro/anti-integrationists, left/right wing and large/small states (Kohnstamm and Durand, 2003; Magnette, 2004, p. 215). Institutional actors also promoted their institutional interests, such as the European parliamentarians and commission (Stuart, 2003, p. 18), as well as the 'common good' (Dobson and Follesdal, 2004). Foreign ministers were brought in at the last minute and government 'hard lines' were introduced (Göler, 2004, pp. 281–2) and sometimes actively encouraged (Magnette, 2004, p. 217).

CIVIL SOCIETY WITHIN THE CONVENTION PROCESS

By giving civil society a place in the Convention the Laeken declaration accorded civil society its first formal role in treaty reform. Civil society contributions were intended to 'serve as input into the debate' (European Council, 2001, p. 5). Civil society was envisaged as a vehicle for citizen participation, to bring citizens' views to the Convention's attention, to stimulate debate and later on to translate the Convention's work to citizens (ECOSOC, 2002a, p. 2). The Convention's very success was linked to being open and receptive to civil society (The European Convention, 2002a).

Vice president Jean-Luc Deheane formalized civil society's role (see Annex II in The European Convention, 2002b). Civil society could contribute through the following avenues:

* internet forum;
* civil society contact groups;
* Convention Observers – social partners, ECOSOC and Committee of the Regions;
* civil society plenaries – 24 and 25 June 2002;
* national debates;
* conventioneers;
* Futurum website (this was aimed primarily at individual citizens).

Civil society's formal participation came at the end of the listening phase in June 2002, through the two-day plenary sessions. Prior to these plenaries, eight thematic civil society contact groups were created. These contact groups were then left to decide who should speak at the plenaries, which Lombardo (2003, p. 27) argues led towards a bias of expert, well resourced, Euro groups speaking at the plenaries: 'It was a gathering of the Commission's payroll of funded lobby groups the usual suspect saying the usual things. Naturally these represented "Euro" viewpoints rather than varied national voices'. The Internet forum provided another outlet for CSOs to articulate opinions. Some civil society sectors were poorly represented in this forum, such as asylum groups, and the majority of civil society participants were once again Euro-groups (Lombardo, 2003). The forum came to be seen as a 'comedy' (Magnette, 2003, p. 32) and as a 'black hole' (Interview, European civil society organization, 2004) because:

a) no feedback was given to the participating organizations;
b) the effectiveness of the advertisement of its existence was questionable;

c)   vast numbers of contributions made it unlikely that they would all be listened to. (Scott, 2002, p. 2; Lombardo, 2003)

The forum also required CSOs to have Internet access, presenting a barrier to those without Internet facilities (Lombardo, 2003, p. 26). Futurum was a message posting website where anybody could post his/her thoughts on the EU, which made it hard both to monitor and to feed into the debate.

The observers and the conventioneers were intended to act as intermediaries in stimulating the national debate and in conveying views from civil society to the Convention. In particular, the ECOSOC (2002b, p. 1) was a pivotal 'bridge between the Convention and civil society'. It carried out eight information and dialogue sessions with civil society, however once more these meetings were only 'open to *European* civil society' (ECOSOC, 2002c, p. 1). National Economic and Social Councils, instead, were meant to engage national and grassroots civil society. The UK does not have an Economic and Social Committee, closing off a further potential avenue for British CSOs.

In practice, the real lobbying occurred outside of the formal channels 'in the usual way of personal contacts and the effect of NGO campaigns' (Berger, 2004, p. 8) and occurred as 'business as usual' (Shaw, Hoffman and Bausili, 2003, p. 17). The civil society contact group, a collection of European CSOs, argued CSOs had to be *proactive* to influence the Convention. This same contact group also viewed the Convention experience and the outcome as largely positive (Berger, 2004, p. 8). Nonetheless, there was a dissonance between the social and largely substantive concerns of civil society and the focus on institutional issues of the Convention (Shaw, 2003, p. 65; Lombardo, 2003, p. 28). This raises questions about civil society's actual scope for influence.

At the national level, civil society debate was lacking (Shaw, Hoffman and Bausili, 2003, p. 17). Particularly in the UK, there was limited press coverage as the Euro dominated the national debate in a Eurosceptic climate (Keohane, 2002). The Foreign and Commonwealth Office did have an online forum with Convention information and the opportunity to send views to the Minister for Europe. Yet, Miller (2003, p. 13) argued that the 'British government has not organised as many open discussions as some Member States'. Thus, the formal structural opportunities in the Convention that were open to civil society in Wales appeared to be few and far between. The stress on *European* civil society in the Convention is shared in the European Commission's and ECOSOC's conception of civil society and this may have also acted as a barrier to CSOs in Wales. The Convention placed an emphasis on CSOs that could input into the Convention; in other words, those with expertise and EU knowledge, in consequence leading to a de facto focus on Brussels-based organizations. This Brussels bias was maintained as the Convention also spent its entire duration deliberating in Brussels rather than going into the different member states. Implicit obstacles to curtailing participation include the Convention's focus on institutional issues, the need for Internet access and for CSOs to be proactive. This situation is exacerbated given that even 'European' civil society was listened to formally only once in the Convention and with so many other actors the influence of CSOs could only be limited. Equally, a lack of engagement on the regional front is likely given that, as Hoffman (2003) notes, language is important in engaging civil society, with a number of authors finding the language of the Convention to be Euro-speak and legalistic (Magnette, 2003, p. 32).

REGIONS AND THE CONVENTION: WALES

The outlook for the regions at the start of the Convention was not good (Jeffery, 2004, p. 9). Yet, like civil society, regions gained their first ever role in treaty reform in the form of six Committee of the Regions' observers to the Convention. Unfortunately, on this role Jones (2002, p. 7) writes that 'all insiders know it is of little significance', with observers merely having speaking rights. Regional issues and public authorities were instead included in the Convention arrangements for civil society in the plenaries and the forum. Moreover, only one Convention representative, Peter Hain, came from Wales. Though an influential conventioneer (dubbed the 'shadow President' by Magnette, 2004, p. 217), he was there primarily to represent the UK Government. From the outset the Assembly had no formal role in the Convention, and with regional interests lumped together with civil society in forum, regions would likely be competing for attention not transmitting CSOs' ideas.

As a result, the Assembly was reliant on its intermediaries (such as regional Euro groups like the Conference of European Regions with Legislative Power) and the UK government. Consequently, the Assembly had little autonomy in the Convention, making it unlikely it would convey competing civil society claims. Indeed, the approach taken by the Welsh Assembly Government (WAG), perhaps in response to a limited formal position, focused on specifically regional concerns, the place of regional governments in the EU architecture, the policy process and subsidiarity: 'Naturally we are interested in changes in the big picture, but we have a special interest in subsidiarity' (First Minister cited in National Assembly for Wales (NAW), 2002a, p. 1). The most significant opportunity for WAG arose at the end of 2002, with the announcement of a further plenary in 2003 to discuss regional issues. Wales and Scotland drew up a paper on the regions and this was discussed in the Joint Ministerial Committee on Europe (see Clifford, 2004). The UK government took forward many of these points in an agreed regional paper which was submitted by Peter Hain to the Convention. This paper called for reforms such as revamping the Committee of the Regions and involving the regions in policy and consultation (see Hain, 2003).

Part of the explanation for limited Assembly activity at the start of the Convention, apart from their constrained formal role, may be found in their perception of the Convention and other more pressing concerns. At the start of the Convention, following a Cabinet briefing in 2001 (WAG, 2001), the First Minister stressed that 'the Convention is not a decision-making body' (NAW, 2002b, p. 20), downplaying the Convention's final status. During the early life of the Convention the Assembly was also absorbed in a number of other European issues, which arguably reduced Convention involvement at this stage. One such European issue was the debate over WEC, following the Assembly's decision to leave WEC in May 2002. Jones (2002) argues that this dispute absorbed the Assembly's energies to the detriment of their Convention participation. Secondly, the Assembly was heavily immersed in the debate on European Governance during the Convention's first few months (McLeod, 2002). The Assembly's European Governance activities culminated with the signing of a Trans-European Declaration on the European Governance White Paper in May 2002, when the Convention was well underway. The governance debate was separate from the Convention, although it marked an attempt by the European Commission to improve and democratize its policy-making.

The Assembly's role in the Convention suggests that the ability of civil society to use the Assembly as an avenue for Convention engagement would be relatively limited. The Assembly emphasised regional institutional issues, rather than typically civil society issues. Secondly, the Assembly's close nesting with other actors in the proceedings means that they would have been unable to forcefully press other issues that civil society may have brought to the table. This is further complicated by the fact that much of WAG's dealings were through the confidential UK line with the UK government, and much of this is inaccessible to civil society. In order to qualify this bleak statement, did the Assembly try to engage civil society in their Convention activities?

Regional institutional opportunities for civil society: Wales

The Assembly's concerns on the Convention, in response to their limited formal role, entailed that they had little formal consultation with civil society on the

Convention: 'I think the constitutional debate was largely about setting in place the structural building blocks which would allow civic society to contribute . . . there wouldn't be very much that civic society could say in respect of more powers for regions' (Interview, Assembly Member, 2003). There was some consultation on the European Commission's European Governance White Paper, which WAG fed into its Convention approach. The European and External Affairs Committee also invited responses on the European Governance White Paper from seventeen organizations (comprising large, Wales-wide farming, business and public sector bodies) and they received only five responses (from the WCVA, WLGA and three quangos). The responses (see NAW, 2002c) generally focused on the organizations' experiences of EU issues and called for increased structures to involve civil society in EU policy-making, to protect subsidiarity and to simplify the EU, and the paper also recognized WEC's importance. This does give some credence to the idea that CSOs would merely reiterate WAG's Convention concerns on the regions. However, some different concerns are also present.

The Wales forum on European Affairs was convened on the topic of European Governance where the Convention was discussed in relation to arrangements for Welsh representation. Similarly, the civil society/media groups present at this event were large Wales-wide organizations such as Wales Council for Voluntary Action (WCVA), Age Concern Cymru, Wales Trades Unions Congress (WTUC), Welsh Centre for International Affairs (WCIA), the Institute of Welsh Affairs (IWA) and BBC Wales. Convening the WEF for the Convention was suggested to the European and External Affairs Committee back in May 2002 (NAW, 2002d) but it was not carried out. Thus, the Assembly carried out some consultation on the governance debate, which translated into their Convention work. However, this was not completely open, and neither was civil society completely interested or able to respond on broad EU issues, with only five out of seventeen organizations responding to the written consultation. This also demonstrates the lack of civil society interest on things generically European, rather than sector-specific.

There were a number of other events in Wales and the UK that interested groups could have attended, organized by European parliamentarians, the Wales Office, MPs and the European Commission Office in Wales, as well as civil society groups such as the Institute for Citizenship. A number of events were held after the Convention's listening stage, when civil society's formal input occurred. Many of these events were not focused explicitly on the Convention. Instead, events encompassed a more general debate on the future of Europe or issues such as the Euro. The conference held by the Green and European Free

Alliance (Green/EFA) group in Cardiff in July 2002 represented a departure as it was conducted with civil society and the Convention in mind. Groups that attended this were mainly Wales-wide offshoots of UK parent groups and covered a range of social interests including: women, international, trade unions, disability, environment and ethnic minority groups. Their concerns were again wider than the role of the regions, including for example the abolishment of the Euroatom treaty, workers' rights, subsidiarity, openness and need for civil society to have a role in the process.

Similarly the WAG sponsored a WCVA-run Welsh 'Colloquium on Civil Society and Governance' in December 2002. This was organized 'to ensure synergy with key development in the EU surrounding the "Convention on the Future of Europe"' (WCVA, 2002, p. 1). The fact that it was placed on the European Commission governance website, not on Futurum or the forum, suggest that it was more orientated to the governance debate and raising the profile of civil society in Wales and less with influencing EU policy on the Convention. Nonetheless, the representation of fifteen grassroots organizations in Wales in the Colloquium represents a broadening out of the debate. With this limited context for civil society involvement, could the media spur on civil society in Wales' participation?

Regional media opportunities for civil society

The media can also create further opportunities for collective action because it shapes frames in the public sphere (Grimm, 2004). A brief overview analysis of four Welsh newspapers will help shed light on how the Convention was viewed and whether it encouraged civil society participation.[6] Figure 2.1 demonstrates the spread of newspaper articles over time. There are two peaks of newspaper coverage that occur during the reflection and decision-making stages when the Convention was well underway. Thus, it can be assumed that Welsh newspapers did not create much initial awareness. The two clusters of articles are identified with three issues. The first cluster in October 2002 marks the time when Peter Hain became the Secretary of State for Wales (whilst remaining a conventioneer). The second cluster in May/June 2003 is associated with a) the UK debate beginning on the DCT referendum and b) Peter Hain's appointment to Leader of the House of Commons, whilst remaining a conventioneer. These issues can be attributed to the article clusters over time because of the proportion of article content they received.

Figure 2.1 Chronological spread of Welsh newspaper coverage of the Convention and future of Europe, October 2001–July 2003

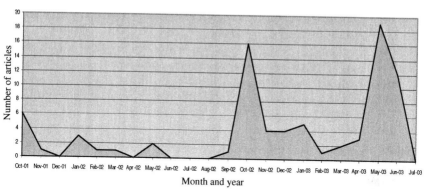

Secondly, the content of articles showed that the topic receiving the greatest coverage was Peter Hain's appointment as Secretary of State for Wales while continuing his role on the Convention, rather than on the Convention itself. The Euro and the actions of British/Welsh representatives on the Convention also had substantial coverage. Moreover, regional rights and institutional issues were given more focus than the Convention's discussion of the EU's policies/values where more civil society concerns may be expected. This is not a conducive setting to facilitate civil society in Wales's Convention participation.

Summary: contextual opportunities for civil society in Wales

Convention related activity in Wales does not seem to offer much scope for civil society participation. Indeed, civil society's involvement appears to emerge through tangential one-off events, although some civil society groups did help to organize and facilitate the debate. Due to the formal limits placed on regions in the Convention, and media sources in Wales, political structures did not offer the prospect of facilitating a widespread debate. However, this stands in comparison to the efforts of other regions that were able to involve their civil society in the Convention debate. For example, the Catalan Convention brought together over 300 politicians, academics, political parties and civil society 'to discuss the future of Europe' (McLeod, 2002, p. 4). The Scottish Parliament also arranged a one-day Convention and the Scottish Executive ran a website and carried out written consultation and seminars with civil society (see Scottish Executive, 2002; Scottish Parliament, 2002, Annex A). Nonetheless, how were groups in Wales actually involved?

DOMESTIC CIVIL SOCIETY ENGAGEMENT

Seventeen CSOs in Wales were interviewed about their Convention involvement.[7] The CSOs had two routes for participation:

a)   via external events and activities outside of their organization and networks, such as involvement with political institutions;
b)   through European/International/British/Welsh networks and parent bodies.

The latter is important as European civil society groups were charged with aiding the national debate. It is essential to note that much of CSOs' participation has been traced following the interviews. Therefore, the extent of participation may be underreported.

Nine groups had some contact with the Convention, with six of these having external involvement outside of their civil society partners/networks. Three CSOs were especially proactive. Among these the intermediary group had discussions with AMs, European Commission officials and the Secretary of State for Wales. The women's group also had contact with AMs and the MP conventioneers. Finally, another CSO sent in a submission to the Internet forum. Two additional CSOs attended the Green/EFA event and one of these also attended the WEF. The last group's staff member had some informal contact with the European Commission office in Wales on this issue. Thus, on the Convention civil society activity was not solely gathered around the Assembly and crosses governance tiers, perhaps in response to the Assembly's limited role.

One of these proactive CSOs viewed the Assembly as accessible because of the WEF consultation: 'it was probably a bit more open in fairness, at least they [the Assembly] did make an attempt to consult'. Similarly, the women's group found access to MP conventioneers relatively easy as they attended a public meeting of the European and external affairs committee. However, there was some divergence over the accessibility of the European level structures. As one CSO discovered, 'for us to feed directly into Europe was very difficult' (because they were not a European group). This shows the role of the EU's conception of civil society acting as a barrier. Nonetheless, the Internet forum user perceived access via the forum as straightforward: 'It was just so easy to make a submission to the Convention, and the Convention really laid over backwards, fell over backwards to encourage people to make a submission' (interview, civil society group, 2004). Thus, despite the negative political and media context for civil society in Wales to contribute, if you were aware of the Convention then these structures were not a barrier to collective action (although they may have limited participation) but obstacles may instead lie elsewhere.

Seven CSOs participated via parent groups or other civil society groups and five of these received information from their partners. The importance of this route is evident in studies of national civil society involvement in EU issues, with the smaller groups often working through or leaving the EU-level work to such bodies (Warleigh, 2001, p. 630; Fairbrass and Jordan, 2002). Involvement varied from, in one case, the British parent group requiring its committee in Wales to discuss the issue, to one CSO attending an event organized by another civil society group. Only one CSO was proactive in contacting its European networks on this issue and in organizing a related event. This demonstrates that some British and European parent groups and networks did try to engage their Welsh group subsidiaries in the Convention. The lack of Welsh groups proactively contacting their parent groups on this matter moreover illustrates an issue of supply-side engagement on the part of Welsh CSOs. Responses reflected the idea that Welsh, British and even European parent bodies/networks should, and would, deal with a European event like the Convention. Accordingly, groups felt that as long as some participation was occurring, even if it did bypass the regional level, this was more important than their group actually contributing: 'We would probably tend to say that we would trust our partners to actually make our voice heard at that particular level' (interview, religious group, 2003).

Some of the participating CSOs do concur with the Assembly's focus on the role of the regions in the EU architecture and subsidiarity, but there are also other wider issues raised by the CSOs. Thus, the business group was, among things, concerned about over-regulation and the effects on the business environment. The concerns of the trade union and the women's group were similarly focused on the effect/influence/discussions of the Convention on a policy area. The trade union promoted the social model, while the women's group wanted gender equality to be part of the constitution. The intermediary and pro-European groups focused more on institutional/power issues. The intermediary group wanted to secure provisions to allow for regional civil society to input into EU policy-making processes. In the same vein, another group wanted the EU to be more transparent and accountable, for competencies to be defined, to improve the definition of the role of regions, to address questions of legitimacy at sub-member state level to allow for secession of regions and to give the European Parliament a permanent home. Overall, the concerns raised by these CSOs are largely along the lines brought up by other CSOs in the Convention process.

CSOs' participation was concentrated among one or two individual group members. Two groups did make an effort to consult their committees, and a further two CSOs spread information to their members on how to participate (through an event or email actions). This concentration means that the role of civil society in Wales in connecting citizens with the EU through the Convention is limited. All of these groups, bar one, were engaged in EU policy-making outside of the Convention. The one that was not usually involved did have very marginal involvement with staff attending the Green/EFA event in Cardiff. This suggests that the Convention did not particularly reach out to those not usually engaged in EU issues.

How do these groups compare with the non-involved organizations in terms of resources and size, and did they want to participate and what would have been their concerns? A fairly straightforward reason for non-involvement, which was also cited by some of the involved groups (showing the precarious nature of their actual participation), was that they were not aware of the Convention. Indeed, five of the interviewees had no prior awareness of the Convention. Many of these groups had found out about the Convention through the media and had rather shaky knowledge of it: 'But much of the information we have got hasn't risen above the tabloid level of Britain in Europe, and Britain out of Europe, all that fairly sort of superficial rubbish on both sides' (interview, trade union, 2004). As many more organizations were aware of the Convention than participated it is evident that being slightly aware did not result in internalizing the Convention's work to their own organization's activities.

Aside from a lack of awareness, non-participating CSOs brought up similar obstacles to action, namely that groups would not make much difference, and that the lack of previous experience and the broad nature of the Convention was outside their organization's core remit:

> I think you would like to see such and such and you know you've got as much chance as a snowflake in the equator. (Interview, community/heritage group, 2004)

> A statutory body which might be interested in that trend, but for whom that trend is not really vital is probably going to shy away from taking that up. (Interview, statutory body, 2004)

> I don't think I have the experience and the language to have had a valid input. (Interview, environment group, 2003)

Groups also cited resources issues such as personnel, money and time as reasons for not getting involved. Moreover, two groups who were normally involved in EU policy-making did not contribute, one because the Convention was not its core business and the other because it did not feel it could make a difference.

Among the non-involved groups, six CSOs would have liked to participate. This suggests that more could have been done to engage civil society here. However, CSOs again seemed to acquiesce with the notion that the topic may have bypassed them and should be dealt with higher up in their organization. Indeed, twelve out of the total seventeen groups had British/European partners who were involved in the Convention:

> If the [European and international branches of the organization] had any input into it then really whatever we would have said would have just been repeating it . . . if you have too much consultation then I think you can't see the woods from the trees and you know if people are merely repeating the points that other people made more succinctly then all you are doing is clogging up the system. (Interview, environmental group, 2003)

A couple of groups generally concurred with the concerns of WAG in the Convention in that they would have wanted the role of the regions in EU policy-making improved. However, many of the other non-involved groups were concerned with specific clauses or policy areas pertinent to their group, thus suggesting the need for further civil society involvement.

In demographic terms the non-involved groups include all of the local and regional groups, most of the groups outside of south Wales and all bar one of the 'Welsh' groups (i.e. without a UK or European parent body). Staffing was important as all the involved CSOs with the exception of three bodies had staff, and those without staff either had other resources (entrepreneurial/expertise) or lack of staff had severely constricted their involvement.

Among the involved groups similar obstacles were encountered to the non-involved groups which limited the scope of their participation. Internal material concerns such as time and resources (people and financial) were present. External structural concerns included questioning how groups in Wales could have an influence, lack of awareness of events/Convention activities and recognition of the limited role of the Assembly as opposed to the UK Government in the EU. The perceived barriers towards regional civil society groups engaging in the EU were also again mentioned. The perception of the Convention itself, together with how the media and the government presented it and, more broadly, conceptions of Europe in the UK were most commonly mentioned as barriers to participation for civil society generally.

CONCLUSION

Despite articulating the need for civil society involvement to create a successful constitution the Convention did not re-engage with civil society on the ground. The Convention did, however, represent a broadening out of the process of treaty reform previously unseen in the EU. The formal opportunities granted to civil society in the Convention came early on in the Convention process and seemed to be dominated by Brussels-based European groups that had both expertise and resources to participate. The national civil society debate, to be organized by the member states and conventioneers, appeared to be similarly wanting. In Wales the Assembly had little formal input and as a result concentrated its efforts on regional institutional issues through the UK government late in the Convention. Although some previous consultation had been carried out on the European Governance White Paper that fed into the Assembly's Convention approach, formal opportunities for civil society to input through the Assembly were limited and inclusive politics was a little wanting, in comparison to the activities of other regional authorities. There was also a range of 'Convention' related events in which civil society in Wales could have participated. The brief analysis of some Welsh newspapers further serves to demonstrate the uninviting atmosphere for civil society with coverage peaking towards the latter stages of the Convention and focus on regional rights and institutional issues rather than civil society issues.

The views and activities of the interviewed CSOs demonstrate that participation by these groups was largely indirect and one-off. However, it does seem that the political context and institutions did not entirely constrain their actions, with groups in some cases choosing not to get involved, although this may be down to a lack of awareness. Therefore, participation seems to be also linked to interplay of group-specific, supply-side factors such as levels of awareness, staff and communication structures with European and British partners. Nonetheless, one CSO did encounter barriers at the European level in the form of the EU's institutional discourse on civil society. The lack of awareness about the special Convention mechanisms, together with a sizeable number of groups who would have liked to participate, suggests that more could have been done to engage civil society groups in Wales in the Convention. This article directs attention to CSOs' organizational structures and cultures of where it is appropriate to engage in EU issues. Perhaps unsurprisingly, given the Assembly's limited legal EU mandate, many of these groups prefer to delegate EU issues to their upper echelons. The key point about the limited nature of CSO participation is not necessarily that some issues were not raised in the Convention, but that civil society, and through these vehicles, citizens, largely did not debate and participate in the process, which was necessary to give the constitution their support. Without such local and broad participation by civil society in the EU's constitution-making process the constitutional outcome's legitimacy is compromised. The continued calls on the need for a debate on the EU among EU member states, following the French and Dutch public rejection of the constitutional treaty demonstrate that the Convention did not entirely live up to its promise.

NOTES

[1] Hereafter referred to as the Convention.

[2] See for example IWA's quarterly monitoring reports on the National Assembly for Wales and Scott (2003).

[3] Nevertheless, the Assembly must abide by EC obligations and has the power to implement European Community (EC) policies (106.1 Government of Wales Act) and create subordinate legislation to carry out that legislation when European orders have been designated to it under section 2 (2) of the European Community Act of 1972. Moreover, the Assembly is permitted to have an EU representation in Brussels and to have a Standing European Committee. The UK government does involve the Assembly Cabinet in EU policy decisions that affect devolved areas and Wales, as laid down in the Memorandum of Understanding and individual concordats (these are codes of good practices not legally binding rules).

[4] WEC announced it would close in November 2005. See *www.wales.gov.uk/ themes-mergers/content/responses/wales-euro-centre-e.htm.*

[5] In other words, there would be no voting, but at the same time a minority could not stop the majority from forging a 'consensus'.

[6] Four Welsh newspapers – the *Western Mail, South Wales Echo, South Wales Evening Post* and *Wales on Sunday* on the database Lexus Nexus were searched for the key words: 'European Convention'; 'future of Europe'; 'draft constitution'; and 'draft treaty'. By excluding irrelevant articles, 81 articles were identified within the time frame. The time frame of Oct 2001–July 2002 gives insight into the debate both preceding and following the Convention (although it is recognized that the future of Europe debate had been started with the Nice Treaty of 2000). It is also conceded these papers only compromise a small proportion of newspaper readership in Wales. Nonetheless, it gives some insight into the framing of the Welsh debate.

[7] These interviews were carried out from November 2003 to May 2004. Sampling included both snowball and stratified sampling to speak to a range of groups who varied in size, function, resources, sector, geographical remit and Convention participation. The sample is not representative of civil society in Wales at large but it meant to provide a snapshot of civil society participation and to explore civil society perceptions and experiences.

REFERENCES

Anheier, H. K. (2004). *Civil Society: Measurement, Evaluation, Policy*, London: Earthscan.

Beetham, D., Byrne, I., Ngan, P. and Weir, S. (2002). *Democracy Under Blair: A Democratic Audit of the United Kingdom*, 2nd edn, London: Politico's Publishing.

Berger, N. (2004). 'A participatory democracy? Organized civil society and the "New Dialogue" ', paper presented at 'Towards a European Constitution: from the Convention to the IGC & beyond', Federal Trust Conference, London, 1–2 July 2004, 1–14. *www.fedtrust.co.uk/default.asp?pageid=187&mpageid=78&msubid=187&groupid=6* (accessed 9 October 2004).

Bulmer, S., Burch, M., Carter, C., Hogwood, P. and Scott, A. (2002). *British Devolution and European Union Policymaking*, Basingstoke: Palgrave Macmillan.

Chaney, P. and Fevre, F. (2001). 'Ron Davies and the cult of "inclusiveness": devolution and participation in Wales', *Contemporary Wales*, 14, 1, 21–49.

Clifford, D. (2002). 'A view from the foothills', *Agenda*, spring 2002, 44–6.

Clifford, D. (2004). 'How devolution changed European policy', *Agenda*, spring 2004, 47–9.

Cook, D. (2006). 'Civil society in Wales and European Union policy-making: the case of the European Convention. A contextual analysis of opportunity, behaviour and democratic effects', unpublished Ph.D. thesis, University of Glamorgan.

Day, G., Dunkerley, D. and Thompson, A. (2000). 'Evaluating the "new politics": civil society and the National Assembly for Wales', *Public Policy and Administration*, 15, 2, 25–37.

Dobson, L. and Follesdal, A. (2004). 'Introduction', in L. Dobson and A. Follesdal (eds), *Political Theory and the European Constitution*, London: Routledge, pp. 1–9.

Drakeford, M. (2006). ' "Infiltration or incorporation": the voluntary sector and civil society in post-devolution Wales', in G. Day, D. Dunkerley and A. Thompson (eds), *Civil Society in Wales: People, Policy and Politics*, Cardiff: University of Wales Press.

Editorial Team (2002). 'Civil society and the Convention', *Centre for Applied Policy Research; Convention Spotlight*, 2002/6, 1–3, *http://www.cap.uni-muenchen.de/konvent/ spotlight/Spotlight_06-02_en.pdf* (accessed 3 August 2003).

Eriksen, E. O. (2004). 'The EU and the right to self-government', in E. O. Eriksen, F. E. Fossum and A. J. Menèndez (eds), *Developing a Constitution for Europe*, London: Routledge, pp. 35–58.

European Commission (2001). *European Governance: A White Paper*, *http://europa.eu. int/eur-lex/en/com/cnc/2001/com2001_0428en01.pdf* (accessed 11 November 2003).

The European Convention (2002a). 'The secretariat: speeches delivered at the inaugural meeting of the Convention on 28 February 2002', CONV 4/02, Brussels: the European Convention, 5 March 2002, *http://register.consilium.eu.int/pdf/en/02/cv00/00004en2.pdf* (accessed 18 January 2005).

The European Convention (2002b). 'The secretariat: follow-up to inaugural session of Convention', CONV 8/02, Brussels: the European Convention, 8 March 2002, *http://register.consilium.eu.int/pdf/en/02/cv00/00008en2.pdf* (accessed 24 April 2005).

European Council (2001). 'Declaration on the future of the European Union', Annex I to 'Conclusions of the presidency', Laeken, 14–15 December 2001, 1–5, *http://europa. eu.int/constitution/futurum/documents/offtext/doc151201_en.htm* (accessed 13 April 2002).

European Economic and Social Committee (ECOSOC) (1999). 'Opinion of the Economic and Social Committee on: "the role and contribution of civil society organizations in the building of Europe" ', CES 851/199 D/GW, 22 September 1999.

European Economic and Social Committee (2002a). 'Press release: European Convention/EESC: Mr Jean-Luc Dehaene takes stock at the half way stage of the Convention's work', no. 79/2002, 18 November 2002, Brussels: ECOSOC, 1–2, *www.esc. eu.int/press/cp/docs/cp_ces79-2002_cp_en_x.pdf* (accessed 17 May 2005).

European Economic and Social Committee (2002b). 'Press release: ESC members stress their specific value to the European Convention', no. 12/2002, 22 February 2002, Brussels: ECOSOC, 1, *www.esc.eu.int/press/cp/docs/cp_ces12-2002_cp_en_x.pdf* (accessed 25 September 2004).

European Economic and Social Committee (2002c). 'Press release: European Convention: Jean-Luc Dehaene welcomes the European ESC's initiatives for organised European civil society', no. 23/2002, 27 March 2002, Brussels: ECOSOC, 1, *www.esc.eu.int/press/cp/docs/cp_ces23-2002_cp_en_x.pdf* (accessed 25 September 2004).

Fairbrass, J. and Jordan, A. (2002). 'The Europeanization of interest representation: the case of United Kingdom environmental policy', in J. Fairbrass and A. Warleigh (eds), *Influence and Interests in the European Union: The New Politics of Persuasion and Advocacy*, London: Europa Publications.

Goehring, R. (2002). 'Interest representation and legitimacy in the European Union: the new quest for civil society formation', in J. Fairbrass and A. Warleigh (eds), *Influence and Interests in the European Union: The New Politics of Persuasion and Advocacy*, London: Europa Publications.

Göler, D. (2004). 'Comment on "Time was of the essence: timing and framing Europe's constitutional convention" ', in C. Closa and J. E. Fossum (eds), *Deliberative Constitutional Politics in the EU*, ARENA report no. 5/04, August 2004, Oslo/Zaragoza: ARENA/University of Zaragoza, *www.arena.uio.no/cidel/Reports/ Albarracin_Ch12.pdf* (accessed 22 May 2005).

Grimm, D. (2004). 'Treaty or constitution? The legal basis of the European Union after Maastricht', in E. O. Eriksen, F. E. Fossum and A. J. Menèndez (eds), *Developing a Constitution for Europe*, London: Routledge.

Hain, P. (2003). 'Europe and the regions', UK government submission to the European Convention, *www.scotland.gov.uk/about/FCSD/ExtRel1/00014768/page2053631259.doc* (accessed 5 August 2003).

Hoffman, L. (2003). 'The Convention on the future of Europe: thoughts on the convention model', in J. Shaw, P. Magnette, L. Hoffmann and A. Vergés Bausili (eds), *The Convention on the Future of Europe: Working Towards an EU Constitution*, London: The Federal Trust for Education and Research.

Jeffery, C. (2004). 'Regions and the European Union: letting them in and leaving them alone', paper presented at 'Towards a European Constitution: from the Convention to the IGC & beyond', Federal Trust Conference, London, 1–2 July 2004, *www. federaltrust.co.uk/default.asp?pageid=187&mpageid=67&msubid=277&groupid=6* (accessed 20 May 2005).

Jones, H. C. (2002). 'Editorial: Europe's crossroads', *Agenda*, spring 2002, 1–8, *www.iwa.org.uk/debate/europescrossroads.htm* (accessed 6 April 2004).

Keohane, D. (2002). 'EPIN briefing note: the UK and the Convention', The Centre for

European Reform, December 2002, *www.epin.org/papers/NatDebandPositions/08_ Keohane_UKdebate.pdf* (accessed 13 September 2004).

Kohnstamm, M. and Durand, G. (2003). 'The Convention on the future of Europe, commentary: common nonsense – defusing the escalating "big versus small" row', *European Policy Centre; The Europe We Need, www.theepc.net/europe/print_ europe. asp?SEC = &SIBSEC = &SUBSUBSEC = &SUBSUBSUBSEC = &REFID = 1163* (accessed 19 August 2003).

Lombardo, E. (2003). *The Participation of Civil Society in the Debate on the Future of Europe: Rhetorical or Action Frames in the Discourse of the Convention?*, working paper, University of Zaragoza, 1–40, *www.unizar.es/union_europea/files/work-Papers_UE.pdf* (accessed 14 May 2004).

McLeod, A. (2002). *Regional Parliaments and the Convention*, constitutional online papers, The Federal Trust for Education and Research 05/02, *www.fedtrust.co.uk/ constitutionalpapers* (accessed 6 March 2005).

Magnette, P. (2003). 'Will the EU be more legitimate after the Convention?', in J. Shaw, P. Magnette, L. Hoffmann and A. Vergés Bausili (eds), *The Convention on the Future of Europe: Working Towards an EU Constitution*, London: The Federal Trust for Education and Research.

Magnette, P. (2004). 'When does deliberation matter? Constitutional rhetoric in the Convention on the future of Europe', in C. Closa and J. E. Fossum (eds), *Deliberative Constitutional Politics in the EU*, ARENA report no. 5/04, August 2004, Oslo/Zaragoza: ARENA/University of Zaragoza, *www.arena.uio/cidel/Reports/ Albarracin_Ch9.pdf* (accessed 22 May 2005).

Meyer, D. S. (2003). 'Political opportunity and nested institutions', *Social Movement Studies*, 2, 1, 17–35.

Miller, V. (2003). 'The Convention on the future of Europe: the deliberating phase', *House of Commons Library Research Papers*, paper 03/06, 14 February 2003, London: House of Commons Library.

National Assembly for Wales (2002a). 'Press release: regions must play their part in the future of Europe says First Minister', 17 October 2002, Cardiff: NAW, *www.wales.gov.uk//assemblydata/N0000000000000000000000000002880.html* (accessed 9 June 2003).

National Assembly for Wales (2002b). 'The official record', plenary meeting, 19 March 2002, Cardiff: NAW, *www.wales.gov.uk/assemblydata/3CA0A6E90000E93 B600000 B4400000000. pdf* (accessed 17 February 2005).

National Assembly for Wales (2002c). 'European and external affairs committee: White Paper on Governance – written submissions', paper EUR 01–02, p. 3, 13 February 2002, Cardiff: NAW, *www.wales.gov.uk/assemblydata/3C67E53D000F2 B5F0000642 D00000000. html* (accessed 12 September 2003).

National Assembly for Wales (2002d). 'European and external affairs committee: the future of Europe debate by Clifford, D.', paper EUR 03–02 p. 3, 8 May 2002, Cardiff: NAW, *www.wales.gov.uk/assemblydata/3CD26882000E443D000051AB00000000.html* (accessed 19 November 2003).

Osmond, J. (2003). 'Laying the foundations', in J. Osmond and J. B. Jones (eds), *Birth of Welsh Democracy: The First Term of the National Assembly for Wales*, Cardiff: Institute for Welsh Affairs/Welsh Governance Centre.

Pietzyek, D. I. (2003). 'Democracy or civil society?', *Politics*, 23, 1, 38–45.

Regan, E. et al. (2003). 'The proposed treaty establishing a constitution for Europe', *Inter Parliamentary Research Network Briefing*, briefing 03/01, 7 November 2003, 1–78, *www.scottishparliament.uk/business/research/briefings-03/iprn03-01.pdf* (accessed 22 June 2005).

Royles, E. (2003). 'Objective 1' in J. Osmond and J. B. Jones (eds), *Birth of Welsh Democracy: The First Term of the National Assembly for Wales*, Cardiff: Institute for Welsh Affairs/Welsh Governance Centre.

Royles, E. (2004). 'Civil society and Objective 1', *Contemporary Wales*, 16, 1, 101–21.

Scott, A. (2003). 'Europe', in J. Osmond and J. B. Jones (eds), *Birth of Welsh Democracy: The First Term of the National Assembly for Wales*, Cardiff: Institute for Welsh Affairs/Welsh Governance Centre.

Scott, J. (2002). 'The culture of constitution-making? "Listening" at the convention on the future of Europe', *German Law Journal*, 3, 9, 1 September 2002, 1–7, *www.germanlawjournal.com/print.php?id=193* (accessed 11 May 2005).

Scottish Executive (2002), 'Consultation responses', *www.scotland.gov.uk/about/FCSD/ExtRel1/00014768/page1795179484.aspx* (accessed 12 December 2003).

Scottish Parliament (2002), 'European Committee: report on the future of Europe', paper 705, Edinburgh: Scottish Parliament, 1–26, *www.scottish.parliament.uk/business/committees/historic/europe/reports-02/eur02-06-01.htm* (accessed 14 June 2005).

Shaw, J. (2003), 'Process, responsibility and inclusion in the EU constitutionalism', *European Law Journal*, 9, 1, 45–68.

Shaw, J., Hoffman, L. and Bausili, V. (2003). 'Introduction', in J. Shaw et al. (eds), *The Convention on the Future of Europe: Working Towards an EU Constitution*, London: The Federal Trust for Education and Research.

Stuart, G. (2003). *The Making of Europe's Constitution*, Fabian Society pamphlet 609, London: Fabian Society.

Wales Council for Voluntary Action (2002). 'Welsh colloquium on civil society and governance', The Office of Eluned Morgan MEP, European Parliament, Brussels, 3 December 2002, *www.wcva.org.uk/images_client/ACF4E89.rtf* (accessed 16 March 2005).

Warleigh, A. (2001). ' "Europeanizing" civil society: NGOs as agents of political socialization', *Journal of Common Market Studies*, 39, 4, 619–39.

Welsh Assembly Government (2001). 'Welsh Assembly Government Cabinet meeting: the regional dimension of European governance by European and external affairs department', CAB (01–02) 20, 10 December 2001, Cardiff: WAG, *www.wales.gov.uk/organicabinet/content/CabMeetings/papers/CAB_01-02_20.pdf* (accessed 12 December 2004).

3. CULTURAL PERSPECTIVES IN THE NATIONAL ASSEMBLY FOR WALES: IDENTIFYING PATH-DEPENDENCY, CRITICAL MOMENTS AND CRITICAL JUNCTURES

Kerry E. Howell

ABSTRACT

This article analyses perceptions of institutional culture in the National Assembly for Wales (NAW) between 2001 and 2002. Assembly Members (AMs) were posed a number of questions concerning the NAW's institutional culture during the first term of devolution for Wales. The article explores the extent to which AMs considered that the NAW embodied the same values and cultural perspectives as Whitehall/Westminster and whether a 'path-dependency' existed that related to pre-devolution perspectives. The investigation provides insight into changes taking place in the NAW and identifies AMs' perceptions of their roles in the new constitutional arrangements. To investigate these issues, the author has undertaken an empirical study and uses an orientation framework and historical institutionalism to analyse the data and assess the existence of general, as well as sub-cultural perspectives in the NAW.

INTRODUCTION

Through an empirical study of Assembly Members (AMs) and historical institutionalism this article provides conclusions regarding the existence of a specific culture in the National Assembly for Wales (NAW) during the early years of its first term. Because the NAW is a new and evolving institution this study uses historical institutionalism to assess 'path-dependency' in relation to culture, 'critical moments' and 'critical junctures'. A set of interviews and a survey provide a perspective on the early years of the Assembly in relation to the evolving institutional structure and culture. Through assessing primary and secondary data and taking into consideration the compromise in the Government for Wales Act (1998) this article investigates whether path-dependency can be identified.

Initially, the article defines culture and outlines the methodological approach and methods of data collection. Difficulties regarding the limitations of the data have to be acknowledged, but through a qualitative and inductive approach the study has aimed for validity and in-depth understanding. To enable analysis, the methodological approach provides a categorization of the data based on interpretations of 'political culture' as outlined by Rosenbaum (1975). Secondly, the article assesses further conceptualisations of culture and sub-cultures through identifying norms, values, etc. Thirdly, the analysis considers that aspects of culture may be rendered explicit through path-dependency, critical moments and critical junctures. Consequently, the article explains 'historical institutionalism' and indicates how this will assist in an analysis of political sub-cultures and institutional culture in the NAW. This is achieved in the fourth section of the article through an analysis of a set of interviews and survey of the NAW membership. Finally, concluding remarks are made in relation to path-dependency, institutional culture and the NAW.

METHODOLOGICAL APPROACH AND MODE OF ANALYSIS

The article uses both primary and secondary data in a qualitative analysis of the NAW. The study analysed the results of interviews with eight AMs, one civil servant and a survey of AMs' perceptions regarding institutional culture and change in the NAW. The survey investigated the devolution agreement and the way AMs envisaged the future; this provided indications of cultural perspectives and outlined aspects of path-dependency. The survey provided a more general perspective than the interviews and asked AMs to agree or disagree with three statements.[1] The statements posed were as follows:

1. the existing arrangements between the National Assembly for Wales and Whitehall/Westminster provide the starting point for a transition toward greater legislative powers for the Assembly;
2. the existing arrangements between the National Assembly for Wales and Whitehall/Westminster provide the starting point for a transition toward tax-raising powers for the Assembly;
3. as it stands the constitutional arrangements between the National Assembly for Wales and Whitehall/Westminster need revisions if the Assembly is to function as a fully democratic institution.

Responses to both the survey questions and interviews are reported in later sections of the article. The interviews were undertaken to ascertain perceptions of culture within the NAW and how interviewees thought this had developed in relation to future directions. The interview sample attempted to provide perspectives from each major political affiliation, in other words Conservative, Labour, Liberal Democrat, Plaid Cymru – as well as the civil service.[2] The sample was small but the study concentrated on validity, and through inductive procedures constructed an understanding of a specific situation and precise historical moment. In analysing situations and moments, reliability and generalization are limited. However, this methodological approach enabled an in-depth understanding of political/institutional culture in the NAW during the first two years of devolution. AMs were asked questions based around whether Whitehall/Westminster perspectives of politics were dominant in the NAW, or whether a new distinct structure and system had emerged. Indeed, the interviewer did not explicitly make enquiries regarding what kind of culture existed or had existed. However, through questions about AMs' internal and external relationships, cultural perspectives began to emerge through 'orientations' toward structure, systems and activities. Furthermore, the perspectives identified through the interviews underpinned issues and considerations relating to 'path-dependency' identified in secondary data (see Chaney et al., 2001; Chaney and Fevre, 2001; Hazell, 2000, 2003a; Morgan, 1999; Richard Commission, 2004; Osmond, 1994, 2001, 2002, 2003, 2004; Trench, 2001, 2004).

During the interviews,[3] AMs used concepts such as inclusiveness, transparency, openness, etc. to explain the culture of the NAW in terms of structure, political systems and activities. Indeed, it is likely that AMs gave the party-line and usually this would detract from the quality of the data. However, when one considers 'path-dependency', some taken-for-granted 'shared basic assumptions' (Schein, 1997) emerged from research participants. The 'emerging stable relationships' drew on pre-devolution ideas and through shared learning in terms of concepts such as inclusiveness, transparency and openness, the membership developed cultural perspectives (Schein, 1997, p. 17). The data indicated that sub-cultural perspectives were drawn together through democratic ideals such as inclusive democracy and transparency and even though the realities of government and politics may detract from these ideals, they were still important for AMs and remained the basis of an overall cultural perspective within the NAW.

Because the NAW is a political institution, this article argues that a general culture and sub-cultures within the Assembly have incorporated forms of political culture. Rosenbaum (1975, p. 4) outlined two conceptualizations of what he labelled 'political culture'. The first is psychological and subjective and concentrated on what an individual 'feels and thinks about the symbols, institutions and rules that constitute . . . the psychological dimension of a person's civic life; we ask what bonds exist between him and the essentials of his political system and how these bonds effect his behaviour'. The second concentrated on positivistic notions of objectivity through the analysis of large masses of citizens 'or the collective orientation of people to their . . . system'.

Even though this study used a survey of AMs, this article concentrates on Rosenbaum's first definition and analyses the interviews through specific categories. The categories are drawn from Rosenbaum (1975) and use the core components of political culture (pp. 6–7). These include: 'orientation toward government structures; orientation toward the political system; and orientation toward political activity'. During the interviews, AMs were asked how they evaluated NAW norms and preferences in relation to alternative structures (Regime Orientation); their thoughts on transparency, inclusiveness, etc. in relation to the political system and civic life (political identification, trust and 'rules of the game'); and understandings of expertise and their impacts on the political process (political competence and efficacy). From this analysis conclusions are drawn regarding the political/institutional/organizational culture of the developing NAW in terms of values, norms, assumptions and beliefs.

POLITICAL, INSTITUTIONAL AND ORGANIZATIONAL CULTURE

Institutional culture is closely linked with the idea of organizational culture, which in political institutions incorporates dimensions of political culture. Studies and theoretical concerns have moved beyond structure in terms of authority, rules and rational choice and have emphasized values, norms, assumptions and beliefs (Schein, 1997; Hofstede, 1984). Commentators have realized that structure only partially provides a theoretical framework for explaining human behaviour in organizations (Dawson, 1996; Dirsmith and Covaleski, 1985; Fox, 1974; Gouldner, 1954). Furthermore, Schein (1997) considers culture to be an institutional process through which behaviour is transformed and refined over time. Behaviours are passed on through the organization and provide accepted values and norms for new recruits and ongoing decision-making as well as daily interaction. Consequently, Schein argues that culture is intrinsic for an institution because it defines or influences norms and behaviour. Trice and Beyer (1984, p. 654) have argued that culture incorporates the 'system of . . . publicly and collectively accepted meanings operating for a given group at a given time'.

In such a way, 'values and beliefs are both created by and revealed to members of organisations and those with whom they interact' (Dawson, 1996, p. 142).

However, within organisations/institutions sub-cultures exist through 'a distinct set of meanings shared by a group of people whose forms of behaviour differ to some extent from those of the wider society' (Turner, 1971, p. 1). Although Turner concentrated on industrial organizations, it is possible to extrapolate this analysis to different types of organization or groups within organizations. Organizations/institutions can encompass different types of culture which reflect 'their particular history and circumstances of definite groups within organisations . . . [and that] these vary in their dynamics and in their attitude towards the structure and functioning of the organisation' (Salaman, 1979, p. 184).

This article examines the extent to which AMs expressed the views of specific sub-cultures and how far these sub-cultural perspectives fit with a general or developing cultural perspective in the NAW. This was investigated and analysed through 'orientations' toward the institution. Furthermore, the analysis is enhanced through investigations of path-dependency, critical moments and critical junctures, and their existence in the NAW.

PATH-DEPENDENCY, CRITICAL MOMENTS AND JUNCTURES

This article draws on aspects of 'historical institutionalism' as outlined by Bulmer (1994; 1997), Bulmer et al. (2001), Bulmer and Burch (2001), Hall and Taylor (1996), March and Olsen (1999), Peters (2001) and Pierson (1996). Building on the qualitative methodological approach explained above, the article agrees with March and Olsen (1994; 1996) who argue that the idea of values is being lost in the social sciences. Positivist objectivity is 'inherently incapable of addressing the most important questions of political life, given that it could not integrate individual action with fundamental normative premises or with the collective nature of most important political activity' (Peters, 2001, p. 26). The methodological orientation I apply to the research allows an analysis of sub-cultural perspectives in the NAW in terms of path-dependency, critical moments and critical junctures. The study draws on historical institutionalism in attempting to identify how institutional settings mediate political differences; this includes both formal organizations and informal rules that structure organizational conduct. Historical institutionalism identifies 'the formal rules, compliance procedures, and standard operating practices that structure the relationship between individuals in various units of the polity and economy' (Hall and Taylor, 1996, p. 19).

As noted above, institutions incorporate formal and/or informal procedures, routines, norms and conventions embedded in an organization's structure of polity (Hall and Taylor, 1996). These range from rules embedded in the constitution to accepted conventions or informal agreements. Historical institutionalism analyses institutions by taking into consideration 'path-dependency'. This is where ideas incorporated in the formation of an institution are endogenous to present and future decisions. Institutions only change in relation to past decisions; change is 'path-dependent in that initial choices determine later developments and once a particular pathway is selected, alternatives tend to be ruled out thereafter' (Bulmer and Burch 2001, p. 81). However, there are opportunities for departures from a particular pathway through 'critical junctures' or 'moments when substantial institutional change takes place thereby creating a "branching point" from which historical development moves onto a new path' (Hall and Taylor, 1996, p. 942). Bulmer and Burch (2001) take this idea a little further and make a distinction between a 'critical moment' and 'critical juncture'. A critical moment is a potential critical juncture; however it may simply be part of the ongoing path-dependency. 'A "critical moment" is when an opportunity arises for significant change. Such opportunities may not be realised and exploited but if they are, the outcome is a "critical juncture" at which point there is a clear departure from previously established patterns' (Bulmer and Burch, 2001, p. 81).

Overall, the aim of the empirical work here is to provide some insight into whether the NAW may be seen as a critical moment or critical juncture and investigate pre-devolution and post-devolution path-dependency in the evolving institution. This may provide some understanding of the culture in the NAW and ideas regarding existing and future norms as understood by individual AMs.

PATH-DEPENDENCY AND DEVOLUTION FOR WALES

This article investigates issues relating to the development of devolution for Wales and the path-dependencies that may have underpinned this process. It argues that through the survey, interviews, pre-devolution and post-devolution literature, path-dependency, critical moments and critical junctures may be rendered explicit. Because the Assembly is a political institution, many arguments for the creation of the NAW were based around political culture and values relating to democratic deficit, accountability and autonomy. Even if this is not categorically distinguishable at a general level, for many years Plaid Cymru, the Welsh Liberal Democrats and the Welsh Labour Party called for accountability and democratic control of the Welsh Office (WO). For those involved in the devolution 'Yes' campaign, these ideals were paramount and reflected certain values that were held by elements of the political elite. One might argue that even though distinct sub-cultural perspectives existed in terms of party differences between and within parties, eventually a unified cultural perspective developed.

The NAW could be perceived as either a critical juncture or critical moment, in relation to the path-dependency and cross-party or general cultural perspective outlined in the Parliament for Wales Campaign's Democracy Declaration of 1994 (see Osmond, 1995). This declaration was approved by a Constitutional Conference of 250 people who represented local authorities, political parties, trade unions and churches in Wales. Osmond (1995, pp. 171–2) writes that: 'the conference registered a land-mark in Welsh politics. A strong intellectual case for legislative and financial powers for a Parliament was made, as well as internal democracy in its elections and procedures.' Important areas for the declaration were an elected parliament, cultural diversity, gender balance, responsibility and greater democracy in terms of electoral procedures and representation, (see Osmond, 1995, pp. 187–8). Furthermore, due to political expediency and Proportional Representation (PR), the idea of inclusiveness was included in arguments for an assembly. Indeed, the term 'inclusiveness' has involved much analysis and could be seen as the basis of a path-dependency. Chaney and Fevre (2001, p. 43) argue that 'the legacy of the term is likely to be twofold. As a notion that helped deliver devolved government, and following devolution, as an idea that pointed the way towards a more democratic process'. Effectively, inclusiveness becomes part of the dialogue in arguments for an assembly; this study assesses the longevity of this and ideals such as transparency, inclusiveness and openness in the early years of devolution.

The eventual political compromise established a NAW with secondary legislative powers; therefore the assembly had political legitimacy but was initially incapable of fully functioning as a legislative institution. As noted by Hazell (2001), the settlement was 'not working and the National Assembly . . . [was] beginning to put together the case for Wales to be given powers closer to those enjoyed by Scotland' (p. 264). Indeed, in 2000 this deficiency led to calls for a review of Assembly procedure. This involved evidence from the four parties, which agreed a common agenda for improvement and prepared the way for both the initiation of the Welsh Labour/Liberal Democrat coalition and Richard Commission (Osmond, 2001). In this context, there were many issues for which there was cross-party support which reflected areas identified in the 1994 Democracy Declaration which indicated aspects of path-dependency.

In addition, the interviews reported on in this article identified that aspects of political culture were important factors for AMs in 2001–2. Transparency, inclusiveness and accountability, etc. were still priorities, but how far the realities of politics and the objective of a functioning government undermined this was unclear. For instance, for Osmond (2002, p. 20), the culture of the National Assembly had 'further underpinned the creation of a stronger executive machine capable of developing policy and pushing it through'. Devolution was a process with groups and sub-groups emphasizing their own cultural perspectives and ideals to ensure these were involved in critical moments and junctures. Osmond (2004, p. 47) identified an important factor regarding the NAW in terms of path-dependency, and a critical juncture when he argued that 'the coming of the National Assembly . . . opened up a civic space for a truly Welsh politics . . . for the first time'. What this will involve is unclear. However, we can look at the ideals of the early years and attempt to identify direction and consequences outlined by this path-dependency.

Research examining political culture and governance before devolution found Welsh structures to be anti-democratic and centralised (Bradbury, 1998; Morgan and Mungham, 2000). Chaney et al. (2001) argue: 'thus it was frequently claimed that devolved government would be judged by its ability to bring about accessibility, representativeness, legitimacy, openness, participation, innovation, inclusiveness and accountability'. However, even though these themes continued to be used in arguments for devolution this does not mean they have been realised in a post-devolution situation. Evidence has suggested some 'discontinuity with . . . pre-devolution politics and . . . the experience of the past four years shows that constitutional change has already had a significant and positive impact on the role of women in politics and increased the legal rights afforded to citizens and advanced the promotion of equality of opportunity' (Chaney, 2003, p. 13). Hazell (2004) expected that given the historical impetus, the Richard Commission would recommend more powers for the NAW. In 2004 the Richard Commission pointed out that devolution did not begin in 1999 but that the NAW had brought a 'new dynamic to the process'. The Richard Commission considered that the present system was confused and unworkable and that since 1999 the NAW had increased its policy development capability so should be awarded primary powers. In addition, it advised a clear separation between the Welsh Assembly Government and the National Assembly (Richard Commission, 2004). When the Richard Commission report was published, it was unclear whether the Labour Government would act on the Commission's recommendations (Hazell, 2004). The White Paper (2005) incorporated some (though not all) issues outlined by the Richard Commission, but the extent to which this finally becomes legislation remains to be seen.[4]

Overall, groups with sub-cultures existed within institutions/organizations and if the NAW is facilitating the above ideals, from where do they emanate? Indeed, what were the main differences between sub-cultures and to what extent could these be identified? Schein (1997, p. 15) writes that 'in spite of such conflict one will find that organisations have common assumptions' and in new institutions these needed to be developed through the formation of 'shared basic assumptions', adaptation and integration (Schein, 1997, p. 5). Through the research interviews, the present study investigated the level of adaptation, integration and intelligibility of 'shared basic assumptions', as well as cultural differentiation in terms of party sub-groupings, in the early years of devolution. As noted above, to assist analysis this article categorised the data in three specific areas based around orientations to structure, system and efficacy and competence.

ORIENTATIONS TOWARDS GOVERNMENTAL STRUCTURES

This section evaluates AM orientations toward a 'specific institution' and the ramifications of these orientations for individual, sub-group and group cultural perspectives (Rosenbaum, 1975, p. 6). Through the survey and interviews this section attempts to identify AM orientations toward government structures and the linkages and changes to the institutional culture. Individual AMs were asked to evaluate their responses to governmental institutions in terms of the differences between Whitehall/Westminster and the NAW and the transition from the Welsh Office to NAW as outlined in the Government of Wales Act (1998).

Orientations to governmental structures were identified through the survey where 91 per cent of respondents considered that existing arrangements between the NAW and Whitehall/Westminster provided a starting point for a transition toward greater legislative powers for the NAW. On the issue of constitutional arrangements 86 per cent thought revisions were needed if the NAW was to function as a fully democratic institution. When asked about tax raising powers, 64 per cent believed that the existing relationships provided the basis for more powers to be transferred to the NAW. The large percentage of AMs agreeing with the first two statements arguably acknowledges the path-dependency prefigured in the Democracy Declaration and gives a strong indication of ideas relating to the future of the NAW. Furthermore, the survey results provide insight into AM conceptualizations of efficacy and indicate that, in general, AMs were (in 2001–2) pursuing changes to the NAW that would extend their power-base and enhance the government structure and specific institutional/political culture. The survey identifies concerns with the Government of Wales Act (1998) and the initial workings of the institution. The results illustrate a general perspective that the post-1999 devolution compromise is unworkable and further reform is necessary. Initial and subsequent actions by AMs that were discussed in the above section substantiate these survey findings (see Hazell, 2000; Trench, 2001; Hazell, 2003b; Trench, 2004). Indeed, the interviews identified differing orientations to the structure but rendered explicit a general discontent with the constitutional agreement and governmental structures of the NAW.

An orientation regarding structure was outlined by Plaid Cymru AM (a) when he argued that the emergence of the NAW was the result of a developing consciousness in terms of the need for alternative structures to meet political aspirations that existed in Wales; aspirations the structures did not fulfil during earlier Conservative administrations prior to 1999. He saw the NAW as part of an ongoing evolution of Welsh consciousness in relation to Whitehall/Westminster and the EU (interview with author, 2001). Corresponding with the survey results, Plaid Cymru AM (a) thought that a pre-devolution perspective underpinned the NAW and provided the basis of path-dependency. As the Democracy Declaration and the Richard Commission (2004) identify, in the NAW at least, such consciousness was an integral part of the devolution process and indicates an intrinsic aspect of path-dependency.

Conservative AM (b) thought there was more openness and transparency in the NAW. However, he did note that Whitehall/Westminster had existed and functioned for a long time. What he meant by this was enigmatic but he could have been intimating that the Whitehall/Westminster system worked well; so why not emulate it? A slightly different perspective was outlined by Conservative AM (a) who did not think devolution would come of age until a Conservative Government was in Westminster. He said, 'an incoming Conservative Government would take a very positive view towards the NAW and give it a positive role within the British constitution'. What is meant by a 'positive role' is opaque. However, David Melding (AM) has argued that Conservatives should support devolution and that 'commentators should not rule out . . . the possibility that the next and most vital advance for devolution in Wales will be instigated by the Conservative party'.[5] Furthermore, Conservative AM Glyn Davies argued that 'whether we like it or not, the National Assembly is here to stay and the Conservative Party's commitment to it is the measure by which our commitment to Wales will be judged' (cited in Hazell, 2001, p. 262).

The Liberal Democrat AM interviewed thought the NAW was developing its own institutional culture and pointed out that the NAW subject committees were unique and that how they operated did not correspond with Whitehall/Westminster institutional culture. In this context, the Liberal Democrat interviewee started to lean toward the idea that a critical juncture had occurred in terms of the structure and, given this structure, a different system and institutional culture would emerge. Conversely, Labour AM (c) argued that devolution and the NAW were elements of a critical moment and if a critical juncture was to materialize certain strategies needed to be pursued. He thought the structure was closed and still represented a Whitehall/Westminster institutional culture.

Labour AM (b) was more optimistic than both Labour AM (c) and the Liberal Democrat AM. He thought that a distinct institutional culture already existed, and that the Assembly's structure allowed for the further development of a different institutional culture. He thought the structure of the institution under-pinned the political procedures and cultural norms in the context of policy-making, stating: 'in Scotland a unified system made their institution distinct, in Wales it was diversity' (interview with author, 2001). He further considered that the NAW was a critical juncture *and* an institution which for the first time provided the Welsh people with a national symbol; where the focus was the representation of the people of Wales. He saw the NAW as an institution that reflected and/or constructed cultural perspectives through the values it embodied. In this context, we observe a distinction between individuals at the centre of the process and those on the periphery. For AMs at the centre, government structures could be more open and inclusive than for those at the periphery.

With the distinction between the Labour Party AMs we can observe different sub-cultural perspectives, in a particular political affiliation, which both relate to the general culture of ensuring a democratic, accountable and policy driven institution. Each considered that the NAW should have greater powers; however one considered the NAW a critical moment and the others a critical juncture. Path-dependency, it seemed, was uncontested.

A general cultural perspective and path dependency stemmed from the 1994 Democracy Declaration and although compromised in the Government of Wales Act (1998) (evidenced in secondary legislative powers), these were intensified following AM unity in overturning the single corporate body structure of the Assembly. In 1999 the NAW legislative and executive functions were combined. However, by the end of the first term the structure had 'moved as far as it possibly could in separating its administrative and legislative roles' (Osmond, 2004, p. 48). This identified the close links between governmental structures and the political system and the fact that there is some overlap between the two. The next section identifies and discussed these interactions in more detail.

ORIENTATIONS TOWARD THE POLITICAL SYSTEM

This section deals with issues relating to the political system in terms of 'political trust' and 'rules of the game' (political process). 'Political trust' involves issues regarding collaboration between groups, group membership and political motives. 'Rules of the game' relate to the expression of political opinions, mechanisms for political decisions and attitudes to political dissent (Rosenbaum, 1975, p. 9).

As with structure, AMs with similar and different affiliations agree in certain contexts but disagree in others. This illustrated aspects of sub-culture between and within parties. For instance, one interpretation of the political system was identified by Labour AM (a) when he explained that even though the NAW possessed a distinct political system that incorporated inclusiveness, he thought that politics in the Assembly were still confrontational. Ultimately, he stated that the political system 'was not as confrontational as Westminster but still involved politics with an edge'. He did not think one could have a chamber 'where people stand up and be reasonable with each other all the time because this blurred the edge of debate'. In 2005 it became clear that the level of confrontation changed during the first two terms of the Assembly. In the first term, the corporate body involved openness and the governing coalition encompassed an embryonic form of government and opposition. Indeed, this was the situation at the time of the research interviews. However, following the election of a Labour majority in 2003, one might argue that a more confrontational system was implemented and this given, the extent or existence of an inclusive political system was unclear.

The interviews identified a distinction between Labour AM (a) and Labour AM (b). Both identified inclusiveness, transparency etc., but Labour AM (b) went further and considered that a political system based on Proportional Representation (PR) provided diversity and because of this, as well as the scale of government, the NAW involved inclusiveness: 'I know it's an over-used phrase but inclusiveness was to be a new focus. Focusing on PR means that diversity and inclusiveness were built into the foundations of the NAW, this was clearly a deliberate attempt to promote diversity.' Hazell (2003a, p. 286) has argued that 'the way the new assemblies go about their business is very different from Westminster. They are . . . more open and accessible to outside organisations and individual citizens and seek to be a lot more participatory in the way they operate.' In this context, we observe the basis for the NAW's institutional culture and its 'path-dependency'. Through both the structure and voting procedures, a break with the former political system could be observed in the early development of the NAW. The realities of government bring about changes in the political system and in certain instances inclusiveness may not be possible. Policy needed to be developed and implemented if the NAW was to have an impact on Welsh society in terms of the economy, education and health etc. However, the way this was done was important for all those involved in the Assembly and ideas such as inclusive democracy, openness, transparency and political trust were endogenous to present – and one might speculate, future – policy mechanisms. Changes to the NAW involved critical moments, for example coalition and Labour administrations, the Richard Commission, but still incorporated pre-devolution path-dependency which underpinned the notion of NAW as critical juncture.

A counter argument and different sub-cultural perspective was identified by Conservative AM (a) who argued that openness and trust did not indicate the basis of interaction between AMs nor exemplified the political system in the NAW. This AM argued that unless there was a significant change in the Labour Party it would use 'every trick in the book' to limit devolution; the rhetoric would be pro-devolution but the reality was an anti-devolution Labour Party and First Minister (FM) who would not challenge this cultural perspective. Of course, as with the other parties, there were competing sub-cultural perspectives within the Labour Party. For instance, Labour AM (c) considered the political system brought about by elected devolution to be an empty shell, with clashes of interest and ideological positions still existing. However, Conservative AM (a) went further than this when he indicated that little had changed between the NAW and earlier administrative devolution. Like the Welsh Conservative Party in general (see Osmond 2001, p. 38 and discussion above), Conservative AM (a) illustrated a pro-devolution perspective but one with distrust for the Labour Party and argued that if successful devolution was to be realised a Conservative government was required. This, of course, is exactly the cultural relationship between Conservative and Labour one would expect in Whitehall/Westminster; a 'path-dependency' was already in place for the government/opposition structure that the political system eventually accentuated.

However, Conservative AM (b) indicated a different 'orientation' toward the political system and considered that the NAW promoted openness, accessibility and immediacy of access. This represented a qualitative difference between the political system and institutional culture of the NAW from that expressed by Whitehall/Westminster. Transparent information and accessibility to policy-making institutions provided plurality and diversity; again an example of the path-dependency of devolution and critical juncture between the NAW and the ideals of the previous mode of administration. As noted above, when discussing orientations to the structure, the changes brought about by the Assembly in relation to Welsh politics had a big impact on Welsh Conservatives and may have prompted a critical moment or juncture in the way that their party now perceived the future of devolution.

The existence of path-dependency relating to political trust, openness, democracy and transparency in relation to the 'rules of the game' was emphasized by the Liberal Democrat AM when he agreed with Labour AM (a) and (b) in considering that 'politics in the NAW were not as confrontational as Whitehall/ Westminster and were based around consensus rather than conflict'. As noted in the section above, he further argued that the NAW membership was given a set structure, and the political system and institutional culture were growing out of this, while AMs were, at the same time, investigating strategies for how the structure could be improved. Indeed, the outcome of these strategies may be observed through the resignation of Alun Michael, the Assembly review of procedure, coalition government, the re-assessment of corporate government and the Richard Commission.

Plaid Cymru AM (a) thought that lobbying in Cardiff was more open and inclusive than in Whitehall/Westminster and that the political experience was similar to that in Brussels. Labour AM (a) noted that outside organizations fully interacted with the NAW. He thought that any organization (professional or other) that had contact with this institution would think the NAW accessible and open. However, only individual AMs could identify whether they engaged with external groups in a competent manner, which begins to deal with issues raised in the next section where we discuss expertise, competence and efficacy.

ORIENTATION TOWARD POLITICAL ACTIVITY

This section investigates levels of competence and expertise in relation to how AMs felt about the efficacy of their individual actions in relation to the problems regarding secondary legislative powers and political expertise. It concentrates on areas relating to civic participation, political activity and identified considerations regarding political change (Rosenbaum, 1975, p. 9).

In general, interviewees thought that during the first two years of the NAW, AMs were on a steep learning curve as they acclimatised to the structure and system. AM expertise was becoming apparent and this confidence was assisting the emergence of distinct modes of policy-making and culture. One civil servant interviewed considered that during the second year the NAW had overcome some of its initial difficulties, as its committees became more focused. Following the resignation of Alun Michael and the stability brought about by Rhodri

Morgan, there was significant cultural change; and if there was to be concerted expertise and efficacy in policy development, political stability was crucial. However, Plaid Cymru AM (b) argued that competence and efficacy were limited in the early years, stating: 'it was the same civil service and the same way of doing things in government. Of the original sixty members, only seven were previously MPs, so in other words fifty-three were new to this level of politics'. Plaid Cymru AM (b) thought the levels of competence and efficacy were linked to the deficiencies in the institutional structure. In this context, he argued that 'in the NAW no one knew what their functions were'. However, Plaid Cymru AM (b) believed that the system could be changed and that AMs could precipitate or impact on this change.

Such arguments were echoed by Labour AM (c) when he considered that in the short life of the NAW little had changed between AMs and Whitehall/ Westminster. However, tensions were developing as AMs became more confident. There needed to be more astute utilization of political resources, the relationships between the NAW and Whitehall/Westminster needed to evolve and that the former should be more assertive and challenge existing arrangements. Labour AM (c) thought a critical juncture was still to be achieved and unless AMs were more proactive, the impetus of the critical moment would be lost. Plaid Cymru AM (a) thought a critical juncture had been achieved and that a distinct institutional culture existed but this needed to be developed through extensions in the powers available to AMs. For instance, he thought that on one level there had been little change between AMs and Whitehall/Westminster; however, he also noted that tensions were beginning to develop as AMs 'find their feet in the ongoing interactions'. Labour AM (c) suggested that AMs remained 'timid in the face of Whitehall; they need to be more assertive!' Both Labour AM (a) and (b) thought that through the creation of the Assembly a critical juncture had been realized and a distinct institutional culture existed in the NAW and this would continue to develop. This meant ensuring that the AMs' expertise continued to develop and that efficacy matched this, and so expertise developed further again. By 2003–4, these concerns were being made explicit by the Richard Commission (2004).

The Richard Commission (2004) is perceived as another stage in the process of devolution and linked to a path-dependency related to the development of primary legislative powers. The Commission identified a number of proposals based on initial path-dependency, the most important involving (full) legislative devolution, clear division of responsibilities with Whitehall/Westminster and the view that the Assembly not Westminster should have the most influence on Welsh policy. It argued that Welsh expertise had grown and efficacy needed to match this.

Overall, views on efficacy and competence were closely linked with orientations toward governmental structure and the political system and ultimately illustrated that cultural dynamics were interactive, iterative and process-based. Orientations identified political/institutional culture which enabled values, norms and beliefs, which allowed individuals to build identities and argue their individuality and own understandings of politics and society in general. As expertise grew and links with the electorate and interest groupings developed, efficacy became more apparent.

CONCLUDING OBSERVATIONS

During this study it became evident that the links between orientations to governmental structures, the political system and AM political activity were closely interrelated. For instance, AM perspectives regarding structure were influenced by the system and their perceived activities. However, each of the areas informed the analysis when identifying political/institutional culture. Through this analysis sub-cultures were identified in relation to an over-arching cultural perspective, which involved the quest for an inclusive, democratic, transparent and functioning assembly.

Through an analysis of orientations to governmental structures AMs perceived the NAW as the foundation of devolution. Each position identified an interpretation of path-dependency in relation to the NAW, one position understanding the institution as a critical juncture that does not require further development and the other as a critical moment with the emphasis on development toward a critical juncture. However, in general, AMs saw the NAW as part of a process and a critical juncture as the eventual outcome. Indeed, all AMs considered that opportunities existed to build on the foundations of the NAW, in the pursuit of a distinct institutional culture, enhanced political system and greater expertise and efficacy. This was evident in the Richard Commission (2004), which was itself based on a number of critical moments. However, whether the Richard Commission will incorporate a critical moment or juncture is not yet clear.

Orientations to the political system were based on the perceived structure and further outlined sub-cultural perspectives. Overall, AMs argued that the political system should be based on a democratically accountable institution that was open to civil society. Each understood the NAW from a specific perspective. However, each considered the NAW as part of the process toward the formulation and creation of a Government for Wales. Consequently, in terms of orientation to individual political activity, AMs behaved in ways that embedded specific cultures in the NAW that ensured extensions of the institution's powers.

Policy-making was seen as necessitating stability and being able to return to routines of behaviour based around inclusiveness, transparency and non-confrontational politics that provided cognitive templates and indicated AMs' self-images. This provided the bottom-line for AMs and outlined the basis for institutional culture, in other words the extension of powers for the NAW with these powers being organized and utilized in an open, inclusive and democratic fashion. This also identified pointers regarding institutional direction and continuity. The NAW had begun to provide certainty about the present and future but at the same time world-views emerged that allowed the construction of self-identities. Path-dependency was in place, which determined decision parameters and identified the way forward and future policy.

The NAW adhered to a specific path-dependency. This path-dependency indicated why other devolved institutions have different structures and institutional cultures. Institutions have different objectives, which the contextual situation, historical process and institutional culture mediate. In 2001–2 most interviewees expressed democracy, accountability, openness, inclusiveness, transparency and non-confrontational politics as necessary elements of the workings in the NAW. Given the realities of policy-making and government the extent that AMs can adhere to these ideals is difficult to ascertain. However, during the early years, most expressed these values as the basis of the NAW's institutional/political culture, even though there were different sub-cultural perspectives regarding how far they had been realized. Values that produced the basis of path-dependency developed cultural tenacity, which reflected the ideological premise or initial ideas on which the institution was based. These early tensions and their ramifications have informed pre-devolution and post-devolution debates. Indeed, the ramifications can be seen in the discussions and conclusions of the Richard Commission (2004). However, issues relating to these will need be developed in a further article.

NOTES

[1] Sixty questionnaires were sent to AMs, twenty-four were returned.
[2] Semi-structured interviews were undertaken in 2001–2 with Peter Black AM, Andrew Davies AM (Economic Development Minister), Glyn Davies AM, Ron Davies AM, William Graham AM, Carwyn Jones AM (Open Government Minister), David Lloyd AM, Dafydd Wigley AM and a civil servant of the Local Government Finance Division.
[3] All quotations are from research interviews undertaken (*c.*2001) by the author unless otherwise stated.
[4] Article written and submitted before publication of White Article and Government of Wales Bill (2005).
[5] 'Conservatives should finish the job', *Agenda*, IWA, Autumn 2001, cited in Osmond 2001, p. 38.

REFERENCES

Bradbury, J. (1998). 'The devolution debate in Wales during the Major governments: the politics of a developing union state?' *Regional and Federal Studies*, 8, 1, 120–39.

Bulmer, S. (1994). 'The governance of the European Union: a new institutionalist approach', *Journal of Public Policy* 13, 4, 351–80.

Bulmer, S. (1997). *New Institutionalism, the Single Market and EU Governance*, Arena Working Paper WP 97/25, Oslo.

Bulmer, S. and Burch, M. (2001). 'The Europeanisation of central government: the UK and Germany: historical institutionalist perspective' in G. Schneider and M. Aspinwall (eds) *The Rules of Integration: Institutionalist Approaches to the Study of Europe.* European Policy Research Unit Series, Manchester: Manchester University Press, pp. 73–96.

Bulmer, S., Burch, M., Carter, C., Hogwood, P. and Scott, A. (2001). *European Policy-Making Under Devolution: Britain's new multi-level governance*. European Policy Research Unit (EPRU) Book no. 1/01 Manchester: Department of Government Manchester University.

Chaney, P. (2003). 'Women and constitutional change in Wales', European consortium for political research, Department of Politics, School of Social and Political Studies, University of Edinburgh, 28 March–2 April.

Chaney, P. and Fevre, R. (2001). 'Ron Davies and the cult of inclusiveness: devolution and participation in Wales', *Contemporary Wales*, 14, 21–49.

Chaney, P., Hall, T. and Pithouse, A. (eds) (2001). *New Governance – New Democracy?*, Cardiff: University of Wales Press.

Dawson, S. (1996). *Analysing Organisations*. Basingstoke: Macmillan Business.

Dirsmith, M. W. and Covaleski, D. (1985). 'Informal communications, non-formal communications and monitoring in public accounting firms', *Accounting Organisation and Society*, 10, 2, 149–69.

Fox, A. (1974). *Beyond Contract: Work, Power and Trust Relations*, London: Faber and Faber.

Gouldner, A. W. (1954). *Patterns of Industrial Bureaucracy*. New York: Free Press.

H. M. Government (2005). *Better Governance for Wales*, White Paper, London: HMSO.

Hall, P. A. and Taylor, R. C. R. (1996). 'Political science and three new institutionalisms', *Comparative Political Studies*, XLIV, 936–57.

Hazell, R. (ed.) (2000). 'The state of the nations 2003: the first year of devolution in the United Kingdom', Exeter: UCL Constitution Unit, Imprint Academic.

Hazell, R. (2001). 'Dilemmas of devolution: does Wales have an answer to the English question?', WGC St David's Day lecture, Cardiff: Welsh Governance Centre, Cardiff University.

Hazell, R. (2003a). 'Conclusion: the devolved scorecard as the devolved assemblies head for the polls', in R. Hazell (ed.) *The State of the Nations 2003: The Third Year of Devolution in the United Kingdom*, Exeter: UCL Constitution Unit, Imprint Academic.

Hazell, R. (ed.) (2003b). 'The state of the nations 2003: the third year of devolution in the United Kingdom', Exeter: UCL Constitution Unit, Imprint Academic.

Hazell, R. (2004). 'Conclusion: the unfinished business of devolution', in A. Trench (ed.) *Has Devolution Made a Difference? The State of the Nations 2004*, Exeter: UCL Constitution Unit, Imprint Academic.

Hofstede, G. (1984). *Cultures and Organisations: Software of the Mind*, London: Harper Collins.

March, J. G. and Olsen, J. P. (1994). *Democratic Governance*, New York: Free Press.

March, J. G. and Olsen, J. P. (1996). 'Institutional perspectives on political institutions', *Governance*, 9, 274–64.

March, J. G. and Olsen, J. P. (1998). *The Institutional Dynamics of International Political Orders*, Oslo: Arena Working Papers, WP 98/5.

Morgan, K. O. (1999). 'Welsh devolution: the past and the future', in B. Taylor and K. Thompson (eds) *Scotland and Wales: Nations Again?*, Cardiff: University of Wales Press.

Morgan, K. O. and Mungham, G. (2000). *Redesigning Democracy: The Making of the Welsh Assembly*, Bridgend: Seren.

Mulhern, F. (2000). *Culture/Metaculture*, New York: Routledge

Osmond, J. (ed.) (1994). *A Parliament for Wales*, Llandysul: Gwasg Gomer.

Osmond, J. (ed.) (1985). *The National Question Again: Welsh Political Identity in the 1980s*, Llandysul: Gomer Press.

Osmond, J. (1995). *Welsh Europeans*, Bridgend: Seren.

Osmond, J. (2000). 'A constitutional convention by other means: the first year of the National Assembly for Wales', in R. Hazell (ed.) *The State of the Nations 2000: The First Year of Devolution*, Exeter: UCL Constitution Unit, Imprint Academic.

Osmond, J. (2001). 'In search of stability: coalition politics in the second year of the National Assembly for Wales', in A. Trench (ed.) *The State of the Nations 2001: The Second Year of Devolution*, Exeter: UCL Constitution Unit, Imprint Academic.

Osmond, J. (ed.) (2002). Engaging with Europe: Monitoring the National Assembly for Wales: March to June 2002, Cardiff: Institute of Welsh Affairs/Strategy Wales.

Osmond, J. (2003). 'From corporate body to virtual parliament: the metamorphosis of the National Assembly for Wales', in R. Hazell (ed.) *The State of the Nations 2003: The Third Year of Devolution*, Exeter: UCL Constitution Unit, Imprint Academic.

Osmond, J. (2004). 'Nation building and the Assembly: the emergence of a Welsh civic consciousness', in A. Trench (ed.) *Has Devolution Made a Difference? The State of the Nations*, Exeter: UCL Constitution Unit, Imprint Academic.

Peters, B. G. (2001). *Institutional Theory in Political Science: The New Institutionalism*, London: Continuum.

Pierson, P. (1996). 'The path to European integration: a historical institutionalist analysis', *Comparative Political Studies*, 29, 2, 123–63.

Richard Commission (2004). *Commission on the Powers and Electoral Arrangements of the National Assembly for Wales*, Cardiff: National Assembly for Wales.

Rosenbaum, W. A. (1975). *Political Culture*, London: Thomas Nelson and Sons.

Salaman, G. (1979). *Work Organisations: Resistance and Control*, New York: Longman.

Schein, E. H. (1997). *Organizational Culture and Leadership*, San Francisco: Jossey-Bass.

Trench, A. (ed.) (2001). *The State of the Nations: The Second Year of Devolution in the United Kingdom*, Exeter: UCL Constitution Unit, Imprint Academic.

Trench, A. (ed.) (2004). *Has Devolution Made a Difference? The State of the Nations*, Exeter: UCL Constitution Unit, Imprint Academic.

Trice, H. M. and Beyer, J. M. (1984). 'Studying organizational culture through rites and rituals', *Academy of Management Review*, 9, 650–66.

Turner, B. (1971). *Exploring the Industrial Sub-culture*, London: Macmillan.

4. WALES, ART, NARRATIVE AND DEVOLUTION

William Housley

ABSTRACT

This article reports on a study carried out on art and devolution in Wales. It explores practitioners' understandings of visual art in Wales and the notion of Welsh art as national parameters that are both recognized and contested. The paper analyses examples of artistic narrative as a means of describing the character of these understandings and the various discourses utilized by artists in negotiating the relationship between the creative self and wider social, cultural and national boundaries. The article argues that recent developments in Wales and the attempts to construct a national visual story overlook the sociological reality of contestation and alternative understandings circulating within the art scene in Wales. However, it also acknowledges that homogenized fictions are inevitable features of national social/cultural forms that have been marginalized. To this extent the article explores the narrative of the creative self in relation to wider discourses of nation in terms of a case study that has resonance with the study of culture, marginalized collective experience and national renewal and re-invigoration and cultural modernization in Wales, the UK and beyond.

INTRODUCTION

During the course of this article I intend to explore some issues relating to the visual arts and wider changes within the national context of Wales. The article draws from a study on art and devolution that explored the perceptions and expectations of a number of established artists working within Wales. The study explored the relationship between art and Wales through a detailed analysis of accounts generated through in-depth interviews. Whilst this article, in line with the study,[1] represents an exploratory analysis, it aims to identify important themes, issues and perspectives that constitute this relatively unexplored domain of sociological interest.

Whilst the focus of this research was directed towards the context of Wales it has resonance with other parts of the United Kingdom and Europe. At a general level the project was concerned with documenting artists' expectations and perceptions of devolution in Wales in relation to the organization of the visual arts, funding, cultural identity and representation. This approach draws on Becker's notion of 'art worlds' which consist of 'all those people and organizations whose activity is necessary to produce the kinds of events and objects which that world characteristically produces' (Becker, 1976, p. 41). It also acknowledges the sociology of cultural display and institutions as identified by Zolberg (1981) in her study of professionalization and American art museums. Whilst focusing on individual elite artists, the article acknowledges the location of practitioners within a form of life rather than spaces of individuated practice. Bourdieu's (1977) concept of habitus is useful for understanding how art can be understood through the concept of a field of social practices. It has led some, drawing from the art historian Panofsky, to rule out the study of art through individuals, groups or patrons. The study of artists in this research is not the study of individuals; rather it is a focus on artists as social and cultural agents who are active within the field. The preoccupation with the whole sometimes leads to a lack of focus upon creative practitioners as agents. In the case of under-researched art worlds it is imperative to understand the creative practitioners as well as the field of a particular art world. This article begins with the creative practitioners of the art world in Wales but situates them within a wider field of relations which they themselves readily acknowledge and refer to.

The research aimed to explore artists' (and people engaged in the production, management and exhibition of artistic products) expectations and perceptions of devolution and change within the United Kingdom. The contributions, concerns and insights of the artistic community are often ignored during times of social and political change whilst the products of art are, paradoxically, used as a means of interpreting historical events. This research sought to identify the changes that members of the artistic community expect to take place within the artistic community itself, the changing relationship and profile of the arts with Welsh institutions and the general public and policy formation within the new devolved Assembly. The study also sought to identify and profile the artistic community's perception of devolution as an opportunity for art to take a greater role in Welsh life and raise its profile as an important area of social, cultural and economic activity.

WALES AND NATIONAL IDENTITY

Theoretical and empirical work in the area of national identity and Wales has developed in recent years. Nationalism in Wales has been explored as a social construction (Denney, Borland and Fevre, 1991). Work by Fevre et al. (1997, 1999) has developed the exploration of nationalist groups and organizations and has understood some of their activities in terms of the protection of monopolies in social and economic resources. Further work on national identity in Wales has explored the relationship between configurations of identity and the challenge of 'inclusive politics' within new devolved political frameworks (Chaney and Fevre, 2001). More recent work has explored the construction and negotiation of Welsh national identity within primary schooling and childhood (Scourfield, Davies and Holland, 2004). This work seeks to relate notions of national identity in relation to an emerging devolved civic sphere in Wales. Additional socio-logical work has explored the more mundane aspects of nationalism (Billig, 1995) and its interactional and situated characteristics in relation to Wales and identity (Housley and Fitzgerald, 2002).

Despite the plethora of sociological work on national identity in post-devolution Wales, little focus has been directed towards the cultural sphere and the relationship there between different forms of identity construction and representation. A notable exception to this point is Dicks' work on heritage, territoriality and imagined communities (1996, 1997, 1999). Through a 'museo-graphical case study' of the Rhondda Heritage Park, Dicks' work demonstrates how specific forms of representation of community and the Rhondda, in which marginality and peripheral (Welsh working class) experiences are paramount, is colonized through specific territorial discourses of 'Britishness' and 'Rhondda Valleyness'. In many respects this article builds on the work above by exploring notions of Welsh cultural identity through a consideration of the visual arts. More specifically it does so through a reconsideration of the representations and understandings of the visual arts in Wales as understood by prominent art practi-tioners; in other words a concern with the actual producers and creators of artefacts. The creative activity of these cultural producers, whilst appropriated, is not necessarily translated into the recognition of a legitimate artistic voice and source of knowledge and insight concerning a changing cultural identity within the space and place that they live, work and create. These voices become increasingly important in the context of post-devolution Wales where the revital-ization of the visual arts has been associated with a wider transcendence of a colonized state of mind (Lord, 2000, p. 9; Adams, 2003, p. 7). This process of cultural renewal during a time of democratization and devolution has been seen to be associated with the creation of new forms of cultural identity and the shaping of new contours of cultural citizenship in Wales. The visual arts and their social and economic organization are seen as an important form of life where such processes can be seen to unfold. This has, at times, taken on a contested character within which various forces of 'cultural modernisation' (Housley, 2006) are seen to be at work.

WALES, ART AND IDENTITY: SOME COMPARISONS

In terms of social-cultural precedent, some comparison to other nations pursuing forms of national renewal and re-invigoration can be located. The intellectual debate in Ireland during the early part of the twentieth century testifies to this. The Celtic revival of the 1880s explicitly sought to recover and construct a distinct Irish culture. An important aspect of this process was the construction of a national artistic tradition. The initial means through which this was to be realized was the establishment of a national art collection. According to Herrero (2000, p. 61) this was seen to encapsulate two functions. First it was a means of constructing an authentic and distinct Irish-Celtic visual narrative and a means of helping Ireland ascend 'modernity's hierarchy of nations'. Furthermore, it was the opinion of Irish intellectuals of the time (in particular the ideas of Hugh Lane writing in a letter to the *Irish Times*, 15 January 1903) that the establishment of a national collection and the physical establishment of a national gallery would help alleviate the paucity of art education in Ireland. For Lane, the establishment of a contemporary school of modern Irish art was central to the modernization process and the securing of Ireland's place alongside other established 'modern' nations. Herrero (2000) asserts that this was a form of practice associated with what Bauman (1987, 1992) has described as the 'legislators of modernity'. For Herrero (2000) the active practice of pursuing such a course of action was an important process in establishing a form of cultural modernity for Ireland. This process was characterized by public debate concerning what the collection should include. The debate polarized around two principal positions; namely an 'introspective position' and an 'internationalist' position. This account of Irish intellectuals, the establishment of national collections and artistic practice has strong parallels with the experience of Wales. In terms of the national context of Wales, attempts at legislation are observable and institutions developed and their consequences experienced. These processes have also been polarized around what Herrero describes as internationalist vs introspective lines and what I have identified as the universal vs particular dimensions of the visual arts in Wales

(Housley, 2006). The potential within this debate for transcending such dichotomies by appreciating the existence of other forms of cultural understanding remains, at least at this stage of cultural re-invigoration in Wales, a possibility.

ANALYTICAL AND METHODOLOGICAL APPROACH

Whilst the policy context and general profile of the visual arts and culture are of importance, this article seeks to explore the field of the visual arts in Wales in terms of a detailed analysis of prominent artists working and living in Wales. The method for selecting the artists interviewed involved the use of publicly available information provided by established institutions in Wales (e.g. the Royal Cambrian Society for the Visual Arts) and contacting well-known and established artists living and working in Wales. Over twenty-two in-depth inter-views with elite artist practitioners were undertaken. To this extent the article draws from data gathered from figures established within the art world. This clearly confines the validity of any observations in terms of the generalizability of artistic perceptions and understandings to a type of 'core group' (Collins and Evans, 2002). However, they do represent a systematic analysis of narratives provided by members of a recognisable 'group'. Consequently, this article works with a series of exemplars grounded in a number of case-centred studies of prominent artistic practitioners. The examples of artistic world-view in post-devolution Wales presented in this article are representative of a systematic analysis of the general data which yielded three principal art world view types. The interview data discussed in this article were theoretically sampled and selected from a wider data set. The limitations and constraints of the article prevent a presentation of all the corpus of material. This work provides detailed enquiry into this under-researched form of life, practice and social perception and perspective within a peripheral European setting. It does so by examining the discourses and understandings of practitioners and thereby initiates the mapping out of an unexplored set of discursive constructions. The relationship between cultural activity and peripheral economic location is one that demands examin-ation. However, whilst this is a latent theme of this article it is one that is not taken up; this deserves far more detailed attention and serves as a basis for ongoing and future research. This article examines artists' accounts and narrative in relation to identity and the social, cultural and political parameters of a peripheral, submerged and problematic national experience.

The notion of narrative used here is one that is couched within the analytical framework of narrative analysis (Gubrium, 1993; Plummer, 1995) and the notion of accounts and categorization articulated within the work of Harvey Sacks (1992). This article therefore understands artists as knowledgeable agents whose accounts of art world-views form critical resources for understanding art worlds and practices. They also represent a crucial means through which the creative self is displayed. The focus here is on the discursive representations and understandings displayed in the artists' narrative rather than the social organization of talk-in-interaction.

The analysis of these accounts will initially take the form of exploring their topical organization, content and the display of art world perspectives in relation to the context of national parameters, identity and political processes. This article seeks to explore the perceptions and expectations of visual artistic practitioners in relation to these matters through the analysis of these narratives. To this extent the article follows Maines' observation that:

> Narrative structures can be thought of as kinds of information technologies insofar as they are a mechanism for processing information . . . Unlike those formed of wire, computer chips, or paper, however, narrative structures are formed by history. They begin with humans trying to make sense out of problematic situations and emerge years later as forms of meaning that contain the criteria for evaluating the credibility of information. They possess reified truth claims and taken-for-granted properties of what-everybody-knows. Like public opinion . . . narrative structures are tied to a society's social structure, and thus their agency derives in part from the legitimising processes that inhere in societal institutional arrangements. (2001, p. 220)

The analysis of artistic narrative in Wales has been explored from a more literary, as opposed to sociological, perspective in the form of Tony Curtis's *Welsh Artists Talking* (2000). In many respects the narratives produced in this book have much affinity with some of the analysis and discussion presented in this article. However, I intend to explore these narratives from a more sociological angle. In terms of the genesis of this project it was my intention to explore art in terms of *artists'* expectations and perceptions. This approach is one that is shared and consistent with Curtis's straightforward and unambiguous approach. Furthermore, the concern with the narrative and voices of artists connects with important sociological work on the collective character of telling as a site through which wider representations, concerns and understandings of particular social groups can be grasped.

NARRATIVE AND THE CONTESTED REALITY OF WELSH ART

In terms of self, creativity and identity and national forms of categorization it would be tempting to establish a matrix of types, upon which various quantified descriptive instances could be mapped, in order to establish a quantified portrait of national self-categorization and its relation to creativity and artistic practice. However, in terms of the corpus of interviews of an artistic 'elite group' such a manoeuvre achieves little. Rather the narrative forms of understanding and description will be attended to in order to flesh out and render visible the perceptions that such artists possess. These accounts are rich sources of data for exploring art worlds and practice in relation to wider configurations of social and national identity. The following data provide a means of beginning to explore such issues. The data represent responses to questions and discussion concerning the creative self and other matters in terms of a changing national context. Furthermore, the examples presented here represent forms of narrative in relation to art-in-Wales that reflect and display three principal ways in which art is represented within the wider corpus of interview data, gathered and analysed during the course of the study. The narrative examples do not reflect these types ideally but they do display how these types can be heard and observed within the general data and the specific examples presented in this article.

Extract 1: Artists in Wales or Welsh art? (Artist A)

Talking about art in Wales in a kind of general sense is it possible from your point of view from your experience to talk about 'Welsh art' or is it only possible to talk about artists in Wales?

I think the second (. . .) I think you can only really talk about artists in Wales. Because I am one of the few artists in Wales who paint in Welsh.

Right. Can you tell us what you mean by that?

My knowledge of Welsh is not very great but there are people who are fluent in Welsh who paint in English or American. But I happen to paint in Welsh. When I say that I've been told I paint in Welsh. Because my pictures do reflect Wales. And they tie up with Welsh poetry and that sort of thing (. . .) that's what I'm told. It's rather nice to be told I paint in Welsh. All these other sort of fashionable avant-garde artists now (. . .) God knows what they paint in! It has certainly got nothing to do with Wales. There is no school of Welsh art there never really has been. We have a small school in North Wales but the Welsh Arts Council soon put the kiss of death on that.

In terms of this narrative and account, the interviewed artist responds to the opening question concerning whether it is possible to talk of 'Welsh art' or 'artists in Wales'. In terms of creative others the second applies, however in terms of *A*'s self-definition he refers to himself as being one of the 'few artists who paint in Welsh', although his understanding of the Welsh language is not as it might be. Thus, *A* understands Wales being mainly characterized by artists living in Wales rather than 'Welsh artists' which is viewed as a rare phenomenon. This provides a form of self-definition that he not only subscribes to but also embodies. Clearly, this is an idiosyncratic and potentially contradictory state; Welsh being a language and painting being a practice that produces a profound visual effect. However, for *A* this apparent oxymoron is transcended. His art, as described by 'others', is linked with the language of poetry and the Cymry; the two as a seamless and unproblematic reality. This self-categorization is made firmly within the, rare, rubric of the Welsh artist. This form of self-categorization and understanding is not only located in terms of others but also contrasted with other contemporary artists in Wales. *A* asserts that 'there is no school of Welsh art there never really has been'. He also asserts that localized attempts to establish a college of Welsh art in his vicinity of Wales were contested and stifled by other agencies active within the cultural field.

Thus, this form of self-categorization of creative act and artefact in terms of national structures is one that, on the one hand, preserves a notion of artists living in Wales but, on the other, displays a unique (or at least not commonplace) claim to being a Welsh artist. This is a rare quality embodied by *A*. Thus, the particularism of the concept of Welsh art as opposed to the universalism of artists and art in general is negotiated by the fact that such an embodiment is rare, unique and not common. This condition is explained by the fact that a school of Welsh art has, in terms of their perceptions, never existed and that attempts to do so have been stifled. This explanation is qualified in later accounts during the course of the same discussion. For *A*, this is both due to historical reasons and contemporary practices. Historically *A* refers to the lack of patronage in Wales and the relationship of the Welsh aristocracy with the Welsh people. Contemporarily, whilst there are Welsh artists and artefacts, an attempt to unify or present a consistent visual presentation or narrative of such social facts had, until the contribution of Lord (2000), been noticeable by its absence. The following account is initiated through a response to a question concerning the establishment of a recognized national collection of Welsh art.

Extract 2: Welsh art as problematic/possible (Artist A)

Oh, well, no not really but they're damned if they're going to have a room for Welsh art. There is no room for Welsh art in the whole of Wales. There is no room for Welsh art in the National Museum. And they're buggered if there is going to be one as far as I can find out.

Do you think that that also extends to other aspects of art? For example there isn't any kind of definitive Welsh school of art in Wales as far as I understand.

There's no Welsh school of art (. . .) no. But there are Welsh artists. And how on earth can a country get interested in art if they cannot see the contribution over the last three hundred years of artists in Wales? And it is hopeless (. . .) they can't do it if they can't see what's going on. If there was a gallery of Welsh art in the National Museum of Wales of the last three hundred years mini buses of school children would come down from around the valleys and say: Damn we didn't know about this! And they would be interested as they see it. That is what is so pathetic.

In this account, which follows the previous discussion, the poor visibility of Welsh art is located and perceived in terms of contemporary practices – in this case there being no gallery or any visible organization for Welsh art. This point is one that connects with wider current debates in which prominent artists in Wales and members of the Welsh Assembly have sought to explore ways in which the artistic legacy of Wales can be mirrored in the form of a designated space in the national gallery. Clearly, there are others who see such a manoeuvre as 'nationalistic' and limited in scope; one that does not fit well with more 'international'[2] theories of curation, organization and display. In terms of the account produced here this is almost a call for recognizing the (contested) category of 'Welsh art'. The artist proposes that this category could be recognized not only through a process of historical recuperation but also a syntagmatic visual display and tangible location within a national institution. Furthermore, it may be observed here that the discourse of Welsh art and artist is one that is not exclusionary in principle but merely one that reflects or asserts a reality of nationhood and national experience – an imagined reality in which the next generation would be able to recognize their own visual heritage. This constitutes an account of national renewal and the recognition of submerged traditions, narratives and understandings that have been previously denied and currently thwarted. In this narrative Welsh art, both its potential recovery and potential realization, are couched in terms of a counter-hegemony; one potentially connected to post-colonial aspirations and the return of the repressed. In the following account, a different understanding of Welsh art and art in Wales is presented. Here the possibility of Welsh art and art in terms of a universal set of signifiers is displayed.

Extract 3: Art, space and place (Artist B)

As a practitioner (. . .) as an artist (. . .) do you think it's possible to talk about Welsh Art or is it only possible to talk about art in Wales? Or is that too much of a hard and fast distinction?

Well (. . .) they probably both exist as concepts. I think that in many areas of the world (. . .) like in Mexico for instance (. . .) there would be such a thing as Mexican Art. In Santa Fé they have what they call 'Western Art'. And in Wales there is bound to be Welsh Art just like in Yorkshire there *is* local art (. . .) based locally. And then there is art that transcends borders and is about human beings and our life our being and that inevitably transcends nationality. Now personally I think that that is greater because of its transcendence that that is a greater form of art. So every locality has its what you might call parochial art. And then every so often someone working that parochial art does it so incredibly well that it transcends the barrier of parochial art and becomes something else. But I suppose they just coexist. But specifically in Wales I think that if a nation can only boast the art of its nationality (. . .) that is if it can only boast parochial art (. . .) that isn't much of a recommendation really.

So do you think there is a kind of tension between art as a universal enterprise and framing it within a category or a national identity or whatever?

Can I just add to that? Just to say that although I would tend to say that universal art (. . .) or you might say art that is unrestricted (. . .) is greater than parochial art (. . .) just to stress that point (. . .) that sometimes parochial art can arise to become profound. But ultimately it's a silly restriction to put a stamp of any particular nation on art that happens to come from there is a silly thing.

In terms of art that that is done Wales (. . .) for example (. . .) thinking about it in a wider sense (. . .) though your work addresses transcendental issues which are perhaps of interest and of significance to human beings rather than specific sections of the population or groups and so forth (. . .) Is there any way in which your experience of being located in Wales does that have any effect on the type of work that you do? Perhaps in the past or the way you've developed or where you're going (. . .) is there any way in which your location does affect your work?

I think there probably is an effect. But it's no more specific than a kind of psychic gloominess. There is a gloom. I think in this weird magical country of mists and heavy layers of cloud and hills. I think the gloom finds its way into my work. The ephemeral uncertainty.

The environmental in one sense?

Yes it's just that. Because that moulds a population as well. The weather changes the psychology of a nation doesn't it?

In terms of the account provided here the concepts of Welsh art and artists living in Wales are understood to be ones that can 'co-exist'. In terms of the notion of national frames of artistic practice this is a form of life that is readily recognized and compared to 'Mexican art' and, in Sante Fé, a form of artistic practice denominated as 'western art'. The account provides for an understanding in which Welsh art is a perfectly realisable and recognizable concept and practice. However, the notion of Welsh art being 'just like in Yorkshire' interpolates the notion of the visual nation as one that can be equated with the local or regional. Here, art is based in terms of the locale, as opposed to art that might resonate with notions of people, nation and submerged, sidelined, unrecognized experiences. Thus the potential for Welsh art *is* recognized but within the terms of a particular discursive construction; that of the local as opposed to the national. The second part of this account (l. 10–19) responds to the question by displaying an understanding of art in Wales as a concept that reflects a universal conceptualization of art. Here art, wherever it may be produced, transcends borders and is 'about human beings and our life our being', a concept of spirituality and the aesthetic that transcends nationality. In terms of this account, it is the universal power of art to transcend boundaries that is of significance (l. 12–14). The account continues by building on a mode of discursive representation in which Wales as a locale is then connected to a third part of a discursive chain, in this case the parochial (Wales → local → parochial). This form of discursive constitution of nation is specified in terms of Wales 'specifically' (l. 16) and not at the level of nations in general. It is qualified in terms of the assertion that 'if a nation can only boast the art of its nationality (. . .) that is if it can only boast parochial art (. . .) that isn't much of a recommendation really' (l. 18–19). Clearly, the notion of Welsh art, though not necessarily other forms of art couched in national criteria, is viewed as one that is local and parochial; particular as opposed to universal. The following account provided by a different artist represents a different framing of creative-self in relation to artistic practice and identity.

Extract 4: Constructing identity and locating the creative self (Artist C)

I'll just shift topic, but I would like to come back to that. Do you see yourself as an artist in Wales or as a Welsh artist?

Well at the moment both. Going to London was interesting because there are more artists there than anywhere else and it's a very sort of cut and thrust place, you're very much aware of how people promote themselves as artists and as people as well, that's so much a part of it, especially nowadays. And everyone really is in the business of exploiting whatever, and rightly so as well, of exploiting whatever they have in their life that makes them different from every other artist that's around. Because that enriches their work if it is genuinely a part of them and part of their work it's a case of promoting it. If you go to London it's such a multinational and multiracial place, and the artistic community is even more so or at least as much so that people are in the business of saying 'I'm from here, this is me, this is what I bring to the picture, to this cultural pot that you are dipping into' so people are really quite upfront about it, where they're and what they're about. So in a way that did make me think about my own relationship to where I'm from.

By going away?

Well, by going to London specifically, but by going away generally, yes. It made me realize that the work I want to make is about the sort of places where I've lived. That hasn't always been Wales. It's been to do with the kind of places that have been important to me, which have often been coastal, isolated or remote countryside, the wilder parts of the world. And I have become aware that that is what I want to talk about even if it's not where I'm making the images that I want to deal with, just because they are important to me.

Do you think there is such a thing as Welsh art as an artist?

Well, on a basic level yes, of course. Are you saying that there are themes in Welsh art that make them different from themes that are in other art? That there is something inherent in the style and the approach of a style?

If you like.

In the visual arts I don't really know whether that's true. It's not as strong a tradition in Wales as say music or writing. Or at least it doesn't have as high a profile, but I think that's changing. But I don't define myself in relation to other Welsh artists any differently than I do to other artists that I'm interested in. Obviously there are Welsh artists who are very definitely addressing Welsh issues, but that is a different thing. When you say is there such a thing as Welsh art, I kind of think that that's meaningless. Is there a kind of school, a style, a way of thinking about work which is inherently Welsh I'm not sure that that's true.

In terms of the narrative presented here the creative self is located within a wider art world that allows the condition of being a Welsh artist and an artist in Wales. The relationship between the creative self, location and identity figure prominently within this account. Recent experience of working in London is referred to, here the art world is characterized in terms of 'cut and thrust' and the profile of a multicultural demographic is alluded to. Furthermore issues of identity are seen to be important within this art world (l. 13, 14). This includes where one is from, self-definition and what one brings to the cultural pot of this multicultural scene. Thus various biographical and reflective resources are central to this *presentation* of creative self in this dense and busy art world. In this scene, the business of presenting your creative self is central to promoting oneself as an artist (l. 5) and of using various cultural resources in order to accomplish not only visibility but *difference*. Difference can be understood in terms of achieving recognition of unique creative quality. This is the hard currency of creative cultural capital. Thus, in terms of this narrative, it is not merely a question of promotion leading to visibility or a high profile but also of exploiting resources (these may be biographical, where you are from as well as your work) as a means of accomplishing difference. Difference is therefore not merely accomplished in terms of works of art but also in terms of the biographical details, geographical details or 'whatever'. Indeed the accomplishment of identity as well as the production of works of art, in this scene or 'field' (Bourdieu, 1977), are presented as equally important: 'people promote themselves as artists and as people as well, that's so much part of it nowadays' (l. 6). In terms of the artist's experience of the London art scene he suggests that this stimulated reflection on his own biography and identity.

This identity is one that does not exclusively link with the national parameters of Wales. It is one that includes Wales but also links with remote parts of the countryside, and isolated coastal areas. Within this narrative the possibility of 'Welsh artists' is acknowledged although it is one that is not of primary importance in terms of the creative self being presented. The notion of 'Welsh art' is viewed as meaningless (although this is prefaced by a view that this may change). However, what is of interest here is the way in which other forms of creative endeavour (e.g. poetry, music) are able to be subject to national parameters and boundaries. Art and visual art in particular is seen to have a problematic relation with the parameters of nation proffered in this account.

WELSH ART, ACCOUNTS AND TYPE

In terms of the exemplar narratives analysed and discussed in this paper a number of points can be advanced. First, whilst artists' experience and perceptions of the creative self in relation to wider social categories and processes are unique, they also exhibit certain typical characteristics. These typical characteristics do not constitute a single homogenous type. Rather they can be subdivided into particular positional/perspectival types. The importance of these types is twofold. First, they represent a way of beginning to understand the discursive charac- teristics of the visual arts in Wales and secondly display the type of discursive moves and cultural understandings that can be inferred and associated with this particular art world. In some respects these can be understood not merely as types but forms of social representation or frames that find resonance within elite artists' accounts.

Welsh art

Within this discursive representation, grounded as it is in lived experience, the notion of being submerged, peripheral and contested is evident. In the case where this form of representation is exhibited in its most pure form (extract 1) the phenomenon of 'Welsh art' is understood and portrayed as a rare entity. It is also constituted in terms that are deeply embedded and connected to Welsh life, landscape and, in an attempt to overcome the dichotomy and compartmentalization of the verbal and the visual, language. Its contested nature and submerged, even oppressed, character is made recognizable through accounts that relay stories of organizational interference (by organizations viewed as sometimes colonial in attitude and action or at least unsympathetic). This sense is also relayed through accounts of a lack of organic organization in terms of grounded and culturally aware sites of artistic pedagogy, for example designated, established and developed art colleges in Wales. These narratives both seek to recuperate a submerged history of Welsh art production and identify agencies of cultural hegemony that exclude national facts and cultural 'realities'.

Art in the locale

Within this discursive frame, artistic and creative practices occur within a whole range of locales: the city, the region and the nation. Whilst some nations can legitimately claim a national narrative for art others cannot. In the example here 'Wales' is linked to localism and parochialism. This is in stark contrast to the previous narrative form. Furthermore, art in the locale is a legitimate cultural and spatial formation that is not at odds with the principles of universalism and transcendence. Certain national parameters are viewed as restrictive, parochial and limiting. This discursive framework negates the 'potential' and 'actual' levels of experience being authentically accorded to the creative self within a meaningful national/cultural milieu as a primary or central concern of artistic endeavour. Furthermore, the principle of locale can also invoke notions of landscape and other geographical features in a way that does not necessarily equate with notions of national identity, although in the case of Wales and other national communities, landscape represents a powerful resource for national forms of identity appropriation, construction, collective memory and representation (Schama, 1995).

Art as universal/transcendental

Art as universal is commensurate with certain modern ideas concerning the conceptualization of artistic practice. In terms of the creative self and the negotiation of national parameters the universal language of artistic endeavours and products overwhelms the particular considerations of national circumstances, experiences or influences. This represents one form of narrative of the creative self in which autonomy of the created and creator is assumed. However, not only does it eschew the many consequences of purely national concerns but it is also associated with social processes, for example, the allocation of scarce resources, patronage and so forth. In many respects the frame and social representation of art in terms of universalism provides an 'othering device' in talk and accounts of art, identity and Wales. It is the antithesis to all those accounts that seek to situate artistic practice and organization in terms of national contexts or experiences. The notion of universalism does not fit well with the post-modern ethic of diversity, plurality and the rejection of grand-narratives. However, the notion of cosmopolitanism may provide a means through which such accounts of national-cultural experience can re-engage with values and principles that stand outside particular concerns. This could be a discursive means of straddling the universal and the particular during a period of cultural modernization in Wales. Within this paper, and the data set as a whole, cosmopolitanism was not an idea that had explicit purchase, although it may provide a means through which the universal vs particular may be negated. However, this discussion remains outside the parameters of this specific paper.

CONCLUSION

None of the exemplar narratives in this article represent a 'pure form' of the narrative 'repertoires' or reflect the discursive positions described above. This is, of course, to be expected, such accounts are principled positions that are renditions, stand on behalf of – and report and reflect on – experience, practice and expert understandings. The readings of doubt and methodological scepticism do not form a focus for this specific article. The negotiation of the creative self in relation to frames of national identity conforms, in part, to specific biographical profiles. Time, history and experience are central components to the stories told here. However, the positioning of narratives, an expression of certain biographical details, is merely one part of the story. These narratives form meaningful accounts and attempts to account for both a contested history of creative production in Wales and the contemporary cultural field during a time of cultural and political reflection and change. As such they are worthy of the most careful consideration and scrutiny as such narratives can also be understood to represent collective 'positionings' (Maines, 2001). The frames of the reflective-creative self in relation to a changing apparatus of national definition is of import. In terms of the exemplar narratives explored here the tension between universalism and particularism features heavily. Furthermore, a notion of nation as parochial and nation as an important but submerged discourse of self-understanding and cultural articulation is also observable. The contested character of the field reflects contemporary social facts. The notion of Wales in the cultural sphere is not only contested but is also 'up for grabs'. Thus, these exemplar narratives are not only passive reflections but represent accounts of 'structuralized' cultural practice (Thomas, 1937) that report on the way in which cultural institutions and artistic traditions are constantly being negotiated and are the product of a variety of sustained social processes and interactions. They form understandings and experiences that mobilize and make use of contested historical accounts and sociological profiles in order to situate the creative self in both contemporary circumstances and current debates. These current debates (a room for Welsh art in the National Gallery, the distribution of resources, the promotion of specific representation(s) and the character of creative careers) are therefore both reflected and constituted by such accounts. They are constituted both in terms of the situated enunciation of narrative in the interviews and their articulation and re-articulation by prominent artists within other domains of social commentary. Thus, this article analyses and reports on the character of such narratives and recognizes their wider circulation and uses. These narratives display not only collectivized positions but also the circulation of discursive types that enable an understanding and contestation of the discursive and practical field of art in Wales. These narratives also report on the presentation of the creative self in relation to wider social structures, parameters and scenes.

To this extent these narratives of the creative self, by prominent artists in Wales, represent crucial data for explaining, exploring and understanding artistic endeavour within post-devolution Wales. The practice of 'telling' as reflected in other works (e.g. Curtis's *Welsh Artists Talking*) provides a resource through which the often relegated voices of artists can be both heard and mobilized as a means of contributing to this ongoing cultural debate. These strong narratives, like visual representations, become powerful resources for informing, shifting and shaping the discourse and contours of debate and cultural decision making (e.g. debates and consultation organized by the Institute for Welsh Affairs, the National Assembly and BBC Wales). To this extent the narratives explored here represent typical discursive positions that are in circulation both in print, by word of mouth and other forms of social network. Indeed many of the narrative accounts reflexively display their positioning in terms of other cultural networks, artists and art scenes. Thus, whilst they are situated accounts, for members they are positioned and connected to wider sets of collective experience and understanding. A crucial feature of the accounts reported within the limitations of this article is the contested character of 'Welsh art'. It is characterized by contested boundaries ranging from explicit scepticism to individual embodiment. It may well be worthwhile to theorize that the narrative reality of contested boundaries reflects certain cultural and social realities of post-devolution Wales as well as the contested character of artistic practice in general. Clearly, a creative space in which a national conceptualization of visual narrative can be advanced is one that is questioned as well as promoted. However, it also displays the way in which the discursive construction of such a tradition in Wales and other nations is founded upon a diversity of views and understandings. The development of a coherent narrative for the visual arts in Wales has now been established in the form of Peter Lord's book *Imaging the Nation* (2000) and calls to establish a place for Welsh art in the National Gallery. Thus the emergence of a visual narrative for Wales is well underway. This represents an explicit and conscious attempt at imagining a 'visual nation' in a space where it had not previously been acknowledged. A crucial feature in building up and operationalizing such strong narratives is recognition. There was simply no narrative through which creative artefacts and individuals in Wales, both past and present, could be represented. It may well be that such intellectual work can be compared to ideal typical legislative function of the modern intellectual (Bauman, 1987). Indeed, the construction of a story, a presentation of a story for the visual arts in Wales, is realized within a context of difference, debate and rancour. However, by analysing the perceptions and expectations of artists in Wales we not only learn a great deal about art, identity and the nation but also the manner in which discursive representations of cultural sites, spaces and places are never 'true' or 'accurate'. They are always partial 'will to truths' that impose a version of events and discursive frames upon, in this case, a national story. They are themselves social, cultural and political acts that promote certain world views and discourses concerning national identity and understanding. The picture from Wales is, I would suggest, little different from other historical and contemporary (e.g. Brit Art) attempts at imaging, 'branding' or 'legislating' through various creative practices in terms of maintaining necessary national 'fictions', boundaries of experience and collective historical understanding. In the case of Wales this process is, however, tainted by other historical experiences, that testify to a submerged, sidelined and ignored visual story that has as much right to expression (and surely contestation) as other national fictions in other parts of the world. In many respects the discourse of art in Wales is one shaped by the experiences of the periphery and economic decline. In terms of this location, visual culture provides a resource through which new forms of national expression/prestige and identity can be realized.

Indeed, in terms of contemporary conditions in Wales, as in other parts of the world, visual culture and sites for the display of visual culture have been used and are being used to promote certain notions of identity, from post-devolution national identities to multiculturalism. The visual arts alongside other creative endeavours are also being marshalled as a resource for the regeneration of areas of economic decline. The new demand for the consumption of 'art' and its wider aesthetic and spiritual function in societies experiencing religious decline represents a powerful resource for social integration. Consequently, the fact that the narratives of visual culture are highly contested by the artists themselves demands examination. It suggests that such narratives for visual culture (and consumption) do not always equate with the understanding and experiences of the artists. In this respect the attempts to construct or legislate meta-narratives for various national visual cultures submerges (some) of the voices of those who produce the visual products, especially those whose biography and identity claims do not fit neatly with the contours of the new narrative. Furthermore, a concern with the creative production of artefacts by highly creative individuals as opposed to mere consumption or re-production represents a form of resistance to the colonization of the life-world by the market, rudderless consumption and its resultant waste (Bauman, 2003). In short, certain strong visual narratives can be used by legislators in constructing certain versions of events and spaces through which collective experiences and understandings can be displayed and inform other (e.g. educational) practices. Thus it is important that such voices are heard in order to inform a narrative of a visual nation; voices that report on the contested character of artistic practice and national cultural appropriation as diverse rather than monolithic, contested rather than passively accepted, productive as opposed to all consuming, vibrant rather than dull. The cultural modernization of Wales and the agents and institutions associated with this process can learn from other precedents. However, in terms of late modernity, the legislation of visual narratives should be open to participatory scrutiny. A crucial dimension of such participatory scrutiny is to be found in the voices of those who produce visual artefacts in the first place. Whilst the discourse of '(post)modern cultural legislation' denies the author such rights, it does so by excluding valuable insights and understandings that if allowed visible and audible expression will surely result in a form of visual narrative of cultural renaissance and regeneration that represents both the unique collective experience of Wales and the diversity of late modern Welshness (Fevre and Thompson, 1999). This manoeuvre would avoid the polarising effects of introspection vs internationalism and represent a more pluralistic path for the management and promotion of the current cultural renaissance in Wales.

NOTES

[1] The study referred to here, 'Art and devolution in Wales: expectations and perceptions', was funded by the British Academy small grants scheme. Thanks are extended to the British Academy for their support.
[2] Ironically, postmodern theories of curation and display, which question established cannons and hierarchies, are increasingly international and almost universally acknowledged.

REFERENCES

Adams, H. (2003). *Imaging Wales: Contemporary Art in Context*, Bridgend: Seren Books.
Bauman, Z. (1987). *Legislators and Interpreters: On Modernity, Postmodernity and the Intellectuals*, Oxford: Polity Press.
Bauman, Z. (1992). *Intimations of Postmodernity*, London: Routledge.
Bauman, Z. (2003). *Liquid Love*, Oxford: Polity Press.
Becker, H. (1976). 'Art worlds as social types', in R. Peterson (ed.), *The Production of Culture*, California: University of California Press.
Billig, M. (1995). *Banal Nationalism*, London: Sage.
Bourdieu, P. (1977). *Outline of a Theory of Practice*, Cambridge: Cambridge University Press.

Chaney, P. and Fevre, R. (2001). 'Welsh nationalism and the challenge of "inclusive" politics', *Research in Social Movements Conflict and Change*, 23, 227–54.

Collins, H. M. and Evans, R. (2002). *The Third Wave of Science Studies: Studies of Expertise and Experience*, Cardiff: Cardiff School of Social Sciences, working paper 25.

Curtis, T. (2000). *Welsh Artists Talking*, Bridgend: Seren Books.

Denney, D., Borland, J. and Fevre, R. (1991). 'The social construction of nationalism: racism and conflict in Wales', *Contemporary Wales*, 4, 149–65.

Dicks, B. (1996). 'Regeneration versus representation in the Rhondda: the story of the Rhondda Heritage Park', *Contemporary Wales*, 9, 56–73.

Dicks, B. (1997). 'The life and times of community: spectacles of collective identity at the Rhondda Heritage Park', Ph.D. thesis, University of Wales, Cardiff.

Dicks, B. (1999). 'The view from our hill: communities on display as local heritage', *International Journal of Cultural Studies*, 2(3), 349–68.

Fevre R., Borland J. and Denney D. (1997). 'Class, status and party in the analysis of nationalism: lessons from Max Weber', *Nations and Nationalism*, 3, 4, 559–77.

Fevre R., Borland J. and Denney D. (1999). 'Nation, community and conflict: housing policy and immigration in north Wales', in R. Fevre and A. Thompson (eds) *Nation, Identity and Social Theory: Perspectives from Wales*, Cardiff: University of Wales Press, pp. 129–48.

Fevre, R. and Thompson, T. (eds) (1999). *Nation, Identity and Social Theory: Perspectives from Wales*, Cardiff: University of Wales Press.

Gubrium, J. (1993). *Speaking of Life: Horizons of Meaning for Nursing Home Residents*, New York: Aldine de Guyter.

Herrero, M. (2000). 'Towards a sociology of art collections', *International Sociology*, 17(1), 57–72.

Housley, W. (2006). 'Wales, identity and cultural modernization', *Contemporary Wales*, 18, 156–67.

Housley, W. and Fitzgerald, R. (2002). 'National identity, categorisation and debate', in S. Hester and W. Housley, *Language, Interaction and National Identity*, Aldershot: Ashgate.

Lord, P. (2000). *Imaging the Nation*, Cardiff: University of Wales Press.

Maines, D. R. (2001). *The Faultline of Consciousness: A View of Interactionism in Sociology*, New York: Aldine de Gruyter.

Plummer, K. (1995). *Telling Sexual Stories: Change, Power and Social Worlds*, London: Routledge.

Sacks, H. (1992). *Lectures in Conversation*, vols. I and II, London: Blackwell.

Schama, S. (1995). *Landscape and Memory*, New York: AA Knopf.

Scourfield, J., Davies, A. and Holland, S. (2004). 'Wales and Welshness in middle childhood', *Contemporary Wales*, 16, 83–100.

Thomas, W. I. (1937). *Primitive Behaviour*, New York: McGraw-Hill.

Zolberg, V. L. (1981). 'Conflicting visions in American art museums', *Theory and Society*, 10, 103–25.

5. CONSTITUENCY REPRESENTATION IN WALES: THE ROLES, RELATIONSHIPS AND REGULATION OF MEMBERS OF PARLIAMENT AND THE NATIONAL ASSEMBLY

Jonathan Bradbury

ABSTRACT

Devolution has ushered in a new era of constituency representation in Wales. Prior to 1999 MPs were the sole parliamentary representatives in their constituencies. Now the sixty members of the National Assembly (AMs) all have the right to engage in constituency work as well. The novel usage of a mixed member proportional (MMP) electoral system, by which forty are elected as constituency AMs and twenty as regional list AMs, also means that there are members elected to different types of constituency. This article explores the character of this new era of constituency representation up to 2004. It draws on evidence from members themselves and addresses the following aims: to clarify the extent of local representative work carried out by different types of member; to consider different perspectives on the qualitative nature of that work; to assess the nature of multi-level and multi-member relationships over constituency representation; and, to explore MPs' and AMs' attitudes to the regulation of their roles. The article concludes by discussing perceived problems in constituency representation and arguments for reform.

INTRODUCTION

Devolution ushered in a new era of constituency representation in Wales. Prior to 1999 MPs were the sole parliamentary representatives in their constituencies. They saw the constituency role as an important part of their work, providing a casework service for individual constituents, as well as advice and support for local organizations and businesses. Such work was often linked to the chances of success in sustaining local party as well as electoral support (Buck and Cain, 1990; Searing 1994; Rush, 2001). After 1999 devolution ushered in a new tier of representatives. The sixty members of the National Assembly (AMs) all had the right to engage in constituency work as well. The novel usage of a mixed member proportional (MMP) electoral system, by which forty were elected as constituency AMs and twenty as regional list AMs, also meant that there were members elected to different types of constituency. MPs and constituency AMs served constituencies with coterminous boundaries, while list members theoretically served all of the constituencies in their respective electoral regions. A regulatory approach was adopted that meant there were no constraints on any members' activities. Candidates could stand for election at both tiers and/or stand for both constituency and list election. Lord Elis-Thomas, the presiding officer, also ruled in 1999 that all AMs were equal and would receive equal office and staff allowances.

The article explores the character of this new era of constituency representation up to 2004. It draws on evidence from members themselves relating primarily to the conduct of their welfare casework roles. Section one seeks to clarify the extent of local representative work carried out by different types of member, and considers different perspectives on the qualitative nature of that work. Section two assesses the nature of multi-level and multi-member relationships over constituency representation, and explores MPs' and AMs' attitudes to the regulation of their roles. The article concludes by discussing pereceived problems in constituency representation and arguments for reform.

In examining these issues it is important to recognize that constituency representation and the need for regulation became politically contentious in a number of ways. First, there were suggestions that the devolution of executive responsibility for many services left MPs with a much reduced role. More prominently, it was alleged by the Labour Party that constituency AMs did more constituency work than List AMs and had different approaches to the role. There was a strong party dimension to this allegation for while constituency AMs predominantly represented the Labour Party, the other parties dominated the list seats (see Table 5.1). Peter Hain and Rhodri Morgan (2005), Labour's Secretary of State for Wales and Assembly First Minister respectively, argued that while constituency AMs offered a traditional service, list AMs did not. They cited a leaked memo from Plaid Cymru List AM Leanne Wood as evidence that opposition list members undertook less local work, and when they did it was politically motivated and targeted on constituencies for electoral purposes.

Secondly, these views were closely linked to perceptions of competitive relationships between different types of member, and led to debate over electoral rules and the possibiliy of guidance on member roles. No changes were made affecting multi-tier relationships. Even so perceptions of tensions between

Labour MPs and constituency AMs were such that the Wales Labour Party issued a code of conduct on their behaviour towards one another. More significantly, between 2004 and 2005 perceptions of tensions between Labour constituency AMs and list members of other parties contributed to a rethink of regulation at the devolved level. As part of the 2005 Government of Wales Bill Labour proposed that candidates could not stand both for constituency and list seats at the same election (see Wales Office, 2005). It was argued that the abolition of dual candidacy would remove the incentive for list members to target constituency seats given that they would now be forced to be either constituency or 'pure' list candidates. Morgan hoped also that the Assembly would introduce guidance that would regulate the roles of list AMs (Hain and Morgan, 2005). On this there was a precedent. In 1999 the Scottish Parliament had introduced guidance that required all MSPs to call themselves constituency or list members and never just the 'local' member. List MSPs were required to conduct local work in more than two constituencies in their region and to inform constituency MSPs of their work. Where a party had more than one list member elected in a region allowances were reduced for the second and subsequent members (Scottish Parliament, 2000).

Table 5.1
National Assembly for Wales, 1999 and 2003 elections

	Constituency	Regional list	Total
1999 elections			
Conservative	1	8	9
Labour	27	1	28
Liberal Democrats	3	3	6
Plaid Cymru	9	8	17
2003 elections			
Conservative	1	10	11
Labour	30	0	30
Liberal Democrats	3	3	6
Plaid Cymru	5	7	12
Others	1	0	1

Source: Electoral Commission 1999, 2003.

The constituency role of MPs received little further public debate, but the criticism of list AM approaches to constituency representation was greeted sceptically by many commentators. In an early analysis Lundberg (2002) drew comparisons with the MMP electoral system in Germany, where direct and list MPs had learned to live with competition. The regulation of candidacy and guidance on the roles of elected members had simply never been seriously discussed. Opposition MPs on the Welsh Affairs Committee later argued that party political competition over constituency representation could easily have been foreseen in 1999 and was an inevitable characteristic of MMP (Hain and Morgan, 2005). Wyn Jones and Scully (2005) argued that there was little international precedent for abolishing dual candidacy. They suggested that the proposed ban appeared partisan in that it impacted unfairly on opposition parties by raising difficult questions as to whether to stand their best candidates in constituencies or on lists. In that good candidates may not get elected this could also have adverse consequences for the quality of representation. On a different tack the Richard Commission in 2004 commented that if relationships between the different types of member were irredeemably poor then it simply added to their argument that MMP should be replaced by Single Transferable Vote (Richard, 2004).

The analysis presented here draws on findings from postal questionnaire surveys that were sent to MPs and AMs in 2002 and 2004, as well as semi-structured follow-up interviews. There are caveats to the value of this evidence. The small number of survey respondents presents problems for how far statistical analysis can be taken, but generally it should be noted that survey response rates compared to most member surveys were good (see Appendix). Equally, findings are based on data that was self-reported by members and not verifiable by independent analysis. Nevertheless, efforts have been made to explore the validity of conclusions on the basis of both quantitative and qualitative evidence. Interim reports from the research have been fed into debates about electoral arrangements in both Wales and Scotland (Bradbury et al., 2003; Bradbury and Russell, 2005a, 2005b). This article brings together some of the main findings to provide an overall appreciation of the roles, relationships and attitudes to regulation during this period, and concludes on the importance to be attached to perceived problems and arguments for reform.

1. THE CONSTITUENCY ROLES OF MPS AND ASSEMBLY MEMBERS

The survey evidence, as might be expected, revealed variations in the behaviour of individual MPs and AMs, but the data overall suggest four key features of MPs' and AMs' constituency roles. First, the commitment of all types of member to playing a constituency role appears to have been very strong. Table 5.2 indicates that virtually all MPs; constituency and list AMs considered helping to solve constituents'; problems to be 'very important', exceeding the perceived importance of all of the other roles open to members. Secondly, this was reflected in high levels of service. In 2004 all types of member claimed to average just under or just over a constituency surgery a week, the mean number of surgeries per month being 3.8 for list members, 4.3 for MPs and 5.0 for constituency AMs. The mean number of hours per week spent on both overall and specific types of constituency duties was also high, with work on individual casework averaging out at just under two days a week. List AMs actually had the highest level of commitment, according to this indicator (see Table 5.3).

Table 5.2
Percentage of MPs and AMs ranking local and other roles as 'very important', 2004

	Welsh MPs	Constituency AMs	List AMs
Help solve constituent problems	93.8%	95.0%	100.0%
Hold government to account	68.8%	42.1%	90.0%
Work on Westminster/Assembly committees	57.1%	70.0%	50.0%
Provide leadership to local party	75.0%	65.0%	70.0%
Contacts with local interest groups	56.3%	30.0%	33.3%
Promote business/government funded projects in constituency/electoral region	43.8%	50.0%	50.0%
Attend local community meetings/functions	62.5%	55.0%	30.0%

MPs, n = 14–16; Constituency AMs, n = 19–20; List AMs, n = 9–10

Table 5.3
Mean number of hours per week spent on constituency duties by MPs and AMs, 2004

	MPs	Constituency AMs	List AMs
Casework individual constituents	12.2	12.0	13.9
Deal local groups/businesses	4.5	5.2	6.6
Attend community meetings	5.0	4.6	4.2
Attend local party meetings	2.4	2.6	2.8
Promote business/public spending in constituency	3.5	2.2	3.7
Total on these five activities	27.6	26.6	31.2

MPs, n = 13–14; Constituency AMs, n = 17–20; List AMs, n = 9–10

Thirdly, however, there were variations in the level of demand upon different types of member. As Table 5.4 shows, whilst demand on MPs and constituency AMs was comparable in 2002, by 2004 constituency AMs received roughly 50 per cent more enquiries than MPs. This resulted from a moderate decline in demand on MPs between 2002 and 2004. This was acknowledged by some MPs, and indeed welcomed by those who were in relatively 'safe' seats and/or held either ministerial or senior Parliamentary positions at Westminster. But the majority of MPs were keen to assert the continued significance of their constituency role. Interview evidence suggested that many MPs went on 'publicity drives' to try to attract new work. More strikingly, in both 2002 and 2004 constituency AMs received roughly double the number of enquiries from local constituents than that were those received by list AMs. In this case, differences in demand between constituency and list AMs were largely acknowledged in interviews.

Table 5.4
Mean number of contacts (letters/e-mails/phone calls) from individual constituents per week received by MPs and AMs

	2002	2004
Labour MPs	103.0	86.4
Constituency AMs	107.3	129.4
List AMs	52.3	60.5

2002: MPs, n = 15; Constituency AMs, n = 22; List AMs, n = 11
2004: MPs, n = 11; Constituency AMs, n = 16; List AMs, n = 10

Finally, there were also possible variations in the extent of the role played by list members relative to whether they stood as both constituency and list candidates at elections, or just as list candidates. Table 5.5 compares the behaviour of the majority of list members, who were defeated constituency candidates in 1999 or 2003, and the much smaller grouping of 'pure' list members, who had simply stood as list candidates, and who could therefore be assumed to have no electoral interest in a particular constituency. The data on surgeries, time spent on constituent casework and communications received show stark differences, with a much smaller level of local work conducted by pure list members. Nevertheless, the figures are small and the only 'pure' list AMs were both from the same party and standing in regions where their party had little chance of winning a constituency. Therefore the evidence is interesting but inconclusive.

Table 5.5
Levels of casework activity by different types of List AM, 2004

	Mean number of surgeries per month	Mean number of hours per week spent on casework	Mean number of communications per week
AMs that did not stand for constituency in 2003 election	2.0	6.5	37.5
AMs that stood for constituency in 2003 election	4.2	15.7	66.3

List AMs that did not stand for constituency n = 2; List AMs that stood for constituency n = 8

Documentary and interview evidence revealed more about the qualitative nature of services provided to constituents by constituency and list AMs. Official data show that all members, whether constituency or list, opened local offices and employed staff who conducted constituency work. The key finding from the interview evidence suggests, however, that while there were generally accepted images of the routine constituency service offered by both MPs and constituency AMs, there were contested views of what list AMs provided. On the one hand, Labour constituency AMs felt that list AMs did not provide region-wide services, as evidenced either by their relative absence from a constituency because it was a 'safe' Labour seat, or because of their extensive attention to one seat in order to promote themselves ahead of a future election in which they intended to stand. Second, it was alleged that they did not provide proper constituency services in that they cherry-picked local issues for their political campaigning value and prioritized local media work.

Constituency AM interviewees grumbled about the activities of list AMs from all opposition parties. The case of Clwyd West, where in 2003 the Labour candidate won the constituency but then saw the second, third and fourth place candidates all win list seats, was frequently cited as an illustration of how an elected constituency Labour AM can potentially face targeted competition from a variety of defeated constituency candidates who then become list AMs and refocus on trying to win the constituency seat four years later. However, constituency AMs' main specific complaints were against the targeting activities of Conservative list AMs in four of the five electoral regions, the only exception being South Wales East. They were accused of acting as shadow constituency AMs, claiming all the rights to local representation without any of the obligations that came with specific accountability to a constituency electorate.

In contrast, list AM perceptions of their approaches to constituency representation were rather more complex. Conservative and Liberal Democrat list members in the relatively compact South Wales West claimed that they did treat the region as a large constituency, visiting all parts of it. However, in some cases it was argued that regions were simply too big for list AMs to offer region-wide constituent-based services, with Mid and West Wales being a prime example. Conservative and Plaid Cymru list AMs suggested that during the 1999–2003 term, where there were two of them from the same party, they divided the region between them, each claiming to serve several constituencies. Even where a list AM accepted that he/she did more work in a specific constituency, mitigating explanations were offered. It was argued that often the seat was not actually clearly winnable. Work focused on a particular constituency was more to do with the convenience of basing an office close to the AM's home, and constituent demand that arose from being well known in that constituency because of previous service, for example as a councillor, or party supporters who would rather come to them than to the constituency AM.

Even so, Conservative list AMs provided some confirmation of the fact that they targeted constituencies for political reasons. They cited the two powerful influences of internal party candidate selection rules and party attitudes to devolution and electoral reform. First, the Conservative Party was the only one of the major parties that required its candidates to be chosen first as a constituency candidate before being able to stand for selection as a list candidate. This gave a powerful incentive to Conservatives elected as list AMs to focus on a particular constituency to gain a constituency candidate selection at the next election, and thereby facilitate list selection again as well. Specifically, there was then also a strong incentive to focus work on the constituency which was most winnable but which also would generally have a large constituency association membership. This would maximize the chances of either winning a constituency or amassing the party member support necessary for achieving a high place on the party's regional list. Secondly, the Conservative Party was the only party where scepticism over the electoral system gave a particular incentive to list AMs to wish to become a constituency AM and thus be seen as a 'proper' member. Equally, the party was the only one where it was acceptable to level hop and seek a Westminster seat while still in the National Assembly. Several Conservative AMs stood in the 2005 UK general election as part of a continuous process of standing as a candidate in a particular constituency, thus incurring the resentment of incumbent Labour MPs as well as AMs.

Constituency and list AMs' perceptions of the roles of list AMs were sharply contrasting. Nevertheless, an important finding is the confirmation that list AM representation across their regions was generally uneven. The differences of opinion were rather over the reasons for this, calling into question whether the non-provision of a region-wide service was a bad thing or simply an inevitable consequence of the factors legitimately influencing list AMs. Only in the case of Conservative list AMs was there some convergence of evidence between alleged constituency targeting and acknowledged electoral incentives for doing so. Survey data suggests that there was no conclusive evidence that this meant that Conservative list AMs actually conducted more local work than list AMs from other parties overall. Meanwhile, list AMs interviewed universally refuted the notion that their constituency work involved cherry-picking issues for political campaigning purposes only.

Overall, we should highlight three primary characteristics of the local constituency roles of MPs and AMs. First, contrary to some expectations all types of member perceived for themselves a strong constituency role. Secondly, this said, demands on list AMs and MPs were somewhat less than on constituency AMs. Finally, AMs' perceptions of the constituency roles of list AMs differed. While there was some agreement over the uneven geographical coverage of list AMs across their regions, there was considerable disagreement between constituency and list AMs over the extent and reasons. Ultimately, this was related to disagreement over what should have occurred. While many constituency AMs asserted that list AM representation should be region-wide and of a lesser order than constituency AMs in any one constituency, list AMs maintained their right to conduct representation as they pleased.

2. MEMBER ATTITUDES TO RELATIONSHIPS AND REGULATION

Given near universally high levels of commitment among the different types of member to constituency work what were the perceived relationships between them over doing that work? The relationships between MPs and constituency AMs were the principal early concern. A key consideration here was the fact that they both received constituent enquiries that related to policy issues in the other's jurisdiction. By 2004 MPs reported that around a quarter of their postbag related to Assembly matters, with Westminster enquiries representing around 12 per cent of constituency AMs' postbags. How did they each deal with this situation?

The findings reveal some ambiguities in approaches (see Table 5.6). Only around 50 per cent of MPs always or often forwarded enquiries to their constituency AM. Party competition was a key factor, but many Welsh Labour MPs who had a Labour constituency AM also did not forward enquiries. MPs interviewed had a variety of attitudes. Some were positive towards devolution but nevertheless found reasons not to pass on enquiries: they did not want to be seen as 'passing the buck' by constituents; the devolution settlement did not clearly demarcate responsibilities between MPs and AMs, meaning MPs often felt a responsibility to respond; and new MPs elected in 2001 wished to establish their local political profile by taking on any enquiries. But less benevolent attitudes were also often evident: some MPs treated enquiries relating to the Assembly in the same superior vein as they did those relating to local authorities, and a minority simply wished to ignore devolution. Constituency AMs in part also took an all-purpose approach to representation; 60 per cent of constituency AMs took Westminster-related inquiries up directly with UK ministers. However, they appear to have been more respectful. By 2004, 80 per cent always or often forwarded Westminster enquiries to their MP, with those who did not largely explained by party affiliation. In effect, whilst in practice dealing with most cases themselves, AMs appear to have at least copied in their MP party colleague.

Table 5.6

MPs' actions when approached about a matter where responsibility rests with the Welsh Assembly; Constituency AMs' actions when approached about a matter where responsibility rests with Westminster, 2004

When approached about a matter where responsibility rests with the Welsh Assembly/Westminster, do you . . .	MPs	AMs
Pass the letter on to the other constituency member?		
Always	3 (20.0%)	6 (30.0%)
Often	4 (26.7%)	10 (50.0%)
Rarely	4 (26.7%)	2 (10.0%)
Never	4 (26.7%)	2 (10.0%)
Total replied	15 (100.0%)	20 (100.0%)
Take the matter up with the minister in the other jurisdiction?		
Always	8 (53.3%)	4 (22.2%)
Often	4 (26.7%)	7 (38.8%)
Rarely	1 (6.7%)	6 (33.3%)
Never	2 (13.3%)	1 (5.6%)
Total replied	15 (100.0%)	18 (100.0%)

Differences in approaches to forwarding enquiries relating to each other's jurisdictions did not appear, however, to have much impact on perceived relationships. Some relationships between members of different parties were perceived as very competitive, as were some between some Labour MPs and AMs. But most of these members appear to have either tolerated each other's behaviour or agreed that each should take up any enquiry irrespective of the jurisdiction it related to so long as the other member was kept informed. Overall, a majority of MP–constituency AM relationships were perceived as cooperative (Table 5.7).

Most interest focused on relationships between constituency and list AMs. Here the survey evidence suggests that party affiliation mattered a great deal. Relations between constituency and list AMs of the same party were generally cooperative. Indeed constituency and list AMs both in the Liberal Democrats and Plaid Cymru often shared office resources and liaised over dealings with local groups and public meetings. Members tended to hold their surgeries separately, although this often still reflected a coordinated approach to covering different parts of the constituency over a given time period. Equally, they did not liaise in detail over constituent enquiries, largely because of data protection legislation. In contrast, relations between constituency and list AMs of different parties were rarely viewed as cooperative, and 50 per cent or more of both constituency and list AMs viewed them as competitive (Table 5.8). This confirms generally held views about the tensions between constituency and list AMs.

Table 5.7

Perceptions of cooperation and competition in relationships between MPs and Constituency AMs over local representation, 2004

	MPs' perceptions	AMs' perceptions
Entirely/very cooperative	11 (68.8%)	14 (70.0%)
Fairly cooperative	2 (12.5%)	3 (15.0%)
Sometimes cooperative, sometimes competitive	1 (6.3%)	1 (5.0%)
Fairly/somewhat competitive	0 (0.0%)	0 (0.0%)
Very competitive	2 (12.5%)	2 (10.0%)
Total	16 (100.0%)	20 (100.0%)

Table 5.8

Perceptions of cooperation and competition in relationships between Constituency and List AMs from other parties over local representation, 2004

	Constituency AMs' perceptions	List AMs' perceptions
Very cooperative	0 (0.0%)	0 (0.0%)
Fairly cooperative	3 (17.6%)	0 (0.0%)
Sometimes cooperative/sometimes competitive	4 (23.5%)	5 (50.0%)
Fairly competitive	2 (11.8%)	3 (30.0%)
Very competitive	8 (47.1%)	2 (20.0%)
Total	17 (100.0%)	10 (100.0%)

Finally, it is important to consider approaches to relationships between MPs and list AMs. In practice, most MPs rarely passed on Assembly enquiries to list AMs of their own parties and never to list AMs of other parties. This was reciprocated by list AMs. Perceptions of relations were accordingly cool. In 2004 more than 70 per cent of MPs considered that they had competitive relationships with list AMs of other parties. A strong influence here was the fact that MPs often faced list AMs who had fought elections in their constituency. Interview evidence again emphasised perceptions of particular competition from Conservative list AMs. Perceptions of competitiveness were reciprocated by list AMs although less strongly. Around 50 per cent of list AMs thought relations were very or fairly competitive (Table 5.9).

Table 5.9
Perceptions of cooperation and competition in relationships between MPs and List AMs of different parties over local representation, 2004

	Welsh MPs' perceptions	List AMs' perceptions
Very cooperative	0 (0.0%)	0 (0.0%)
Fairly cooperative	2 (15.4%)	2 (22.2%)
Sometimes cooperative/sometimes competitive	1 (7.7%)	2 (22.2%)
Fairly competitive	3 (23.1%)	3 (33.3%)
Very competitive	7 (53.8%)	2 (22.2%)
Total	13 (100.0%)	9 (100.0%)

Given the extensive competition over constituency representation the obvious question arises as to what attitudes developed towards regulation of member roles. This met with varying answers. On the one hand, MPs and constituency AMs generally considered that the arrangements for regulating their relations were adequate. Even where members were from different parties they felt that any new rules would serve little purpose, reflecting largely sanguine attitudes to the political impulses for dealing with constituent enquiries irrespective of the level of government concerned. On the other hand, list and constituency AMs had very different views of whether there was a need to introduce regulation of local roles at the devolved level. By 2004 practically all list members supported or were indifferent to the statement that existing guidelines on the roles of list and constituency AMs were adequate. Meanwhile, 75 per cent of constituency AM survey respondents, predominantly representing Labour, considered existing guidelines on roles to be inadequate (Table 5.10).

One way of assessing AMs' views further was to ask them whether they agreed with a series of statements that related to the guidance for members used in the Scottish Parliament. Table 5.11 shows that this revealed more clearly the divisions of opinion. List AMs strongly supported equal formal and legal status and equal allowances, and strongly opposed being required to work in more than two constituencies. Meanwhile a majority of constituency AMs did not agree with equal formal and legal status between constituency and list members and did not believe that they should have equal allowances. A majority also felt that list members should be obliged to do local representative work in more than two constituencies. The one area of possible consensus was that constituency and list members should term themselves as such and never as simply the 'local' member.

Table 5.10

AMs' views on whether the guidelines relating to responsibilities of List and Constituency AMs are adequate, 2004

	Strongly agree	Agree	Neither agree	Disagree nor disagree	Strongly disagree	Total
All members	4 (13.3%)	6 (20.0%)	4 (13.3%)	4 (13.3%)	12 (40.0%)	30 (100.0%)
Constituency	2 (10.0%)	2 (10.0%)	1 (5.0%)	5 (25.0%)	10 (50.0%)	20 (100.0%)
List	2 (20.0%)	4 (40.0%)	3 (30.0%)	0 (0.0%)	1 (10.0%)	10 (100.0%)
Conservative	1 (25.0%)	1 (25.0%)	1 (25.0%)	0 (0.0%)	1 (25.05%)	4 (100.0%)
Labour	1 (6.3%)	0 (0.0%)	1 (6.3%)	4 (25.0%)	10 (62.5%)	16 (100.0%)
Liberal Democrats	1 (25.0%)	3 (75.0%)	0 (0.0%)	0 (0.0%)	0 (0.0%)	4 (100.0%)
Plaid Cymru	1 (16.7%)	2 (33.3%)	2 (33.3%)	1 (16.7%)	0 (0.0%)	6 (100.0%)

Interview evidence suggested that many Labour constituency AMs considered the key issue to be that the presiding officer, Lord Elis-Thomas, had established an unwarranted compliance to his ruling on equal status. Some specifically favoured the introduction of Scottish-style guidance; others a broader debate about roles that recognized the inequality of burdens placed upon constituency and list AMs. Some suggested that introducing inequality into office and staff allowances need not necessarily mean actually reducing list AM allowances. Rather, constituency AMs believed that they alone should have theirs increased. A common complaint was the inability to afford premises that were both in central locations and on the ground floor, thus guaranteeing access for the disabled and elderly. Constituency AMs also suggested that the demand placed upon them justified more casework staff, to parallel the resources provided to MPs.

At the time of the 2004 interviews the proposal to abolish dual candidacy had just been made. It actually received less than wholehearted support among Labour constituency AMs. One Labour AM suggested that it would inconvenience list AMs in having to make a choice of whether to stand as a list or constituency candidate. However, given the strong motivation for list AMs to still serve their party interests in target seats, it was unlikely to change list AM approaches. Regulation of AMs once they had been elected was a much more strongly favoured course of action. List AMs were well aware of constituency AM views and responded robustly. One Conservative list AM interviewed asserted the purpose of list AMs as being to avoid a situation in which Labour dominance meant that there were not sufficient opposition members to effectively scrutinize the executive. List AMs' capacity to play their role in the checks and balances of the Assembly would then be undermined if they were not granted equality of status with constituency AMs. He claimed that MMP actually worked quite well except for the 'immaturity' of the constituency AMs. Another Conservative list AM suggested that it might be useful to have a grown-up discussion about a protocol on local representation, but not on the basis of assumptions that list AMs should not exist and did not try to do a decent job. A Plaid Cymru list AM suggested that obvious Labour party self-interest made the proposal to abolish dual candidacy 'pathetic, trivial and of no interest to the public'. Many list AMs were supportive of STV at least partially because it elected all AMs on the same basis, and thereby ended any notion of them being 'second class' members.

Table 5.11

AMs' views on local representation after devolution, 2004

(i)   Constituency and regional members should have equal formal and legal status
(ii) Members' allowances for constituency and regional list members should be the same
(iii) AMs should always call themselves constituency or regional member as appropriate but never the local member
(iv) Regional list members should be required to work in more than two constituencies

	(i) Equal status	(ii) Equal allowances	(iii) Specific member titles	(iv) Regional AMs in more than two constituencies
All AMs				
Strongly agree	11 (36.7%)	10 (33.3%)	9 (31.0%)	7 (24.1%)
Agree	3 (10.0%)	5 (16.7%)	9 (31.0%)	6 (20.7%)
Neither agree nor disagree	1 (3.3%)	1 (3.3%)	3 (10.3%)	5 (17.2%)
Disagree	4 (13.3%)	4 (13.3%)	4 (13.8%)	3 (10.3%)
Strongly disagree	10 (33.3%)	10 (33.3%)	4 (13.8%)	8 (27.6%)
Constituency AMs				
Strongly agree	2 (10.0%)	1 (5.0%)	8 (42.1%)	7 (35.0%)
Agree	2 (15.0%)	4 (20.0%)	6 (31.6%)	6 (30.0%)
Neither agree nor disagree	1 (5.0%)	1 (5.0%)	0 (0.0%)	4 (20.0%)
Disagree	4 (20.0%)	4 (20.0%)	3 (15.8%)	1 (5.0%)
Strongly disagree	10 (50.0%)	10 (50.0%)	2 (10.5%)	2 (10.0%)
List AMs				
Strongly agree	9 (90.0%)	9 (90.0%)	1 (10.0%)	0 (0.0%)
Agree	1 (10.0%)	1 (10.0%)	3 (30.0%)	0 (0.0%)
Neither agree nor disagree	0 (0.0%)	0 (0.0%)	3 (30.0%)	1 (11.1%)
Disagree	0 (0.0%)	0 (0.0%)	1 (10.0%)	2 (22.2%)
Strongly disagree	0 (0.0%)	0 (0.0%)	2 (20.0%)	6 (66.7%)

Total, n = 29–30; constituency, n = 19–20; regional, n = 9–10

Overall, three points on attitudes to regulation need to be emphasized. First, relationships between Labour MPs and Labour constituency AMs were on the whole cooperative. The issue of regulating multi-level relationships over constituency representation was one that was not seriously raised. Secondly, in contrast there was considerable competition in relationships between constituency and list AMs. Nevertheless, there was a wide divergence of opinion over the need to regulate members' roles, with list AMs favouring the status quo and Labour constituency AMs strongly in favour of new regulation. Finally, whilst Labour constituency AMs raised one or two cheers for abolishing dual candidacy they mainly supported the introduction of guidance that more directly regulated the behaviour of list AMs. List AM perceptions of partisan and spiteful influences in the advocacy of these changes cemented their support for the status quo, or else a shift to STV.

CONCLUSION

In contrast to the former era of MP monopoly provision, the new era of constituency representation was a marketplace in which there were a number of different types of representative supplying a constituency service from which constituents could choose. In this new marketplace MPs' approaches were marked by considerable continuity. They had to make changes, which some resented. On the whole, however, MPs appeared to sustain their commitment to the constituency role, adapted to the new situation and/or were generally sanguine about the arrival of AMs as 'new kids on the block'. Regulation of relationships with AMs was not on the political agenda.

In many ways AMs' adoption of constituency roles also showed considerable continuity with previous practice. Both constituency and list AMs utilized time-honoured practices for organizing constituency services, meeting and responding to constituents. However, what was striking was the depth of constituency AM feeling (predominantly Labour) that the new marketplace of constituency representation was rigged against them. They felt that list AM approaches were illegitimate, and that relationships over local representation were such that regulation of member roles was required. Intriguingly, there appeared to be greater support for Scottish-style guidance than for the abolition of dual candidacy but, whatever the precise form, regulation of relationships between different types of AM was definitely on the political agenda. An assessment of this deeply felt attitude and its consequences became the key focus of debate. Were Labour arguments valid or were they as critics have suggested a reflection of the Wales Labour Party's inability to adjust to pluralism, and a readiness to resort to institutional devices to safeguard local party fiefdoms? The answer is that there are arguments in support of both perspectives. On the one hand, it could be argued that Labour complaints were unjustified. The Assembly electoral system has a proportion of list seats that is very close to the lowest level acceptable to acknowledge it as an MMP system (Farrell, 2001, pp. 114–15). This was of Labour's own making for the simple purpose of creating an electoral system that would give the other parties more of a stake in the Welsh Assembly but which through the much greater proportion of constituency seats would still provide for a majority Labour administration. It might be expected that Labour constituency AMs might be open to competition from opposition list AMs for their constituency seats, and that defeated Labour constituency candidates would have no second route to election through list representation. But there was a simple pay-off here: the vulnerability of individual Labour constituency AMs was to be borne for the sake of legitimizing the Assembly with other parties while sustaining Labour Party power overall. Consequently, it may be worth reminding Labour AMs that whilst they may have felt individual resentments at 'unfair' competition from list AMs, the electoral arrangements were created with their party's strategic aims in mind. They are in danger of being seen to want their cake as well as to eat it.

In such a system, any mechanism that sought to overcome problems experienced mainly by Labour constituency AMs would be open to perceived partisanship. This was a factor in the thinking of Lord Elis-Thomas in his disinclination to introduce Scottish-style guidance. He was concerned that in a chamber half the size of the Scottish Parliament any discrimination against list, and therefore opposition, AMs would be seen as unfair and would have damaging effects on Assembly proceedings (Elis-Thomas, 2005). Such concerns were easily extended to cover the potentially discriminatory impact on opposition parties of the abolition of dual candidacy. On the other hand, Labour could reasonably claim that they should receive credit for introducing MMP when a simple plurality system would have been substantially more in its interests. Equally in practice, while Labour was the largest party after both the 1999 and 2003 elections, it did not do as well as had been expected. It did not have a majority between 1999 and 2003 and MMP clearly diminished Labour's prospects of a guaranteed hold on power. In such a context it is not surprising that the strategic gains for Labour were less clear. Meanwhile, Labour candidates' defeats in 'safe' seats such as the Rhondda, Llanelli and Islwyn in 1999, without compensatory list election, underlined their sense of greater individual vulnerability. Labour candidates realised that they only had prospects of being elected in constituency seats (with the possible exception of one list seat in Mid and West Wales) compared to many opposition party candidates having genuine opportunities in both constituency and list elections. In the context of what they felt to be a competitive electoral system, in which Labour was not guaranteed success, this appeared patently unfair.

The individual prospects for Labour candidates in Wales can be seen as a distinctive problem if we compare with other MMP systems. To return to the case of Germany, it should be noted that candidates from the major parties have a chance of being elected by either means. This is for two reasons. First, 50 per cent of the seats are list seats, meaning there are sufficient to go round. Secondly, party competition throughout Germany is based predominantly on two major parties. Thus, most constituencies are won by a major party candidate, but the defeated major party candidate as long as (s)he is high up the party list is also able to get elected as well as many minor opposition party candidates on the list (see Patzelt, 2007). In contrast, in Wales Labour's success as the only major party in constituency seats is relatively very high and the proportion of list seats is relatively very low. Labour would have to lose a significant number of constituency seats before becoming eligible for many list seats.

If it is accepted that at an individual level Labour candidates experienced unequal prospects and that resulting resentments created problems for the smooth operation of the Assembly, then a case can be made that it was right to address that inequality. Even so, whether the abolition of dual candidacy and the possible introduction of Assembly guidance are appropriate revisions is difficult to say. For, as we have seen, constituency AMs doubted whether abolition of dual candidacy would reduce the targeted constituency work of list AMs. Equally, evidence from Scotland suggests that while the Parliament guidance on member roles was ultimately accepted by list MSPs, this was largely because it was easily circumvented. Labour constituency MSPs considered it inadequate for curbing perceived list MSP targeting of their constituencies (Bradbury et al., 2003). It is questionable, therefore, whether such devices can effectively address the problems perceived by (Labour) constituency AMs. On the other hand, the abolition of dual candidacy on its own could be an effective reform in that it might reduce some of the incentives for perceived excessive list AM targeting, while leaving well alone any questioning of the equal status of list AMs (Bradbury and Russell, 2006).

The ultimate test of reform is that it addresses problems perceived by (Labour) constituency AMs without creating any new ones perceived from an (opposition) list AM perspective. It is important, therefore, that future assessments focus: first, on the extent to which it manages to curb perceived constituency work

targeting without diminishing list AMs' capacity to provide constituency representation overall; and secondly, the extent to which it manages to reduce
perceptions of individual inequalities between the prospects of candidates
without affecting the strategic interests of any one party. Failure to achieve this
balance of concerns would leave constituency representation of continuing
importance in the bedding-down of devolution in Wales, potentially re-igniting
wider debates about the reform of MMP, or indeed the introduction of STV.

ACKNOWLEDGEMENTS

The author acknowledges the Economic and Social Research Council for its
financial support of the project 'Multi-tier politics and its impact on local
representation' (grant number L219252103). He also acknowledges Dr Meg
Russell (University College, London), who co-directed the project, Professor
James Mitchell (University of Strathclyde), who was a research partner, Oonagh
Gay (House of Commons Library) and Professor Robert Hazell (University
College, London), who took part in the research 2002–3, and Guy Lodge and
Akash Paun who were research assistants.

APPENDIX: SURVEY RESPONSE RATES

1. Members of Parliament

	2002	2004
Labour	15 (44.1%)	12 (35.3%)
Conservative	0 (0.0%)	0 (0.0%)
Lib Dem	2 (100.0%)	2 (100.0%)
Plaid Cymru	4 (100.0%)	2 (50.0%)
Total	21 (52.5%)	16 (40.0%)

2. Members of the National Assembly for Wales

	2002	2004
Constituency members	24 (60.0%)	20 (50.0%)
Regional List members	11 (55.5%)	10 (50.0%)
Labour	16 (57.1%)	16 (53.3%)
Conservative	4 (44.4%)	4 (36.4%)
Liberal Democrat	4 (66.7%)	4 (66.7%)
Plaid Cymru	11 (64.7%)	6 (50.0%)
Others	Not applicable	0 (0.0%)
Total	35 (58.3%)	30 (50.0%)

REFERENCES

Bradbury, J. and Russell, M. (2005a). *The Local Work of Scottish MPs and MSPs: effects of non-coterminous boundaries and AMS*, commissioned report to the Arbuthnott Commission on Boundary Differences and Voting Systems, Edinburgh: Scottish Parliament.

Bradbury, J. and Russell, M. (2005b). *Better Governance for Wales: the Proposal to Abolish Dual Candidacy in National Assembly Elections*, written evidence to the Welsh Affairs Committee, *Better Governance for Wales, First Report 2005–6, Government White Paper*, HC 551, evidence 89–93.

Bradbury, J., Gay, O., Hazell, R., and Mitchell, J. (2003). *Local Representation in a Devolved Scotland and Wales, Guidance for Constituency and Regional Members: Lessons from the First Term*, ESRC Devolution Policy Papers, Swindon: ESRC.

Buck, J. and Cain, B. (1990). 'British MPs and their constituencies', *Legislative Studies Quarterly*, 15, 1, 127–43.

Elis-Thomas, D. (2005). *Interview with Lord Elis-Thomas*, 10 January 2005.

Farrell, D. (2001). *Electoral Systems, a Comparative Introduction*, Basingstoke: Palgrave.

Hain, P. and Morgan, R. (2005). Oral evidence to the Welsh Affairs Committee, *Better Governance for Wales*, First Report 2005–6, Government White Paper, HC 551, evidence 63–79.

Lundberg, T. (2002). 'Putting a human face on proportional representation: early experiences in Scotland and Wales', *Representation*, 38, 4, 271–83.

Patzelt, W. (2007 forthcoming). 'The constituency work and roles of MPs at the federal and state levels in Germany', *Regional and Federal Studies*, 16, 4.

Richard, I. (2004). *The Report of the Commission on the Future Powers and Electoral Arrangements of the National Assembly for Wales*, Cardiff: National Assembly.

Rush, M. (2001). *The Role of the Member of Parliament since 1868, from Gentlemen to Players*, Oxford: Oxford University Press.

Scottish Parliament (2000). 'Relationships between MSPs: guidance from the presiding officer', Annexe 5 of *Member's Code of Conduct*, Edinburgh: Parliament.

Searing, D (1994). *Westminster's World, Understanding Political Roles*, Cambridge, Mass.: Harvard University Press.

Wales Office (2005). *Better Governance for Wales*, London: HMSO.

Wyn Jones, R. and Scully, R. (2005). 'Electoral arrangements and electoral politics after the White Paper', written evidence to the Welsh Affairs Committee, *Better Governance for Wales*, First Report 2005–6, Government White Paper, HC 551, evidence 14–16.

6. GREEN AND PLEASANT LAND: BUILDING STRONG AND SUSTAINABLE LOCAL ECONOMIES IN WALES

Molly Scott Cato

ABSTRACT

This article discusses the impact on economic development in Wales of climate change and proposes an alternative trajectory based on the principle of bioregionalism. The National Assembly for Wales has made clear its commitment to sustainability and yet this is not linked up with economic development, which is still following the business-as-usual model and relying on growth bought at the expense of carbon dioxide emissions. This article offers a green critique of economic growth, identifying what types of growth are possible within an ecologically balanced economy. The following key sectors for economic development are identified: biofuels, windpower, organic farming and waste management.

INTRODUCTION

The objective of this article is to discuss the issues of green economics and green business in the context of the Welsh economy. The Welsh Assembly Government has made a strong commitment to sustainability and makes great play of being the only government in the world to have this built into the heart of its decision making. For academics and activists in Wales with an interest in the environment the following quotation is nearly as well-worn as Brundtland's definition of sustainability:

Uniquely among EU Nations, the National Assembly for Wales has a binding legal duty to pursue sustainable development in all it does. This is built into its constitution through section 121 of the Government of Wales Act [the Assembly shall make a scheme setting out how it proposes, in the exercise of its functions, to promote sustainable development] . . . All Ministers are responsible for integrating these principles into our work.[1]

Yet in the arena of economic policy we find the dedication to business-as-usual effectively unchallenged. In spite of being given the seal of approval by Forum for the Future,[2] the Assembly Government's economic development strategy document, *A Winning Wales* (2002), is couched in the old discourse of growth, innovation and competitiveness which a truly sustainable economy needs to evolve beyond. The issue of sustainability is on the policy agenda, and as Bishop and Flynn (2004, p. 110) observe, adding explicit commitments to sustainable development 'may mean that the Assembly is placing a "soft" sustainability commitment on ASPBs' (Assembly sponsored public bodies), but without evidence of policy changes this may amount to little more than 'shallow mainstreaming' such that 'the expectation of what ASPBs will deliver is limited and a business-as-usual scenario will prevail'. Policies such as the subsidising of north–south air travel within Wales (WAG, 2004) make it clear that environmental policy is not joined up with economic policy.

Presently, there are as many definitions of sustainability as there are newly converted believers in climate change. This has led some commentators to suggest not only that these definitions delay the process of operationalization, but also that without a challenge to the given economic and political power structure an ecological economics may not even be possible (Özkaynak, Devine, and Rigby, 2004). Accordingly, this article uses the insights developed by green economists over the past thirty years to trace a path of economic development for Wales that would truly reflect a commitment to 'strong sustainability' and one which certainly does challenge existing assumptions about what an economy is for. Green economists have concluded that sustainability requires that our economy is based in our ecology; allowing our decisions about economic development to be shaped by the planet and its natural cycles. This is what a fully rounded definition of sustainability requires (Barry, 1999).

The key concept underlying the development of sustainable economies is that of the bioregion. Bioregions are natural social units determined by ecology rather than economics, entities that can be largely self-sufficient in terms of basic resources such as water, food, products and services.[3] Ecology demands that we recognize our part in a complex web of natural systems and this should reflect the places we choose to live and how and where we choose to access our resources. Unlike political boundaries, bioregional boundaries are flexible, but should be guided by the principle of subsidiarity in the case of any individual resource or service. Thus, within the bioregional approach beginning with the local is a principle that trumps principles such as price or choice (Desai and Riddlestone, 2002). Such a view has an impressive pedigree, dating back to early critics of industrial capitalism such as William Morris (Delvaux, 2005). Curtis describes such a system of interrelated but independent local economies as 'eco-localism' and argues that it includes: 'local currency systems, food co-ops, micro-enterprise, farmers' markets, permaculture, community supported agriculture (CSA) farms, car sharing schemes, barter systems, co-housing and eco-villages, mutual aid, home-based production, community corporations and banks, and localist business alliances' (2003, p. 83).

Rebuilding strong local economies within our bioregions will present political as well as practical challenges:

A world economy that was sustainable would therefore be almost the exact opposite of the present unsustainable one. It would be localized rather than globalised. It would not have net capital flows. Its external trade would be confined to unimportant luxuries rather than essentials. Each self-reliant region would develop to a certain point and then stop, rather than growing continuously. Investment decisions would be made close to home. And assets would be owned by the people of the area in which they were located. (Douthwaite, 2005)

This is certainly a radical vision which has far-reaching political as well as economic implications. However, as the following discussion asserts, the ecological realities we are facing require us to revise our economic paradigm in the ways suggested by this sort of vision.

THE ECONOMIC IMPACT OF CLIMATE CHANGE

While bioregionalism represents a vision for policy-makers to move towards, the most urgent environmental problem facing us is climate change and so the first challenge for policy-makers is to consider the economic implications of an economy that is massively less reliant on the production of carbon-dioxide (CO_2) pollution. The UK government's target of 60 per cent reductions by 2050 (based on an assumption of a planetary carrying capacity of CO_2 of 550 parts per million) is nowhere near being reached; yet many climate scientists believe that reductions of 80 or even 90 per cent are more realistic (using a carrying-capacity assumption of 450 ppmv) (Hillman, 2004).

Until fairly recently it would have been necessary to spend some time in an article such as this justifying the reality of climate change, but we are no longer arguing about theories; we are living with the reality. Yet the links between the need to reduce carbon dioxide emissions and the way we manage and direct our economic activity are not being made. Figure 6.1 illustrates the carbon cycle, the natural process of fixing of carbon from the atmosphere and its release after a certain length of time – short in the case of cattle eating grass, very long in the case of fossil fuels. Climate change is the result of the burning of fossil fuels that have stored carbon for thousands of years, thus disrupting this natural cycle.

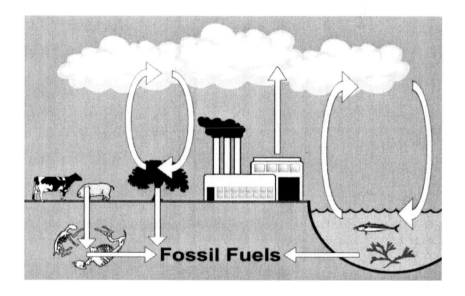

Figure 6.1. The carbon cycle
Source: Reproduced with permission from Environmental Practice at Work *www.epaw.co.uk*

From an economic development perspective the important point is that there are three main systems producing greenhouse gases that are part of our broad economic activities: the growth and decay cycle of living organisms, our interaction with the land via agriculture, and our use of fossil fuels. Of these it is the third that is mainly causing the breakdown in the natural system. Any economic activity that adds to the downwards arrows in Figure 6.1 by absorbing carbon dioxide (such as planting trees) – or, reduces the size of the upwards arrows in the diagram by reducing the emissions of carbon dioxide (such as switching from fossil-fuel intensive agriculture to organic agriculture) is in a sector that is bound to grow in the future. The current commitment to business-as-usual and the failure at the policy level to make the connections between climate change and economic development are resulting in business in Wales failing to establish a place in this new market.

Now that climate change is being taken seriously by world governments businesses are having to pay for their impact on the carbon cycle. This has begun with the Climate Change Levy[4] and initial carbon trading schemes, but it is a sure prediction that the costs to business will increase over coming years. So moving the Welsh economy towards a carbon-neutral position, or better still, investing in low-carbon sectors, would be both economically and ecologically desirable. Wales has many natural advantages in this respect; particularly its energetic natural environment and its sparsely populated land-mass, much of which can sustain tree growth.

Climate change is going to have a major impact on the future path of globalization, and especially on the world trade system. Reports such as *Collision Course* (Simms, 2000) have painted a disturbing picture of the environmental cost of the expansion in global trade. For example, OECD data show that the Asian Tiger economies of Indonesia, Malaysia, the Republic of Korea and Thailand increased their carbon dioxide emissions by between 100 and 278 per cent. Climate change means an end to this economic paradigm, one that achieves growth at the expense of CO_2 emissions. In the new paradigm which takes carbon limits seriously,[5] every gram of CO_2 will have to have achieved its maximum in terms of increasing well-being, and this cannot be said of the exhaust gases of trucks moving manufactured goods from the factories of China across the developed world.

This is the source of the pressure to re-localize our economies, and in the case of Wales this means building a system of strong, local economies where as many of our needs for goods and services as possible are met from as close to home as possible. Within the new paradigm trade is organized according to the principle of 'trade subsidiarity', a straightforward extension of the concept of 'subsidiarity' into the realm of production and consumption, so that we naturally tend to look to purchase goods produced as close to where we live as possible (see Cato, 2003; Woodin and Lucas, 2004). Key challenges emerging from the latter approach include: how realistic it is for complex items such as machine tools or computers to be made in each individual region and what the natural size of the market might be for such goods. In response, Hines (2000), a leading proponent of the re-localization of our economics, makes a strong argument for government action to strengthen and protect local economies; he notes that: 'the essence of these policies is to allow nations, local government and communities to regain control over their local economies; to make them as diverse as possible; and to rebuild stability into community life'. The most important policies are systems of tariffs, subsidies and import and export quotas, to encourage local production. In this respect Hines also suggests a policy of 'site here to sell here', in other words producers would be required to make goods within defined economic areas, balancing the needs of consumers in those areas with those of employees. On the capital side he proposes the grounding of capital through exchange controls, limits on consumer credit, and the imposition of taxes on speculative financial transactions.

Away from such issues, a more sophisticated debate is currently taking place around the concept of 'burden-shifting'. The movement of much of our heavy industry and production to poorer countries, especially China, has meant that many goods consumed in the UK are no longer produced in the UK, meaning that CO_2 emissions associated with this production are now counted in other countries' emissions totals. The problem with CO_2 burden-shifting is that it creates the false impression that a high-consuming country is managing to reduce its emissions – when in fact all that has happened is that its consumption has continued unchanged, and thus its emissions have continued, but the responsibility for counting those emissions has been shifted to another country. Because high consumption of consumer goods is a major driving force in increasing emissions, this very much distorts how we perceive responsibility for emissions and our performance in cutting them. To gain a real sense of our CO_2 emissions it is important that the CO_2 embodied in goods consumed in the UK but manufactured elsewhere should be included in UK emissions totals. Figures from Best Foot Forward[6] suggest that alongside our net per capita emissions of CO_2 of 9,029 kg we should add CO_2 embodied in net imports of 2,132 kg – a 23.6 per cent increase (for further details see Cato, Fitzgibbon, Kemp and Whitelegg, 2004).

The first official recognition in the UK of the importance of carbon neutrality in future economic development was made by Chancellor Gordon Brown, in a speech in which he acknowledged the unavoidable link between climate change and the structure of the economy:

Since 1997 the UK economy has enjoyed high growth, averaging growth of 2.8 per cent a year, or 17 per cent in total. In the same period carbon dioxide emissions have remained about the same. So the carbon intensity of the British economy – carbon emissions per unit of GDP – has fallen by nearly 15 per cent. (Brown, 2005)

This will be the focus of economic development in the twenty-first century, increasing GDP while reducing CO_2. Thus the remainder of this article attempts to apply this new basic assumption of economic policy to the Welsh economy.

Economic growth or economic contraction?

The most basic assumption of economic policy, one that is challenged by those adopting a strong view of sustainability, is the beneficial nature of economic growth. Orthodox economists are beginning to question the ability of a booming economy to generate happiness (Easterlin, 2004; Layard, 2005; Graham, 2005), the so-called well-being agenda, while for green economists the ending of economic growth is a necessary condition for ensuring the balance with our eco-system that sustainability requires (Worldwatch Institute, 2004). The classic green critique of the concept of growth is *The Growth Illusion* by Douthwaite (1992), whose subtitle summarizes the argument of the book as a whole: 'how economic growth has enriched the few, impoverished the many and endangered the planet'. But even Douthwaite makes the point that there are different kinds of growth and lists conditions that economic activity should meet for it to be considered 'good growth'. The latter includes economic activity that does not rely on increased use of energy or raw materials and transport, and has a neutral impact on waste production and pollution (Douthwaite, 1999).

Ekins (2000) contextualizes such concerns and distinguishes between four types of economic growth, as summarized in Figure 6.2. We can see clearly from this figure that, historically, the economy has relied heavily on Type 1 growth, demanding more from the planet to generate higher levels of consumption and return on investment. In the debate over climate change the emphasis has shifted to Type 2 growth, relying on ingenuity to overcome the negative consequences of increased production and consumption. Ekins is keen to point out the sceptical response from many to this suggestion that technology can guarantee business as usual, emphasizing again the difficulty of circumventing the second law of thermodynamics. Type 3 growth, in human welfare, is often more apparent than real, since for example a new 4×4 vehicle may generate immediate well-being but only at the cost of later environmental destruction. Moreover, it is frequently achieved at the cost of other generations, other species or the planet itself. Type 4 growth is the type that green economists have no argument with since it represents the natural ability of the planet to regenerate itself. Again, remembering the importance of living in balance with nature, such growth can be beneficial, for example the use of biomass to generate fuels, when the carbon dioxide produced in burning can be reabsorbed by the next round of tree growth.

Figure 6.2. Ekins's typology of economic growth and consequent environmental problems

Type of growth	Environmental problem	Green economists' verdict
Growth of the economy's biophysical throughput (Type 1)	Increases entropy manifest as growth in waste and pollution	Detrimental
Growth of production (Type 2)	Tends to rely on Type 1 growth or technological advance	Suspicion
Growth of economic welfare (Type 3)	Can be limited by negative environmental externalities and unequal distribution	Approval in theory; scepticism in practice
Environmental growth through increase in ecological capital (regeneration) (Type 4)	None, because nature manages to circumvent the second law of thermodynamics and decrease biospheric entropy	Approval, subject to genuine respect for natural cycles and biodiversity

Ekins provides some useful clarification of what we mean by growth, in contrast to standard accounts which tend to be based on very narrow measures. Historically standard accounts have used gross national product (GNP) but more recently (since the abolition of the distinction between domestic and foreign earnings) they have often centred on gross domestic product (GDP). The argument that these standard and money-based measures of economic activity distort economic performance and do not reflect well-being is now becoming mainstream. The critique has four strands: the problem of the exclusion of unpaid economic activity, such as housework; the addition of negative activity, such as environmental disasters, on the positive side of the balance-sheet; the inadequacy of a summary measure that indicates nothing about distribution; and the sole focus on flows rather than stocks of wealth (Waring, 1989; Anderson, 1991). The Welsh Assembly Government has responded to this debate by reporting a range of alternative indicators, although economic policy still focuses on the GDP, which is drawn from the old discourse and again measured only in monetary terms.

Green economists are developing other measures, such as the Index of Sustainable Economic Welfare (ISEW), which deducts negative economic activity such as crime-fighting and pollution control, and adds in unpaid activity such as housework (see Jackson and Marks, 1994). Research commissioned by the Countryside Council for Wales (2003) from BRASS[7] of Cardiff University produced data for the ISEW for Wales between 1990 and 2000, compared with GDP. They found that after 1992 the GDP trend was steadily upwards whereas the ISEW lost over £1bn between 1997 and 1999. They conclude that:

the trend in the ISEW for Wales is not encouraging, with this socio-economic measure showing little evidence that Wales is developing in a sustainable manner. The maintenance of current patterns of consumption and activity are expected to increase the gap between the ISEW and GDP. (Countryside Council for Wales, 2003)[8]

The data are presented in Figure 6.3.

Figure 6.3. Comparison of ISEW and GDP for Wales, 1990–2000

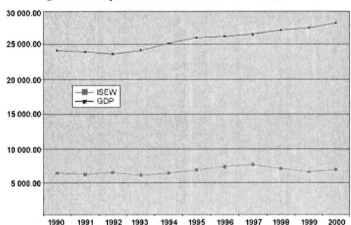

Source: Countryside Council for Wales (2003), *An Index of Sustainable Economic Welfare in Wales 1990–2000*, Bangor: CCW.[9]

In conclusion it appears that climate change is forcing economists and policy-makers alike to ask questions about what our economy is for rather than blindly following the path of maximizing growth.

GREEN JOB CREATION: QUALITY AS WELL AS QUANTITY

Much of the early opposition to the linking of sustainability and economic policy focused on the potential of green policies to reduce employment, despite the fact that as long ago as 1994, Friends of the Earth argued that 'the UK economy could gain in the order of 33,000 to 78,000 additional jobs directly through environmental policy by 2005; the sectors they considered including renewable energy, recycling, public transport and organic farming' (FoE, 1994). This argument now appears to have been concluded by the understanding that greening the economy will be a labour-intensive process. Evidence of this shift in official thinking includes 'The Green Jobs Strategy for Scotland' that was first raised by Green MSP Robin Harper in 2002 and has since been taken up by the Scottish Executive (2005a). Their consultation report estimated a growth in offshore wind production of 185 MW in the UK by 2007 and a near doubling in the waste and recycling sector by 2010. This is what is meant by 'green growth' and, based on the shortcomings of traditional approaches to economic development noted above, it is a priority that the Welsh Assembly Government undertakes a similar assessment of the opportunities for green growth.

In the UK as a whole, the report called *Best of Both Worlds* (Fitzgibbon, 2004) identified how a million extra jobs could be created as a consequence of a green industrial revolution (see Figure 6.4). The principal focus of this key publication was to explain how moving towards a truly sustainable economy would lead to job creation on a large scale, producing whole new areas of employment in sectors such as the mending of goods and the repair of machinery and equipment.

Figure 6.4 Creating a Million Extra Jobs through a Green Industrial Revolution

- 30,000 UK jobs in wind energy leading to a trebling of employment in the energy sector.

- Unsustainable farming practices have cut farming jobs by two-thirds in 50 years – while devastating the environment.

- Organic food production employs 20–30 per cent more people per hectare than chemical- and mechanical-intensive farming.

- Sustainable agricultural practices could create 40,000 new jobs.

- Banning throwaway containers for beer and fizzy drinks would create up to 4,000 jobs.

- More UK jobs in repair of cars and white goods would lead to more skilled jobs tied to the UK.

- Recycling offers to create 14,000 extra jobs in London alone.

Source: Fitzgibbon (2004).

But from a green perspective the quality of those jobs matters as well as the quantity. Schumacher (1979) developed the Buddhist idea of 'right livelihood' to describe work that was simultaneously enriching for the individual and beneficial for the community, while not causing environmental destruction. Recent research (Cato, 2004a) into economic development in the valleys of south Wales highlighted that for most of the era of Conservative government the only regional policy was inward investment. The conclusions were that the policy was of limited social and economic benefit and of vast public expense. 'Back-of-envelope' calculations of costs per job indicate rates as high as £90,000 per job created at the Bridgend Ford plant compared with £4,600 on average per job created in England. Sony's Pencoed factory alone received £15 million in Regional Selective Assistance (RSA) during 1984–99, and between 1988 and 1998 almost £800m in RSA payments were made in Wales, compared with £1.4 billion spent by all the RSAs in England between 1994/5 and 2000/1 (for more details see Cato, 2004a).

An equally serious effect of this policy was the manner in which it undermined the confidence of local people in their ability to solve their own economic problems, and destroyed their self-esteem by requiring unskilled, low-grade and poorly paid work for which they had no respect. The search for 'foreign saviours' was carried out to the cost of the 'local heroes' who, recent analysis concludes, would offer more to their local communities in the long run (see Cato, 2001). There has been a change of emphasis since elected devolution, but what has often not changed is the sort of business to whom Wales's economic future is entrusted. The emphasis is still on globalization, on export-led growth, and on expansion: 'Wales has to become a world-class location, attracting new business from and exporting to, the rest of the world' (WAG, 2004, p. 23). Businesses with a good product, a loyal and productive workforce, and with a market for their goods and services are not supported but face increasing pressure from the need to extract shareholder value and the impossibility of competing with Chinese wage-rates.

For the contemporary policy-maker environmental problems can seem a long way off but a more immediate incentive to reinforce local production and distribution systems may emerge for an economy which, like Wales, finds itself at the edge of the European economy. Wales is increasingly dependent for its basic requirements on oil-based distribution systems that look increasingly unreliable in the era of 'peak oil', when many commentators believe we have already passed the point of maximum oil production (FEASTA, 2003). In such a context increasing Welsh reliance on imported food is not only a wasted business opportunity but also short-sighted. Figures from the Office of National Statistics show that food imports into the UK rose by 24.6 per cent between 1992 and 2002. The annual balance of payments deficit in food moved from £4.7bn to £9.8bn during the same period. In response, the UK government is seemingly unconcerned: a statement from DEFRA of July 2003 noted that 'National Food security is neither necessary nor is it desirable'.[10] This attitude seems irresponsible in view of the increasing competition for the oil on which food transport relies, as well as the reduction in transportation that will be required to tackle climate change. It also undermines rural economies, which have always been based in agriculture, and devalues the contribution farming makes to the national economy.

KEY SECTORS FOR DEVELOPMENT

Having explored the academic and policy literature this discussion now turns to a series of policy recommendations for the Welsh economy that draw upon leading practices and debates. Key sectors in which Wales has a strategic advantage that is enhanced in an era of carbon-limited economic activity are identified and briefly described.

Biofuels

An important sector of the green economy where Wales could have a real competitive advantage is in biofuels. Biofuels represent a huge and renewable supply of energy stored in plant form – an amount equal to several times the world's primary energy consumption. Solar energy is fixed in plants and trees and can be converted into heat by burning. There is nothing new about this; it is the oldest form of energy and the most widespread in the world. What is new is the realization that biofuels are sustainable because the CO_2 emitted when they are burned is the same as that absorbed during the plant's growth, enabling another carbon cycle to be created so long as enough new plants are grown to reproduce those cut down for fuel.

Wales's competitive advantage in this sector lies in the large expanse of undeveloped land available for cultivation. There is huge potential for producing faster-growing fuel crops which can thrive in soil of quality too poor for agricultural crops. Biomass is not only about large trees; shrubby crops are faster-growing and can also be used to provide heat and electricity. One example is Pembrokeshire Bio Energy; this organization is a cooperative launched by farmers in Wales in autumn 2004 to produce, market and supply biofuels, primarily wood chips for heating. The crops are various forms of reeds and willows which are fast-growing and make good fuel. Symbolically, the new Welsh Assembly building will be heated by wood chips. The UK biomass industry is well positioned for expansion: the use of biofuels for electricity generation has been supported through the non fossil-fuel obligation;[11] and EU set-aside subsidies favour energy crop production: currently, energy coppice attracts annual payments of around £140 per hectare.

Scotland is developing its biomass sector and could provide an example for Wales to follow.[12] It already has 17 per cent forest cover compared to a UK average of 11 per cent and it is estimated that the social and environmental benefits provided by Scotland's forests are worth over £100 million per year. Around 40,000 jobs in Scotland depend on the forest industries and the sector contributes around £811m annually to total output. Biofuels can also be used to power vehicles, in this case biodiesel or bioethanol. Wales has the UK's first community biodiesel recycling plant at Ammanford at the western end of the south Wales Valleys. Sundance Renewables recycles used vegetable oil into fuel that can be used in any diesel car. It offers the advantages to the local economy typical of a social enterprise: providing high-quality empowering employment; creating self-reliance to replace dependence on imported mineral diesel; reducing environmental impact by taking used vegetable oil out of the waste stream; and providing a service to local businesses.

Windpower

Wind energy is another green sector where we might follow Scotland's example; three-quarters of the UK's installed renewable energy generation capacity is in Scotland (Scottish Executive, 2005b). The main brake on the further development of wind power in the UK is now the planning process, with a campaign by local communities against the destruction of their visual amenity gaining momentum. It is clear that the way the sector is presently structured local communities have much to lose and little to gain from a windfarm development in their backyard. This suggests the need for a change in ownership patterns in the wind energy sector. A recent UK government Department of Trade and Industry seminar focused on sharing the experience of Denmark, where much of the wind-energy capacity is organised by the community that uses the energy or benefits from its sale. The Global Watch[13] mission visited Denmark in October 2004 under the auspices of Cooperatives-UK. The support of the UK government suggests that they recognize the need to offer local communities the value of windpower if the large-scale expansion they plan is to succeed. Wales is already well-placed in terms of community windfarm development: the UK's first community windfarm, Bro Dyfi, opened near Machynlleth in April 2003. The company has 59 shareholders, with holdings ranging from £100 and a maximum of £1000. The single turbine, known as *Pŵer Pobl* or People Power, has a maximum output of 75Kw, enough for nearly fifty households.

Organic farming

Organic farming is another sector that would be prioritized in a green economy: this is clearly a key economic sector from a green perspective. Organic agriculture is sustainable and the produce demands a price premium. This form of agriculture would also benefit Wales's natural heritage and wildlife, thus having other benefits in terms of well-being and the tourism industry. The large size of the market, the large proportion of imports and the price premium all indicate this is a market ripe for expansion (see Figure 6.5).

Because of pressure from Green MSPs, Scotland again appears to be leading the UK in this sector, with over 425,000 hectares of land (8 per cent of the total) in conversion or in organic production, which represents 57 per cent of the total in the UK. Of this, 304,000 hectares are supported by the Organic Aid Scheme, which offers assistance in the first five years of organic production or conversion.[14]

Figure 6.5 Organic agriculture: a profitable and growing market.[15]

- UK demand for organic produce is growing at 15 per cent per year; up to two-thirds of UK organic produce is imported.
- The UK organic market is predicted to be worth more than £1billion this year.
- 80 per cent of organic fruit and vegetables and 85 per cent of cereals are imported.
- 45 per cent of vegetables which can be produced in the UK (potatoes, carrots, cauliflower, cabbage, broccoli, lettuce) are imported.
- Each year £136 million is spent removing pesticides and nitrates from drinking water in the UK.
- Welsh agriculture is a major contributor to climate change as it is grossly fossil fuel dependent. Organic farming and local markets are more fuel-efficient.

A report from Richard Blacklaw-Jones (2004) of the Organic Centre Wales in Aberystwyth discusses the health and economic advantages of encouraging local procurement of organic produce focusing especially on hospitals and schools.

This draws on the idea of bioregionalism, as outlined above, for it advocates local procurement as a strong basis for a local economy. Such procurement of organic food has several advantages: the food is of better quality because it has travelled shorter distances; local jobs are protected both in the production and preparation of food; less carbon dioxide is needlessly produced in transporting food over long distances. It is an issue that has been put into practice by Powys Food Links, a local procurement project growing out of collaboration between the Soil Association and Powys County Council in 1998 which aims to assist producers to sell more produce locally, increase local awareness of local food and drink and help consumers buy it directly, thus keeping more value in the local economy. The purchasing routes supported by this project include direct marketing by producers, box schemes, farmers' markets, farm shops, mail order and local shops.[16]

Wealth from waste

Again, drawing on the bioregional vision, the new target for waste management is Zero Waste (see Murray, 2002), recognizing the need to find new uses for old products and to manage the problem within the local economy rather than seeking to dump waste elsewhere. In the area of waste management the challenge for the Welsh Assembly Government is to make good its commitment to sustainability by adopting a Zero Waste vision for Wales. This offers great business opportunities which are currently being lost, for example by the export of waste vegetable oil to Germany to be turned into biodiesel before being reimported into the UK and mixed with mineral diesel for resale. It has been estimated that for the UK as a whole, an intensive recycling programme would create 15,000 jobs in collection and sorting and 25,000 to 40,000 jobs in manufacturing and reprocessing (Murray, 1999). The waste market alone was worth a total of £4.6bn in 2000 (Fitzgibbon, 2004).

The zero waste concept also has implications for other businesses which will be made to take responsibility for materials used in their products that cannot be recycled or reused. This will take us to an economy of reusable spare parts, like those presently being developed by Ford, and where biodegradable components become the norm, such as the plant-based plastics used to make doors on Volkswagen cars. It will also take us into an economy where reuse and repair become sources of employment, replacing our throwaway economy.

Wales has a poor record for recycling: the latest edition of *Key Environmental Statistics for Wales*[17] shows an average rate for domestic recycling of only 7 per cent for Wales as a whole, and the worst unitary authorities only achieving less than 3 per cent. The Welsh Assembly Government has adopted a very unambitious target of 15 per cent. This seems tame given the fact that the waste sector is bound to grow as pressure from Europe to reduce dumping leads to increases in the Landfill Levy. The potential for jobs growth via locally based economic activity in reuse, repair and recycling is vast.

CONCLUSION

The vision of an alternative economics paradigm presented in this article is a challenging one, yet it has enormous positive potential:

> Eco-localism suggests ultimately a radical reorganization of economic life across the globe, disassembly of globalization, re-orientation to a broader range of human needs and values and environmental imperatives than is present in conventional economic theory or policy. To this extent, eco-localism is not only a more explicit normative theory, it may also be a more useful positive economic paradigm.

Thus Curtis (2003, p. 100) concludes one of the few developed academic analyses of the existing movement to link ecological concerns with economic needs through the development of bioregional economies. The present discussion has worked from this vision to draw out its implications for economic development in Wales, and has highlighted specific business opportunities that could be encouraged and supported. The perspective that has been offered is neither sanguine nor complacent about the challenges faced by Wales, and acknowledges the dedicated work being carried out already by those creating projects in fields such as eco-housing, biofuels, community recycling, organic food supply and community currencies. Nevertheless, many future challenges remain in fully translating the vision of a green economy into practice.

A whole range of recent natural events from the 2003 heatwave in Europe to the 2005 hurricane season in the Caribbean have increasingly convinced policy-makers of the reality of climate change. However, the economic consequences of the realization, namely that we cannot use fossil fuels and the earth does not have the ability to absorb pollution to generate economic growth ad infinitum, are so unpalatable for those who live within the conventional economics paradigm that they are left vacillating. From the perspective of green economics the route out of the policy wilderness begins with the realization that economic growth is not necessary and may not even be beneficial. Thus by beginning to embed our economy in our ecology and respecting the natural cycles and the need for planetary balance we can create the sort of sustainable Welsh economy that has been outlined in this article. Unless we make rapid strides along this road the future will be grim for ourselves and our children. But if we do take those steps, Wales will have a bright future. We have all the resources necessary to build a successful new economy: water, land, renewable energy and an intelligent, well-educated population. The realities of climate change and resource depletion mean that one day all economies will have to become sustainable: it is important that we begin the process of transforming Wales into such an economy, and devolution has given us the power to do so.

It is a criticism commonly made of the green vision for the economy that life would be dreary and joyless. From the perspective of the green economists themselves, nothing could be further from the truth. As Richard Douthwaite writes:

Making one's own region sustainable along these lines might seem to involve turning it into a grim, restrictive place but I think that's wrong and that it will become a liberating and joyous one instead. Certainly, the only way for an area to escape from a system that continually impoverishes the periphery by taking resources to the centre, wherever that centre may be, is to build a protective niche within which its local economy can develop diversity and become more sustainable. (Douthwaite, 2005, p. 123)

This comment was made in the context of Ireland, which has seen all the negative consequences of rapid economic development both environmentally and socially in recent years. Perhaps this is the lesson from Ireland we should ask our policy-makers to learn from, rather than imitating the now rather forlorn 'Celtic tiger'?

ACKNOWLEDGEMENTS

The author wishes to thank the anonymous reviewers of *Contemporary Wales* for the helpful and supportive suggestions for changes that have greatly strengthened the argument. She is also grateful to the Network of Development Researchers of the University of Wales, and Alan Thomas in particular, for the invitation to the colloquium at Gregynog that led to the writing of this article.

NOTES

[1]   Taken from the Welsh Assembly Government's website: *www.wales.gov.uk.*
[2]   Forum for the Future describes itself as 'the UK's leading sustainable development

charity' whose 'object as a charity is to promote sustainable development and to educate different groups in sustainable development, in order to accelerate the building of a sustainable way of life', see *www.forumforthefuture.org.uk.*

[3] Clearly 'basic resources' is a subjective concept, with one person's life of paradise being another's hair-shirt. The idea relates to that of trade subsidiarity, where the more complex or luxurious the product the more likely it is to be found outside the local economy (see Cato, 2003, for a further discussion). For a discussion of how a consumer culture itself defines what are basic needs see Cato, 2004b.

[4] The Climate Change Levy, which came into effect on 1 April 2001, is a tax on users of energy in the non-domestic sector (industry, commerce and the public sector) which aims to encourage these sectors to improve energy efficiency and reduce emissions of greenhouse gases.

[5] This might not only be carbon trading but carbon taxes and even rationing.

[6] An Oxford-based sustainable development consultancy responsible for the creation of ecological footprint analysis and whose aim is 'to help regions, organisations and communities to reduce their "ecological footprint" through the delivery of a wide range of analytical tools and consulting services'.

[7] Centre for Business Relationships, Accountability and Society.

[8] See *www.brass.cf.ac.uk/projects/03Measuring_Sustainability—Developing_Sustain-ability_Indicators—Key_Findings.html.*

[9] Research conducted by Prof. Max Munday and Annette Roberts of the Centre for Business Relationships, Accountability and Society.

[10] See comments by James Paice MP, Hansard, (19 Jan. 2005), 673, col. 875.

[11] Replaced by the Renewables Obligation in April 2002, which, according to the DTI website, 'is the Government's main mechanism for supporting renewable energy . . . it provides a substantial market incentive for all eligible forms of renewable energy'.

[12] Data from Scottish Forest Industries Cluster: *www.forestryscotland.com.*

[13] A service offered by the DTI to ensure that UK businesses keep abreast of innovation and development taking place in other countries.

[14] See *www.scotland.gov.uk/Topics/Agriculture/Agricultural-Policy/15869/OAS/OrganicAS.*

[15] Information from the Soil Association.

[16] For more information, see *www.foodlinks.powys.gov.uk.*

[17] Wales Assembly Government, 2004 edition, available at *www.wales.gov.uk/keypubstatisticsforwales/content/publication/environment/2004.*

REFERENCES

Anderson, V. (1991). *Alternative Economic Indicators*, London: Routledge.

Barry, J. (1999). *Rethinking Green Politics: Nature, Virtue and Politics*, London: Sage.

Bishop, K. and Flynn, A. (2004). 'Sustainable development in Wales: schemes and structure, debate and delivery', *Contemporary Wales*, 17, 92–112.

Blacklaw-Jones, R. (2004). *Local procurement of organic food in Pembrokeshire: the health and other benefits of doing so*, Aberystwyth: Organic Centre Wales.

Brown, G. (2005). Speech by the Rt Hon. Gordon Brown MP, Chancellor of the Exchequer, at the Energy and Environment Ministerial Roundtable, 15 March, *www.hm-treasury.gov.uk/newsroom_and_speeches.*

Cato, M. S. (1997). *Climate Change is Here, Now*, London: Green Party.

Cato, M. S. (2001). 'Inward investment and economic regeneration: listening to workers in Rhondda-Cynon-Taff', *Local Economy*, 16, 3, 198–220.

Cato, M. S. (2003). *Trade Subsidiarity: Trade Justice from a Planetary Perspective*, Aberystwyth: Green Audit.

Cato, M. S. (2004a). *The Pit and the Pendulum: A Cooperative Future for Work in the Valleys of South Wales*, Cardiff: University of Wales Press.

Cato, M. S. (2004b). 'Sen and the art of market-cycle maintenance', *Sustainable Economics*, 12, 5.

Cato, M. S., Fitzgibbon, S., Kemp, P. and Whitelegg, J. (2004). 'The international challenge of climate change: UK leadership in the G8 and EU', submission to the House of Commons Environmental Audit Committee from the Green Party of England and Wales, *The International Challenge of Climate Change: UK Leadership in the G8 and EU*, fourth report of the session 2004–5 (March 2005).

Countryside Council for Wales (2003). *An Index of Sustainable Economic Welfare in Wales 1990–2000*, Bangor: CCW.

Curtis, F. (2003). 'Eco-localism and sustainability', *Ecological Economics*, 46, 83–102.

Delvaux, M. (2005). ' "Oh Me! Oh Me! How I Love the Earth": Williams Morris's *News from Nowhere* and the birth of sustainable society', *Contemporary Justice Review*, 8, 2, 131–46.

Desai, P. and Riddlestone, S. (2002). *Bioregional Solution for Living on One Planet*, Schumacher Briefing no. 8, Totnes: Green Books.

Douthwaite, R. (1992). *The Growth Illusion: How Economic Growth has Enriched the Few, Impoverished the Many and Endangered the Planet*, Totnes: Green Books.

Douthwaite, R. (1999). 'The need to end economic growth', in M. S. Cato and M. Kennett (eds), *Green Economics: Beyond Supply and Demand to Meeting People's Needs*, Aberystwyth: Green Audit.

Douthwaite, R. (2005). 'Why localisation is essential for sustainability', in *Growth: The Celtic Cancer: Why the Global Economy Damages our Health and Society*, FEASTA Review no. 2, Dublin: FEASTA.

Easterlin, R. A. (2004). 'The economics of happiness', *Daedalus*, 133, 2, 26–33.

Ekins, P. (2000). *Economic Growth and Environmental Sustainability: The Prospects for Green Growth*, London: Routledge.

FEASTA (2003). *Before the Wells Run Dry: Ireland's Transition to Renewable Energy*, Dublin: FEASTA.

Fitzgibbon, S. (2004). *Best of Both Worlds: Green Policies for Job Creation and Sustainability*, London: Green Party, available at *www.greenparty.org.uk/files/reports/2004*.

Friends of the Earth (1994). *Working Future? Jobs and the Environment*, London: FoE.

Graham, C. (2005). 'The economics of happiness', *World Economics*, 6, 3, 41–56.

Hillman, M. (2004). *How We Can Save the Planet*, Harmondsworth: Penguin.

Hines, C. (2000). *Localization: A Global Manifesto*, London: Earthscan.

Jackson, T. and Marks, N. (1994). *Measuring Sustainable Economic Welfare: A Pilot Index: 1950–1990*, York: Stockholm Environment Institute.

Layard, R. (2005). *Happiness: Lessons from a New Science*, Harmondsworth: Penguin.

Murray, R. (1999). *Creating Wealth from Waste*, London: Demos.

Murray, R. (2002). *Zero Waste*, London: Greenpeace Environmental Trust.

Oswald, A. J. (1997). 'Happiness and economic performance', *Economic Journal*, 107, 445, 1815–31.

Özkaynak, B., Devine, P. and Rigby, D. (2004). 'Operationalising strong sustainability: definitions, methodologies and outcomes', *Environmental Values*, 13, 3, 279–303.

Schumacher, E. F. (1979), *Good Work*, London: Cape.

Scottish Executive (2005a). *Going for Growth: A Green Jobs Strategy for Scotland*, Edinburgh: Scottish Parliament.

Scottish Executive (2005b). *Scotland's Renewable Energy Potential: Realising the 2020 Target*, Future Generation Group Report 2005, Edinburgh: Scottish Parliament.

Simms, A. (2000). *Collision Course: Free Trade's Free Ride on the Global Climate*, London: New Economics Foundation.

Waring, M. (1989). *If Women Counted: A New Feminist Economics*, London: Macmillan.

Welsh Assembly Government (2002). *A Winning Wales: The National Economic Development Strategy of the Welsh Assembly Government*, Cardiff: WAG.

Welsh Assembly Government (2004). *Intra-Wales Scheduled Air Services Consultation Document*, Cardiff: WAG.

Woodin, M. and Lucas, C. (2004). *Green Alternatives to Globalisation: A Manifesto*, London: Pluto.

Worldwatch Institute (2004), *State of the World: The Consumer Society*, New York: Worldwatch Institute.

7. WALES'S CHANGING POPULATION: A DEMOGRAPHIC OVERVIEW

David Dunkerley

INTRODUCTION

The aim of this article is to provide a brief demographic outline of Wales, providing a backdrop to related articles on the lifecourse. The presentation is largely on the basis of statistical information derived from official sources such as the national census.[1] By their very nature such statistics are 'cold' and detached, possessing none of the rich qualitative material that is found in other articles in this issue. Nevertheless, the statistics do provide a profile of Wales that suggests a nation divided geographically and along lines of age, religion, ethnicity, health and household formation. The profile also enables interesting comparisons with the rest of the UK and European countries.

General trends are largely consistent with the rest of the UK (e.g. an ageing population, a growing population and a more culturally diverse population) but specifically there are notable exceptions such as the relatively poor state of health of the population of Wales. Such consistencies and differences are explored in detail below.

POPULATION

Along with the rest of the UK, successive decennial censuses indicate that the population of Wales continues to rise. By 2001 (the last census year) the population of Wales stood at 2,910,200, a modest increase over the previous twenty years (2,813,500 in 1981 and 2,873,000 in 1991). Over the fifty years since 1951, the population had grown by more than 300,000. Such bland global figures, however, disguise some interesting developments when compared with the distribution of population by nation within the UK and, indeed, within Wales itself. As a proportion of the population of the whole of the UK, Wales stands at 4.9 per cent, a small decrease on both 1981 and 1991 when the population of Wales comprised 5 per cent of the UK population. Both England and Northern Ireland have seen their proportions grow over the same period while Scotland has experienced a proportional decline from 9.2 per cent in 1981 to 8.6 per cent in 2001.

The pattern of population change within Wales itself is more complex. About two-thirds of the population live in south Wales with the highest populations in 2001 being found in Cardiff (307,000), Rhondda Cynon Taff (RCT) (232,000) and Swansea (224,000). In terms of inhabitants, the smallest of the 22 unitary authorities was Merthyr Tydfil with a population of 56,000.

Those unitary authorities experiencing the greatest socio-economic difficulties have also experienced a proportional decrease in population. Included here are Merthyr Tydfil, Blaenau Gwent and RCT. With a small number of exceptions such as Cardiff, the proportional increase has been in the more rural authorities such as Powys, Carmarthenshire and Pembrokeshire. Remarkably, Ceredigion's population increased during the twenty year period (1981–2001) by more than a quarter and 14 per cent in the previous decade.

Wales is also following the general UK trend of having an ageing population. The overall increase in the population of Wales between 1981 and 2001 of just over 2 per cent is not matched equally by age group. Most dramatically, there has been an increase in the proportion of those of retirement age (currently taken as 60 for women and 65 for men) of 9.1 per cent in that period, a proportionate decrease of 5.8 per cent of children and young people under the age of 16 and a rise of 2.9 per cent of those of working age. The absolute numbers reveal the stark reality that in 2001 Wales had 59,000 more people of retirement age than in 1981 (roughly equivalent to the total population of Merthyr Tydfil) and 38,800 fewer young people under the age of 16. According to the mid 2002 population estimates (*Regional Trends*, ONS, 2004a) a fifth of the population of Wales is now of retirement age although, again, there are variations by unitary authority. For example, those of retirement age comprise 26.5 per cent of the population of Conwy compared with 16 per cent of Cardiff's population. Furthermore, Wales has a slightly older population than the rest of the UK (20.2 per cent and 18.4 per cent of pensionable age respectively). Figures produced by Eurostat in 2003 show that Wales – at 17.4 per cent – has a higher proportion of the population aged 65 and over than all of what were then the 15 EU member states with the exception of Italy with 18.2 per cent.

Unsurprisingly, the density of the population of Wales varies along the urban–rural continuum. At the extremes, in 2002 there were 2,222 people per km² in Cardiff compared with a mere 25 per km^2 in Powys. Blaenau Gwent, Caerphilly, Cardiff, Merthyr Tydfil, Newport, RCT, Swansea and Torfaen all have a population density in excess of 500 per km^2. Wales is far less densely populated than the UK as a whole (141 people per km^2 and 244 per km^2 respectively).

The death rate (i.e. deaths per 1,000 of population) for the whole of Wales in 2001 was 11.8, the highest of all UK nations (for the UK overall the figure was 10.2) but, again, there are substantial differences by authority. Conwy, for example, had a rate of 15.1 compared with 9.6 in Cardiff. Other areas experiencing a higher than average death rate include Anglesey, Blaenau Gwent, Carmarthenshire, Denbighshire, Merthyr Tydfil and Powys. This higher rate might be expected where the population is older (as in the rural authorities) but in Blaenau Gwent and Merthyr Tydfil a range of social indicators may be contributors.

HOUSEHOLD COMPOSITION

In 2001, the population of Wales of almost 3 million were living in 1.2 million households. Of the latter, 29 per cent comprised households of persons living alone, a proportion that grew in the previous decade from 25 per cent in 1991 but still slightly lower than the English counterpart (30.1 per cent). About a half of the one person households were made up of people of pensionable age in Wales.

A further 28 per cent of households were made up of families with dependent children. Although the majority of these households contained married couples (17 per cent of all households) the trend is for this to be a declining majority since in 1991 married couple households formed 23 per cent of all households. As this household profile has declined, households with lone parents and dependent children have increased to 7.3 per cent of the total (5 per cent in 1991) as have households with cohabiting couples with dependent children (still only 3 per cent of the total number of households but double the position of 1991). In Wales lone parent households with both dependent and non-dependent children account for 10.6 per cent of all households, rather higher than the English figure of 9.5 per cent.

Compared with England, there are small differences in the profile of the marital status of the population of Wales. The figures in parenthesis show the English equivalent:

- single and never married (aged over 16 years) – 28 per cent (30.2 per cent);
- separated people – 1.9 per cent (2.4 per cent);

- married – 44.5 per cent (43.5 per cent);
- divorced – 8.7 per cent (8.2 per cent);
- widowed – 9.4 per cent (8.3 per cent).

The latest figures available show that in Wales in 2003 the proportion of live births outside marriage equalled that of live births within marriage (*Digest of Welsh Statistics*, NAW, 2003). This is part of a consistent trend shown, for example, by 56 per cent of live births being within marriage in 1998 with the numbers dropping by one or two percentage points each year since then. The 2001 Census indicated that 48.3 per cent of births occurred outside marriage, a much higher figure than for the UK as a whole where the figure was 40.1 per cent. Within Wales there were very large variations – 63.5 per cent of live births were outside of marriage in Blaenau Gwent in 2001 compared with 35.2 per cent in neighbouring Monmouthshire. Furthermore, 18 per cent of babies were born to lone mothers in Wales in 2001 (compared with 13 per cent in England and 14 per cent in Scotland). Out of every 1,000 live births in Wales in 2001, 35 were to teenagers (28 in England).

HEALTH AND WELL-BEING

Across Wales 12.5 per cent of the population reported that their health was not good (in the 12 months prior to 29 April 2001) compared with 9.0 per cent in England. In each of the Welsh unitary authorities poor health was reported above the English average, with Merthyr Tydfil having double the proportion (18.1 per cent) of the latter. Monmouthshire had the least proportion of the population stating that their health was 'not good' – 9.5 per cent. Additionally nearly a quarter (23.3 per cent) of the population of Wales cited having 'limiting long-term illness' that included disability limiting daily activities or work. 30 per cent of the population of Merthyr Tydfil, 29.4 per cent from Neath Port Talbot, 28.3 per cent of Blaenau Gwent and 27.2 per cent of RCT were in this category. Even in those authorities with the least proportions (such as Cardiff, the Vale of Glamorgan and Monmouthshire) close on a fifth of the population experienced limiting long-term illness. Over half of the households of Blaenau Gwent and Merthyr Tydfil had individuals so defined.

'WELSHNESS'

Although the 2001 census did not include a category of national identity as 'Welsh' 14.4 per cent of respondents (some 417,800 people) chose to write 'Welsh' on the form. It is interesting to compare this figure with the 2001/2002 Annual Local Area Labour Force Survey where respondents were specifically asked about their national identity. In this case, the figure rose to 69.2 per cent of respondents across Wales but with major differences in different geographical locations. The lowest proportions of people identifying themselves as Welsh were in Flintshire (43.3 per cent) and Conwy (49.5 per cent); the highest in Merthyr Tydfil (87.0 per cent), Blaenau Gwent (85.2 per cent) and RCT (54.3 per cent).

Three quarters of the residents in Wales in 2001 were actually born in Wales (nearly 97 per cent had been born in the UK). It is interesting to note that since the Second World War there has been a consistent increase in the proportion of those living in Wales who were born in England. Less than one in seven residents was born in England in 1951 compared with a fifth in 2001. Again, there are considerable differences across Wales and these differences mirror the response to national identity. The lowest proportions of Welsh-born residents in 2001 were to be found in Flintshire (51 per cent) and Conwy (54 per cent), followed by Powys with 56 per cent. The highest proportions were to be found in south Wales – Blaenau Gwent and Merthyr Tydfil (92 per cent), Caerphilly and RCT (90 per cent) and Neath Port Talbot (89 per cent).

Perhaps unexpectedly, there is a link between age and whether born in Wales or not. Younger people are more likely to have been born in Wales. In fact, 87 per cent of young people under the age of 16 years were born in Wales compared with 74 per cent of those between 16 and 34 years, and 71 per cent aged between 35 and 64. Variations do exist, most markedly in the cases of Conwy and Denbighshire where English-born residents of retirement age out-numbered, in absolute terms, those born in Wales.

The 2001 census also shows that of the 2.8 million people who were born in Wales and living in the UK as a whole, 22 per cent of them were living in England. This percentage has changed little since 1951 (23 per cent) although in 1991 20 per cent were resident in England. The most likely destinations in 2001 for these Wales-born individuals were London and the South East (29 per cent) and the South West (18 per cent). Those with higher educational qualifications and higher socio-economic status were more likely to be living in England. Thus, 10 per cent of those men of working age born in Wales and living in Wales were graduates compared with 38 per cent of those born in Wales and living in

England. Similarly, 22 per cent of women born in Wales and still living in Wales were categorized in the managerial and professional class compared with 49 per cent of Welsh-born women living in England. (*Annual Local Area Labour Force Survey*, ONS, 2001/02).

The 2001 census indicated an increase in the use of the Welsh language in Wales. This was the first census to ask respondents about their knowledge of Welsh at different levels of knowledge, understanding and application although since 1891 a basic question on speaking Welsh had been included. Indeed, in that year 54 per cent of the population declared that they could speak Welsh. This figure had sunk to 19 per cent in 1981 and 1991 but increased to 21 per cent in 2001. 16 per cent stated that they could speak, read and write Welsh while 24 per cent said they could understand Welsh. The introduction of Welsh as part of the national curriculum in Wales has obviously played a key role in this increased use and understanding of the Welsh language. In fact, 39 per cent of children aged 10 to 15 years could speak, read and write Welsh, decreasing to 25 per cent for those aged 16 to 19 years and declining further in adulthood with only 11 per cent in the 35 to 49 age bracket. Throughout the population of Wales men have fewer Welsh language skills than women and amongst younger people this difference is most pronounced with the proportion of boys aged 10 to 19 years who were able to speak, read and write Welsh seven percentage points lower than girls of the same age.

In general, the north and west of Wales had the largest proportion of the population who could speak, read and write Welsh. In both Gwynedd and the Isle of Anglesey over half the population stated they had this ability (61 per cent and 51 per cent respectively). The south-east of Wales and the border areas posted much lower figures with Monmouthshire and Blaenau Gwent having only 7 per cent of their respective populations speaking, reading and writing Welsh. Similarly, 69 per cent of the population aged 3 or over could speak Welsh in Gwynedd but only 9 per cent in Monmouthshire and Blaenau Gwent.

ETHNICITY

Table 7.1 shows vividly that the population of Wales is overwhelmingly 'white' as described by respondents' ethnicity in the 2001 census. Whereas 96 per cent of the population of Wales gave their ethnic origin as 'White British', the parallel figure in England was 87 per cent. Only 2.1 per cent of the population of Wales are from non-white ethnic backgrounds, just 61,580 people. This proportion has increased from 1.5 per cent in 1991 and is largely as a result of increases in the proportion of Indian, Pakistani and Bangladeshi people. Indeed, the largest non-white group have Asian descent headed with about a third each defining themselves as Indian or Pakistani.

Table 7.1
Distribution of ethnic groups in Wales, April 2001

	Numbers	%
White British	2,786,605	95.99
White Irish	17,689	0.61
Other white	37,211	1.28
Total white	2,841,505	97.88
Mixed	17,661	0.61
Indian	8,261	0.28
Pakistani	8,287	0.29
Bangladeshi	5,436	0.19
Other Asian	3,464	0.12
Total Asian or Asian British	25,448	0.88
Black Caribbean	2,597	0.09
Black African	3,727	0.13
Other black	745	0.03
Total black or black British	7,069	0.25
Chinese	6,267	0.22
Other	5,135	0.18
All non-white	61,580	2.12
Total	2,903,085	100.00

A significant proportion of the non-white population described themselves as being of 'mixed' ethnic origin while over 7,000 people declared their ethnicity as 'black'.

The non-white population of Wales is largely concentrated in the south Wales urban areas, especially in the coastal cities. Thus, Cardiff's non-white population accounts for 8.4 per cent (25,700 people) of its total and the figure for Newport is 6,600 (4.8 per cent). Only three other authorities have a non-white population exceeding 2,000 (Swansea, RCT and the Vale of Glamorgan). The lowest proportion of non-white residents is on the Isle of Anglesey (0.7 per cent). The 2001 census figures indicate that about a half of the black and Asian population of Wales lived in Cardiff, as did a third of the mixed and Chinese groups.

RELIGION

Information on the religious profile of Wales is not as accurate as other social indicators because provision of this information in the 2001 census was voluntary. In fact, 8.1 per cent of the population (234,100 people) chose not to answer the question relating to religion.

Table 7.2
Distribution of religious affiliation across Wales, April 2001

	Residents of Wales		Percentage of those with stated religion
	Thousands	Percentage	
Total	2,903.1	100.0	
Religion not stated	234.1	8.1	
No religion	537.9	18.5	
Total with stated religion	2,131.0	73.4	100.0
Christian	2,087.2	71.9	97.9
Buddhist	5.4	0.2	0.3
Hindu	5.4	0.2	0.3
Jewish	2.3	0.1	0.1
Muslim	21.7	0.8	1.0
Sikh	2.0	0.1	0.1
Other religions	6.9	0.2	0.3

Clearly, Wales remains a predominantly Christian country although there are interesting variations in the proportions who declared themselves as Christians. These range from a low of 64.2 per cent in Blaenau Gwent to a high of 79.4 per cent in Anglesey. Similarly in Wales as a whole 18.5 per cent of the population stated that they had no religious affiliation ranging from 12.9 per cent in Flintshire to around a quarter of the population of RCT and Blaenau Gwent.

Only 1.5 per cent of the population (43,800 people) declared themselves as belonging to non-Christian faiths. By far the largest group is Muslim but still only comprising 0.7 per cent of the population. Over the last century the Jewish population of Wales has halved to its present level of 2,300 people. Again, the geographical distribution of the non-Christian followers is uneven although there is a clear pattern of the south having the largest concentrations. Thus, Cardiff had 17,300 people (or 5.7 per cent of the population) of non-Christian faiths followed by Newport with 4,400 (3.8 per cent) people and Swansea with 3,800 (1.7 per cent). No other local authority had more than 2,000 people of a non-Christian faith.

The 'white' population of Wales was older than the population of other ethnic groups. 'White Irish' comprised the oldest group with 32 per cent of white Irish people being above working age. This compares with 5 per cent of the 'mixed' population and 3 per cent of Bangladeshis. 47 per cent of the 'mixed' group were aged under 16 years. In terms of religious groups, between 5 and 6 per cent of Muslims, Hindus and Sikhs were pensioners, compared with 24 per cent of Christians and 30 per cent of Jews.

DISCUSSION

This brief demographic outline of Wales paints a picture of a diverse nation possessing considerable differences by geographical area. This is consistent with a country with a relatively small population and one that is largely rural but with population concentrations in a small number of cities in the south. Those areas of greater population density inevitably display different characteristics from their rural counterparts. Similarly, those areas of relative economic deprivation are different on a range of dimensions from relative prosperous areas. By way of example, then, it is unsurprising to find a younger population in urban areas, a less healthy population of economically poor areas, a more 'Welsh' population in areas of low geographical mobility or a more culturally diverse population in denser population centres. More surprising findings relate to comparisons with the rest of the UK especially with regard to household composition, health and geographical mobility. This is not the place to account for similarities and differences; rather the aim has been to present an objective account of the changing and current patterns of the population profile.

NOTE

1   The 2001 census provides most of the statistical material in this article along with profiles specifically focusing on Wales provided by the Office for National Statistics (ONS). Unless otherwise specified, the individual statistics cited can be accessed through ONS as indicated in the references section.

REFERENCES

National Assembly for Wales (2003). *Digest of Welsh Statistics*, Cardiff: NAW, *www.wales.gov.uk/keypubstatisticsforwales/topicindex/topics.htm*.
National Assembly for Wales (2003). *2001 Census of Population, Statistical Bulletin*, Cardiff: NAW, *www.wales.gsi.gov.uk/statistics*.
National Assembly for Wales (2004). *Digest of Local Area Statistics*, Cardiff: NAW,

www.wales.gov.uk/keypubstatisticsforwales/content/publication/compendia/2004/dwla s2004/dwlas2004-ch1/dwlas2004-ch1.htm.

Office for National Statistics (2001). *Census 2001 Wales*, London: ONS, *www.statistics. gov.uk/census2001/profiles/W.asp.*

Office for National Statistics (2002). *Annual Local Area Labour Force Survey, Wales,* London: ONS.

Office for National Statistics (2003). *Census 2001 Commentary on Wales*, London: ONS, *www.statistics.gov.uk/census2001/profiles/commentaries/Wales.asp.*

Office for National Statistics (2004a). *Regional Trends*, 38, London: ONS.

Office for National Statistics (2004b). *Wales: Its People*, London: ONS, *www.statistics. gov.uk/focuson/wales/default.asp.*

8. TEMPORALITY AND NATIONALITY

Andrew Thompson

But do you know what a nation means? says John Wyse
Yes, says Bloom
What is it? says John Wyse
A nation? says Bloom, a nation is the same people living in the same place
By God, then, says Ned, laughing, if that's so I'm a nation for I'm living in the same
place for the past five years.
So of course everyone had a laugh at Bloom and says he, trying to muck out of it:
Or also living in different places.
That covers my case, says Joe.
What is your nation if I may ask?, says the citizen.
Ireland, says Bloom. I was born here. Ireland.
(James Joyce, *Ulysses*)

ABSTRACT

*This article deals with three aspects of the temporality of national identification.
The first section underlines that self-understanding is a product of momentary
interactional encounters; though people routinely speak of 'just having' a nationality,
it is in these situations that they actively establish themselves as, for example,
British or Welsh. The principle that nationality is constituted in these instances
informs the remainder of the analysis, but in the subsequent sections of the article
the discussion is more closely focused on specifying the implications of biography and social change for self-understanding. Where the 'development' of
national identity has been the subject of research, of which there are surprisingly*

few cases, the spotlight has almost without exception been on childhood and early adolescence. In contrast, the second section of the article explores how nationality is experienced at different points across the lifecourse. The third dimension I address is the historical moment at a given time and the effect of wider processes of cultural, political and social change over time. Overall, the intention is to explore the situational character of nationality by grounding it in individuals' lived-through experiences over time. Throughout, I stress that self-understanding is an interactional accomplishment, not a uniquely individual condition.

INTRODUCTION

It is appropriate that Joyce set the above interaction within a bar. For it is one of the few ordinary social contexts within which such an extraordinary conversation could imaginably occur. People do not typically experience such pointed questioning about such taken-for-granted subjects, encounters with social scientists aside. Yet, while deliberation on what a nation is, or what it means to belong to one, would not be expected to detain most people for very long as they go about their day-to-day lives, national identification, by which I mean the ways in which nationality is, variously, constituted, negotiated and ascribed, is certainly far from absent from everyday life.

Dependent on context, people may read as markers of nationality accents, names, behaviour, mannerisms, physical characteristics, dress and, in contexts where ethnic geography 'really matters', to borrow from Richard Jenkins (2001), even the specific localities in which people live. As social acts, identification and categorization of self and others can occur because people have available to them ready-made ethnic and national categories. When, then, judgements about ethnicity or nationality are made on the basis of accents or names, or when ethnic or national categories are deployed in observing behaviour, people are seeing things *as they are*. Though these acts may not be literally everyday occurrences, what renders these phenomena meaningful, and which makes such common-sense judgements possible, is a contextual stock of knowledge that is both acquired from others and forged in and across people's everyday lives in particular places.

We see this at work in, for example, Northern Ireland, where by relatively early in their lives young people display an extensive repertoire of lay socio-logical skills that they use to attribute ethnicity and nationality (Bell, 1990; McGrellis, 2004). Equally, as Jonathan Scourfield, Andrew Davies and Sally

Holland (2003) show in their study of the negotiation of nationality by children in Wales, the participants in their study were, in their own way, adept at identifying among other things Davies' accent as 'more Welshy' and, though it is left unspoken, identifying him as coming from a particular part of the country. Studies also highlight that in all manner of commonplace settings people invoke nationality to make sense of situational encounters or to interpret what is happening in a situation as being about nationality. In his research in the city of Cluj in the Transylvanian region of Romania, in which around 20 per cent of the population identify as ethnic Hungarian, Jon Fox (2004) explains that the failure to perform in 'proper' Romanian such an otherwise ordinary task as requesting books in the university library may lead an ethnic Romanian observer to identify a person as 'Hungarian', even if he or she is a Romanian citizen.

The following discussion is concerned with national identification as a situational social act that occurs within everyday life *over time*. It is largely, though not exclusively, concerned with national identification as a mode of self-understanding, of defining or situating oneself in particular moments and times (Brubaker, 2004). For much of the time nationality is not an everyday issue to the extent that it becomes part of conscious deliberations or reflective moments; as an occasioned occurrence self-understanding is episodic. It becomes salient only in those comparatively fleeting instances when, for example, our sense of who we are is called into question by others or when it becomes relevant for how we interact with others. It is, I will suggest, a response to situational social occurrences. Though over the last decade or so more attention has been given to *what* happens in those everyday contexts in which nationality is of significance for self-understanding, the relevance of *when* they occur has, with some interesting exceptions (Fox, 2003; Todd, 2004), been relatively neglected.

RESEARCH METHODS

The following discussion draws on interviews with 33 men and women living in Pontypridd, aged between 59 and 81 years old.[1] The main aim of the research, and the rationale underpinning sample selection, was to examine the ways in which national identification may be viewed as a product of biographical experiences. Specifically, the intention was to consider how moments and transitions over the lifecourse influence self-understanding and to examine how these instances, in turn, might be understood within the wider historical moment in which they occur. Each participant was interviewed twice, with the first interview lasting for typically two hours and the second for between one-and-a-half and two hours. The purpose of the two-stage interview format was twofold. Firstly, to use the initial interview to gather base-line biographical information from the participants on areas such as family, schooling, work and travel and also to pose questions intended to establish how they gained information about, and thus interacted with, the world beyond their locality, while largely reserving more directed questions about nationality for the second meeting. The second reason for undertaking the interviews in two stages was that it would allow time to identify accounts of experiences elicited in the first interview and to revisit these in the follow-up interview by asking the participant to say something more about particular incidents and the context in which they occurred.

MOMENTS OF IDENTIFICATION

As a category that people use to identify themselves and others, or that others use to position them, nationality – as with other aspects of social identity – is a relatively transitory phenomenon that individuals experience in moments. Outside of the kinds of occasions, when, to borrow from Rogers Brubaker (2004), 'groupness' *happens*, for much of the time people may be only be fleetingly conscious of nationality or of reading a situation as being about nationality. The significance of these moments for identification is nevertheless worth stressing for at least two reasons.

First, because in instances when they are required to do so, people very often account for their nationality with reference to place of birth, ancestry or simply because that is the way they 'feel'. Thus, by way of illustration, take the following examples: a woman in her late seventies remarked that 'of course I was born here and have lived here for many, many years so that makes me Welsh'; a woman in her early sixties commented 'I live here, I feel Welsh and my accent is Welsh; so that's it really'; a man in his late fifties responded that 'I think it was how I felt myself . . . I am just Welsh'; a man in his sixties declared that 'you just become Welsh and you really cannot describe it really. I was born here and I am Welsh.' Being born in a particular country may well give an individual the right, if it can be put that way, to claim a certain nationality, but birthplace in itself does not *cause* national identification, any more than does family pedigree, accent or 'feeling'. Identification, instead, has to be actively done. Richard Jenkins puts it particularly well when he suggests that identity 'is not "just there", it must always be established' (1996, p. 4). Birthplace, for example, is only relevant for national identification, for self-understanding, when individuals make it so, when others make reference to it to challenge an individual's claim to a nationality, or when it is invoked to legitimate a claim, as the account below highlights:

> I felt inadequate when I worked in north Wales that I could not speak Welsh. Many of the lads would speak to me in Welsh when I first started and I could not answer them. They would make jokes such as 'you call yourself Welsh?'. I found a vast difference between north and south Wales because of the language and their accent. Despite this I am still Welsh and although I cannot speak it [Welsh] – it really does not make me less Welsh.

Though factors such as birthplace, ancestry, or in the case of Wales being a Welsh speaker, are cited as 'giving' people their nationality, and spoken of in a manner that suggests their nationality is, to come back to Jenkins's point, 'just there', their bearing on nationality, for national identification, is present only in those moments when they become relevant to particular situations. More generally, while individuals view nationality as something they become 'aware of' in passing moments, it is, instead, in these instances that nationality is constituted. Nationality is not something that individuals simply *have*; a person is not 'just Welsh'. They are so because in moments across their lives they establish themselves as such.

Secondly, the moments in which individuals are prompted to identify themselves and others by nationality, or are given cause to think about 'who they are', are not limited to the timetabled occasions – such as sporting events or days of national celebration – when it would be expected, if not necessarily guaranteed, to happen (cf. Fox, 2004). The experiences of the participants in this study, for example, highlight the variety of instances in which people are categorized by their nationality and in which they make sense of occurrences with reference to the category of nationality. Moving outside of the locality in which they live, and especially outside of Wales, is a recurring feature of participants' accounts. One man explained that he visited relatives in England quite frequently when he was young, and at these times he was made very conscious of his 'Welsh' accent:

> I felt different at quite a young age. I was about ten years of age. I was different because of the speed that I spoke and the way I spoke and my accent. My dad was in the Army and he was friendly with a Cockney and he used to say to me dad 'slow down Taff because they won't be able to understand you'. I think it is the way we speak.

Others similarly spoke of a time when they, or others they knew, were encouraged to modify or 'lose' their accent in order to progress in their new careers in England. A man in his sixties told of how a relative who had moved to London felt that because her accent identified her as Welsh this was preventing her from getting the jobs she wanted: 'apparently she used to practice in the mirror and talk with a very posh accent. That was over fifty years ago. She felt because she was Welsh she was not accepted in London and as soon as she changed her accent she became part of the place she lived.' Another man in his late sixties, who had worked in England for a number of years, remembered the following incident as one of the first times when he was aware of being addressed as Welsh:

> At first when I moved up they asked me to change my accent and the funny thing was there was a Scot and a man from Liverpool who also had broad accents. Of course, I was a little angry at the comment and I think it went along the lines of 'in order to get on here you will have to change your accent' and I said 'No. You have to learn how to understand me.'

Not all such moments occur outside of Wales. One woman explained how on a shopping trip to Cardiff the shop assistant had 'said to me I have a strong Welsh accent. She comes from Cardiff and not England.' Trips to north Wales tend to have the opposite effect, leading these participants to feel 'inadequate', 'alien', 'embarrassed' or 'inferior' when they were spoken to in Welsh but had to reply in English. For example, a woman in her late seventies remembered how on a trip to north Wales, 'I felt embarrassed that I could not even speak a word of Welsh not even "hello". It never really bothered me before but I said to my friend "eh, it's all Welsh up here". Funny isn't it? I don't know what it was but it made me feel awkward.' As this woman's comments indicate, people attribute meaning to differences in accent or provide motives for behaviour in large part because they feel that others are doing the same with them (this applies also to some situations described by participants who had temporarily lived in England). The following remark by a man in his seventies is characteristic of similar observations by other individuals: 'you can definitely feel the difference between the north and south and I don't think you are truly accepted there because you cannot speak the language. I think they know who we are and I feel they treat us differently. See, you go into a shop and ask for something then they will speak to their friend in Welsh so we cannot understand.'

Accounts such as this also provide some indication of how categorization and identification by group, ethnicity or nationality happen in everyday life beyond the occasions where individuals are openly addressed by nationality. Thus, in the case of the man quoted at the end of the paragraph above, he explains that conversing in Welsh in the presence of non-Welsh speakers is something Welsh speakers *as a group* do, and do for a reason. Participants made passing references to characterizations of numerous national groups. 'The English', for example, are 'aloof' and 'arrogant'. As one man commented on his experiences in the army, 'the English thought they were superior to everyone. They were arrogant. Perhaps these days it has changed, but the English hated the Welsh and they treated us like second-class citizens.' For another Second World War veteran who had been stationed in Germany after the War, 'the Germans were a different race to us'. Americans, as one man who had served with US soldiers in the Second World War stated, 'were very loud to be honest, just like they are today'. Identification and categorization may be situational, but the knowledge that people use to categorize others is, generally speaking, not. The latter is what they bring to the situation when they do the former. The categories *may* be refined (such as when one man qualifies his view of 'the English' on the basis of practical experience to 'the southern English') though it is more likely that when individuals come to be known as persons rather than as members of groups they are seen as exceptions to the rule; it is not necessarily the case that the category will be subject to wholesale revision. Again, the categories *may* be contingent on particular historical moments – Germans may not now be a 'different race to us' – but they are more likely to be taken as timeless (the man who said this about 'the Germans' insists they still are 'different').

'DEFINING MOMENTS' ACROSS THE LIFECOURSE

Where research focuses on the development of national identification as a process that occurs over time attention has overwhelmingly been on early and middle childhood (Stephens, 1997; Barrett, 2000; Scourfield, Davies and Holland, 2003). This raises two issues. The first is, quite simply, what happens beyond this point? The second is the relationship between what occurs in the early stages – in childhood and early adolescence – and the life experiences later. In the cases of those either born in, or who had moved to Wales early in their lives, childhood is associated with qualitatively different experiences to those they connect with the period (usually in late adolescence) when they recollect first identifying as Welsh. The general view is that, in many respects, their childhood experiences had little bearing on their outlook as adults. They describe childhood as a period when they were largely unaware of the matters that concerned their parents, a condition sustained by, as they saw it, the relationship between children of their generation and their parents. One of the most striking themes of the participants' accounts of this period is how their childhood and early adolescent worlds and horizons centred on a very restricted geographical space, with, for many, a trip to Barry Island the furthest they travelled until late adolescence. News about the world beyond their immediate localities was limited. One man, for example, remembered that the only reason he was able to read a newspaper as a child was because his mother used it as a tablecloth and he could read it while he ate his dinner. Generally, there is a sense of being disconnected from the adult and wider world.

Childhood is, however, arguably much more relevant for national identification than the participants' narrative accounts would at first suggest. Specifically, it is in childhood that they first learn to categorize by national differences and to think of themselves and others as belonging to national groups. These categories are encountered through others, typically through interaction with adults. Given their views on their childhood, however, it is interesting how many of the participants had specific memories of their parents speaking about Wales, Britain or, in some cases, Ireland.[2] A man in his early seventies told of how he 'learned about Britain from my father who would take the Daily Herald paper . . . He was against the monarchy and would often tell me about things that was going on in the world . . . I cannot remember the exact stories he told me but I just picked up on things he would say. I was about eight at the time.' Adults, particularly parents, did not just provide information about others; they are also instrumental in teaching young children how to categorize themselves. One woman in her early sixties remembered that when she joined her new school after moving to Wales (at seven years old) the teacher 'introduced me as Paula from England'. Another woman also in her sixties remarked that a teacher had told her that because her parents were English she was also English. In another case, a man in his early seventies recounted how he had been teased at school by other children about being English (because it had come out that he was born in London) and how he had returned home from school to ask his grandfather if he was English (who told him that it came down to what he 'felt' he was).

Schooling, though dismissed by many participants as teaching them little beyond literacy and numeracy, is also significant for a number of reasons. In classes on history and geography, Britain was, for the majority, the principal frame of reference. As a woman in her late seventies recounts: 'I remember our history was always about British history and I think our teacher Mr Edwards told us we were British and we are proud Britons. Funny what sticks in your mind.'

Wales, by contrast, receives little mention, though some schools and, more particularly, some teachers placed more emphasis on teaching aspects of Welsh history (I return to this point in the subsequent section). Most remember taking part in activities to celebrate St David's Day, although the day is largely remembered because school shut early. Those who attended Catholic schools, by comparison, have few memories of St David's Day celebrations, of Eisteddfod activities, or any Welsh-language lessons (the others generally speak of having one half-hour per week Welsh class), but did celebrate St Patrick's Day and spoke of learning about Ireland and Irish culture through their Irish-born teachers. In the case of these participants, therefore, schooling did not afford even the minimal opportunities for constituting themselves as Welsh; instead, Ireland was more likely to be discussed, just as it was at home:

I went to a Catholic school which predominately focused on religion and Ireland. Wales as a country never existed in my schooling and even our school concerts focused on Ireland . . . So part of my childhood and early adult years was a belief that I was to feel Irish and the concept of being born in Wales never came into the equation . . . bloodline was the significant thing. (woman, sixties)

There is evidence, then, that by adolescence at least some working knowledge of nationality has been acquired. However, this information is, largely, imparted to them by adults. Up until late adolescence and early adulthood there is relatively little exposure to the kinds of situational encounters in which they might actively identify themselves by nationality, or more particularly be required to do so by others. For many participants the situation begins to change in this later period of their lives as a consequence of, in the first instance, increased geographical mobility and the new experiences and possibilities for interaction this brings. Many of the men served in the British Army, either during the Second World War or for national service, some of the older women had gone 'into service' as maids in London, while others moved out of Wales, usually to England, for periods as a result of their husband's work. Moving outside of the localities in which they had grown up, and which, as I have noted, they only rarely left as children, puts them in situations where they are categorized by others as Welsh (or sometimes have their Welshness called into question by those from other parts of the country), where they identify others by nationality and, often, identify themselves to others as Welsh. For example, one man in his seventies recollects his experiences of this in the Army: 'there was . . . a guy from the Valleys and we called each other Taff. It is funny when you think and this was ludicrous. The north Walians would rib me and the essence of their conversation was that we were not Welsh. I was always defensive and would say to them just because you cannot speak Welsh does not mean you are not Welsh.' Categorization is just as apparent in interaction with those of different nationalities. When asked who he associated with in the Army he replied: 'The Scots definitely and the English were quite hostile to the Welsh. There was lots of ribbing with the English guys to the Welsh.' For some, interaction with others carries added complexities. One of the women, in her late seventies, had been born in England and lived there until she met her husband (from the Valleys, but stationed in a barracks near her home), with whom she later moved to Wales. She describes how some 'poked fun' at her accent in her new home, but explains that, shortly after, her family in England remarked how she had 'lost' her original accent: 'I think I was about twenty three years of age. It was somebody who worked for [name of employer] and he said "look out, Taffy's coming" . . . My brothers thought I had developed a Welsh accent and they told me to speak in my own accent.' Geographical mobility is associated with what the participants view as the time when they first identify themselves as Welsh. The significance they confer on these dramatic changes to their personal circumstances may be partly attributable to them being more memorable than the day-to-day experiences of their lives previously. That said, it was evident that the move away from home exposed aspects of their selves that hitherto they had been largely unaware of, or at least had given comparatively little thought to, such as their accents, mannerisms and, above all, their nationality. That others categorize them by their nationality, and the relative frequency with which this happens, ensures that nationality becomes an increasingly meaningful sociological category.

Interaction with children and, later, grandchildren also produces situations in which the participants are given cause to reflect on their nationality. This is especially evident in the case of the women, though a number of the men made similar references to how observing a more pronounced Welsh dimension to their children's and grandchildren's education compared to their own experiences of school made them think more about their own Welshness. More specifically, these experiences cause them to reflect on how Wales is changing by placing themselves, their children and grandchildren within a narrative of wider cultural and social change. Indeed, often this narrative includes their own parents and grandparents, particularly when speaking of the fortunes of the Welsh language. A woman in her seventies, for example, commented that 'it wasn't until I had the children that . . . I felt more Welsh and they did not have much Welsh at school . . . It has been only these past few years that I have thought about my fathers' family and the Welsh [language] in their family.'

Such reflections are not limited to the later stages of the lifecourse, but they are made possible by living through change, by life experiences. Adulthood does not necessarily bring greater 'technical' knowledge about nationality, such as on national history, but it does progressively broaden practical or applied knowledge through interactional encounters with those of different nationalities and of what it is to be Welsh. It is from this acquired stock of applied knowledge that the participants draw in making sense of nationality, particularly Welsh nationality, when they need to do so. As adults the participants continue to learn about nationality from others, including how others perceive them and how significant others, such as immediate family or friends, talk about or display their nationality, just as they did as children, but their situational encounters, and the expanding base of practical knowledge of nationality on which they can draw, encourage a greater degree of reflexivity about their nationality. This reflexivity is only in part a product of general changes across the lifecourse. It also, as I will argue in the next section, needs to be contextualized within the wider historical moments through which the participants have lived.

IDENTIFICATION AND SOCIAL CHANGE

The question must be raised as to how we social scientists can deduce the meaning of a social act if we do not know the history of the individual leading up to it or the history of the social system. Social acts may only be understood and explained by analyzing the conditions prevailing at their conception and this implies undertaking a biographical analysis. (Rosenthal, 1997, p. 36)

Biographical analysis may not be the only way to 'deduce the meaning of a social act' – ethnography, in particular, produces some revealing studies of the situated meaning of ethnicity and nationality[3] – but it does encourage closer inspection of the 'here-and-now' in which identification and self-understanding are temporally situated. The discussion in the preceding section argues for the importance of taking into account the 'history of the individual'. Yet, the emphasis is on 'stages' in the individual's own life and only more generally on lifecourse transitions; how might a focus on social change – the 'history of the social system' – contribute to the analysis of national identification? One way it may do so is by underlining that the historical moment through which individuals are living, while not determinant, has a bearing on self-understanding. To come back to Rosenthal's point, social acts – in this case, the act of locating oneself socially – need to be understood within the framework of the wider social context *at that time*.

All the participants speak of how they have become more aware of being Welsh in recent years. While this is certainly worthy of investigation, in a period when, as one woman in her early sixties puts it, 'it is really popular to be Welsh', it is not likely to be an exceptional occurrence. It is rather more interesting when one knows that for many of them when they were children, to draw on the words of a woman in her seventies, 'Wales never really existed as a conversation', or as one man also in his seventies says of his school teachers, 'I don't think Wales existed in their minds to be honest.' Equally, the wearing of replica shirts of the Welsh national football and, more pervasively, rugby teams as items of everyday clothing (before the latter reached its current heights), or the flag waving and the 'valley chic' t-shirts that Rebecca Edwards (2006) describes in her article elsewhere in this volume, are only really sociologically significant when seen in the context of a longer term process of cultural and social change. Reading Edwards's essay alongside a much earlier one, Isabel Emmet's (1978) discussion of the 'Blaenau Boys', based on research originally undertaken in the mid 1960s, goes some way to exposing the scale of the cultural change that has taken place in the last forty years or so. Using Michael Billig's (1995) concept of 'banal nationalism' to describe the way that the Welsh flag or other icons now adorn everything from key rings to underwear, we still have to ask *how* this came to happen.[4]

How Wales, as perceived by the participants, has changed, and more particularly how the status and 'manner' of being Welsh have been transformed, is vividly laid out in the participants' narratives. In particular, what comes through strongly in these accounts is the way in which the wider social context – such as the embedded, banal Britishness the participants view as being largely beyond reflection until the 1960s and early 1970s – at times constrains and in other periods is seen to enable Welsh national identification, or at least a more positive evaluation of Wales and of being Welsh. While as I pointed out in the previous section, many of the participants remark that they identified themselves as Welsh in their late adolescence and early adulthood, which for some would have been in the 1940s but for the majority would have been in the late 1950s, Britain and Britishness were present in their worldview in ways that Wales and Welshness were not. The following remarks, the first from a man in his late seventies and the others from two men and a woman in their sixties, illustrate what for many participants was a common experience:

When I was growing up the feeling was more British and especially with the war, and Britain was a powerful country then. In school we learned about Britain in history . . . I never did anything about Wales at school and the focus was more on Britain and that was it really.

The curriculum was not Welsh at all, and focused on Britain and the rest of the world . . . Wales must have been a second thought or something that wasn't really taken seriously.
I don't think being Welsh was taken very seriously by the teachers at all and to us it wasn't something to feel any pride about, being Welsh . . . there was more of a focus on Britain and we learned about some historical figures such as queens and kings . . . It was like Wales was a forgotten country.

When we were young nobody thought of themselves as Welsh so we must have been British . . . When I think back I would question whether Wales had a history. It was non-existent.

Today, by contrast, it is Britishness that is becoming 'non-existent'. Participants, for example, remark that 'today people say I am English or Irish and you hardly ever hear British being mentioned', that 'people have now become more into their own country like being Welsh or English and I don't think people say British anymore', or, again, that 'today . . . there is a lot on the news about Scotland, England and Wales and to me it feels like being British is not something that people see themselves as anymore'. Where once it was the Union Jack and the red-white-and-blue bunting that adorned their streets to commemorate, among other events, the Battle of Britain, VE Day, the coronation of Queen Elizabeth and Charles and Di's wedding, now, as a woman in her seventies remarks, 'there are [Welsh] flags everywhere, on cars and buildings and you can even buy fridge magnets [with the Welsh flag on them]'. Many of the participants talk of people today being 'flag mad', so much so that for one man 'with so many people taking an interest in their country and flag waving we are getting dull like the Americans'. Numerous explanations are offered for this transformation, such as the improving fortunes of the Welsh language, the number and better quality of television programmes about Wales and life in the country, and devolution. The most common account, however, is that Wales is 'just there' in a way that it hitherto was not. Where Wales was once a 'forgotten country', now, as one woman puts it, 'being Welsh is everywhere', or as another suggests, 'there is far more access to Welshness'.

The current context nevertheless does not *compel* the participants to identify more strongly with Wales and with being Welsh, any more than the cultural and political conditions of the period through which they lived their childhoods and part of their adulthoods *made* them British. It is clear from their comments that change has not passed them by, and that particular changes are the subject of conversation, whether the decision of their children to send grandchildren to Welsh medium schools, the knowledge that their grandchildren listen to music by bands from Wales, or that their children and grandchildren know more about 'their country' than they did at the same age. Situational differences are actively noted and are meaningful to a degree that might not be expected among young people for whom the Welsh flag on a fridge magnet, stamped on a cup, on the car in front or on the bedroom window of a house across the street are familiar and for much of the time unnoticed features of the everyday context in which they have grown up. 'Wales' has certainly become an increased, visible presence in their everyday lives.

It is not, however, 'just there'. It is evident in their support today for the Welsh language, and in the pleasure they derive from the knowledge that their grandchildren are learning to speak it (and the way some view this as 'bringing back' Welsh into their families). It is present, too, in the regrets of non-Welsh-speaking participants (which accounts for all but a handful of the group) about not being able to speak 'their' language, in their remarks that, were they able to roll back the years, they would learn the language or, at the very least, that they would have sent their own children to Welsh medium schools. Its influence is apparent in the pride with which they refer to Wales now being 'its own country' or how 'Wales and its flag is definitely on the map', and in their views on devolution, whether as positive development because 'we have our own voice', as one woman puts it, or in the expressions of discontent that 'what this country needs is what Scotland has got', as a man in his seventies comments. The significance of the changes the participants have observed lies, then, in the manner in which they become incorporated into their actions, their opinions and, ultimately, how they identify themselves.

CONCLUSION

> The 'nation' is a grand generalization that does not discriminate among, and says nothing about, its individual members. By contrast, the individual is highly specific and is distinguished from other individuals in innumerable and very particular ways. Why, then, do individuals elect to identify themselves (to themselves as well as to others) in terms of the nation? (Cohen, 1996, p. 802)

If not, in the end, what *any* study of nationality must address, dealing with the issue so succinctly put by Anthony Cohen is surely one of the principal concerns to which those studying nationality must direct themselves. National identification, as a social practice that people engage in, is not only about declarative acts, but also about the ways in which people use 'nationality' as a readily available category to identify others and to make sense of their own everyday experiences. I have touched on this aspect of national identification in the preceding discussion; it is considered more closely elsewhere (see, for example, Thompson and Day, 1999; Kiely et al., 2001; Thompson, 2001; Fox, 2003). The main focus of this paper, however, has been with self-identification, the subject of the problem posed by Cohen.

My answer to Cohen's question comes in two parts. The first is that people identify themselves by nationality because they *can*. Even if they might struggle to proffer a precise definition of 'nation', they often have a good working knowledge of its general field as a category, as the participants' comments at the start of the opening section highlight. Thus, when prompted to do so, they can talk on a general level about deriving their nationality from their country of birth or from their parents. So, there is an understanding of the generalities of the nation as a category that is acquired over their lives, beginning, as I have suggested, in childhood. Moreover, as a category that they can use to identify themselves, 'nation', like other similar categories such as 'race' or 'class', is available to them to use for this purpose. They are exposed to it throughout their lives. In particular moments, such as the present, it is seen, as one woman said of 'being Welsh', to be 'everywhere'. Yet, turning to the second part of my answer, nationality is not an abstract phenomenon, even if 'the nation' *is* a 'grand generalization'. *Being* Welsh has been part of the participants' lives, intermittently integrated into everyday occurrences such as their schooling, work, personal relationships and leisure pursuits. My concern in this article has been to show not only that self-identification is actively constituted in particular moments in their everyday lives, but also to highlight how this occurs in situations over time.

NOTES

[1] The interviews were undertaken by Catherine Davies.
[2] Six participants had Irish parents, and in four of these cases both parents were Irish.
[3] Arguably the finest of which is Brubaker et al. (2006).
[4] See Davies (2006) for an interesting application of the concept of banal nationalism to account for the 1997 devolution referendum.

REFERENCES

Barrett, M. (2000). 'The development of national identity in childhood and adolescence', inaugural lecture, 22 March, University of Surrey.
Bell, D. (1990). *Acts of Union*, London: Macmillan.

Billig, M. (1995). *Banal Nationalism*, London: Sage.

Brubaker, R. (2004). *Ethnicity Without Groups*, Cambridge, Mass.: Harvard University Press.

Brubaker, R., Feischmidt, M., Fox, J. and Grancea, L. (2006). *Nationalist Politics and Everyday Ethnicity in a Transylvanian Town*, Princeton, NJ: Princeton University Press.

Cohen, A. P. (1996). 'Personal nationalism: a Scottish view of some rites, rights, and wrongs', *American Ethnologist*, 23, 4, 802–15.

Davies, R. (2006) 'Banal Britishness and reconstituted Welshness', *Contemporary Wales*, 18, 106–21.

Edwards, R. (2006). " 'Everyday, when I wake up, I thank the Lord I'm Welsh'': reading the markers of Welsh identity in 1990s pop music', *Contemporary Wales*, 19, 144–61.

Emmett, I. (1978). 'Blaenau boys in the mid-1960s', in G. Williams (ed.), *Social and Cultural Change in Contemporary Wales*, London: Routledge.

Fox, J. (2003). 'Nationhood without nationalism: being national in everyday life', unpublished Ph.D. thesis, Los Angeles: University of California.

Fox, J. (2004). 'Missing the mark: nationalist politics and student apathy', *East European Politics and Societies*, 18, 3, 363–93.

Jenkins, R. (1996). *Social Identity*, London: Routledge.

Jenkins, R. (2001) 'The limits of identity: ethnicity, conflict and politics', paper given to international symposium on ethnic identities and political action in post-cold war Europe, Greece: Democritus University of Thrace.

Kiely, R., Bechhofer, F., Stewart, R. and McCrone, D. (2001). 'The markers and rules of Scottish national identity', *Sociological Review*, 49, 33–55.

McGrellis, S. (2004) *Pushing the Boundaries in Northern Ireland: Young People, Violence and Sectarianism*, Families and Social Capital ESRC research group, working paper no. 8, London: London South Bank University.

Rosenthal, G. (1997). 'National identity or multicultural autobiography: theoretical concepts of biographical constitution grounded in case reconstructions', in A. Libelich and R. Josselson (eds), *The Narrative of Lives*, London: Sage.

Scourfield, J., Davies, A. and Holland, S. (2003). 'Wales and Welshness in middle childhood', *Contemporary Wales*, 16, 83–100.

Smith, A. (1995). *Nations and Nationalism in a Global Era*, Cambridge: Polity.

Stephens, S. (ed.) (1997). 'Children and nationalism', special edn, *Childhood*, 4, 1.

Todd, J. (2004) 'Social transformation, collective categories and identity change', Institute for the Study of Social Change discussion paper series, working paper 2004–3, Dublin: University College.

Thompson, A. (2001). 'Nations, national identities and human agency: putting people back into nations', *Sociological Review*, 49, 18–32.

Thompson, A. and Day, G. (1999). 'The local construction of national identity', in R. Fevre and A. Thompson (eds), *Nation, Identity and Social Theory*, Cardiff: University of Wales Press.

9. 'EVERYDAY, WHEN I WAKE UP, I THANK THE LORD I'M WELSH': READING THE MARKERS OF WELSH IDENTITY IN 1990s POP MUSIC

Rebecca Edwards

ABSTRACT

This article will explore the role of music in constructions of national identity, and specifically the role of popular music as an expression of identity in Wales in the late 1990s. During this time, a number of bands from Wales achieved widespread success outside Wales. Newport was hailed as the 'new Seattle'[1] and the phrase 'Cool Cymru' came into use. It will look at how the three most commercially successful bands from Wales at this time, Manic Street Preachers, Stereophonics and Catatonia, came to be identified as Welsh, and how and where their music was used. Dai Griffiths and Sarah Hill rightly acknowledge that the bands tended not simply to 'name Wales' in their songs (2005, p. 225). Instead, the association between the bands and Wales took place in three key ways: through the discursive media world around the bands to Wales and to each other; through symbols (words, pictures, voice and language) used by the bands; and, most importantly, the way the music itself was used in public spaces. None of the three existed in isolation from each other; they were often closely entwined with the fans of a band understanding symbols, seeking out interviews and programmes which involved the group and attending gigs and public events.

MUSIC AND NATIONAL IDENTITY

It is not only national anthems and the appropriation of folk music patterns that can represent ideas of identity, but also popular music. As flags and symbols can act as a visual marker, so popular music can act as an aural marker, though with the important distinction that it is a less clearly defined beast as it is likely to be unconnected with official state bureaucracy or power. Moreover, unlike folk music, it does not necessarily follow traditional patterns, nor use traditional instruments. Popular music is played in stadiums and arenas, at national and local events and at festivals, as expressions of collective grief and celebration.[2] Whilst formal national anthems are mentioned when considering ideas of identity, popular music is often ignored or overlooked, even when the author is considering the 'everyday'. In *Banal Nationalism* Michael Billig makes a powerful and persuasive argument for the reader to 'look and see the constant flaggings of nationhood' (1995, p. 174), from the language of the news referring to 'us' and 'them', to emblems of the state visible on its buildings and its representatives: 'the metonymic image of banal nationalism is not a flag which is being consciously waved with fervent passion: it is the flag hanging unnoticed on the public building' (Billig, 1995, p. 8). Yet, within his discussion, music is referred to solely in the guise of the national anthem with reference to it being a requisite emblem of a nation. There is no consideration of the everyday role of music in constructing identity.

Other theories of the construction of national identity have offered a variety of factors as central to its explanation and understanding, from formal education systems (Gellner, 1983), mass literacy and printing (Anderson, 1991), to the invention of tradition (Hobsbawm, 1992). The representation, or 'flagging', of the nation through music and song is often only briefly mentioned by theorists. Hobsbawm's discussion of the invention of tradition sees music appear only in the guise of anthem or folksong (1992, p. 6). Anderson, commenting on national anthems 'sung on national holidays', argues that '[n]o matter how banal the words and mediocre the tune there is in this singing an experience of simultaneity. At precisely such moments, people wholly unknown to each other utter the same verses to the same melody. The image: unisonance' (Anderson, 1991, p. 145). Such a feeling of unisonance will be explored further below with relation to popular music. It must be remembered that all music and songs, including anthems, must be absorbed into the imagining of the nation. When discussing the Welsh national anthem, 'Hen Wlad fy Nhadau' ('Land of my Fathers'), Smith reminds us that it was 'by no means an automatic choice as a national song until the last decade of the nineteenth century, by which time the trappings of an invented history were themselves disseminated and used' (Smith, 1999, pp. 81–2).

Within musicology and cultural studies, there is a growing body of work exploring the relationship between music and identity, both in 'classical' music and within popular music and culture. A number of works have looked specifically at England and constructions of identity (Hughes and Stradling, 2001; Bracewell, 1997; Zuberi, 2001). Bracewell and Zuberi particularly explore associations between popular culture and popular music, through film, journalism, art and imagery. Connell and Gibson (2003, p. 118) argue successfully that '[m]usic, alongside national artistic traditions, common religions, ethnic identity and a range of visual symbols (flags, emblems, crests, currency, figureheads) is embedded in the creation of (and maintenance of) nationhood'. Gilroy has demonstrated how 'the musics of the black Atlantic world were the primary expressions of cultural distinctiveness' seized upon by black migrants to Britain after 1945 (1993, pp. 81–2). Connell and Gibson point out that the linking of music to place 'can only be a contested enterprise' (2003, p. 143) but this reflects the contested nature of identity itself.

The most common site for popular music to be associated with identity and place is through music scenes, many of which are associated with place, such as 'Madchester', grunge in Seattle, Northern Soul and Mersey Beat in the north of England. In the early 1990s, the term 'Britpop' began to appear in the music press, referring to a number of young guitar bands, largely based in London or Manchester, who presented a markedly English identity (see Harris, 2003). This phrase spread to the mainstream media, becoming associated with the rise of New Labour and 'Cool Britannia'. Blur, Oasis and the other bands associated with Britpop did not have to sing specifically or explicitly about England – the references were there in a multitude of ways, including imagery (visual images and also aural signifiers, such as Blur and Suede's London/'estuary English' accents), musical references, use of irony, association with each other through personal relationships and musical projects. The iconography and imagery was particularly clear, with various groups and magazines frequently using the red, white and blue of the Union Jack, colours also associated with The Kinks, The Who and The Jam – groups who were closely associated with constructions of Englishness. Blur used imagery of dog racing (*Parklife*) and steam trains (*Modern Life is Rubbish*), the voice of Phil Daniels (another Who/mod connection, via the film *Quadrophenia*) talking about bin men and feeding pigeons, all of which combine to play the music itself in an imagined location. They were linked with Damien Hirst, one of the most famous of the group known as the Young British Artists (YBAs), Hirst directing the video for their single 'Country House'. This video featured the actor Keith Allen, who had starred in the 1994 film *Shallow Grave*, and who collaborated with Hirst and Alex James (of Blur) under the pseudonym Fat Les to release the single 'Vindaloo' in 1998, in support of the England football team competing in the World Cup.[3] They returned in 2000, releasing 'Jerusalem' as the official Euro 2000 England anthem. These events were reported widely in the press, and illustrate how music (and musicians) became associated with place. Iconography, images, sounds, personal associations and collaborations combine and become emblematic of a time and constructions of identity.

MUSIC FROM WALES AND THE MEDIA

Towards the end of the 1990s, the phrase 'Cool Cymru' appeared frequently within the media, broadly used to describe a rethinking of Welsh identity along the lines of 'Cool Britannia' (see *Western Mail*, 1998c). While the *Western Mail* had previously reported a 'South Wales [sic] band explosion', which made reference to the 60Ft Dolls, Catatonia and Gorky's Zygotic Mynci (*Western Mail*, 1994), it had also referred to 'Cymrock' (*Western Mail*, 1996) and later 'Taff Rock' (*Western Mail*, 1997a). The real catalyst for the writing in the national British press came from an article in the *New York Times* which hailed bands from south Wales as 'making loud guitar rock as if they were the next Seattle' (*New York Times*, 1996). The phrase itself, 'Cool Cymru' (and very occasionally Cŵl Cymru), first appeared in the press in *The Times* in 1998, in an article which reported that Ron Davies (then Secretary of State for Wales) wanted to 'create a new symbol for the nation' (*The Times*, 1998). Peter Hain MP was quoted in the same piece as saying that 'modern Wales is about Manic Street Preachers and Catatonia rather [than] women in shawls and rain-sodden valleys'. The phrase appeared at the opening of the piece, with no explanation, suggesting that the reader might already be familiar with its meaning. 'Cool Cymru' found its way into magazines and newspapers, becoming so well known that it appeared (also without explanation) in the National Assembly's *Plan for Wales* in 2001 (p. 21). It referred primarily to the increased exposure and success outside Wales of several bands from Wales, including Manic Street Preachers, Stereophonics and Catatonia, but was also associated with the release of three films set in south Wales (*House of America*, *Twin Town* and *Human Traffic*), the 1997 referendum vote for devolution and the holding of the 1999 Rugby World Cup in Wales. In 1999, Wales's most famous musical son, Tom Jones, enjoyed something of a renaissance after the release of his *Reload* album, which included collaborations with members of Manic Street Preachers, Catatonia and Stereophonics. Other bands from Wales who were successful at this time included Super Furry Animals, Gorky's Zygotic Mynci, 60Ft Dolls, Derrero and Topper. None of these bands shared a particular musical style, and there is nothing in the music itself which is distinctly or recognizably Welsh in origin, other than recording and performing partially in Welsh in the case of Super Furry Animals, Gorky's Zygotic Mynci and Topper.[4] When reviewing the 1997 *Dial M For Merthyr* compilation, which included tracks by Stereophonics, Catatonia and Manic Street Preachers, one commentator remarked that 'the "Welshness" of these bands is derived purely from an accident of birth rather then any particular sonic or cultural similarity' (NME, 1997a). All of the bands were covered by the music press, particularly the weekly 'inkies', *New Musical Express* (*NME*) and *Melody Maker*, which generally focus on what is termed 'indie music' (see Shuker, 2002, pp. 6–11 and Hibbett, 2005, pp. 55–77). The vast majority of what may be identified as 'Welsh' in the music of Cool Cymru came from outside of the music itself. There were occasional exceptions, such as Catatonia performing with the Pontardulais Male Voice Choir at Margam Park, and their song 'Bulimic Beats', which opens with a harp playing.

Before 'Cool Cymru', musicians from Wales were often subject to derisory jibes from the music press. In his television series exploring music in Britain, John Peel commented that Wales 'went through a very long period of being just about as *un-cool* as it's possible to be' (*Sound Of The Suburbs*, Channel 4, 1999).[5] According to Simon Price '[o]ne of the biggest jokes of all was the Welsh music scene. It was a widely held truism that, in forty years of pop culture, all that the alleged Land of Song had given the world was Tom [Jones] and Shirley [Bassey], Shaky [Shakin' Stevens] and Bonnie [Tyler], and (God preserve us) The Alarm' (1999, p. 24). As Price goes on to argue, this summation of music from Wales unfairly ignores Welsh-language music which had some excellent bands who were championed by Peel, but who largely went unnoticed in the general music press.

In 1991, Manic Street Preachers began to receive attention in the music press, and at this time bands from Wales were indeed something of a rarity. The Manics found themselves continually mocked, not only for their eye-liner, slogans and musical similarity with The Clash, but because of their origin in south Wales. Neither their Welsh background nor any expression of Welsh identity appeared in their lyrics. Richey James, one of the band's two lyricists, commented that '[i]f I tried to write a Springsteen-esque lyric about Wales it'd be "I went to the Pontypool factory/Then drove up Caerphilly mountain/And drank tea from a plastic cup". You can't do it.' (*Melody Maker*, 1992a). Until 1996, the association between the band and Wales came from interviews and press articles, rather than from their work. The group's other lyricist, Nicky Wire, has spoken of the band's experience of prejudice against them because of the Welsh background in their early years:

You've only got to look at the headlines, from 'You Sexy Merthyr F**kers' [censored on tape] to 'Boyos from Blackwood' – leeks and daffs you know? – I wouldn't call it full-on racism because I don't think we were ever treated in a full-on racist way, but there was definitely an *unbelievable* bias against us because we were just Welsh . . . but that gave us so much strength. (BBC Radio Wales, *Dragon's Breath*, 2001)[6]

In their initial interviews and reviews in the music press, their background was constantly referenced, sometimes in the headings or photograph captions ('Taffer than the rest' (*Melody Maker*, 1992b), 'The leek shall inherit the earth' (*Melody Maker*, 1992c) and in the body of the articles themselves. A typical early interview began with the journalist setting the scene:

> You have to keep reminding yourself that they have dropped out of a poop hatch called Wales, a country whose contribution to rock'n'roll has been, to say the most, negligible. John Cale, Steve Strange, Darling Buds, Harry Secombe, Max Boyce, Shakey, Racing Cars and Man. Perhaps the last maddened teenage roar before the end of the millennium could only come from Britain's last remaining cultural void. (*Melody Maker*, 1991)

Stuart Cable of Stereophonics later commented that '[t]he Manics turned people's heads towards South Wales [*sic*]' and that they paved the way for other bands from south Wales (*Western Mail*, 1997a).

The 1996 *New York Times* article hailing Newport as a 'new Seattle' excited interest in both the national press and the music press, and was eagerly taken up by other journalists. By October 1996, the *Guardian* rather breathlessly encouraged readers to 'Dial the code 01633 and six more figures. Chances are you'll get through to an aspiring pop icon because there are rather a lot of them in Newport at the moment' (*Guardian*, 1996). In May 1997, the *Telegraph Magazine* ran a six-page piece entitled 'Move over Seattle, here comes Newport', which ran with the sub-heading 'The town that died when coal collapsed is mining a fertile new seam – of raw rock and punk talent' (*Telegraph Magazine*, 1997). And just a couple of weeks previously the *Melody Maker* front cover ran with 'Never Say Dai: Why it's *finally* cool to be Welsh' (emphasis in original). Inside there was a double page spread, a mixture of cliché, band biographies and hype of bands from across Wales and publicizing the Cardiff Bay Big Noise Festival taking place that Saturday and a Radio 1 documentary, *Made in Wales*, to be broadcast the following day (*Melody Maker*, 1997a).

Both Stereophonics and Catatonia were included within this article, and both were closely associated with Wales by the press from the beginnings of their careers, but not in the negative and mocking way in which Manic Street

Preachers had been. Reviews in the music press had an optimistic feel to them (see *Melody Maker*, 1997b; *Melody Maker* 1999e). Reports in the *Western Mail* were affectionate, repeatedly referring to Stereophonics as 'Cwmaman boys', (see, for example, *Western Mail*, 1997b and 1997c). It ran a number of articles which referred to the band's background as a sign of their authenticity, describing how they 'keep in touch with their roots' (*Western Mail*, 1997d) and how '[t]here are real people behind that mammoth sound' (*Western Mail*, 1998a). The *Melody Maker* and *NME* continued to use Wales-related puns as headings to articles, as they had with Manic Street Preachers, including 'Shine on you crazy Dai men!' (*NME*, 1999a), however there was little in the text of the articles that was scornful.

Catatonia's association with Wales was perhaps inevitable given that the verses of the title-track of their 1998 breakthrough album, *International Velvet*, were sung in strict Welsh meter, followed by the English-language chorus 'Every day when I wake up/I thank the Lord I'm Welsh'. The references to Welsh musical history were still to be found. Catatonia's singer, Cerys Matthews, was variously described as 'Cardiff's greatest singing export since Shirley Bassey' (*Evening Standard*, 1999), 'this generation's Bonnie Tyler' and 'the anti-Nerys Hughes' (*Q*, 1999), again illustrating a constant placing of the band as Welsh in the press. The *Melody Maker* even mocked-up a photo of Matthews wearing a dress made from the Welsh flag (*Melody Maker*, 1999a).

In addition to the bands individually being associated with Wales, they were frequently associated with each other, and stories about the different bands often reported together. Occasionally it was because they were playing gigs together, such as when Manic Street Preachers toured with Catatonia and Super Furry Animals in December 1996. Often, there was no link but a variety of stories about different bands from Wales were reported together (see for example 'Cymru as you are', *Melody Maker*, 1999a, and 'Welsh round-up', *Melody Maker*, 1999b).

'Cool Cymru' was however a contested area in the media. It has been described as a media invention, a lazy journalistic device for pigeonholing a number of bands that happen to have come from Wales, and rarely used by the bands themselves. Adam Walton of BBC Radio Wales said it 'sucked from day one' and Curig Huws from the band Murry The Hump argued that it was 'just journalists trying to find connections between bands that are not necessarily connected apart from where they come from' (*Western Mail*, 1999a).

WALES IN SONGS

The naming of Wales in songs by these groups was rare, but references to Wales were made in a variety of ways, including artwork used on albums and singles, as well as lyrics. Until the release of their 1996 album *Everything Must Go*, there was scant reference to Wales, or any expression of specifically Welsh identity, in Manic Street Preachers' songs, and any association between the band and Wales came from the press. Nicky Wire has since said that the Manics' early single 'Motown Junk' is about Wales (BBC Radio Wales, *This Is My Truth Tell Me Yours*, 1997). However, as Price has argued, with its lyric about being 'numbed out in piss towns' it could be said to be about a place *like* south Wales (Price, 1999, p. 22), such as the post-industrial areas of the Midlands, the north of England and Scotland, all of which lost much of their economic power and jobs in the 1980s. Elsewhere in their work there was one critical reference on their third album, *The Holy Bible* (1994) in the song 'PCP' to the Welsh-language movement, with the lyric 'systemised atrocity ignored/as long as bi-lingual signs in view'. The release in May 1996 of the album *Everything Must Go* saw more explicit references made to Wales than their previous releases.[7] These different expressions of, and references to, Welsh identity were neither simple nor always obvious. On *Everything Must Go* they were related to a working-class, post-industrial south-Welsh identity, expanding on their next album *This Is My Truth Tell Me Yours* to include other aspects of Welsh identity. None of these references are necessarily immediate, although they are deliberate, and were discussed by Nicky Wire in radio and press interviews but would perhaps not be obvious to the casual observer.

The first single released from their 1996 album was 'A Design for Life' which opened with the lines 'Libraries gave us power/Then work came and made us free', acknowledged by its author, Wire, as being inspired by the inscription above a library in Newport, 'Knowledge is Power', and was described by him as being 'the nearest song ever [by the Manics] to writing about Wales' (BBC Radio Wales, *Libraries Gave Us Power*, 1997). In addition, the album notes included a dedication: 'Inspiration – Tower Colliery, Cyon [*sic*] Valley'. The Wales which the Manics made reference to at this point was primarily the post-industrial south Wales that they come from; ostensibly working class, a history of autodidacts and powerful oration, with a strong awareness of politics, and arguably almost a folk memory. This shift in the band's attitude towards Wales was noted in the music press, who referred to them as 'adopted godfathers of the new Taffia' (*Melody Maker*, 1997c). The third single released from the album, 'Australia', featured 'Can't Take my Eyes Off You' as its b-side. By releasing a song already so closely linked to Welsh football,[8] and by playing it at gigs (especially in Wales) it can also be seen as a flagging of the group's Welshness – an aural flagging. It is a constructed national identity which is both masculine and working class. Their live concerts, along with those of Catatonia and Stereophonics, were frequently punctuated by cries of 'Wales! Wales!' between songs, a cry normally associated with rugby and football supporters. Another aural marker of the band's identity was the playing of 'Hen Wlad fy Nhadau' (à la Jimi Hendrix playing 'The Star Spangled Banner' at Woodstock) as the introduction to another song at their Christmas gig in Cardiff, in December 1996.[9] If this was intended as an ironic comment it was completely lost on the audience who sang along. From December 1995, the band began playing gigs with a Welsh flag draped over one of their amps. Nicky Wire also collected the band's Brit award in 1997 draped in a Welsh flag, which was copied elsewhere by fans at festivals and gigs (Price, 1999, p. 27.; Griffiths, 2001, p. 215; Middles, 1999, p. 189).

Their 1998 album, *This Is My Truth Tell Me Yours*, contained many themes which could be identified as Welsh, and were broader than those which they had used before. The album cover featured the three remaining band members standing on a beach in north Wales, with the mountains of Snowdonia clearly visible in the background. The inside cover featured the poem *Reflections* by R. S. Thomas, a poet more usually associated with rural, religious, Welsh-speaking Wales. For the first time the promotional material was bilingual, albeit grammatically incorrect (*Western Mail*, 1998b). In an interview with BBC Radio Wales, Nicky Wire had said that '[i]n some ways I think this is the first Welsh folk album'. Elsewhere in the interview he discussed the formation of the Welsh Assembly and Welsh themes on the album, such as the drowning of Tryweryn,[10] again outside of their more usual post-industrial south Wales references, and also of the great Welsh artists who have suffered from alcoholism, including Richard Burton, Dylan Thomas and Rachel Roberts (BBC Radio Wales, *This Is My Truth Tell Me Yours*, 1997). References to post-industrial, socialist, south Wales are however by no means absent. Nicky Wire said that he chose the title of the album after hearing a recording of Aneurin Bevan speaking those words, played at his monument near Ebbw Vale during a celebration of the centenary of his birth in 1997 (BBC Radio Wales, *This Is My Truth Tell Me Yours*, 1997). The artwork for the singles released from the album included a quotation from actor Anthony Hopkins and a photo of volunteers for the International Brigades in Spain, taken from *Miners Against Fascism* by Hywel Francis (1984). Lyrics included a quotation from one of the volunteers, '[i]f I can shoot rabbits, I can shoot fascists', also taken from this book (Francis, 1984, p. 215). B-sides from the singles included 'Socialist Serenade' and 'Prologue to History', a reference to Gwyn A. Williams's *When Was Wales?* (1985), and opens with the line 'Were we the Kinnock factor?' alluding to the 1992 *Sun* headline which asked 'If Labour wins today will the last person to leave Britain please turn out the lights?'. Another, entitled 'Valley Boy', was also used (along with 'Valley Girl') as a t-shirt slogan, popular at concerts and worn by Cerys Matthews of Catatonia on the cover of the *Melody Maker* (1999c) with two members of Stereophonics.

With Stereophonics, the link between the band's songs and south Wales was more explicit from the outset. When interviewed, Kelly Jones of Stereophonics located his lyrics in his experience of growing up in south Wales: 'I only write like I do because I've never been anywhere. The stories are based on people I know and things I've seen' (*Melody Maker*, 1997b). The tales of small-town life from their first album *Word Gets Around*, with its dedication to 'the people of Cwmaman', drew comparisons with Bruce Springsteen: 'They've done for rural South Wales [sic] what Bruce Springsteen did for New Jersey. They've taken the apparently parochial, provincial and mundane inside-page headlines in the local paper and turned them into massive, rampant, breathless, bog-eyed anthems' (*NME*, 1997b). In many ways, Stereophonics offered a much more 'real' construction of working-class, south-Welsh identity than the Manics did. Their appearance and dress was undoubtedly masculine, unlike the Manics' make-up, leopard skin and (especially Richey James and Nicky Wire's) blurring of gender and sexual identity. This was clearly reflected within their lyrics too, which reflected personal experience rather than the south-Walian folk identity of the Manics at this time. As Jones acknowledged, the lyrics of their debut album were very much concerned with the everyday, and local characters ('Walks like Chaplin'), tragedy ('Local Boy in the Photograph') and scandal ('A Thousand Trees'). Again, these songs could come from almost anywhere *like* south Wales, but coupled with the specific references to their origin in Cwmaman in the press, they are tied to the place. Unlike Manic Street Preachers, the references to Wales are not made in the band's artwork, although the band's merchandise did include a t-shirt which bore the legend, 'You Can Take the Boy Out of Wales, but You Can't Take Wales Out of the Boy'.

In contrast, Catatonia's music itself contained scarce references to Wales or identity, generally being more concerned with love and relationships. The song 'International Velvet' was the only track on their breakthrough album to be sung (partially) in Welsh, or to mention Wales. In the artwork used for the singles taken from the album, 'Mulder and Scully' featured a spaceship hovering over Cardiff, and one of the covers for 'Strange Glue' showed a red dragon striving towards a city, Godzilla-like.

Voice and language also played a role in the placing of these bands, though arguably more in the *type* of Welshness presented. Of these bands, only Catatonia ever sang in Welsh, and only Cerys Matthews's accent could be identified as Welsh, reflecting their background.[11] Both Manic Street Preachers' James Dean Bradfield and Stereophonics' Kelly Jones sing in voices best described as 'mid-Atlantic' and always in English, reflecting their origin in the industrial valleys of south Wales, the region identified by Zimmern (1921) as American Wales.[12] However, it is *how* the music was used and *where* it was played that tied it to Wales and to 'Cool Cymru'.

'WA-LES! WA-LES!' – SPORT AND MUSIC AND PUBLIC SPACES

The significance of 'A Design for Life' and its association with Wales goes beyond the opening lyrics. The b-side of the single remixed the song as an instrumental piece and was later taken by the Welsh Tourist Board to soundtrack its campaign, featuring adverts screened in cinemas and on national TV networks, showing rural and coastal landscapes of Wales. Another single, 'Australia', was used to try to attract Australian visitors to Wales for the Rugby World Cup in 1999.[13] Robin Gwyn of the Wales Tourist Board was quoted as saying that the music was used to 'show that Wales can be contemporary, it's not all just heritage and culture' (*Western Mail*, 1999a). It was reported that the Wales Labour Party had also wanted to use 'A Design for Life' as their campaign theme for the Welsh Assembly elections, but permission was refused (*Melody Maker*, 1999a). In television, too, music was used as an expression of a 'new' Wales. The 1998 BBC *Scrutiny* documentary 'Cool Cymru' followed the attempts of the Welsh Development Agency to attract inward investment and made use of this new Welsh music. The film opens with the usual shots of Wales (hills, farms, former mining towns) accompanied by the loop from Catatonia's 'International Velvet' with the chorus 'Everyday, when I wake up/I thank the Lord I'm Welsh'. In one of the first sequences, Elfyn Llwyd MP talks about his opinion of what it is to be Welsh, concluding that 'to be Welsh is to be cool'. The use of this music encourages the viewer to make a link between these newly successful bands, and a bringing of new jobs and industry to Wales, implying cultural and economic regeneration.

Music played an important role in films coming out of Wales at this time. *Twin Town* (1997) and *House of America* (1997) both used Welsh bands in their soundtracks. *Twin Town* included songs by Manic Street Preachers, Super Furry Animals and Catatonia, though the soundtrack was by no means completely

Welsh. In *House of America* music played a central role in establishing place and identity. Its writer, Ed Thomas said that:

> There are two musical canons in the film for the Lewis family. Dad is into the Velvet Underground and the whole Beat Generation thing, Mum is wedded to Tom Jones – also very apt, the Boy from Nowhere who found the American Dream in Las Vegas. And there's the music for the kids . . . What's happening in Wales at the moment is fantastic, and I think *House of America* rightly capitalises on that. The fact that there are bands like Catatonia who go for that slightly American guitar sound fitted into our needs brilliantly. (*Western Mail*, 1997e)

Similarly, Patrick Jones's play *Everything Must Go*, performed in 1999 in Cardiff and London, used an entirely Welsh soundtrack (*Gair Rhydd*, 1999), including a reworking of the Catatonia chorus from 'International Velvet' sung by a school choir.[14] Jones released an album of poetry and music later that year, entitled *Commemoration and Amnesia*, which included contributions from members of Manic Street Preachers, Catatonia and Super Furry Animals. In 2000 the film *Camgymeriad Gwych/Beautiful Mistake* was released. It featured John Cale performing with, amongst others, James Dean Bradfield (Manic Street Preachers), Catatonia, Gorky's Zygotic Mynci, Super Furry Animals and Patrick Jones. The film was comprised of footage of the bands performing with Cale, cut with clips of everyday life in south Wales, with Cale providing a commentary as part of the soundtrack.

Away from film and television, at the huge gigs at Margam Park, the Millennium Stadium and Morfa, the use of the bands at major sporting events had two major effects: to prove the genuine popularity of these groups on a mass scale, and to link sport and music. National identity and sport are closely linked in popular culture, and the bands becoming closely associated with sporting events served to tie them further to ideas of Welsh identity. Sport fans have long had songs and chants. Welsh football supporters adopted the Andy Williams song 'Can't Take My Eyes Off You' after it was used in a BBC Wales advert for a match in 1993 (see also Blake, 1999, p. 113). Further, no Welsh international rugby match today would be complete without an accompaniment of 'Calon Lân', 'Cwm Rhondda' and 'Delilah'.

At national sporting events, bands began to play a central role. Stereophonics played before Wales played South Africa at Wembley in 1998. In March 1999, singer Kelly Jones appeared in an advert for BBC Wales's coverage of the final five nations match between England and Wales. He was shown busking in Twickenham, singing a song which ended with the lines 'As long as we beat the

English/We don't care.' The *Melody Maker* reported that the story was played to a 'thrilled audience' in Scotland, and that it was 'believed the band would quietly drop it for the [tour] dates in England' (*Melody Maker*, 1999d). In September 1999, Cerys Matthews took part in the opening ceremony for the Rugby World Cup in Cardiff.

As music became a part of sporting events, so highlights of Welsh sporting history became part of gigs, especially the Stereophonics gig at Morfa Stadium, Swansea in the summer of 1999, and the Manic Street Preachers 'Manic Millennium' concert. A fortnight after the Morfa Stadium gig, the following review was published in the *NME*:

> We're staring at the video screens at Morfa stadium, shortly before the Stereophonics encore. The crowd is in raptures, but not just about the music. Rather they're raving over the highlights of Welsh cultural history that are reeled around us. And in particular we're watching footage of the rugby lads on form. Which naturally involves the national team putting it up the English again and again.
>
> You can't *not* be moved by this. Such a noise, so much jubilation from 50,000 people. They're calling it the biggest public convergence in Swansea this century. People from every social and generational area have scrawled 'PROUD TO BE WELSH' on their flags to complement their Cool Cymru and valley chic t-shirts.
>
> In a few minutes they'll be letting rip with a glowering Welsh national anthem 'Hen Wlad fy Nhadau' before the fireworks show and the ultimate all-thundering Welsh rugby standard 'Bread of Heaven'. (*NME*, 1999b)

This was pop concert as triumphant sporting event. The rules are the same – clothing and flags showing your allegiance, screens showing the game and the crowd erupting at the winning try, national anthem, sporting anthems and pop anthems merging into one; Anderson's 'unisonance' but with a pop soundtrack, the imagined community assembled. And all of it taking place in a sporting arena. Again, it is a very masculine identity, and very working class. The Catatonia 'Home Internationals' at Llangollen and Margam Park had a similar feel, and received similar reviews in the music press with mention of the flags, chanting and singing, 'a back-up choir of thousands' singing 'International Velvet' along with the band (*Melody Maker*, 1999e). The 'Manic Millennium' concert that took place in the Millennium Stadium on 31 December 1999 took a similar format to Morfa, with clothing, flags and the use of large screens showing classic moments of victory in Welsh sport, hymns and arias and the chanting 'Wales! Wales!'. The DVD of this concert includes footage of flags for sale in Cardiff Central station, as they are on match days, fans wrapped in flags or wearing their rugby and football shirts (Manic Street Preachers, *Leaving the 20th Century*). The visual flaggings are clear, flags waved and flags worn, the 'valley chic' t-shirts, the sport on the huge televisions. But the aural flaggings are of importance too. After all, the concerts at the Morfa and the Millennium stadiums, Llangollen and Margam Park, were primarily *musical* events.

After the gig at Morfa, there was some discussion in the music press over whether the display of flags constituted racism. It began with the *NME* printing a letter from a reader, Boris from Telford, who complained that he had felt intimidated by the flags and singing, particularly the 'chanting of "Wales" throughout the day and singing a song "slagging off the English" ' (*NME*, 1999c).[15] The debate continued in the *NME* letters page for several weeks, and led to an editorial under the unfortunate heading 'Is Wales the new Germany?' (*NME*, 1999d). The *Western Mail* responded with indignation, and showed pictures from the gig of people waving and wearing their flags (*Western Mail*, 1999b). It is clear from letters to both *Melody Maker* and *NME* that it was not only the visual markers of Welsh national identity which upset some readers, but the aural markers which they reported as being intimidating – the chants and the songs. The reviews of these concerts describe a form of unisonance, of 'people wholly unknown to each other utter[ing] the same verses to the same melody' (Anderson, 1991, p. 145). However, what is perhaps most interesting is that we can see from the reaction within the music press that this unisonance was not necessarily a harmonious experience, reflecting the contested nature of national identity.

CONCLUSION

This article has illustrated how ideas about identity have been expressed and articulated through the use of popular music and has suggested that 'Cool Cymru' was primarily a musical event. While most common 'flaggings' of the nation and identity given by theorists are visual, 'Cool Cymru' was driven by music. It was through music that it was identified, and this became used as a marker for a 'modern Wales' in politics, television, film and sport. And it was through public uses of the music that it became most strongly associated with ideas of Welsh identity, at huge concerts and sporting events. It is here that we can see Anderson's idea of unisonance, the 'experience of simultaneity', is evident. It is significant that it was *popular* music which provided this soundtrack, rather than the formal national anthems usually discussed, with new music used as a metaphor for a new Wales. Without a doubt 'Cool Cymru' was (and is) a contested term. Nevertheless, the bands involved created a positive soundtrack that reflected the burgeoning confidence of Welsh identity and nationalism during the late 1990s. It will be interesting to see if this aural flagging continues with the new bands coming from Wales, such as Goldie Lookin' Chain, and the role which popular music might play in articulating ideas of identity in the future.

NOTES

1   This is a reference to several successful bands which emerged from Seattle and the surrounding area in the early 1990s, and including Nirvana, Pearl Jam and Soundgarden, which were known in the press as 'grunge' or 'the Seattle sound'.
2   For example, the release of 'Ferry Cross the Mersey' after the Hillsborough tragedy, and 'Candle in the Wind 1997' by Elton John, recorded and released after the death of Diana, Princess of Wales.
3   Allen had also co-written the 1990 England World Cup anthem 'World in Motion' with New Order.
4   For further discussion of the role of the Welsh language in music, see Sarah Hill's thesis ' "Blerwytirhwng?" Welsh popular music, language and the politics of identity' (Cardiff: Cardiff University, 2002); Meic Llewellyn 'Popular music in the Welsh language and the affirmation of youth identities', in *Popular Music*, vol. 19, 3 (2000).
5   All radio and television transcriptions are author's own.
6   Ellipses are editorial.
7   This was the first release after the disappearance of guitarist and lyricist Richey James in February 1995.
8   This song had been adopted by Welsh football fans after its use by BBC Wales in an advert for a Wales game in the early 1990s.
9   The guitarist Titch Gwilym had also done this in the 1970s as had Datblygu in the late 1980s and early 1990s, see discography for further details.
10 The Welsh-speaking village of Capel Celyn, in the Tryweryn valley, was flooded in the 1960s by the Liverpool Corporation to create a reservoir for Liverpool, despite almost all the Welsh MPs voting against it. The slogan 'Cofiwch Dryweryn' (Remember Tryweryn) is still painted in parts of Wales.
11 Members of Catatonia come from west of Swansea, Llanwrst and Cardiff, and all of them speak Welsh as their first language.
12 For further discussion, see Dai Griffiths (2001), and his argument that the Welsh identity of Bradfield must be understood through factors other than his voice.
13 It has also been used by the Australian tourist board in their British campaign.
14 Patrick Jones is Nicky Wire's older brother.
15 This refers to Kelly Jones performing the song from the BBC Wales five nations advertisement mentioned previously.

REFERENCES

Books and Journals

Anderson, B. (1991). *Imagined Communities* (revised and extended edn), London: Verso.

Billig, M. (1995). *Banal Nationalism*, London: Sage Publications.

Bracewell, M. (1997). *England is Mine: Pop Life in Albion from Wilde to Goldie*, London: HarperCollins.

Blake, A. (1999). 'Chants would be a fine thing', in M. Perryman (ed.) *The Ingerland Factor: Home Truths from Football*, Edinburgh: Mainstream Publishing Company.

Connell, J. and Gibson, C. (2003). *Sound Tracks: Popular Music, Identity and Place*, London: Routledge.

Francis, H. (1984). *Miners Against Fascism*, London: Lawrence and Wishart.

Gellner, E. (1983). *Nations and Nationalism*, Oxford: Blackwell.

Gilroy, P. (1993). *The Black Atlantic: Modernity and Double Consciousness*. Cambridge, Mass.: Harvard University Press.

Griffiths, D. (2001). 'Kelly, Cerys and James Dean Bradfield', in T. Herbert and P. Stead (eds), *Hymns and Arias: Great Welsh Voices*, Cardiff: University of Wales Press.

Griffiths, D. and Hill, S. (2005). 'Postcolonial music in contemporary Wales: hybrids and weird geographies', in J. Aaron and C. Williams (eds), *Postcolonial Wales*, Cardiff: University of Wales Press.

Harris, J. (2003). *The Last Party: Britpop, Blair and the Demise of English Rock*, London: Fourth Estate.

Hibbett, R. (2005). 'What is indie rock?', *Popular Music and Society*, 28, 1, 55–77.

Hobsbawm, E. (1992). 'Introduction: inventing traditions', in E. Hobsbawm and T. Ranger (eds), *The Invention of Tradition*, Cambridge: Cambridge University Press.

Hughes, M. and Stradling, R. (2001). *The English Musical Renaissance 1840–1940, Constructing a National Music*, 2nd edn, Manchester and New York: Manchester University Press.

Middles, M. (1999). *Manic Street Preachers*, London: Omnibus.

Perryman, M. (1999). 'The Ingerland factor', in M. Perryman (ed.) *The Ingerland Factor: Home Truths from Football*, Edinburgh and London: Mainstream Publishing.

Price, S. (1999). *Everything (A BOOK ABOUT THE MANIC STREET PREACHERS)*, London: Virgin.

Shuker, R. (2002). *Popular Music: The Key Concepts*, London and New York: Routledge.

Smith, D. (1999). *Wales: A Question for History*, Bridgend: Seren.

Welsh Assembly Government (2001). *Plan For Wales 2001, www.planforwales.wales.gov.uk/pdf/plan_for_Wales_English.pdf*, accessed 31 March 2005.

Williams, G. A. (1985). *When Was Wales? A History of the Welsh*, London: Black Raven.

Zimmern, A. (1921). *My Impressions of Wales*, London: Mills and Boon.

Zuberi, N. (2001). *Sounds English: Transnational Popular Music*, Urbana: University of Illinois Press.

PRESS

Bigmouth (1998). 'Year of the dragon', by Lisa Symonds, August.

Evening Standard (1999). 'Who's that lady?', by Tim Marsh, in 'Hot tickets', 11 March.

Gair Rhydd (1999). 'From despair to where?', by Alexandra Lewis and Rachel Harding, *GRiP Magazine*, 1 March.

Guardian (1996). 'Into the valley of the 60Ft Dolls', by Caroline Sullivan, 4 October, accessed through LexisNexis, *www.lexisnexis.co.uk*, 9 April 2005.

Melody Maker (1991). 'Manic Street Preachers take no prisoners – Jon Wilde talks to the Welsh renegades', by Jon Wilde, 1 June.

Melody Maker (1992a). 'Singalongamanics', by Simon Price, 29 August.

Melody Maker (1992b). 'Taffer than the rest', by Jon Seizer, 8 February.

Melody Maker (1992c). 'The leek shall inherit the earth', by David Fricke, 6 June.

Melody Maker (1997a). 'Evans sent!', by Dave Simpson, 10 May.

Melody Maker (1997b). 'Feelin' supersonic', by Ben Myers, 29 March.

Melody Maker (1997c). 'Street life', by Simon Price, 4 January.

Melody Maker (1999a). 'Cymru as you are', 17 April.

Melody Maker (1999b). 'Welsh round-up', 29 May.

Melody Maker (1999c). Front cover, 7 August.

Melody Maker (1999d). 'News', 24 April.

Melody Maker (1999e). 'This could be legendary', 29 May.

Melody Maker (1999f). 'I heard the news today, oh boyo', by Mark Rowland, 31 July.

New York Times (1996). 'Critics choice/pop CDs; of reggae and rock from Wales', by Neil Straus, 4 June, accessed from LexisNexis, *www.lexisnexis.co.uk*, 9 April 2005.

NME (1997a). 'Dial M For Merthyr', reviewed by Mark Sutherland, 4 April.

NME (1997b). 'Scandal in the wind', by Steven Wells, 18 October.

NME (1999a). 'Shine on you crazy Dai men!', by Mark Beaumont, 10 April.

NME (1999b). 'Kelly watch the stardom', by Stuart Bailie, 14 August.

NME (1999c). 'Welsh pride or fascism? – an overview of the debate', 11 September.

NME (1999d). 'Is Wales the new Germany?' 21 August.

Q (1999). 'I want to be alone', by Nick Duerden, May.

Sun (1992). 'Would the last person to leave Britain please turn out the lights?', 9 April.

Sunday Times (1995). 'Which side are you on?', by Robert Sandall, 20 August, accessed through LexisNexis, *www.lexisnexis.co.uk*, 9 April 2005.

Telegraph Magazine (1997). 'Move over Seattle, here comes Newport', by Byron Rogers, 24 May.

The Times (1998). 'Davies delivers his call to arms', by Jasper Gerard, 4 April, accessed through LexisNexis, *www.lexisnexis.co.uk*, 9 April 2005.

Western Mail (1994). 'Valleys of the dolls', by Andy Barding, 15 May.

Western Mail (1996). 'Chorus of approval for Welsh pop', 30 April.

Western Mail (1997a). 'Taff rock brings English music press to its knees and begging for more', by Darren Waters, 13 June.

Western Mail (1997b). 'Chasing the American scream', by Rob Driscoll, 3 October.

Western Mail (1997c). 'Prince of darkness entertains shoppers in helter-skelter campaign', 16 August.

Western Mail (1997d). 'The boys are back in town', by Darren Waters, 10 October.

Western Mail (1997e). 'Coping with first album, fame and . . . Cwmaman', by Pauline McLean, 8 August.

Western Mail (1998a). 'There are real people behind that mammoth sound at sell-out gigs', 5 December.

Western Mail (1998b). 'Manics put on report for grammar slip', by Patrick Fletcher, 19 September.
Western Mail (1998c). 'Selling Wales – the hunt for a new image', by Clive Betts, 20 June.
Western Mail (1999a). 'Cooling down Cymru?', by Rhodri Owen, 30 October.
Western Mail (1999b). 'Welsh are a Nazi piece of work say pop fans', by Darren Waters, 28 August.

TELEVISION AND RADIO

Dragon's Breath (2001). BBC Radio Wales, part 3, 28 February.
Libraries Gave Us Power (1997). BBC Radio Wales, 11 May.
Made in Wales (1997). BBC Radio 1, 11 May.
Scrutiny (1998). BBC 2, 19 September.
Sound of the Suburbs (1999). Channel 4, 13 March.
This Is My Truth Tell Me Yours (1997). BBC Radio Wales, 5 May.

DISCOGRAPHY

(Where multi-formats have been released, the compact disc reference number has been given unless otherwise stated).

Blur, *Modern Life is Rubbish* (1993: Food, B000002USH).
Blur, *Parklife* (Food, FOODCD10).
Catatonia, *International Velvet* (1998: Blanco y Negro, 3984208942).
Catatonia, 'Mulder and Scully' (1998: Blanco y Negro, NEG109CD).
Catatonia, 'Strange Glue' (1998: Blanco y Negro, NEG113 – 7" vinyl).
Datblygu. 'Hen Wlad Fy Nhadau' (James and James), *Radio Crymu Playlist* compilation (2003: Ankst Records, ANKST108).
Titch Gwilym. 'Hen Wlad Fy Nhadau' (James and James), *Welsh Rare Beat* compilation (2005: Finders Keepers/Sain Records, FKR003CD).
Manic Street Preachers, 'Australia'/'Can't Take My Eyes Off You' (1996: Epic, 664044 4).
Manic Street Preachers, 'A Design for Life', stealth Sonic Orchestra instrumental version (1996: Columbia, 663070 5).
Manic Street Preachers, 'The Everlasting'/'Black Holes For the Young'/'Valley Boy' (1998: Epic, 666686 2).
Manic Street Preachers, *Everything Must Go* (1996: Sony, 483 930 2).
Manic Street Preachers, *The Holy Bible* (1994: Epic, 477421 2).
Manic Street Preachers, 'If You Tolerate This Your Children Will be Next'/'Prologue to History'/'Montana Autumn 78' (1998: Epic, 664044 2).
Manic Street Preachers, *Leaving the 20th Century* (2000: Epic, 2011269).
Manic Street Preachers, 'Motown Junk' (1991: Heavenly, NVN8 CD).
Manic Street Preachers, *This Is My Truth Tell Me Yours* (1998: Sony, 483 930 2).
Stereophonics, *Word Gets Around* (1997: V2, WR1000432).

Tom Jones, *Reload* (1999: Gut, GUTCD009). Included collaborations with Cerys Matthews of Catatonia ('Baby It's Cold Outside'), James Dean Bradfield of Manic Street Preachers ('I'm Left You're Right She's Gone') and Stereophonics ('Mama Told Me Not To Come').

Various Artists, *Dial M for Merthyr* (1997: Fierce Panda, NONGCD/02 TIDY 003).

10. CHILDREN'S RIGHTS AND WELL-BEING IN WALES IN 2006

Nigel Thomas and Anne Crowley

ABSTRACT

The purpose of this article is to take stock of developments in policy and practice affecting children in Wales since the establishment of the National Assembly in 1999. In the first part the authors review a range of policy initiatives in education, health and social care, and poverty reduction, identifying common themes and considering what can be said about the impact of these policies on practice. They also review developments in governmental structures for children, including the Children's Commissioner, Funky Dragon and changes in Cabinet responsibilities. The second part of the article looks at some indicators of children's well-being in order to assess how the reality of life for children and young people appears to be changing in areas such as health and education, lifestyle, poverty, abuse and bullying, and in relation to particular issues for children in care and care leavers and for refugee and asylum-seeking children. The authors conclude that, despite signs of improvement, on some key indicators Welsh children lag behind their peers in the rest of the UK; and that there is a serious need for better information in the form of a 'state of Wales's children' report. They also conclude that it is encouraging to see distinctive policies being developed in Wales that in important respects put children at the heart of policy-making, and that the 'participation agenda' has caught on in a way that may promise real change.

INTRODUCTION

Our purpose in this article is to try to take stock of developments in policy and practice that affect children's rights and well-being in Wales in the first decade of the twenty-first century. We look first at developments in policy, and then at some indicators of how the reality of life for children and young people appears to be changing on the ground. Finally we attempt to draw some more general conclusions and point to a few questions that may merit further examination.

We take as our starting point the establishment of the National Assembly in 1999. We do so not only because this is a convenient point from which to assess developments in policy, but also because the condition of children and young people was in some ways a core issue for the devolution settlement – as reflected, for instance, in the sheer quantity of policy and strategy documents relating to children and young people that have been produced in the past six years (see below).

Of course, it is not just the policies made by government ministers and Assembly Members that affect the lives of children and young people. Policy-makers at other levels of government, including the local authority, have their own agendas, as do the many non-governmental organizations engaged in activity in this field. However, to a significant extent it is the National Assembly and the Welsh Assembly Government who give the lead and set the tone, as well as holding the purse-strings for many of the key services.[1]

There are a number of signs that issues around the rights and well-being of children and young people may be especially salient in the Welsh political landscape. The pressure for a children's minister and a children's commissioner was particularly strong before 1999, and had already borne fruit in the appointment of a children's minister in the old Welsh Office. In Wales there are comparatively strong links between governmental and non-governmental organizations in the field of child welfare and children's rights, for which Children in Wales provides one focal point. There is also a strong recent tradition of work in children's participation, which we discuss later in this article.

In addition, key players in the new administration such as Jane Davidson[2] and Jane Hutt[3], with a background of working in the voluntary sector on child, youth and family issues, are likely to have had an effect in moving children's issues up the political agenda. It is worth noting too that 'the two Janes' were among an unprecedentedly large number of women in the new Assembly, particularly in the Labour and Plaid Cymru groups. It has been remarked that women politicians tend to be better at recognizing the importance of children's issues.

It could also be argued that for some people the definition of Wales as a nation is tied up with traditions of mutuality and social support, and that the agenda of children's rights and welfare fits well with this, while for others the demand for national self-government is strongly linked with the demand for socially or politically excluded groups, including children and young people, to take a greater part in the life of the nation. In addition to being increasingly recognized as having interests of their own as citizens or potential citizens, children and young people have long been seen as having future economic value. This remains an important element in policy, as we see below.

DEVELOPMENTS IN POLICIES AND STRUCTURES

Policies and their impact

Children and Young People – A Framework for Partnership; Extending Entitlement; Early Entitlement; Cymorth; The Child Poverty Strategy; The National Service Framework for Children, Young People and Maternity Services; Rights to Action; Moving Forward.[4] There has certainly been no shortage of strategies and initiatives to improve the well-being of children and young people, and that is without counting Iaith Pawb, Wales – A Better Country, and all the other policy documents that have more general implications but that include important potential impacts for children and young people.

Several threads run through most of these policies. One thread is a very strong emphasis on collaboration and partnership, not only between public bodies like local authorities and health trusts, but including a whole range of governmental, non-governmental and quasi-governmental agencies who can contribute to promoting the interests of children and young people. This is particularly evident in the arrangements for Children and Young People's Framework Partnerships, for Cymorth and for the new Integrated Children's Centres, where successive policy statements and guidance are increasingly based on assumptions that agencies should and will see themselves as having a collective responsibility for providing services to children and young people that are 'joined-up' both in strategy and in delivery.

A second thread is the set of seven core aims, derived from the United Nations Convention on the Rights of the Child, which are intended to inform all the Welsh Assembly Government's work with children and young people. To quote one recent document, *Children and Young People: Rights to Action*, these aim 'to ensure that all children and young people':

- have a flying start in life;
- have a comprehensive range of education and learning opportunities;
- enjoy the best possible health and are free from abuse, victimisation and exploitation;
- have access to play, leisure, sporting and cultural activities;

- are listened to, treated with respect, and have their race and cultural identity recognized;
- have a safe home and a community which supports physical and emotional wellbeing;
- are not disadvantaged by poverty.

(Welsh Assembly Government, 2004a, p. 1)

The extent to which these ambitious aims are developed in more detail varies from one policy document to another. For example, the 'Rights to Action' document says little or nothing about ensuring that children and young people have their race and cultural identity recognized.

As we noted above, children and young people are also seen as important for their future economic value. Indeed, they are essential to the vision of a vibrant and prosperous Wales laid out in the strategic plan *Better Wales*.

> Learning – for both children and adults – is at the top of the Assembly's agenda. A sound education is essential to becoming a responsible and active citizen and gaining a good job. Indeed, the only way in which we can achieve enduring success as a nation is for life-long learning – in the literal sense – to be embedded in the cultures of the diverse communities and organisations that make up modern Wales . . . If we are to succeed in a knowledge-driven world we must ensure that everyone has the skills and the knowledge to fulfil their potential at all stages of their lives. (National Assembly for Wales, 2000, p. 23.)

The focus on children as part of this vision has been developed by Jane Davidson under the slogan of a 'learning country'. In particular, early years policy has prioritised quality, integrated services and user involvement, aimed at supporting the development of healthier, happier, more socially competent children who, research suggests (see for instance Sylva et al., 2003), will go on to become more economically productive adults. At the same time, policy has focused on providing much needed affordable childcare to support the 'welfare to work' agenda. The emphasis has been different in some respects from the rest of the UK, as Wincott (2004) argues. This may be in part because of the way in which bilingualism tends to politicise early childhood issues. The long tradition of Welsh-medium preschools and playgroups assumes an even greater significance as the Assembly adopts policies to promote the language.

In other ways Wales has followed a different agenda in education from that in England, dispensing with school league tables and at least some of the Standardised Assessment Tests, and opting for a more child-centred Foundation

Phase. In respect of play for children, the Welsh Assembly Government has arguably been the first in the UK to take seriously children's rights to play as set out in Article 31 of the UN Convention, adopting an explicit policy for the promotion of play which was drafted by the agency Play Wales, and insisting that the flagship Integrated Children's Centres now being established in each authority for early years education and childcare must include an element of open access play. This was not without some opposition, as Seaton (2005) notes.

In some respects it is too soon to evaluate the real impact of many of these policy initiatives on practice, let alone on the daily lives of children. Even where policies have been in place for some time, relevant data are often not collected or made available. There is in general too little research in Wales in the field of child welfare, including evaluation of policy. There has never been a government research programme on a comparable scale to those in England and Scotland, and when studies are commissioned by government the timescale has often been too short to produce much of value. The Wales Office of Research and Development for Health and Social Care has been less active in recent years than might have been hoped. Non-governmental research funders such as foundations tend to underspend in Wales, although at least one funding council (the ESRC) is now trying to address this. Nevertheless, some impact of policy on practice is discernable, judging by operational contacts with practitioners and managers. Our impression is that the drive for interagency planning of services is beginning to make a difference to what happens in local areas. 'Partnerships', as opposed to agencies, are evolving into key players in the planning, commissioning and delivery of a range of services. On the other hand, in some local areas partnerships have been slow to establish themselves or to engage with the core business (and budgets) of key agencies in local government and the health service. It is arguable that until they can do this their capacity to have a significant impact on the lives and experiences of children and young people will be questionable.

So far the Welsh Assembly Government has not been active in monitoring the implementation of its policies and evaluating their impact on children, although this may change with draft guidance under Section 26 of the Children Act (2004), which if adopted will put Children and Young People's Framework Partnerships on a statutory footing. From 2007–8, partnerships will be required to produce Children and Young People's Plans for all services provided for children and young people up to the age of 25, setting out their plans for improvements to be made in the well-being of children and young people in accordance with the Assembly Government's seven core aims. The Assembly Government is currently working with the Welsh Local Government Association and the Local Government Data Unit to reach agreement on an appropriate set of performance indicators for key areas of activity by which local partnerships can demonstrate progress in achieving these aims. In addition the National Service Framework for Children, Young People and Maternity Services in Wales (Welsh Assembly Government, 2005b) is accompanied by a self-assessment and audit tool designed to assist health services and their partners to monitor and improve their performance in implementing the National Service Framework standards.

At the same time the United Nations Committee on the Rights of the Child Non-Governmental Organisation Monitoring Group in Wales is working to develop a framework for monitoring the implementation of the UN Convention in Wales, and has been invited to participate in a children and young people's reference group advising the Welsh Assembly Government on the core indicators it will use to measure progress against its seven aims for children. The Monitoring Group's report Righting the Wrongs (Save the Children, 2006) appeared after work on this article was completed, but represents a useful overview of progress in key areas. The pioneering work in the Republic of Ireland (Hanafin and Brooks, 2005) to develop a national set of well-being indicators, and the work of Boyce (2005) in Northern Ireland to establish a broader range of children's rights indicators, should influence what is done in Wales. Until there is a robust framework for measuring changes to the lives and circumstances of children and young people in Wales, it will remain very difficult to evaluate the impact of the Welsh Assembly Government's policies.

Governmental structures for children

The other respect in which things have clearly changed is in structures. The Gulbenkian (1996) inquiry into effective government structures for children set out a strong case for developing special governmental structures and activities for children because of children's vulnerability and lack of power. Many of its recommendations have now been implemented in Wales. There is an overarching strategy for children and young people, on paper at least. There is an Assembly Government Cabinet sub-committee for children and young people, and a children's minister to champion the interests of children across government. Perhaps most importantly, there is the Children's Commissioner for Wales.

One of the first tasks of the new administration following devolution was to respond to the Waterhouse (2000) report into abuse in children's homes in north Wales. The political climate was such that it was imperative to respond forcefully and positively to the report. Given that the first of Waterhouse's seventy-two recommendations was that 'an independent Children's Commissioner for Wales should be appointed', and that the Care Standards Bill was currently going through Parliament, the decision to add a section to the Bill creating the office of Children's Commissioner cannot have been a difficult one. What was more praiseworthy, and needed more determined pressure, was the decision to go a step further and promote a further parliamentary bill which became the Children's Commissioner for Wales Act (2001), the first specifically Welsh legislation following devolution. This extended the commissioner's functions, and the range of children and young people encompassed by those functions, beyond the narrow focus on the care system implied by Waterhouse and the Care Standards Act (2000). In fact, it produced one of the stronger models of children's commissioner in its range of powers and its independence, in important respects stronger than the office more recently introduced in England, although the lack of power over non-devolved matters remains a serious weakness.

At the time of writing, the commissioner's office has been active for four years. As the first such post in the UK it has been intensely scrutinized, not least because the precise mix of powers and duties is unique. It is probably too soon to say with confidence what difference the commissioner's appointment has made to the lives of children and young people. The present authors are working with a group of children and young people to evaluate the working of the commissioner's office, in what is thought to be the first serious evaluation of an ombudsperson or children's commissioner anywhere in Europe.

Another aspect of effective structures for children is the availability of advocacy and provision for hearing complaints and representations. The Waterhouse report also prompted some expansion of advocacy services, and following the Carlile (2002) review the Welsh Assembly Government gave a commitment to review advocacy arrangements for children and young people. A task group was established whose remit later expanded to take in the recommendations of the children's commissioner's review of complaints, whistle-blowing and advocacy in social services (Children's Commissioner for Wales, 2003), and led to the Advocacy Services and Representations Procedure (Children) (Wales) Regulations 2004.

To inform the review, researchers at Cardiff University were commissioned to undertake a study of advocacy services for children and young people in Wales (Pithouse et al., 2005). This found that children and young people were generally unaware of their right to complain, few children and young people actually made a complaint, some had poor experiences of making a complaint and many were left confused about the process and the outcome. On the other hand, those who had access to an advocate valued the emotional and practical support the advocate brought to the process. However, access and quality of services across Wales varied widely, and difficulties were compounded by short-term contract arrangements and poor monitoring. The low level of complaints by children suggests that complaints procedures remain a blunt instrument to improve the quality of services, let alone to protect our most vulnerable children. In social services, 201 children (from a total of 23,000 children in need) made a complaint in their own right and fewer than 80 received support from advocacy services (2003–4 figures). In the health service, 226 children made a complaint in their own right, and advocacy services are not generally provided. The numbers of complaints to schools and education services could not be ascertained but appeared to be low. The Children's Commissioner (2005) found low levels of awareness among education authorities, and a generally negative attitude towards the consideration of complaints from pupils.

The task group has now recommended reform in the way in which advocacy and children's rights services are commissioned and delivered, with a new integrated regional advocacy service to support children and young people making complaints across health, social care and education, and programmes to develop capacity amongst those working directly with children and young people to listen and take children's concerns seriously.

A final structural change that is worthy of note is the foundation in 2001 of what was originally to be called Young Voice/Llais Ifanc but was eventually born as Funky Dragon/Draig Ffynci, and which is intended to fulfil the role of a children and young people's Assembly. The story of the foundation of Funky Dragon deserves to be told separately, but the organization is already far more independent than appeared to be envisaged by Alun Michael, the First Minister of Wales at the conception (though not by the time of the birth). It is already engaged to a significant extent in policy making, with children and young people attending regular formal meetings with ministers and officials at the highest level.[5] In combination with the growing network of youth forums, and now with the introduction of school councils across Wales, it appears that Funky Dragon may represent something of a sea-change in participation and citizenship for children and young people. We discuss this further later in this article.

At the time of writing it is not clear what will be the effect of recent changes in Cabinet and departmental responsibilities for different aspects of children's services in the Assembly. The relationship between those functions held in the education division and those retained in health and social services has always seemed somewhat arbitrary to the outsider, and the overall strategic direction is only as strong as the collaborative relationship between those divisions. In the civil service, however much it preaches 'joined-up' government, this often seems to be something of a challenge. It would be unfortunate if the new Cabinet arrangements were to lead to an overemphasis on educational priorities at the expense of (a) a holistic strategy for children's services and (b) a serious attempt to address the needs of the most disadvantaged children.

INDICATORS OF CHILDREN'S WELL-BEING

When we come to consider the effects of these policies, it is important to look at a range of indicators of children and young people's well-being. What can these tell us about how life is changing for children and young people in Wales, and how it is different for them than for children in other countries?

In many ways the mechanisms for monitoring outcomes for children in Wales (and across the UK) remain woefully inadequate (Bradshaw and Mayhew, 2005; Williams, 2003). Neither Wales nor the other nations of the UK have implemented a key recommendation of the Gulbenkian report on effective government structures for children, namely to publish an annual report on the state of the country's children. In a recent review Bradshaw and Mayhew note that there are 'entire areas of child well-being for which data is [*sic*] simply not available or where data is not comparable across the UK' (Save the Children, 2005a, p. 5). This makes it very difficult to assess progress towards improving children's well-being and therefore to evaluate the impact of policies. In some areas of children's lives, the lack of data on children in Wales is particularly acute. For example, there is little Wales-specific data on health and well-being, in particular mental health. Crime statistics are only presented on a combined basis for England and Wales. Although it is clear that children's life-chances are heavily influenced by factors such as ethnicity and country of origin, there is a particular dearth of information that can be used to relate outcomes for children to these factors, and we acknowledge that this is a weakness of our review.

What follows is based in large part on Bradshaw and Mayhew's UK review (2005), and the analysis of data specific to Wales produced from that review by Save the Children (2005a). Unless otherwise stated, those are the main sources used. We have also consulted other publications including *A Statistical Focus on Children in Wales* (National Assembly, 2002, in need of an update), the report of the Child Poverty Task Group (Welsh Assembly Government, 2004b), the background report for the National Service Framework produced by the National Public Health Service for Wales (2004), the review carried out by the New Policy Institute for the Joseph Rowntree Foundation (Kenway et al., 2005), and material from the Local Government Data Unit.

Demographic information

As Dunkerley notes elsewhere in this issue of *Contemporary Wales*, we live in an ageing society. In 1971 one in every four people in Wales was a child under sixteen; by 2002 that had fallen to one in every five. Children are also tending to live with older parents. The average age of a first-time mother in England and Wales rose in the same period from twenty-four to thirty years (although the proportion of women who are under twenty-one when their first child is born is higher in Wales than in England – 28 per cent compared to 23 per cent). The proportion of lone parent families in Wales at 7.3 per cent is higher than in England with 6.4 per cent (Scotland 7.0 per cent). Wales also has the highest percentage of babies born to lone mothers: 18 per cent compared to 13 per cent in England, 14 per cent in Scotland and 17 per cent in Northern Ireland.

Poverty

The indicators here are generally poor. The child poverty rate in the UK doubled during the 1980s and continued to rise until 1998–9, although since then the rates have improved. According to data from the Millennium Cohort Study, in 2002–3 Wales had the highest child poverty rate in the UK, with a quarter of children living in households at or below poverty threshold before housing costs compared with a fifth in England (using the 60 per cent median threshold). When housing costs are added, the child poverty rate in Wales rises to 30 per cent, which equates to over 200,000 children living in poverty. The UK continues to have the highest proportion of children living in workless households in the European Union.

More recently published data (Kenway et al., 2005) suggest that Wales has improved faster and in effect 'caught up' with the rest of the UK in the proportion of children facing poverty. However, the fall has been among households closest to the poverty threshold of 60 per cent of median household income. The proportion living in 'deep poverty' has not changed; an analysis of British Household Panel Study data (Adelman et al., 2003), recently updated by Save the Children (2005b), indicates that approximately 60,000 children in Wales live in severe poverty, defined as in households with an income of below 27 per cent of median income, and that this figure has not changed in the last decade.[6]

Health

Health indicators are mixed. The infant mortality and stillbirth rates for Wales were lower than those in England in four of the five years up to 2002. As in the rest of the UK, there is a long-term downward trend in infant mortality, although the rate is still higher than in most other European countries. In 1998 infant deaths in Wales were 5.6 per 1,000 live births; this had fallen to 4.5 per 1,000 by 2002. According to Kenway et al. (2005) the gap in the rate of infant deaths among those from manual and non-manual social backgrounds has widened since the mid 1990s. A comparative study across the UK found that Wales has the highest teenage conception rate, with 35 live births per 1,000 women under twenty, compared to 28 per 1,000 in England. In 2001–2 children in Wales were more likely to rate their health as 'fair' or 'poor' than children living in England or Scotland. Kenway et al. (2005) point to the poor health of children in the Valleys compared to other parts of Wales, using their selected indicators of (a) numbers of decayed, missing or filled teeth among 5-year-olds, and (b) numbers of births to girls who conceived under the age of sixteen. The rate of MMR (measles, mumps and rubella) immunizations in Wales remains slightly lower than in England, having fallen from 90 per cent to 81 percent over six years.

Lifestyle

Lifestyle indicators are generally poor. A range of data suggests that the prevalence of weekly drinking by young people is higher in Wales than in England. In 2001–2, the proportion of boys in Wales drinking on a weekly basis increased with age from 12 per cent of 11-year-olds to 58 per cent of 15-year-olds. The rate for 15-year-old girls, at 54 per cent, was the highest in the UK and sixteen other nations. The proportion of girls experiencing problems due to alcohol or drugs is higher than for boys in Wales and for young people in England. In Wales, 50 per cent of girls are reported as having at some time experienced problems due to alcohol and drugs, compared to 39 per cent of boys in Wales and 43 per cent of girls and 39 per cent of boys in England. In Wales as elsewhere in the UK, more teenage girls smoke regularly than boys (16 per cent as opposed to 9 per cent). As with alcohol, the rates increase with age: among boys, from 6 per cent at thirteen years to 12 per cent at fifteen, and among girls from 12 per cent at thirteen to 22 per cent at fifteen. The trend in Wales is for an increasing proportion of 13- to 16-year-old girls to smoke regularly, contrary to the rest of the UK where there has been a continuing decrease in smoking rates over the last fifteen years.

Childhood obesity levels in Wales, England and Scotland are some of the highest internationally, and Wales itself ranks fifth highest of thirty-five countries, with 2.4 per cent of girls and 5.0 per cent of boys being obese. The proportion of children in Wales playing sport 'most days' decreased dramatically between 1998 and 2001, from 69 per cent to 45 per cent, closing a previous regional difference (in 1998 children in Wales had been more likely than children in England or Scotland to participate in sport 'most days'). In a comparison of thirty-five countries, Wales has one of the worst records of fruit and vegetable consumption by young people, and consumption of soft drinks every day is above average of all the countries (although lower than in England and Scotland).

Mental health

Data on mental health are particularly patchy. There is a downward trend in suicide rates for young men in England and Wales, with a 33 per cent decrease between 1993 and 2002. Among 15- to 24-year-olds in England and Wales in 1999, there was a relatively low rate of suicides of young men compared with Scotland and Northern Ireland. A national survey of looked-after children aged five to seventeen years found that 49 per cent of those in Wales had a mental health disorder, compared to 45 per cent in England and Scotland. Looked-after children in Wales also had higher rates of conduct disorders (42 per cent) than those in England (37 per cent) and Scotland (38 per cent). It appears that boys are more likely to experience mental health problems than girls, particularly conduct disorders, although emotional health issues (including unhappiness) are more prevalent among girls. Older children experience more mental health problems than younger children, irrespective of condition. Suicide is more prevalent among boys than girls and increases with age.

Abuse and bullying

Child protection registrations in Wales decreased from 4.0 per 1,000 to 3.4 per 1,000, between 1999 and 2003. This remains high compared to the rate in England of 2.4 per 1,000. Research in Wales found that children under one year had the highest rates of incidents of severe abuse, at 54 per 100,000 per year (compared to 9.2 per 100,000 for children aged one to four, and only 0.47 per 100,000 for those aged five to thirteen). A survey found that 35 per cent of 11-year-olds in Wales had been bullied at least once in the 'previous couple of months'.

Substitute care and care leavers

The number of looked-after children in Wales increased from 3,574 in 2000 to 4,219 in 2003, a rise from 4.9 to 5.5 per 1,000 children under eighteen. The proportion of looked-after children placed for adoption increased from 3.9 per cent in 2000 to 5.9 per cent in 2003; this is in line with the rise in England from 4 per cent to 6 percent. Care leavers seem particularly badly served in Wales. In 2003, nearly all young people who left care aged over sixteen were aged under eighteen, in contrast to England where more than half were eighteen or over. The proportion in Wales leaving before age eighteen actually increased from 2000 to 2003, while in England the number fell. Since a central aim of leaving care policy has been to challenge policy and practice that leads to the most vulnerable young people leaving home at a much younger age than the rest of the population, this is a particularly alarming trend.

Refugee and asylum-seeking children

A group that is acknowledged to be especially vulnerable, and whose numbers have grown in the period under review, are children seeking asylum or refuge, either alone or as part of a family. Hewett et al. (2005) note that in October 2004 there were 2,232 asylum seekers dispersed to Wales, including 510 families with 1,435 dependants, some but not all of whom would be children. In 2003 it was estimated that seventy separated or unaccompanied asylum-seeking children were being looked after by local authorities in Wales. These authors draw attention to the many ways in which asylum-seekers are disadvantaged, and report that 'virtually all young people said that they felt they were in limbo and were anxious about their future' (p. 3). Particular areas of concern included lack of school places for some children, lack of healthcare (especially for those refused asylum), lack of expertise and specialist services, the effects on children of being moved, the long wait for decisions, racism and harassment.

Education

Several indicators show children in Wales doing less well in education than their peers elsewhere in the UK. For instance, the proportion of boys leaving with no qualifications is 9.2 per cent in Wales compared with 6.4 per cent in England (2001–2 figures). This relative difference has remained since the mid 1990s. The percentage of children in Wales gaining two or more A levels is also lower than elsewhere in the UK. Kenway et al. (2005, p. 36) summarize their more recent findings thus:

• for pupils overall, both at eleven and sixteen, the unambiguous improvements in educational outcomes in the second half of the 1990s generally stalled around 2000;

- pupils from more deprived backgrounds shared in that improvement, although the gap in performance with pupils on average did not narrow;
- the proportion of pupils attaining either no or just a few qualifications at sixteen is higher in Wales than in Scotland or in any of the English regions.

The number of children permanently excluded from school is rising, and boys are four times more likely than girls to be excluded. Truancy rates from secondary schools in Wales are on average higher than in England or Scotland. In 2002–3 the highest rate in Wales was in Cardiff, at 3.4 per cent, and the lowest in Neath Port Talbot, at 0.6 per cent. The rates in special schools are higher, though there was a reduction from 4.1 per cent in 1997–8 to 2.9 per cent in 2002–3. Three-quarters of all children in Wales with a statement of special educational need are educated in mainstream schools.

So, is the well-being of children in Wales improving or getting worse?

Generally, the trends are mixed. There are signs of improvement in line with the rest of the UK and some indicators which are worsening. Table 10.1, taken from Save the Children (2005a), summarizes the indicators that are improving, deteriorating or showing no change. Table 10.2, from the same source, shows at a glance on which key indicators children in Wales are doing better than, similarly to, or worse than the rest of the UK. As one would expect, on many indicators Welsh children are following a similar trend to their peers in the rest of the UK, although on many of the most important indicators, particularly those associated with poverty, they continue to lag behind. There are a few indicators on which the direction of travel is different for children and young people in Wales, notably outcomes for care leavers and smoking among girls. Overall, child poverty rates continue to give substantial cause for concern, educational achievement is not improving as fast as elsewhere in the UK, and lifestyle indicators for children in Wales rank low in comparison to other countries.

Despite the progress noted by Kenway, child poverty remains the 'national disgrace' of Wales (Children's Commissioner for Wales, 2002, p. 15). One in four children in Wales still lives in poverty (a higher proportion than that for pensioners or for adults of working age), and this interacts with other factors to produce a range of poor outcomes for children. The National Public Health Service for Wales (2004) recently noted the massive contribution which poverty and deprivation still make to poor health outcomes. The Assembly, with its limited financial powers, has responded to the problem with a child poverty strategy, as recommended by a strong NGO lobby (Welsh Assembly Government,

2005a). Implementing this strategy depends not only on willingness, but on adequate resources, a well trained workforce and clear accountability for delivering improved services on the ground (Williams, 2003). Unfortunately at the time of writing, nearly twelve months after the strategy was launched, the Assembly Government had still not produced the promised action plan.

Table 10.1
Key indicators in Wales over time

Improving	No change	Deteriorating
Infant mortality	Child mortality	MMR vaccination
Smoking (boys)	Whooping cough immunization	Diabetes
Adoptions (up)	Diphtheria, tetanus and polio	Alcohol consumption
Daycare nursery places	immunization	Obesity
Out of school places	Teenage conception rate	Childminder places
Educational qualifications	Youth crime	Drug and violent crime
Narrowing class differential	Stillbirths	Offending (girls)
in attainment		Playgroup places
Housing conditions		School exclusions
Suicide rate (15- to 24-year-olds)		Child homelessness
		Numbers playing sport
		Smoking (girls)

Table 10.2
Key indicators in Wales compared to UK

Better than UK rate	Similar to UK rate	Worse than UK rate
Infant mortality	Alcohol consumption	Child poverty (before housing costs)
Low birth rates	TV watching (boys)	Teenage conceptions
Diabetes (boys)		Diabetes (girls)
Consumption of sweets		Reporting good health
and soft drinks		Consumption of fruit and vegetables
Some physical activity rates		TV watching (girls)
Bullying		Looked-after children with mental
		disorder/conduct disorders
		Achieving five GCSEs
		Achieving two A levels
		Leaving school with no qualifications
		Leaving care at 16- to 17-year-olds
		Leaving care with one or more GCSE
		Truancy rates
		Unfit housing

Adapted from Save the Children, 2005a

These findings, coupled with the lack of evidence in a number of key areas and inconsistent data collection across the UK highlight the need for a 'state of Wales's children' report. Save the Children (2005a) recommend that the UK government and the Welsh Assembly Government collaborate to set up a new UK survey of children, in which children are the primary unit of analysis and data are collected on their family, school and neighbourhood. These data could then be collated into a regular comprehensive report on the well-being of children in the UK, measuring progress over time and showing comparisons between countries within the UK, and where possible with the rest of Europe. It is also worth noting here the opening recommendations from the Child Poverty Task Group, that the Welsh Assembly Government should 'monitor child poverty over time, utilising a number of different indicators, in order to assess the impact of policy and to allow for UK and international comparisons', and that 'a more detailed profile of the children most vulnerable to severe and persistent poverty in Wales is needed' (Welsh Assembly Government, 2004b, p. 7).

CONCLUSIONS

When the UN Committee on the Rights of the Child made its concluding observations on the 2002 review of the UK's implementation of the Convention, Wales was singled out for praise on two counts: (1) banning physical punishment in all forms of daycare, and (2) creating the office of the Children's Commissioner for Wales – although the Committee expressed the view that the commissioner's powers should be extended to non-devolved matters. The committee also welcomed the positive use of the convention by the National Assembly in its strategy for children and young people.

In policy terms, then, Wales does seem to be getting some things right, and of course one should not be too surprised at the lack of evidence that the wealth of new policies are having a consistently positive impact on the actual lives of children and young people. It is too soon for some effects to show; the resources are not there to deliver certain policies on the ground; policies made in Wales are undermined by other policies made elsewhere, or swept aside by global influences, economic upturns and downturns, and the impact of broader cultural changes, many of them driven by new technology; the list is predictable.

What is perhaps most encouraging about policy and practice in Wales is that children and young people are increasingly at the heart of policy-making, not just in the sense that their interests are being promoted by increasing numbers of those in a position to do so, but also in that they themselves are being given a say in how policies are developed and implemented, and in how services are delivered in practice. The 'participation agenda' really does seem to have caught on, in that it is much better understood by many more professionals – social workers and doctors, civil servants and chief executives – and that participation by children and young people is increasingly becoming an accepted part of practice. This also means that increasing numbers of children and young people have experience of becoming engaged in policy work of various kinds. This of course raises many new questions, some of them not easy to answer. Which young people are involved in participatory work, and how representative are they? Are certain groups – perhaps some of the most vulnerable – being missed out? Is there a danger that participation and consultation becomes a matter of 'rounding up the usual suspects' (as often happens with adult participation too)? Learning how to do all this better is a challenge for everyone. However, we would argue that an approach to planning and monitoring services that puts children and young people at the centre as active participants, if it can be delivered, carries two particular benefits. One is that it helps to move away from a deficit model of childhood and a view of children as 'needy' to one of children as *resourceful*.[7] The other, linked with the first, is that it takes a step further toward real citizenship.

NOTES

[1] Bransbury (2004, p. 176) comments that 'the extent of the dialogue and partnership between WAG and other Welsh organisations, including highly iterative and participative approaches to policy development, seems in a completely different league from that in England and is often observed with envy by local government colleagues on the other side of the border'.

[2] Minister for education and lifelong learning.

[3] Minister for health and social services until 2005; business minister and minister for children at the time of writing.

[4] Many of these documents have catchy titles; although some have disconcertingly similar ones, and the same phrases tend to be recycled or combined in different ways. Who could not be forgiven for confusing 'Rights to Action', which offers an overview of policy and provision of services for children and young people in Wales, with 'Rights Into Action', the first international congress of young disabled people?

[5] Funky Dragon is also notable for being the first organization in the UK to succeed in legally constituting young people under eighteen as voting trustees, after a prolonged discussion with the Charity Commissioners.

[6] In 2003–4 this amounted to £132 a week (or £6,864 per annum) for a family of two adults and two children, and £97 a week for a single parent with two children.

[7] As in the contrast between the 'child in need' and the 'rich child' proposed by Moss, Dillon and Statham (2000).

REFERENCES

Adelman, L. Middleton, S. and Ashworth, K. (2003). *Britain's Poorest Children: Severe and Persistent Poverty and Social Exclusion*, London: Save the Children.

Boyce, S. (2005). *What Kind of Indicators Can Best Monitor the Delivery of the Children's Strategy? Briefing Paper Prepared for OFMDFM by Children's Law Centre and Save the Children*, Belfast: Children's Law Centre.

Bradshaw, J. and Mayhew, E. (2005). 'Is child poverty higher in Wales?', *Wales Journal of Law and Policy*, 4 (1), 112–21.

Bradshaw, J. and Mayhew, E. (2005). *The Well-being of Children in the UK*, 2nd edn, London: Save the Children.

Bransbury, L. (2004). 'Devolution in Wales and social justice', *Benefits*, 12, 3, 175–81.

Carlile, A. (2002). *'Too Serious a Thing': The Review of Safeguards for Children and Young People Treated and Cared for by the NHS in Wales*, Cardiff: National Assembly for Wales.

Children's Commissioner for Wales (2002). *Annual Report and Accounts 2001–2002*, Swansea: Children's Commissioner for Wales.

Children's Commissioner for Wales (2003). *Telling Concerns: Report of the Children's Commissioner for Wales' Review of the Operation of Complaints and Representations and Whistleblowing Procedures and Arrangements for the Provision of Children's Advocacy Services*, Swansea: Children's Commissioner for Wales.

Children's Commissioner for Wales (2005). *Children Don't Complain . . . The Children's Commissioner for Wales' Review of the Operation of Complaints and Representations and Whistleblowing Procedures, and Arrangements for the Provision of Children's Advocacy Services in Local Education Authorities in Wales*, Swansea: Children's Commissioner for Wales.

Hanafin, S. and Brooks, A. (2005). *The Development of a National Set of Child Well-Being Indicators: Executive Summary*, Dublin: National Children's Office.

Hewett, T., Smalley, N., Dunkerley, D. and Scourfield, J. (2005). *Uncertain Futures – Children Seeking Asylum in Wales*, Cardiff: Save the Children.

Kenway, P., Parsons, N., Carr, J. and Palmer, G. (2005). *Monitoring Poverty and Social Exclusion in Wales 2005*, York: Joseph Rowntree Foundation.

Moss, P., Dillon, J. and Statham, J. (2000). 'The "child in need" and "the rich child": discourses, constructions and practice', *Critical Social Policy*, 20(2), 233–54.

National Assembly for Wales (2000). *Better Wales*, Cardiff: National Assembly for Wales.

National Assembly for Wales (2002). *A Statistical Focus on Children in Wales*, Cardiff: National Assembly for Wales.

National Public Health Service for Wales (2004). *A Profile of the Health of Children and Young People in Wales*, www.wales.nhs.uk/sites/documents/368/ChildrenProfile200407.pdf, accessed August 2005.

Pithouse, A., Parry, O., Crowley, A., Payne, H., Batchelor, C., Anglim, C., Aspinwall, T., Davies, L., Larkins, C., Dalrymple, J., Madoc-Jones, I., Holland, S. and Renold, E. (2005). *A Study of Advocacy Services for Children and Young People in Wales*, Cardiff: Welsh Assembly Government.

Save the Children (2005a). *The Well-being of Children in the UK*, summary, London: Save the Children.

Save the Children (2005b). *Britain's Poorest Children Revisited*, London: Save the

Children.

Save the Children (2006). *Righting the Wrongs: The Reality of Children's Rights in Wales*, Cardiff: Save the Children.

Seaton, N. (2005). *Integrated Centres in Wales*, Cardiff: Institute of Welsh Affairs.

Sylva, K., Melhuish, E., Sammons, P., Siraj-Blatchford, I., Taggart, B. and Elliot, K. (2003). *The Effective Provision of Pre-school Education (EPPE) Project: Findings from the Pre-school Period*, summary of findings, London: Institute of Education.

United Nations Committee on the Rights of the Child (2002). *Concluding Observations of the Committee on the Rights of the Child: United Kingdom of Great Britain and Northern Ireland*, New York: United Nations.

Waterhouse, R. (2000). *Lost in Care: Report of the Tribunal of Inquiry into the Abuse of Children in Care in the Former County Council Areas of Gwynedd and Clwyd since 1974*, London: Stationery Office.

Welsh Assembly Government (2002). *Extending Entitlement: Support for 11- to 25-year-olds in Wales – Direction and Guidance*, Cardiff: Welsh Assembly Government.

Welsh Assembly Government (2004a). *Children and Young People: Rights to Action*, Cardiff: Welsh Assembly Government.

Welsh Assembly Government (2004b). *Report of the Child Poverty Task Group*, www.wales.gov.uk/subichildren/content/cptg-rpt-fin-e.pdf.

Welsh Assembly Government (2005a). *A Fair Future For Our Children: The Strategy of the Welsh Assembly Government for Tackling Child Poverty*, Cardiff: Welsh Assembly Government.

Welsh Assembly Government (2005b). *National Service Framework for Children, Young People and Maternity Services in Wales*, Cardiff: Welsh Assembly Government.

Williams, C. (2003). 'The impact of Labour on policies for children and young people in Wales', *Children & Society*, 17, 3, 247–53.

Wincott, D. (2004). *Learning from Devolution: Making Childcare Labour's 'Big Idea'*, ESRC research programme on devolution and constitutional change: briefing no. 4, www.devolution.ac.uk/pdfdata/Wincott_briefing_PDF.pdf, accessed 1 August 2005.

11. AGEING IN WALES: POLICY RESPONSES TO AN AGEING POPULATION

Judith Phillips and Vanessa Burholt

ABSTRACT

Wales is ageing at a greater rate than its counterparts in the UK. Nearly one in four people are over the age of sixty and one in eight are over seventy. The demographic shift over the last forty years, during which the numbers over eighty-five have increased fourfold, has meant that policy-makers have had to turn their attention to issues of ageing and place older people high on the policy agenda. The purpose of this article is twofold: first, we give a broad overview of the issues surrounding the experiences of ageing in Wales and second, we investigate the main social policy responses followed by the Welsh Assembly Government to an ageing population. In conclusion we consider what form a Welsh social policy of ageing in the twenty-first century may take to meet these issues.

INTRODUCTION

The Welsh population is ageing due to a decline in fertility rates since the baby boom eras (people born between 1946 and 1950, and 1961 and 1965) and an increase in life expectancy. By 2040 the number of people over the age of sixty-five in Wales is expected to increase by a half to over 800,000 (ONS/WAG, 2004). It is not the increase in numbers alone that poses challenges for policy but the fact that policy will need to respond to the diversity of ageing alongside increasing proportions of people over the age of eighty requiring some form of daily living assistance. The purpose of this article is twofold: first, we give a broad overview of the issues surrounding the experiences of ageing in Wales and second, we investigate the main social policy responses followed by the Welsh Assembly Government (WAG) in responding to an ageing population. In conclusion we consider what form a Welsh social policy of ageing in the twenty-first century may take to meet these issues.

In outlining the situation of older people in Wales we draw on statistics and literature specifically addressing the Welsh context. Literature on the global experiences of ageing, albeit relevant, is not reviewed. The rationale for this is to highlight the gaps in our knowledge and to establish areas where further work needs to be undertaken to give policy and practice a firmer Wales-specific evidence base (for a more detailed account of research undertaken on ageing and older people in Wales see Phillips and Lambert, 2005.)

Understanding ageing in Wales requires more than just the facts and figures; ageing is shaped by a lifetime of experiences, which can be reflected in literature and poetry, for example through Dylan Thomas's 'Do not go gentle into that good night' or the image portrayed by Emyr Humphreys of Mary Keturah Parry in *Old People are a Problem*. Qualitative, narrative and biographical accounts are also relevant to our perceptions and responses to ageing and older people (Rowles and Schoenberg, 2002).

The experience of ageing will be different for different generations and cohorts. Different world events shape particular memories of cohorts. People over the age of eighty today will remember the Second World War, the 1926 strike, a thriving coal-mining industry and the Welsh-language petition to demand equal status for the Welsh language in every aspect of the administration of the law and public services in Wales. Different local experiences will shape how people age; growing up in the Valleys during the Depression or the years of religious revival; witnessing the Aberfan disaster or the flooding of Capel Celyn to build Tryweryn reservoir will all have had an impact on the experience of ageing. Consequently, we use the terms ageing and older people throughout this article specifically to reflect that ageing is a process and should be considered flexibly. Definitions of old age are socially constructed through retirement (sixty and sixty-five) or often eligibility criteria (SAGA membership starts at fifty). Lifestyles are changing throughout the lifecourse. The challenge for policy is therefore not only to address today's older population but to predict future needs and responses for tomorrow's ageing population.

THE DEMOGRAPHICS OF AGEING

The whole of the UK population is ageing but Wales is ageing at a greater rate than its counterparts in the UK. Nearly one in four people are over the age of sixty and, one in eight are over seventy (compared to the UK as a whole where one in six are over the age of sixty; in England 20.8 per cent of the population are over sixty compared to 22.7 per cent in Wales (ONS/WAG, 2004)). The demographic shift over the last forty years, during which the numbers over eighty-five have increased fourfold, has meant that policy-makers have had to turn their attention to issues of ageing and place older people high on the policy agenda. It is likely that policy-makers will be interested for several years as it is projected that by 2030 there will be an increase in the number of people aged sixty-five and above in all regions of Wales, with the largest increase in the oldest age group seventy-five and over, a development reflecting improvements to life expectancy (ONS/WAG, 2004). In Wales the population of older people (sixty-five and over) as a percentage of the total population in 2041 will be 27.4 per cent (2002-based National Population Projections, Government Actuary's Department).

The diversity of the older population makes this a particularly interesting challenge. Behind the success of longevity lies difference and complexity. There are wide variations in life expectancy and levels of social and economic disadvantage. For example, people living in Merthyr Tydfil are likely to live shorter lives and to experience more ill-health than people living in Ceredigion or Monmouthshire (ONS, 2005). Women outnumber men, with twice as many women over the age of eighty as men. As most family carers, along with the majority in the social care workforce, are women the current world of older people is one of women. Although there will be gradual closing of the life expectancy gap (currently seventy-five for women and eighty for men (ONS/WAG, 2004)) gender imbalance will still shape social policy in coming years. As we note later, this has not been adequately reflected in social policy responses to ageing in Wales.

Gender imbalance among the older members of black and minority ethnic groups (BME) in Wales is not as stark, with larger percentages of men in the older population than women, reflecting historical patterns of in-migration. The number of people in black and minority ethnic groups over sixty has doubled in the past ten years. Just over 2 per cent of the population are from minority ethnic groups. Although Wales has a long history of in-migration of ethnic minority populations, unlike the rest of the UK no one minority group is dominant (ONS/WAG, 2004). Most of the concentrations of BME groups are in the south Wales coastal cities, but many are dispersed in rural areas, presenting a particular challenge to health and social care services (Saltus, 2005). As a whole, BME groups are more likely than other groups to experience ill-health and to have difficulty in accessing health and social care services (Merrell and Kinsella, 2003).

LIVING ARRANGEMENTS

Geography plays an important part in the location of ageing populations in Wales. With in-migration of older people to seaside resorts there are greater concentrations of older people along the north Wales coastline and rural west Wales. In north-west Wales (Anglesey, Conwy and Gwynedd), 26 per cent of residents are over the age of sixty. Within the rural areas of Wales, counties are losing their younger population (for housing or employment opportunities elsewhere), leaving many communities to 'age in place' (Cloke et al., 1997, Jones et al., 2001, cited in Newidiem, 2003). The project Age Balanced Communities in Rural Wales (Newidiem, 2003), demonstrated that in 2000, compared with other authorities, rural authorities lost the greatest proportion of population in the 20–29 year group, and almost 5 per cent of people in the 20–24 year group (Newidiem, 2003). These contemporary migration patterns, when set in an historical context show that Wales has distinct migration patterns that have been stable over time. In particular, the Principality has consistently experienced a net loss of young people aged between sixteen and twenty-four and more recently age between twenty-five and twenty-nine. Throughout the country, the net loss of young people is the greatest in rural authorities and, in contrast, less in valley authorities. Consequently, Cardiff and the south Wales coast have lower proportions of older people.

In Wales, 16 per cent of older people live alone (National Assembly for Wales Statistical Directorate, 2004) with few living within multi-generational households. Most people want to live independently and the majority of older people (91 per cent) do not want to move house (Burholt, 2005) or move from their present community (95 per cent) (Burholt and Naylor, 2005). Different factors are associated with attachment to place; these include the proximity of friends/neighbours and family, the aesthetic qualities of the surroundings, a historical perspective of being born and bred in the area and the suitability of the environment (Burholt, 2006). The use of language is also a significant aspect in attachment to place for older people, encompassing a whole way of life and culture.

LANGUAGE AND CULTURE

The sustainability of the Welsh language and culture is related to the movement of population. Older people living in native areas of Wales[1] with a strong culture and local language are more likely than older people living in other types of communities to be both historically attached and socially integrated into the community. Especially in the north of Wales, the Welsh language serves as a symbol of Welsh identity (Bourhis et al., 1973; Jones and Desforges, 2003), and in those areas with a high level of Welsh communication, and low levels of in-migration, feelings of citizenship and regional identity are fostered (Burholt and Naylor, 2005).

The Bangor (University) Longitudinal Study of Ageing over the last twenty-five years has examined the social networks of older people. It has contributed to a better understanding of the ageing process in a number of ways. It has provided confirmation about the importance of the family in supporting older people. It has also attempted to explain why it is that some older people receive support from family members and others do not. It has drawn attention to the wide range of variation in family forms and support networks that are critical for support in old age (Wenger, Burholt and Scott, 2000).

HOUSING AND CARE

The link between housing and care is vital in older age if older people are to be able to make choices about their living arrangements. In recent years the debate has centred on alternatives to sheltered housing and residential care. 'Extra care' has become a popular concept, with many local authorities shifting their residential provision to a model where older people have their own flats within a communal community and can buy in or be assessed for 24-hour care. Several new private companies have entered the arena of social care housing for older people as well as private developers promoting the retirement village concept. In Wales a number of such examples are to be found in the south.

A study in north Wales identified older peoples' preferences for supported living environments (sheltered housing, extra care sheltered housing and residential care) and compared the importance of privacy and physical space, physical care, domestic services, security, social activities, and control or autonomy in future accommodation. The findings showed that older people rated privacy, physical space and control of life as important, compared with the other domains (Burholt and Windle, 2005).

Home ownership has often been an indicator of wealth in Wales and older people are more likely to be home owners than those under sixty (ONS/WAG, 2004). However, they are also more likely to be living in housing that requires modernization and lacks some important amenity. In Wales, in 1998, 17,500 older households lived in dwellings unfit for human habitation with people over the age of sixty twice as likely to be living in houses without central heating or other amenities (such as hot running water), whilst those over eighty are more likely than others to be living in houses with inadequate insulation (National Assembly for Wales Statistical Directorate, 2004). Despite being home owners, many older people are on low incomes and face difficulties in meeting the costs of repair and improvement (Age Concern Cymru, 2004). A combination of poor housing stock and low levels of income in Wales also increases the likelihood of older people experiencing fuel poverty (Burholt and Windle, 2006).

In Wales, it is estimated that between 1999 and 2000 there were 2,970 excess winter deaths (Friends of the Earth, 2000).[2] A study in rural north Wales found that fuel-poor households had lower incomes, resided in older properties and lacked double glazing and central heating. Older people in the lowest income bands were spending the largest proportion of their income on heating their properties. Some older people do not spend a sufficient amount on energy to be warm in their homes (Burholt and Windle, 2006). In the social housing sector older people are the predominant group, particularly in rural areas (Tai Cymru, 1990). However, housing for which the WAG are responsible does now have to conform to Lifetime Homes Standards which meet the needs of older people.

In terms of socio-economic groupings, geography again plays a crucial influence. Wales has both pockets of poverty and wealth among its older population with one of the lowest GDP figures and the lowest disposable income per head compared with other UK nations and regions. A study on the financial situation of older people in Wales found that 24 per cent of the 895 people interviewed reported that, excluding their home, they had no savings or assets; 34 per cent reported savings or assets less than £6,000 (Help the Aged/Age Concern Cymru/WAG, 2004). Poverty in rural areas may be masked by high income differentials between incomers and long-term inhabitants. Poverty is also concentrated in the oldest age groups with smaller proportions of those people over seventy-five getting income from occupational pensions than those under seventy-five (ONS, 1999). A recent study conducted in Wales shows that within the older population low material resources are associated with older age, poor health, a low level of education, living in a deprived neighbourhood and not being married (never married, divorced/separated or widowed). Overall, the findings suggest that differences in material resources in old age are generally determined by earlier life experiences, for example engagement in the labour market and subsequent ability to save and invest (Burholt and Williams, 2005).

HEALTH

Health is also a key indicator of relative poverty and wealth. Five out of ten people between the ages of sixty and eighty and seven out of ten people over eighty have a limiting long-term illness; much higher than in England (ONS/WAG, 2004). Heart and respiratory diseases as well as arthritis and cancer are major diseases for older people. The Bangor Longitudinal Study of Ageing found that so long as older people remain in good or even moderate health, they continue to live their lives in a similar fashion throughout their lives. They adapt to widowhood, the death of siblings and friends and to declining functional ability. The maintenance of independence is important to older people who tend not to look for, or accept, help unless they need it (Wenger, Burholt and Scott, 2000).

About 20 in 1,000 people over the age of eighty have Alzheimer's disease; and about 5 in 1,000 between the ages of seventy and eighty (ONS/WAG, 2004). The proportions suffering from dementia in Wales are comparable with other European countries and show an exponential increase in prevalence with age. Policy-makers' concern about the ageing population has been focused on the heavy demands that those who develop dementia are likely to make on formal services. Older people prefer to be supported in their own home; therefore mental health service provision should aim for home-based services. Carers value support, especially such as that delivered by Crossroads. This type of service or other family-link and home-based schemes need further development across Wales (Audit Commission, 2000). Despite the high levels of impairment of people with dementia, carers typically receive low levels of regular support from formal services, in particular emergency relief residential care, hospital respite care, day hospital, fostering and incontinence laundry service (Wenger et al., 1998).

Most help for people with dementia comes from someone in the same household, whereas most help for people not suffering from dementia comes from someone in a different household (Wenger et al., 1998). In a study conducted in north Wales approximately one-third of carers of people with dementia were aged seventy or over, and approximately half of the carers were in less than good health (Wenger et al., 1999).

LONG-TERM CARE

During 2003–4, 22,000 older people were in nursing and residential placements; for those in residential care the majority (45 per cent) were placed in the independent sector without nursing care (Local Government Data Unit Wales, 2003–4). There has been limited research on this sector in Wales but patterns mirror those in England, with admission often precipitated by a crisis incident, which usually precludes the older person from involvement in decision-making. In addition, there are a number of barriers to decision-making, including a lack of information, time pressures, limited financial resources and inter-professional disputes. Given that research has long documented the shortcomings in the process of admission (Phillips, 1989) it is surprising that little space has been given to this important area in policy initiatives. This may be short-sighted given the looming crisis of recruitment and retention within the care workforce (ADSS Wales, 2005). The contribution of older people, however, to the socio-economic fabric of Wales is considerable. This can be seen intergenerationally, for example, through grandparenting, or both across and within generations through their role as carers.

CARERS

There are 350,000 carers in Wales, including older people. One in three people over the age of sixty-five who are users of social services have a carer. In line with UK profiles, the majority of carers are older people themselves, either through spouse care (14 per cent of service users over eighty-five have carers over seventy-five years of age) or caring for a disabled younger member of the family. The highest proportions of people providing care are found in areas with higher than average levels of deprivation and long-term illness. Carers in such areas are themselves more likely to be in poor health. Local authorities in the UK with the highest proportions of the population providing intensive unpaid care include Neath Port Talbot and Merthyr Tydfil (Young and Grundy, 2005).

The Carers Strategy (National Assembly for Wales, 2000) states that the needs of carers must be assessed by the NHS and they should be directed to the appropriate services. Social services must also provide assessment for carers (National Assembly for Wales, 2000). The Carers (Recognition and Services) Act (1995) states that carers are entitled (on request) to an assessment of their needs, when an assessment is being carried out for the person they are caring for. Similarly, the Carers (Equal Opportunities) Act of 2004 seeks to reinforce the rights to individual, independent assessment, along with carers' rights to leisure and employment. However, data show that there is limited evidence that carers' needs are being recognized or addressed. The rhetoric of community care and greater support for informal carers is not being realized and few carers receive assessments of their own needs (Parry-Jones and Soulsby, 1999; Robinson, 1999; Seddon, 1999a; Soulsby et al., 2001; Wenger et al., 1999; Audit Commission, 2000; Hardy et al. 1999; SSI/Audit Commission Joint Reviews Team, 1997, SSI/DoH, 1996).

Most carers of working age have to rearrange their working lives to cope in their role (Phillips et al., 2002). The Carers Strategy aims to encourage employers to recognise and respond to carers' needs (National Assembly for Wales, 2000). However, some carers found it difficult to get support from formal services in order to continue in employment. Where support is delivered this is inflexible and unresponsive to the needs of carers in employment (Seddon, 1999b). More adequate assessment, support and protection of employment activity and pension rights for carers of people with dementia are likely not only to enable those who wish to continue caring to do so, but are also likely to make it possible for less immediate relatives to consider providing care (Wenger et al., 1999).

Changes in family structure (increasing divorce rates and declines in fertility), increased labour force participation of women and geographical mobility present issues for the future supply of women as the traditional carer. Although the Carers Strategy addresses the need to look at carers in employment, the extent to which employers have introduced initiatives in Wales is unknown. The inequalities among our ageing population are considerable. The realities of poor housing, the lack of opportunity for employment, and inadequate services are real concerns for policy.

POLICY RESPONSES

It has been argued (Bernard and Phillips, 2000) that social policy in Britain has been bedevilled by piecemeal and ad hoc approaches, narrowly conceived and based on an apocalyptical scenario of old age. It is only since elected devolution that a concerted policy in relation to older people has been articulated in Wales. In this sense Wales leads the world in its vision and strategy for older people. However, the challenge is to implement its vision given that not all powers (benefits and pension provision; long-term care funding arrangements, for example) are devolved to the Assembly Government.

In Britain, public discourse has shifted from valuing a collectivist institutional approach to a more person-centred individualistic approach. In line with UK policy, the health and social care agenda is towards community care, transferring responsibility for care of older people from the state to families and communities. The introduction of terms such as empowerment, advocacy, user involvement, partnership, enablers and navigators has reinforced such erosion and placed the onus on individual responsibility. This has led to policy focusing on planning for 'active' and 'productive' ageing.

Increasingly, the policy focus has been on how we pay for an ageing population and what responsibility individuals have for saving for retirement. The pensions issue, addressed through the Wanless and Turner reports, looks at different scenarios of saving for retirement and extending the working age and applies across the UK. However, the emphasis in the last decade has been on strengthening community care through enabling service users to determine the services they use through direct payments; strengthening the contribution of carers through the Carers (Services and Recognition) Act, 1995 and the Carers and Disabled Children Act, 2000; and encouraging low level preventative services to develop (e.g. partnership and prevention grants). Although these are UK-wide issues they form the context within which policy within Wales has developed.

Questions remain however as to what extent these initiatives have led to the improved quality of life of older people. Evidence from elsewhere in the UK (Scharf et al., 2005; Tanner, 2003) shows that much of the policy development has been to do with 'maintenance' and concentration on individual risk rather than radical change focusing on the quality of life of older people. Wales breaks the mould in this respect. Older people are one of the Welsh Assembly Government priority areas. Social policy measures addressing ageing in Wales have become prominent, raising expectations among older people and raising the profile of older people both in Wales and beyond Offa's Dyke.

The focus of Welsh policy is on citizenship and participation of older people and capacity-building within their communities. Although this was heralded first through the UK 'Better Government for Older People' (BGOP) programme, Wales has taken this approach further with a whole range of initiatives and strategies. The strength of the approach has been to take a broader perspective on ageing, beyond the traditional health and social care territories. Throughout a series of documents, the quality of older people's lives based on their broader social, economic and cultural experiences is highlighted (for example, *the Carers Strategy* (WAG, 2000), *Better Health Better Wales* (WAG, 1998); *Well-being in Wales* (WAG, 2002); *Securing our Future Health: Taking a Long-Term View* (*The Wanless Review of Health and Social Care*), (WAG, 2003a); *Designed for Life* (WAG, 2005a) and the *National Service Framework for Older People* (WAG, 2005c).

The main tenet of policy is the *Strategy for Older People* launched on 30 January 2003 with five broad aims:

* to tackle discrimination against older people, promote positive images of ageing and give older people a stronger voice in society;

- to promote and develop older people's capacity to continue to work and learn as long as they want and to make an active contribution when they retire;
- to promote and improve the health and well-being of older people through integrated planning and service delivery frameworks and more responsive diagnostic and support services;
- to promote the provision of high quality services and support which enable older people to live as independently as possible in a suitable and safe environment and ensure services are organized around and responsive to their needs;
- to implement the strategy with support funding to ensure that it is a catalyst for change and innovation across all sectors, improves services for older people and provides the basis for effective planning for an ageing population.[3]

The strategy set in motion a ten-year implementation plan with the establishment of a new Assembly Government Cabinet Sub-Committee on the needs of older people in order to ensure the wide range of issues impacting on older people are dealt with coherently across the Assembly. This was accompanied by the creation of a deputy minister for older people and the formation of a National Older People's Partnership Forum for Wales; at least 50 per cent of the Forum comprises of older people. Accompanying this is the establishment of a commissioner for older people. The role of the commissioner will be to 'promote a culture of respect for human rights through providing systematic advice and guidance to public bodies' (WAG, 2005b). The functions will be to influence policy and delivery; champion the cause of older people in Wales; offer information, support and advocacy; investigate complaints and promote and enforce older peoples' rights. One of the strengths of this appointment will be the proactive role of the commissioner.

Yet the role of the commissioner in tackling discrimination and promoting older peoples' interests needs to be clear. One of the difficulties comes down to the definitions of which 'older people' the commissioner will address – those over sixty-five, as in the Commissioner for Older People (Wales) Bill? Or fifty – people targeted through the strategy? The extent to which the commissioner is able to influence non-devolved issues, such as the debate on free personal care, and avoid duplication between the commissioner role and other bodies such as the Social Services Inspectorate will be essential if the function is to champion older people.

Further initiatives on a national level include: free bus travel across Wales, subsidies for information technology clubs, training and encouragement for good equity release schemes, free swimming and health promotion. Funding to improve home adaptations was also taken forward in an attempt to support older people to stay independently at home. Regulation and standards in domiciliary and nursing home care were also introduced and a commitment to eliminate all home care service charges for disabled people in Wales also forms part of the plan. Considerable activity around the strategy is concentrated at a local level with councils charged to put in place measures to support the strategy by formulating development plans, appointing an older persons' champion and engaging in project work. A review after one year of implementation demonstrated commitment and enthusiasm at local level, the appointment of champions and the setting up of local forums for older people in most of the twenty-two councils (WAG, 2004a). Local interpretation of the strategy illustrates the flexibility that can develop with the important role of strategy coordinators at local level. For example, Swansea has appointed anti-poverty coordinators across the sector. The voluntary sector also plays a role in the implementation of the strategy through the setting up of Age Alliance bringing all the organizations that work with older people together.

The National Standards Framework for Older People is the latest in a series of policies (*Making the Connections* (WAG, 2004b); *Designed for Life* (WAG, 2005a) and the ongoing remodelling of social care) to address standards and issues around maintaining health, well-being and independence for as long as possible, and to ensure the receipt of prompt, seamless, quality treatment and support when required. The NSF sets out nine standards that can inform a multidisciplinary research agenda:

- rooting out age discrimination;
- person-centred care;
- promoting health and well-being;
- challenging dependency;
- intermediate care;
- hospital care;
- stroke;
- falls and fractures;
- mental health.

There are six cross-cutting themes which underpin all of the standards: equity; person-centred care; engaging older people and carers; whole systems working; promoting well-being and independence and management capacity.

POLICY NIRVANA OR CHIMERA?

One of the strengths of the strategy is its articulated value base. There is a commitment to reflect the United Nations principles for older people, 'tackling discrimination, promoting positive images of older people and giving older people a stronger voice' (WAG, 2003b, p. 14). Principles of citizenship, intergenerational linkage, social inclusion, quality of life and integrated policy underpin the way forward. In a number of senses this strategy heralds a cultural, social and political change. It moves policy from a concentration on concepts of dependency and need, viewing older people as a burden or threat and dependent on the state and families to a position where human rights are in the forefront, promoting social inclusion and citizenship. It is based on the social model of ageing rather than viewing ageing within a medical model of disease and degeneration. It also takes a broader vision of ageing incorporating a view that quality of life requires attention at both broad-societal and local community level. The Communities First Programme (WAG, 2001) places an onus on councils to address the needs of older people in terms of urban renewal. Community plans have to address older people's issues across the board and describe how the connections are being made. Champions are located in every local authority. Participation, consultation, addressing ageism and other forms of discrimination, integrated systems in relation to mobility and transport, to combat poverty and poor housing are laudable aims but can the strategy deliver quality of life for older people?

CHALLENGES FOR THE TEN-YEAR STRATEGY: WELSH AGEING POLICY IN THE TWENTY-FIRST CENTURY?

Given that the baby boom generation will turn sixty-five by 2030, this is a critical time in which to establish and consolidate policies that will support families and communities and empower older people. There are a number of difficulties to be faced:

1. Although premised on principles of integration (see for example, Making the Connections; Link Age Wales) and working together (Age Alliance), the gap between medical and social services – and the medical and social models – is still embedded within organizations. With health free-at-the-point-of-delivery and social care means-tested, administrative integration has remained illusive. The challenge will also be to break down professional barriers and territories and to

enable older people to have a voice. Yet there are real practical difficulties in making these realizations. For example, the difficulties in recruitment and retention of the social care and health workforce in Wales, as in the rest of the UK, threaten developments in person-centred care and the voices that organizations seek to promote. The large number of stakeholders involved also poses issues of accountability;

2. changes in the social context and environment for older people through health, housing and technology etc. are also necessary beyond the strategy. The challenge will also be to provide innovative and creative services at local level, different from current outdated provision. Older people of tomorrow will also require short-term outcomes along with the longer vision if their perceptions of quality of life are to be changed;

3. the provision and funding of long-term care is not addressed in the strategy. Although some of the issues around these lie at Westminster rather than in Cardiff Bay, the continuum of care needs to be seen as a whole. Policy cannot ignore the needs of the very old, those with complex needs and those who are dependent, without family, or where families can no longer cope. Based on current demographic trends and service provision, research by the Personal Social Services Research Unit indicated that demand for social care services is likely to increase by approximately 10 per cent between 2001 and 2010, and by a further 10–15 per cent between 2010 and 2020. This approximates to the need for an additional 5,000 care home places by 2020 (Comas-Herrera et al., 2003). This is being watched by the commercial sector in developing retirement villages and extra care housing, yet more care and repair and staying put schemes need to be developed alongside;

4. new models of how we care for older people need to be developed. Issues of gender and ethnicity are not reflected adequately in the strategy, yet changes in the gender roles and ethnic composition of Wales will have far-reaching consequences. Gender roles are changing as more women enter the labour market and become less available to take on full-time care responsibilities. More ethnic minority groups will age and we need to be able to respond appropriately. In providing care there is an increasing role for assistive technology together with the use of the unified assessment process, care and repair schemes and partnership working. However, there is little evaluation of such schemes in Wales to date;

5. there is a growing need to underpin policy with evidence-based knowledge. Supporting current and future generations of older people to achieve a good quality of life rests on policy that works to achieve this aim. There is a critical need therefore for evidence to support policy decisions around the strategy in particular;

6. the Welsh agenda also should link with the European agenda. There are a number of initiatives, for example co-housing in the Netherlands and transport integration

in Sweden and funding of long-term care in Scotland, from which we can benefit. Engaging in the wider debates around ageing across Europe and beyond will be of significance if Wales is to remain in the policy spotlight.

CONCLUSION

Over the next decade there will be a need for short-term impacts as well as ten-year plans to address the well-being and quality of life of older people in Wales. Alongside, there needs to be flexibility in the strategy to accommodate future projections and changes in lifestyles. The size of Wales can help, as elected devolution can allow closer working relations and partnerships between sectors. However, there is a long way to go before policy around ageing can be seen as a nirvana. One of the fundamental steps will be to increase the participation of older people, not just in relation to the strategy but in relation to all aspects of life. Without such involvement, well-intentioned statements will be vacuous.

NOTES

[1]   Defined as areas where a greater proportion of residents than the county as a whole, read, write and speak Welsh and have a lower rate of in-migration than the county in which they are located.

[2]   This source cited: House of Lords Hansard, Written Answers, Column WA 149, 8 November 2000.

[3]   *Strategy for Older People in Wales* (WAG, 2003b, p. 9).

REFERENCES

Age Concern Cymru (2004). *EnvisAGE*, Autumn, no. 3.

Association of Directors of Social Services, Wales (ADSS) (2005). *Social Work in Wales: A Profession to Value*, Bridgend: ADSS.

Audit Commission (2000). *Learning the Lessons from Joint Reviews of Social Services in Wales, 1999/2000*, Abingdon: Audit Commission Publications.

Bernard, M. and Phillips, J. (2000). 'The challenge of ageing in tomorrow's Britain', *Ageing and Society*, 20, 33–54.

Bourhis, R. Y., Giles, H. and Tajfel, H. (1973). 'Language as a determinant of Welsh identity', *European Journal of Social Psychology*, 3, 447–60.

Burholt, V. (2005). 'The relationships between individual characteristics and attachment to home in old age', paper presented at the 18th Congress of the International

Association of Gerontology, 'Active ageing in the XXI century. Participation, Health and Security', Rio de Janeiro, Brazil, 26–30 June.

Burholt, V. (2006). ' "Adref": theoretical contexts of attachment to place for mature and older people in rural north Wales', *Environment and Planning A*, 38 (6), 1095–114.

Burholt, V. and Naylor, D. (2005). 'The relationship between rural community type and attachment to place for older people living in north Wales, UK', *European Journal of Ageing*, 2, 109–19.

Burholt, V. and Williams, R. (2005). *The Material Resources of Older Men and Women in Wales: Welsh Assembly Government Policy Responses*, Bangor: Centre for Social Policy Research and Development (CSPRD), University of Wales.

Burholt, V. and Windle, G. (2005). *Retaining Independence and Autonomy: Older People's Preferences for Specialised Housing*, CSPRD, University of Wales, Bangor.

Burholt, V. and Windle, G., (2006). 'Keeping warm? Self-reported housing and home energy efficiency factors impacting on older people heating homes in north Wales', *Energy Policy*, 34 (10), 1198–208.

Cloke, P., Goodwin, M. and Milbourne, P. (1997). *Rural Wales: Community and Marginalization*, Cardiff: University of Wales Press.

Comas-Herrera, A. Wittenberg, R. and Pickard, L. (2003). *Projections of Demand for Long-term Care for Older People in Wales to 2020*, Canterbury: Personal Social Services Research Unit, University of Kent.

Friends of the Earth (2000). *Soaring Winter Deaths Emphasise Need for Warm Homes Bill*, London: Friends of the Earth.

Hardy, B., Young, R. and Wistow, G. (1999). 'Dimensions of choice in the assessment and care management process: the views of older people, carers and care managers', *Health and Social Care in the Community*, 7 (6), 483–91.

Help the Aged/Age Concern Cymru/WAG (2004). *For Richer for Poorer the Financial Situations of Older People in Wales*, Cardiff: Help the Aged/Age Concern Cymru/WAG.

Humphreys, E. (2003). *Old People are a Problem*, Bridgend: Seren.

Jones, R. and Desforges, L. (2003). 'Localities and the reproduction of Welsh nationalism', *Political Geography*, 22, 271–92.

Jones, S., Day, G., Morris, E. and Williams, T. (2001). *The Dynamics of Demographic Change and Migration in North-West Wales*, research report for Isle of Anglesey County Council, Gwynedd Council, CELTEC and North Wales Local Employment Observatory.

Local Government Data Unit Wales (2003–4). *Social Services Statistics Wales*, Cardiff: Local Government Data Unit Wales/Welsh Assembly Government.

Merrell, J. and Kinsella, F. (2003). *Identifying the Social Care and Health Needs of Women in Swansea's Bangladeshi Community: Professional and Community Perspectives*, research paper, School of Health, University of Wales Swansea.

National Assembly for Wales (2000). *Caring about Carers: A Strategy for Carers in Wales*, Cardiff: National Assembly for Wales.

National Assembly for Wales Statistical Directorate (2004). *A Statistical Focus on Older People in Wales*, Cardiff: National Assembly for Wales Statistical Directorate.

Newidiem (2003). 'Age balanced communities in rural Wales', report to the Welsh Assembly Government, Cardiff: Newidiem, retrieved 9 August 2005,*www.countryside. wales.gov.uk/fe/fileupload_getfile.asp?filePathPrefix=3586andfileLanguage=e.pdf.*

Office of National Statistics (1999). *Social Focus on Older People*, London: The Stationery Office.

Office of National Statistics (2005). *A Profile of the Health of Older People in Wales: A Report by the Public Health Service for Wales*, Cardiff: National Public Health Service for Wales.

Office of National Statistics/Welsh Assembly Government (2004). *A Statistical Focus on Older People in Wales 2004 Edition*, Cardiff: Office of National Statistics/Welsh Assembly Government.

Parry-Jones, B. and Soulsby, J. (1999). *Transitions in Community Care: Changes in Assessment and Multidisciplinary Practice*, Bangor: Centre for Social Policy Research and Development, Institute of Medical and Social Care Research, University of Wales.

Perry, J. and Burholt, V. (2005). *Promoting the Health of Older People in Respect of Alcohol Use. Report for the Health Promotion Division of the Welsh Assembly Government*, Bangor: Centre for Social Policy Research and Development, University of Wales.

Phillips, J. (1989). *The Process of Admission to Private Residential Care*, Basingstoke: Ashgate.

Phillips, J. and Lambert, S. (2005). *Older people and Ageing Research and Development Scoping Study*, final report, retrieved 5 February 2006, *www.word.wales.gov.uk/content/networks/opan*.

Phillips, J., Bernard, M. and Chittenden, M. (2002). *Juggling Work and Family Life*, York and Bristol: Policy Press.

Robinson, C. (1999). *Comparative Care Management*, final report to Wales Office of Research and Development for Health and Social Care, Bangor: Centre for Social Policy Research and Development, University of Wales.

Rowles, G. and Schoenberg, N. (eds) (2002). *Qualitative Gerontology: A Contemporary Perspective*, London: Continuum.

Saltus, R. (2005). *Scoping Study to Explore the Feasibility of a Health and Social Care Research and Development Network Covering Black and Minority Ethnic Groups in Wales*, retrieved 24 April 2006, *www.word.wales.gov.uk/networks*.

Scharf, T., Phillipson, C. and Smith, A. (2005). *Multiple Exclusion and Quality of Life amongst Excluded Older People in Disadvantaged Areas*, London: ODPM

Seddon, D. (1999a). *Carers of Elderly People with Dementia: Assessment and the Carers Act*, Bangor: Centre for Social Policy Research and Development, Institute of Medical and Social Care Research, University of Wales.

Seddon, D. (1999b). 'Negotiating Caregiving and Employment', in S. Cox and J. Keady (eds), *Younger People with Dementia: Planning, Practice and Development*, London: Jessica Kingsley Publishers.

Social Services Inspectorate/Audit Commission Joint Reviews Team (1997), *Reviewing Social Services: Annual Report 1997*, London: SSI.

Social Services Inspectorate/Department of Health (1996). *Caring for People at Home – Part II: Report of a Second Inspection of Arrangements for Assessment and Delivery of Home Care Services*, London: Department of Health.

Soulsby, J., Seddon, D., Hill, J., Robinson, C., Webb, V., Wenger, G. C. and White, N. (2001). *Assessment and Care Management: The Needs of Older People with Sensory Impairments*, final report to NHS Wales Office of Research and Development, Bangor: Centre for Social Policy Research and Development, Institute of Medical and Social Care Research, University of Wales.

Tai Cymru (1990). *The Demand for Social Housing in Rural Wales*, Rural Survey Research Unit, Department of Geography, University of Wales, Aberystwyth.

Tanner, D. (2003). 'Older People and Access to Care', *British Journal of Social Work*, 33, 499–515.

Welsh Assembly Government (1998). *Better Health Better Wales*, Cardiff: Welsh Assembly Government.

Welsh Assembly Government (2000). *Caring about Carers: A Strategy for Carers in Wales*, Cardiff: Welsh Assembly Government.

Welsh Assembly Government (2001). *Communities First*, Cardiff: Welsh Assembly Government.

Welsh Assembly Government (2002). *Well-being in Wales*, Cardiff: Welsh Assembly Government.

Welsh Assembly Government (2003a). *Securing our Future Health: Taking a Long-Term View (The Wanless Review of Health and Social Care)*, Cardiff: Welsh Assembly Government.

Welsh Assembly Government (2003b). *The Strategy for Older People in Wales*, Cardiff: Welsh Assembly Government.

Welsh Assembly Government (2004a). *Building the Foundations – A Report on the First Year of the Strategy for Older People in Wales*, Cardiff: Welsh Assembly Government.

Welsh Assembly Government (2004b). *Making the Connections Delivering Better Services for Wales*, Cardiff: Welsh Assembly Government.

Welsh Assembly Government (2005a). *Designed for Life: Creating World Class Health and Social Care in Wales in the 21st Century*, Cardiff: Welsh Assembly Government.

Welsh Assembly Government (2005b). *Commissioner for Older People (Wales) Bill*, Cardiff: Welsh Assembly Government.

Welsh Assembly Government (2005c). *National Service Framework for Older People*, Cardiff: Welsh Assembly Government.

Wenger, G. C., Burholt, V. and Scott, A., (1998). 'Dementia and help with household tasks: a comparison of cases and non-cases', *Health and Place*, 4 (1), 33–44.

Wenger, G. C., Scott, A. and Burholt, V. (1999). *The Bangor Dementia Studies – 1989–1999: Final Report to NHS Wales Office of Research and Development*, Bangor: Centre for Social Policy Research and Development, Institute of Medical and Social Care Research, University of Wales.

Wenger, G. C., Burholt, V. and Scott, A., (2000). *The Ageing Process: The Bangor Longitudinal Study of Ageing 1979–1999*, Bangor: Centre for Social Policy Research and Development, University of Wales.

Young, H. and Grundy, E. (2005). *Who Cares? Geographic Variation in Unpaid Caregiving in England and Wales: Evidence from the 2001 Census*, London: ONS.

12. YOUTH POLICY IN WALES SINCE DEVOLUTION: FROM VISION TO VACUUM?

Howard Williamson

ABSTRACT

Devolution heralded the possibility for Wales to determine and develop, amongst other things, a distinctive 'youth policy' based on 'opportunity-focused' principles and aspirations around learning, participation, inclusion and justice. At its inception, in May 1999, the National Assembly for Wales was led by a strong political core which commanded significant credibility across the wider professional field. Political championing of the youth agenda produced a coherent policy vision for youth services, enshrined in 'Extending Entitlement' which, when published in 2000, secured unanimous cross-party political support. That vision (in contrast to the emergent youth policy context in England) saw no need for new structures or new professions. Instead, it made a strong case for strengthening existing youth work and 'youth support' measures to ensure that a package of opportunities and experiences reached young people, in particular those who were more disadvantaged. Regrettably, the vision quickly unravelled and subsequent developments have created confusion, and sometimes cynicism, amongst many of those charged with its delivery in the field. The rhetoric of a world-class service for young people conceals what is now, arguably, a policy vacuum with a confusing array of initiatives, unclear lines of accountability and widespread practitioner disillusionment.

PREFACE

There is an apocryphal story circulating amongst 'traditional' youth work practitioners in Wales that in one relatively small socially disadvantaged community, there are so many recent regeneration and inclusion initiatives that there is virtually one for every household. Each initiative has its coordinator of the requisite partnership, but practice is consigned to committed but under-trained, and often part-time, practitioners. Such are the perceptions of the plethora of measures established by the Welsh Assembly Government: they are long on rhetoric and aspirations but very short on delivery and impact.

The flippant and facetious have, further, already identified some key distinctions between children and youth policy in England and Wales since the inauguration of the devolved National Assembly for Wales in May 1999. England wants to provide the 'best' start in life (Department for Education and Skills, 2003), while Wales seeks to provide a 'flying' start (Welsh Assembly Government, 2003a). England has five core aspirations for children and young people, whereas Wales has seven. Only England has Connexions (its flagship, though now declining 'youth support service'), while Wales is working on *Making the Connections* (Welsh Assembly Government, 2004). This will be achieved by dismantling the 'quangos' and the formation of a Welsh public service through the somewhat Orwellian and disingenuous '1+1=3': the amalgamation of arms-length public bodies and the civil service in Wales to produce a richer blend of public administration. The cynics in the 'youth' field remain unconvinced, and even sceptics are not persuaded by the competence, credibility and capacity of the Welsh Assembly Government to deliver on its rhetorical vision. Yet that vision was an important and powerful one, enshrined in *Extending Entitlement* (National Assembly for Wales, 2000b), which continues to be promoted as the 'flagship' and framework document for youth policy in Wales.

INTRODUCTION

It would be quite possible to write two completely contrasting accounts of 'youth policy' in Wales since the inception of the National Assembly in 1999. Both would take, as their starting point, the publication of *Extending Entitlement* towards the end of the year 2000, and its subsequent debate in plenary by Assembly Members, where it secured unanimous support (59–0). The story since then, however, would diverge – highly dependent on those within the orbit of these developments who were telling it.

One perspective would be that the Welsh Assembly Government has put in place distinctive and innovative structures for the development and delivery of policies directed towards young people. It would proclaim a leading role in youth policy formulation in Europe, assert a coherence in philosophy and practice at both national and local level, and argue for the achievement of an effective platform for engaging with and responding to the needs and aspirations of young people. The other would assert the proliferation of new initiatives at a national level which have patently failed to 'drill down' effectively on the local level. It would deride the establishment of a Youth Policy Team within the Welsh Assembly Government (subsequently the Youth and Pupil Participation Division), alleging chaotic and inappropriate interference on operational matters in relation to those organizations which had previously taken a lead responsibility in different areas of youth policy – within, for example, the voluntary sector, the youth service and the careers service. It would suggest a 'Stalinist' centralizing tendency which had dismantled 'arms-length' (and sometimes oppositional) advocates for young people, and make particular reference to the political decision (in December 2004) to cease funding the Wales Youth Agency. It would maintain that the Assembly had become increasingly strong on political rhetoric and correspondingly weak on making any real practical difference to the lives of the majority of young people in Wales.

The 'truth' of the matter clearly lies somewhere in between, demanding considerable caution about the grand claims of politicians and their civil servants, but equally requiring a tempering of the often polemical critique advanced by practitioners and others outside that orbit. I cannot divorce my own involvement in these developments, which has been considerable. What follows, then, is a description of the range of measures which have been put in place by the Welsh Assembly Government, and a commentary and critique of those 'youth policy' measures in the context of Wales itself and, briefly, in the context of the wider Europe.[1]

ANTECEDENTS

For some years prior to elected devolution in Wales, the landscape of 'youth policy' across the United Kingdom had been shifting – away from a largely punitive and neglectful position (see Williamson, 1993) to one that was more actively, positively and purposefully interventionist. In particular, research that had been conducted in Wales (Istance et al., 1994) had revealed significant numbers of young people outside of education, training and employment; they had, in effect, disappeared from mainstream transition pathways to adulthood. Subsequent research on this issue (see, for example, Macdonald, 1997) confirmed the earlier findings and strengthened the evidence that 'disaffected', 'disengaged' or 'marginalized' young people both caused and experienced a clustering of 'pathologies': not just a lack of educational achievement, but substance misuse, offending behaviour, family breakdown, poor mental health and self-harm. A key plank of the new Labour Government's policy agenda in 1997 concerned young people and social inclusion. Indeed, two of its five manifesto commitments related directly to young people: the 'fast-tracking' of persistent young offenders in the youth justice system, and the movement of a quarter of a million unemployed young adults from welfare to work. These were specifically addressed in the reforms of the youth justice system and the creation of the Youth Justice Board for England and Wales, and in the rapid establishment of the New Deal for Young People (18–24-year-olds), which was rolled out nationally in April 1998. Furthermore, there was the Prime Minister's legendary mantra of 'education, education, education' as the key to realizing individual potential and improving national economic performance. To address these, and other, issues, Tony Blair created the Social Exclusion Unit (SEU). Over the space of a few years, the SEU produced a sequence of policy reports on, for example: truancy and school exclusion, rough sleeping, young people not in education, employment or training, neighbourhood renewal (including young people), teenage pregnancy, and the education of children in care (Social Exclusion Unit, 1998a, 1998b, 1998c, 1999a, 1999b, 2000, 2002). The SEU has been depicted as the de facto 'Ministry of Youth' (Coles, 2000).

Even prior to the election of the new Labour government, there had been a range of campaigns and initiatives on behalf of young people, despite the apparent disinterest of the Conservative administration. These included the production of *Agenda for a Generation* (United Kingdom Youth Work Alliance, 1996), the 'Years of Decision' programme established by the Carnegie United Kingdom Trust (see Smith et al., 1996) and the 'Heirs to the Millennium' event convened by the Conservative MP Andrew Roe, chair of the All-Party Parliamentary Group on children, also in 1996. A receptive government was, therefore, able to draw immediately on a body of thinking about how best to support young people as they 'navigated' the increasingly treacherous waters of transition to adulthood (Furlong and Cartmel, 1997; Evans and Furlong, 1997). And so, as Home Office Minister Alun Michael noted in his keynote address in October 1998 to the inaugural meeting of the Research, Policy and Practice Forum on Young People (which was 'steered' by the Department for Education and Employment, the National Youth Agency and the Joseph Rowntree Foundation), the Labour Government 'hit the ground running'. It had had a long lead-in to tune its ideas, and now it had the power to put them into practice. Alun Michael was, of course, later to become Secretary of State for Wales and the first First Secretary of the new devolved National Assembly for Wales.

DEVOLUTION – A BRAVE NEW WORLD FOR YOUNG PEOPLE?

Shortly before the inception of the National Assembly, Ron Davies, Secretary of State for Wales, had his 'moment of madness' on Clapham Common and tendered his resignation. He was replaced as Secretary of State by Alun Michael, hitherto Minister of State at the Home Office and de facto Deputy Home Secretary. As noted, Michael also inherited, after a protracted contest with Rhodri Morgan MP for the leadership of the Labour Party in Wales, Davies's mantle as First Secretary-in-waiting of the imminent National Assembly.

Alun Michael, as a Westminster MP and Minister, had been closely attached to the emergent 'youth policy' agenda following the election of the new Labour government in 1997. His credentials for such a role were robust, insofar as he had practised as a youth and community worker in Cardiff prior to his election to Parliament. In London, not only had he been one of the architects of the youth justice reforms pioneered by the Prime Minister Tony Blair ('tough on crime, tough on the causes of crime') but he had also taken an active interest in the work of the Social Exclusion Unit. In particular, he kept in close touch with the SEU's Policy Action Team 12, which focused on young people and had commenced its deliberations in 1998, though it did not report until March 2000 (see Social Exclusion Unit, 2000).

On his inauguration as First Secretary of the National Assembly, Alun Michael set about exploring three discrete areas of 'youth policy' development which potentially lay within his devolved powers: 'youth support services', substance misuse, and youth participation. He was also keen to explore a fourth – youth justice – for though this was not constitutionally devolved, he felt that his background in the Home Office would still permit, if this was considered useful, a distinctive approach in Wales. Beyond himself, the key political players were the Education Secretary Tom Middlehurst, the Health Secretary Jane Hutt, and the Deputy Presiding Officer Jane Davidson (subsequently Minister for Education and Lifelong Learning). All had distinguished backgrounds in the Welsh political context *and*, in the case of Hutt and Davidson, in pioneering professional initiatives in Wales. This was a powerful group that commanded considerable respect in the broad 'youth' field and clearly had a strong collective personal/professional, as well as political, mandate to take the youth agenda forward. There was also Wayne David (who has now replaced Ron Davies as MP for Caerphilly) who had previously been an MEP and leader of the Labour Group in the European Parliament. David had stood for the Welsh Assembly and indeed been tipped as a prospective leader of the Assembly should Michael fail to secure a seat through the regional lists. However, David – who had resigned as an MEP

– was dramatically, and unexpectedly, defeated in the Rhondda. The Wales Youth Agency seized the opportunity to contract him as a part-time 'policy consultant', and David's political connections proved invaluable during the period of Michael's tenure as First Secretary. There was, therefore, for the two years between May 1999 and the end of 2000, a powerful 'head of steam' in terms of constructing a robust and coherent framework of policy for young people under the leadership of the Welsh Assembly Government.

The concept of a new 'youth support service' had first been mooted in Westminster during the summer of 1999 in two key policy documents. On the 'social inclusion' agenda, the Social Exclusion Unit had reported on young people outside education, employment or training (the 'NEET's) (Social Exclusion Unit, 1999b). On the lifelong learning and 'employability' agenda, the Department for Education and Employment had produced a white paper on education and skills (Department for Education and Employment, 1999). There was, inevitably, some departmental rivalry about exactly what such a 'youth support service' should comprise. The SEU had a more extensive and holistic model which it felt should be organized strategically by a cross-departmental unit (which eventually took shape as the Children and Young People's Unit). The DfEE, in contrast, was more concerned about the re-engagement of the 'disaffected' in education and training. This position subsequently produced the Connexions Service, launched in England in February 2000. The policy question for Wales was: to what extent should it follow, or mirror, those developments?

In terms of substance misuse, the Welsh Office had already, from the mid 1990s, sanctioned departures from the drugs strategy in England (Department of Health, 1996) and endorsed a more holistic approach to substance misuse (Welsh Office, 1996). However, Blair's appointment of a United Kingdom drugs czar (Keith Hellawell) required Alun Michael to consider the extent to which Wales should remain out of kilter with the emergent United Kingdom ten-year drugs strategy (Cabinet Office, 1998), in which educative and preventative strategies directed towards young people were central. One of Michael's first acts was to disband the cumbersome Welsh Advisory Committee on Drug and Alcohol Misuse (WACDAM) and replace it with a much smaller Substance Misuse Advisory Panel (SMAP), whose task was to align the Welsh strategy more closely with the UK strategy. This was achieved by 2000, when Jane Hutt launched a new 'refocused' strategy for Wales, though it still retained an integrated position on substance misuse (including alcohol) rather than illegal drug misuse per se (National Assembly for Wales, 2000a).

Alun Michael was also keen to strengthen structures for youth participation in Wales. Building on the embryonic work instituted prior to the Welsh Assembly by the then Parliamentary Under-secretary at the Welsh Office Peter Hain, he sought to involve young people in all elements of governance in Wales. To this end, Jane Davidson, who as the 'neutral' Deputy Presiding Officer could not be active on a *party* political front, was enjoined to take the lead on building participatory structures in which young people might become involved. The initial deadline was July 2000, when young people could engage directly (and through email) with Members of the National Assembly. Michael, through Davidson, established a group called Llais Ifanc (Young Voice) under the chairmanship of Wayne David. There were, of course, other traditions in youth participation, not least within the youth service (supported by the Wales Youth Agency) and through the dedicated work of Save the Children Fund, which had already organized a 'Young People Bite Back' event in Aberystwyth. Llais Ifanc, which eventually metamorphosized into the Welsh Youth Parliament, Funky Dragon, had to contend with these 'alternative' approaches on its flanks and to consider how they might be accommodated within an overarching youth participation approach. The challenge was reflected in other developments and did not go away.

Critically, however, there was the need for the Assembly, if it was not to follow emergent developments in England, to construct its own enveloping vision for 'youth policy' in Wales. At an informal meeting between Michael, Middlehurst and Hutt in the autumn of 1999, the idea of adopting unfolding English models was rejected and the decision was made to explore a distinctive Welsh approach. Michael set about convening an inter-professional group to consider what needed to be done. This group was appointed by the end of the year as an Advisory Group, to assist two Assembly officials in devising a youth strategy for Wales.

As the Advisory Group embarked on its deliberations, however, the political landscape within which it was doing so was already shifting. Alun Michael's position as First Secretary was precarious and, as a vote of no confidence in his leadership was imminent, he resigned in mid February 2000, just as David Blunkett (the Secretary of State for Education) was launching the (English) Connexions strategy. Up until this point, the youth agenda in Wales had been developing at least in parallel with a children's agenda, and had arguably held sway. Following the accession to the post of First Secretary (subsequently First Minister) of Rhodri Morgan, whose wife Julie was a former social worker with a children's charity and now a Westminster MP with a close interest in children's issues, the pendulum swung in favour of the children's agenda. Indeed, while Michael had been seen as a 'youth' advocate, Morgan was depicted as a champion for *children*. The children and families division of the Welsh Assembly took over lead responsibility for Llais Ifanc and any proposed collaboration between the two relevant Assembly-supported arms-length bodies, the Wales Youth Agency and Children in Wales, now appeared to be a missed opportunity.

Nevertheless, the youth Advisory Group continued and by the middle of the year had agreed on a working title for its strategy: 'Extending Entitlement'. This was *not*, at the time, related in any specific way to children's rights and the UN Convention that was guiding the development of a children's strategy for Wales and, indeed, soon led to the appointment of a Children's Commissioner, the first in the devolved nations of the UK. Rather, it was premised on the idea that for young adults to acquire the range of skills and competencies that would equip them for future 'life management' (see Helve and Bynner, 1996), they needed to have been exposed to a 'package' of diverse experiences and opportunities: a 'package of entitlement'. At its heart was the prospect of formal educational achievement, but young people also needed to have access to new technologies, away from home experiences, opportunities for international contact, sport and leisure possibilities, and other things. Moreover, while many young people accessed much of this 'package' through family support and self-direction, some young people were unlikely to access it without more strenuous public support. It should be no surprise, the Advisory Group argued, that the young people creating the greater problems for their communities and for themselves were often those with the greatest poverty of opportunities. It was therefore to those young people that such a package of experience and opportunity needed to be most purposefully extended.

There were some critical features to this 'Extending Entitlement' agenda that distinguished it from its 'youth support' counterpart in England and – critically – got lost in subsequent developments. First, it was not exclusively outcome-focused, maintaining that 'the quality of opportunity extended to young people is *sometimes* more important than the specificity of outcome'. Secondly, it saw no need for new structures or new professions, just more effective working together and an enhanced role for the youth service and for the Wales Youth Agency. (In England, by contrast, the Connexions service was establishing a new profession of 'personal adviser' and had significantly sidelined the youth service.) Thirdly, impact measurement would not be at the level of the individual but at the level of the local authority. If local authorities organized their services appropriately and 'reached' more disengaged and disadvantaged young people more effectively, then one would expect, in time, reductions in negative indicators (such as school exclusions or teenage pregnancy) and improvements in positive indicators (such as educational achievement and healthy lifestyles). The strategy from the centre needed to provide relevant incentives to ensure that local authorities adopted the philosophy of 'Extending Entitlement' and restructured their services accordingly.

Extending Entitlement: Supporting Young People in Wales (National Assembly for Wales, 2000b) got off to an inauspicous start. Its lead minister, the Education Minister Tom Middlehurst, resigned the evening before its launch in protest against the coalition agreed between the First Minister Rhodri Morgan and the leader of the Welsh Liberal Democrats Mike German. As a result, the document was launched, rather mutely, by the Assembly's business manager Andrew Davies. It was, however, launched again, some two months later, jointly by the new Education Minister Jane Davidson and the Health Minister Jane Hutt. *Extending Entitlement* was debated in plenary by the Assembly in December 2000 and received unanimous cross-party political support. Davidson took the opportunity to announce some £3m of extra money, over three years, for the Wales Youth Agency to strengthen support for the voluntary sector, expand the training and qualifications of youth workers, and improve the quality of youth information.

These were considered to be exciting times for the youth agenda in Wales. English colleagues, especially those in the youth service, gazed with envy across Offa's Dyke. While they were in retreat and entrenchment, with limited political support and a new competitor profession, youth work appeared to be centre-stage in Wales, at the heart of a coherent philosophical and strategic plan. However, things quickly began to unravel. Early in 2001, the youth information resources were re-directed from the Wales Youth Agency to a newly-formed organization called Canllaw-online. Not that this in itself was a problem – the agency had called, for some years, for the resurrection of Canllaw, which in another form had first been established in International Youth Year in 1985. But it was the first step in the haemorrhaging of the agency which, just four years hence, would cease to exist.

The voluntary youth work sector, subsumed against its wishes within the Wales Youth Agency when this was set up in 1992, struck out once more for independence; the Council for Wales Voluntary Youth Services (CWVYS) was subsequently supported separately by the Assembly. The strategic role of the agency was taken over by a youth policy team within the Welsh Assembly. With the assistance of external consultants, the Youth Policy Team developed *Guidance on Extending Entitlement* (Welsh Assembly Government, 2002). Enabling clauses within the Learning and Skills Act (2001) certainly strengthened, in theory at least, the role of the youth service and the age range to which 'youth support' could apply (up to 25 years of age). However, the Welsh Assembly Government now required all local authorities to establish Young People's Partnerships *under*, not in parallel with, the Children and Young People's Partnerships which were a statutory requirement of the Children and Young People's Framework. Contrary to the view of the original 'Extending Entitlement'

Advisory Group, new structures were being put in place. Furthermore, alongside the *Extending Entitlement* agenda, the Welsh Assembly Government was also developing a 'Learning Pathways 14–19' agenda (see Welsh Assembly Government, 2003b), considering more flexible learning routes and opportunities that would incorporate academic, vocational and civic learning. Again, such developments were commendable, but they introduced the idea of a 'learning coach', which suspicious minds viewed as the introduction of Connexions personal advisers 'by the back door'. The concept of a 'learning coach' had in fact originated with the appointment of two *youth workers* on an alternative curriculum programme, to support young people's learning; the head teacher at the school concerned had used the designation to pre-empt professional rivalry between the teaching and youth work professions. Nevertheless, suspicions were raised. Finally, youth participation was firmly seized by the children's agenda, which invoked Article 12 of the UN Convention as its guiding force. The irony of this was, first, that youth work also had a long tradition in participative practice which had, by and large, been ignored. Secondly, the Welsh Assembly Government had fought for a commitment, through *Extending Entitlement* (and the Learning and Skills Act), to young people up to the age of twenty-five, in contrast to Connexions in England which served young people only to the age of nineteen. Yet 'children' under the UN Convention ended at age 18, begging the question of quite how participative and wider *youth* policy would in fact address the 'chronic crisis of young adulthood' once the 'acute anxieties of adolescence' had passed (see Williamson, 1985).

The bureaucratic, organizational and professional territory was therefore becoming very crowded. There was increasing confusion about divisions of roles and responsibilities, both horizontally across professions and vertically from the Welsh Assembly's Youth Policy Team, through the Wales Youth Agency, to the field. The terrain became even more crowded at the start of 2002 when youth justice, though still a non-devolved function, entered the orbit of the Welsh Assembly Government, at least on the basis of close collaboration and consultation. There was a strong rationale to the proposal by Lord Warner, then Chairman of the Youth Justice Board for England and Wales, to have a 'Wales Committee' co-chaired by himself and the then Welsh Assembly health minister, Jane Hutt. After all, while the 'criminal' dimensions of the youth justice system (the police and the courts) were not devolved, the services that would assist the re-engagement of young offenders and the prevention of further offending (health, social services, education) were. Moreover, Jane Hutt not only had a watching brief on crime issues but had a direct responsibility for the Welsh substance misuse strategy and for mental health – both critical issues in turning the lives of young offenders around. As a result, a high level committee was convened, composed of senior Assembly officials as well as external members from local authorities, probation, education, social services and health. A subgroup was charged with developing an 'All Wales Youth Offending Strategy' which, predictably and commendably, was enveloped within the framework of *Extending Entitlement*, as well as other Welsh Assembly strategies concerning, for example, learning pathways, neighbourhood renewal and community safety. The premise was a simple one: youth offending might be prevented through the more effective extending of entitlement. Indeed, at the second meeting of the 'Wales Committee', the head of the Youth Policy Team made a presentation on the rhyme and reason for *Extending Entitlement*. The All Wales Youth Offending Strategy, jointly produced by the Welsh Assembly Government and the Youth Justice Board, was launched formally in the summer of 2004 (Welsh Assembly Government/Youth Justice Board, 2004).

The final piece in this apparently integrated jigsaw – of youth support, learning pathways and youth justice – was youth participation. Although responsibility for youth participation had shifted significantly in the direction of the children's agenda, there was strong political commitment to ensuring that the 'voice' of young people was heard across the work of the Welsh Assembly Government. To this end, the Youth Policy Team, now re-cast as the Youth and Pupil Participation Division within the Assembly, had established youth forum coordinators within all twenty-two local authorities in Wales and had a shared responsibility for the work of the Welsh youth parliament, Funky Dragon. A participation consortium was set up by the Assembly, through the offices of Save the Children, to orchestrate and coordinate different participative initiatives. Once more the Wales Youth Agency, which had originally had the functions of the original youth participation body, the Wales Youth Forum (which had been set up in 1985) subsumed within its responsibilities, appeared to have been sidelined. There was, unsurprisingly, much chagrin amongst youth workers around these developments, for there appeared to be little recognition of their work in involving young people in decision-making, which had been an integral part of youth work practice over many decades. Indeed, on a broader front, there were growing concerns that the Welsh Assembly Government was seeking to bypass the established structures and practice of youth work and the youth service. It had already set up meetings of All Wales Young People's Organisations (AWYPO), outside of the various groupings convened by the Wales Youth Agency, including the Agency's own Advisory Council for Youth Work in Wales.

Of course, as had always been the case, there were ideological tussles concerning the idea, concept and definition of 'youth work'. For some, this elided comfortably into the idea of 'work with young people' while for others it was a much more bounded concept, governed by distinct and clear values that did not necessarily inform wider practice with young people. Indeed, deep concern had been expressed in some quarters about the wording within the enabling clauses of the Learning and Skills Act where 'youth work' and 'youth support services' were used almost interchangeably. Proponents of 'traditional' youth work maintained that this was inappropriate – that while 'youth work' was part of the lattice-work of supporting young people, not all 'youth support work' was youth work. Yet it was equally possible to argue that so-called 'traditional' youth work had always been closely connected to wider political concerns and policy agendas concerned with social inclusion, promoting better health and combating crime. Early youth work had been about 'child rescue' and the post-war youth service was significantly the outcome of concerns about the poor physical condition of many army recruits and the prospective wayward behaviour of young people (young men) whose fathers were away at war (see Jeffs, 1979). Thus it was perhaps misguided for youth work advocates to press too hard on their focus on the individual and 'personal development' and often to oppose new expectations that they should become more closely involved in school inclusion, health promotion and crime prevention initiatives.

The Wales Youth Agency was, probably too often and too much, perceived to be the stubborn defender of the 'faith' – the protagonist for a purist notion of youth work uncorrupted by these broader social and political imperatives. A review of the agency in 2003 certainly called for it to widen its engagement beyond the youth work field (as, in fact, it had already done with the careers service during the emergence of *Extending Entitlement*). Yet when the Wales Youth Agency sought to engage more closely with a wider field of practice with young people, it was then accused of betraying its primary responsibilities to a *youth work* constituency, which needed its support on matters as diverse as training, information and international work. Thus, as the *Extending Entitlement* momentum gathered pace, the agency was arguably at its lowest ebb, trapped 'horizontally' between its core and wider potential constituencies and 'vertically' between its strategic and operational functions. Stripped almost immediately of some of its roles (despite the promises of the Minister to extend its role), it was losing credibility both with the Assembly and with some parts of the field. In an effort to clarify its place, its then chairman – the legendary Welsh rugby player Gerald Davies – convened representatives of the youth work field under Chatham House rules. This group, however, then took on an identity of its own – as something called the 'Standing Conference', with terms of reference that, to some, looked remarkably like those of the agency itself. The Standing Conference itself denied that there was any competition or conflict of interests with the agency, but this was not the view of the Assembly, which was bemused by the fact that the agency continued to 'service' the Conference. The place and status of the Wales Youth Agency was thereby even further undermined and, to many in the field, it was no great surprise when the Assembly's Education Minister Jane Davidson announced her proposed decision to cease funding the agency from the end of 2005.

The Minister's announcement was met with widespread disdain by the youth work field. Though many in the field had hardly been great supporters and advocates for the agency (and this, in part at least, had contributed to its decline), they now cried out for an independent voice, a representative at arms-length from the Welsh Assembly Government. Moreover, they expressed little confidence in the credibility or competence of those within the Assembly who would take over the roles and functions of the agency. Such views were relayed with some conviction to the minister but she was set on her 'proposed' decision, which was integrally bound up with the First Minister's confirmation, in July 2004, that he would fulfil his promise to execute a 'bonfire of the quangos'. Though the agency was a small fish in a pool that included the Welsh Development Agency (WDA) and Education and Learning Wales (ELWa), it was also to be brought inside the Assembly as part of the mission to establish a Welsh public service, compromising both the existing civil service and a variety of 'arm's length' agencies supported financially by the Welsh Assembly Government.

A WORLD-CLASS YOUTH SERVICE AND A YOUTH POLICY TO EMULATE?

The rhetoric of the Welsh Assembly Government, and particularly the Education Minister Jane Davidson, is that 'youth work' remains centre-stage within the Assembly's flagship youth policy framework, *Extending Entitlement*. As the politician who has routinely represented the UK on youth matters in the European context, the idea and vision of 'Extending Entitlement' has been promulgated across the wider Europe and is well known in many European countries. Indeed, it has come to inform a framework for youth policy standards and development within the Council of Europe (Council of Europe, 2003).[2] Yet it is instructive to 'test' the position in Wales against that broader youth policy work of the Council of Europe, not least its international reviews of national youth policy. Following seven such reviews between 1997 and 2001 (Finland, the Netherlands, Sweden, Romania, Spain, Estonia and Luxembourg), a synthesis report was produced (Williamson, 2002), comparing and contrasting approaches in these different countries and generating some themes and models against which future reviews might consider their findings. These models were concerned both with practice implementation and political commitment. In terms of practice, the themes revolved around five 'C's (the 'components' of youth policy): coverage, capacity, competence, coordination and cost.

In relation to *coverage* – which applies not only to geography but also to social groups – the challenge for Wales is not just to reach the most 'disengaged' but to build an approach which takes account of its striking urban/rural divide. This is a challenge for all countries with a few medium-sized cities but otherwise a dispersed rural population (cf. Sweden or Lithuania). A range of opportunity and experience can be cultivated effectively in the cities but often fails to extend to the countryside. Wales does have some healthy and admirable youth provision in rural areas, not least through Urdd Gobaith Cymru and the Young Farmers' Clubs, but by and large there is little indication that this has been strengthened significantly since devolution. Nor does the aspirational reach of *Extending Entitlement* appear to have made significant inroads into the communities of young people who are most disadvantaged. There are, of course, case study exceptions, but a recent evaluation conveyed some criticisms (albeit rather veiled ones) regarding progress to date (Haines et al., 2004). It is, of course, still relatively early days. Nevertheless it is of some concern that the evaluation should conclude that 'those young people who report higher levels of negative influences in their lives also report lower levels of access to entitlements' and that 'those young people who report higher levels of positive influences in their lives report higher levels of access to entitlement' (Haines et al., 2004, p. 103). It was precisely this polarization of experience and opportunity that *Extending Entitlement* was designed to address and redress – that concerted professional partnership effort should plug the gap when family, school and neighbourhood did not confer such opportunities.

The same evaluation also comments somewhat critically on the issue of *capacity*. This refers to the infrastructure for service delivery. Unsurprisingly, members of Young People's Partnerships were familiar with the objectives of *Extending Entitlement* and were positive about the guidance produced by the Assembly; after all, the two were integrally linked, for YPPs were a product of those deliberations. Yet recent anecdotal evidence points to considerable ignorance about the philosophy and operation of *Extending Entitlement*. Only three of some eighty youth justice workers attending the Cynnydd conference in 2004 knew anything in detail about it, and, similarly, only three participants out of around fifty at a careers service conference had any in-depth knowledge. For a 'flagship' policy of the Assembly Government, this should be a matter of deep concern. In terms of structures, professionals in the field express repeated criticism that they are unclear about their lines of accountability and routinely deplore the 'operational meddling' of Assembly officials. There appears to be immense confusion between the numerous partnerships and groupings that have purportedly been established to advance the aspirations of *Extending Entitlement*, which of course is embedded with, or related to, a range of other Welsh Assembly Government initiatives concerned with learning pathways, community regeneration and community safety. The *coordination and communication* between this plethora of new developments is unclear at the levels of the Assembly and within local authorities and on the ground. This does not bode well for concerted effort and action in relation to young people most in need, despite improvements in information-sharing (or 'keeping in touch') processes.

Of critical importance in any 'youth policy' framework is the *competence* of those charged with its delivery. Reference has already been made to perceptions that, at the level of governance, Assembly officials are not up to the task. At the other end of the line, and despite considerable progress in professional training and workforce development (as a result of more initial training courses in Wales, a 'coherent route' for youth worker training, and the work of the Wales Youth Agency Staff College), recruitment and retention of suitably skilled professionals remains a significant challenge. Yet without a skilled professional base both in youth work and beyond (i.e. amongst other professions working with young people), the prospects of achieving the vision of *Extending Entitlement* are slim. This is not to say that resources are denied to this endeavour. In terms of *costs*, the Welsh Assembly Government makes comparatively generous allocations to its youth-related initiatives. After all, it has a 'state budget' that is pro rata ten times greater than that of Slovenia and even greater than that of other similar size countries (such as the three Baltic States) that have recently become members of the European Union. It is the deployment of resources that is the question, for any highly complex infrastructure – composed of numerous partnerships and coordinators – has the tendency to consume such resources long before they reach their intended destination. From chief officers to grass-roots practitioners, there is a groundswell of complaint concerning 'bureaucratic overload', though its articulation is often muted in contexts where it needs to be said.

This point leads to a more political level analysis of youth policy development – what has been referred to in the work of the Council of Europe as the four (or eight) 'Ds', or the 'dynamic' of youth policy (see below). The essential point is that 'youth policy' can start or stall at any point in a cycle of momentum that, when it works well, should produce an 'opportunity-focused' and effective strategy. It is clear that, in Wales at the start of elected devolution, there was a coherent and constructive relationship between the elements of the cycle: political championship, professional motivation, self-critical dialogue, a determination to make a difference. Though the political championship remains – Jane Davidson is a powerful advocate for young people in Wales, on both formal and non-formal learning agendas – it rests on a much more precarious and often quite cynical platform, which detects more rhetoric than reality. Government ministers in any context tend to be responsive to a coherent lobby from the field, but when the field is divided and disorganized, their lead derives more from political instinct and the advice of their officials. A vicious circle takes hold, inevitably raising 'chicken or egg' questions: the field discerns a level of governance that is 'out of touch', those in government perceive a field that appears reluctant to engage with its agenda.

Figure 12.1: The dynamic of youth policy

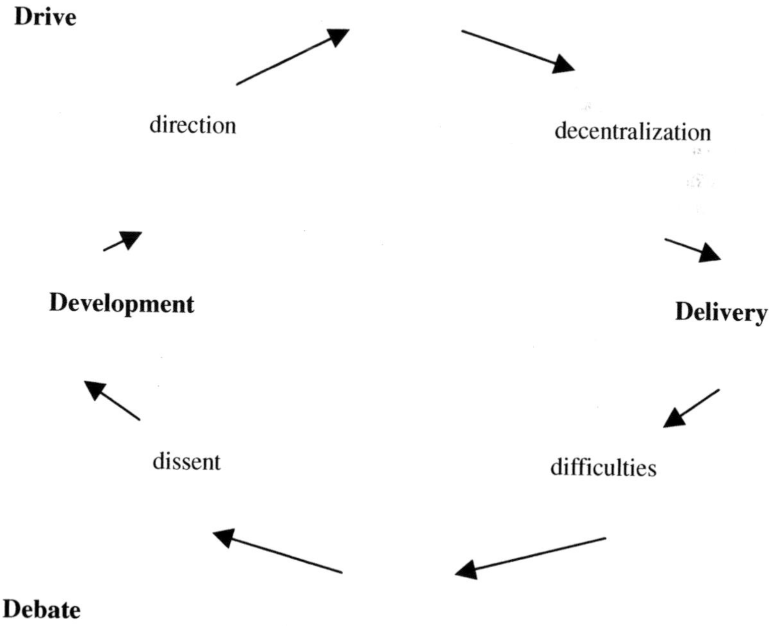

Drive

direction

decentralization

Development

Delivery

dissent

difficulties

Debate

No doubt the Assembly would argue that, from the political centre, a decentralized structure (through the Young People's Partnerships in each local authority) has been established for the delivery of the aspirations of *Extending Entitlement*. Many in the field would argue, however, that this structure has been fraught with difficulties, with a lack of clarity about roles and responsibilities, and the status of different forms of professional involvement and participation. Yet concerns on this front have largely been deflected or ignored, absorbed within general exhortations about 'working together' on behalf of young people in Wales. This has produced a vacuous debate, for legitimate concerns have been dismissed and construed as an unwillingness to work on the *Extending Entitlement* agenda. Indeed, Jane Davidson herself, in justifying the decision to cease funding the Wales Youth Agency, has suggested that youth work, led by the agency, has 'peripheralised' itself. Welsh Assembly Government internal advice to the minister concerning withdrawing the agency's funding speaks of using the 'funding of the Wales Youth Agency for use in supporting the wider *Extending Entitlement* agenda by setting up a branch with the Assembly Government' – as if the agency was not harnessed, and was indeed oppositional, to that agenda. Such insinuation is a far cry from the Assembly's plenary debate in 2000 that saw the agency as the central driver for the development and delivery of that agenda. This is but one example of both perceived, and in part real, dissent within the field and between the field and the Assembly. The agency might well maintain that it is the Assembly that no longer understands how the aspirations of *Extending Entitlement* might be achieved. But there is also real dissent between different elements of the youth service, and between some of those elements and other professions. Elements of the youth service have been demonstrably reluctant to engage with school-based alternative curriculum programmes and with youth offending teams, to the transparent irritation of some of those within the Assembly, at both political and official levels. Such friction, deriving from ideology, perceptions and practical realities, inevitably impedes any consideration of alternative directions to current trajectories. And this, in turn, produces frustration at the highest political level. Wales is not alone; similar processes are currently at play in Lithuania which also, only a few years ago, was celebrating its innovative co-management structures for youth policy (a shared responsibility between government and youth organizations), the formulation of an overarching 'youth policy concept' bordering on formal legislation, and powerful political championship of these ideas. That has also unravelled dramatically in the space of only a few years.

CONCLUSION

The demise of the Wales Youth Agency – just five years after it was heralded as the engine for the delivery of *Extending Entitlement* – is, in many respects, a metaphor for the more general trajectory of 'youth policy' since the inception of the Welsh Assembly Government. It rose on a tide of vision and expectation and has descended into a morass of competing and confusing structures, lacking direction and arguably in a vacuum. The political scientist Kevin Morgan has argued that the 'bonfire of the quangos' will produce less delivery and more navel gazing. Nowhere is this likely to be more apparent than in the youth field, where there is little evidence that the grand rhetoric emanating from the Assembly is likely to be converted into real practice that makes a constructive difference to the lives of (particularly more disadvantaged) young people in Wales.

NOTES

[1] This paper was written in June 2005.
[2] Since 2002, the Council of Europe has conducted a further six national youth policy reviews, of Lithuania, Malta, Norway, Cyprus, Slovakia, Hungary, and a review of Armenia is in progress.

REFERENCES

Cabinet Office (1998). *Tackling Drugs to Build a Better Britain*, London: The Stationery Office.

Coles, B. (2000). *Joined-up Youth Research, Policy and Practice: A New Agenda for Change*, Leicester: Youth Work Press.

Council of Europe (2003). *Standards for Youth Policy Development in Europe: Working Paper*, Strasbourg: Council of Europe Youth Directorate.

Department for Education and Employment (1999). *Learning to Succeed*, London: The Stationery Office.

Department for Education and Skills (2003). *Every Child Matters*, London: The Stationery Office.

Department of Health (1996). *Tackling Drugs Together*, London: HMSO.

Evans, K. and Furlong, A. (1997). 'Metaphors of youth transitions: niches, pathways, trajectories and navigations', in J. Bynner, L. Chisholm and A. Furlong (eds), *Youth, Citizenship and Social Change in a European Context*, Aldershot: Ashgate.

Furlong, A. and Cartmel, F. (1997). *Young People and Social Change: Individualisation and Risk in Late Modernity*, Milton Keynes: Open University Press.

Haines, K., Case, S., Isles, E., Rees, I. and Hancock, A. (2004). *Extending Entitlement: Making it Real*, Cardiff: Welsh Assembly Government.

Helve, H. and Bynner, J. (eds) (1996). *Youth and Life Management: Research Perspectives*, Helsinki: University of Helsinki Press.

Istance, D., Rees, G. and Williamson, H. (1994). *Young People Not in Education, Training or Employment in South Glamorgan*, Cardiff: South Glamorgan Training and Enterprise Council.

Jeffs, A. (1979). *Young People and the Youth Service*, London: Routledge and Kegan Paul.

Macdonald, R. (ed.) (1997). *Youth, the 'Underclass' and Social Exclusion*, London: Routledge.

National Assembly for Wales (2000a). *Tackling Substance Misuse in Wales – A Partnership Approach*, Cardiff: National Assembly for Wales.

National Assembly for Wales (2000b). *Extending Entitlement: Supporting Young People in Wales*, Cardiff: National Assembly for Wales.

Smith, G., Williamson, H. and Platt, L. (1996). 'Growing up in the age of uncertainty', in Carnegie United Kingdom Trust, *The Carnegie Young People Initiative: Years of Decision*, Leicester: Youth Work Press.

Social Exclusion Unit (1998a), *Truancy and School Exclusion*, London: The Stationery Office.

Social Exclusion Unit (1998b). *Rough Sleeping*, London: The Stationery Office.

Social Exclusion Unit (1998c). *Bringing Britain Together Again: National Strategy for Neighbourhood Renewal*, London: The Stationery Office.

Social Exclusion Unit (1999a). *Teenage Pregnancy*, London: The Stationery Office.

Social Exclusion Unit (1999b). *Bridging the Gap: New Opportunities for 16–18 Year Olds Not in Education, Employment or Training*, London: The Stationery Office.

Social Exclusion Unit (2000). *National Strategy for Neighbourhood Renewal: Report of Policy Action Team 12 – Young People*, London: The Stationery Office.

Social Exclusion Unit (2002). *The Education of Children in Care*, London: The Stationery Office.

United Kingdom Youth Work Alliance (1996). *Agenda for a Generation*, Edinburgh: Scottish Community Education Council.

Welsh Assembly Government (2002). *Extending Entitlement: Supporting Young People in Wales – Direction and Guidance*, Cardiff: Welsh Assembly Government.

Welsh Assembly Government (2003a). *The Learning Country: Learning Pathways 14–19*, Cardiff: Welsh Assembly Government.

Welsh Assembly Government (2003b). *Children and Young People: Rights to Action*, Cardiff: Welsh Assembly Government.

Welsh Assembly Government (2004). *Making the Connections: Delivering Better Services for Wales – The Welsh Assembly Government Vision for Public Services*, Cardiff: Welsh Assembly Government.

Welsh Assembly Government/Youth Justice Board (2004). *All Wales Youth Offending Strategy*, Cardiff: Welsh Assembly Government.

Welsh Office (1996). *Forward Together*, Cardiff: Welsh Office.

Williamson, H. (1985). 'Struggling beyond youth', *Youth in Society*, 98, January.

Williamson, H. (1993). 'Youth policy in the United Kingdom and the marginalisation of young people', *Youth and Policy*, Spring, 40, 33–48.

Williamson, H. (2002). *Supporting Young People in Europe: Principles, Policy and Practice*, Strasbourg: Council of Europe.

13. DEDDFWRIAETH NEWYDD A'R GYMRAEG

Colin H. Williams

Mae statws swyddogol y Gymraeg wedi ei ddiffinio gan Ddeddf yr Iaith Gymraeg 1993. Yn ôl y ddeddf hon, dylai'r Gymraeg a'r Saesneg gael eu trin yn gyfartal mewn busnes cyhoeddus ac wrth weinyddu cyfiawnder yng Nghymru. Gwyddom o brofiad nad yw cyd-destun y ddwy iaith yn gyfartal, felly mae'n dilyn y bydd y Gymraeg o dan anfantais strwythurol fel dewis iaith dinasyddion Cymru. Un peth yw egwyddorion deddfwriaeth, peth arall yw profiad bob dydd yr unigolyn. Dymunaf gyfrannu at ein dealltwriaeth ni o'r angen am ddeddfwriaeth newydd i'r Gymraeg drwy dynnu sylw at wendidau yn y system bresennol a chynnig rhai ffyrdd ymarferol o weithredu er mwyn i'r dewis ieithyddol gael ei seilio ar ddisgwyliadau rhesymol. Byrdwn yr erthygl hon yw mai hawl yr unigolyn ddylai fod y sbardun cysyniadol ychwanegol i gyfeirio unrhyw bwyslais pellach ar y Gymraeg. Bydd hyn hefyd yn berthnasol i'r pwyslais diweddar ar hawliau dynol yn gyffredinol, ac yn fwy penodol ar ddeddfwriaeth a chydraddoldeb. Yn bersonol nid wyf yn gyffredinol o blaid rhagor o fiwrocratiaeth, rheoleiddio, deddfwriaeth ac yn y blaen. Mae yna ddigonedd o gyfarwyddiadau gennym yn barod ar sut i fyw. Y sialens yw byw a bod. Ond os ydym am fyw bywyd drwy gyfrwng y Gymraeg neu byw yn ddwyieithog, rwy'n derbyn fod angen cyfnod gweddol hir o ddeddfwriaethu, rheoleiddio a meddwl strategol ynglŷn â'n sefyllfa fel dinasyddion dwyieithog neu amlieithog. Erbyn hyn, dim ond y gyfraith all sicrhau ein hawl i ddefnyddio'r Gymraeg fel mater o ddewis a hawl, ac nad braint mohono.

Felly ar y cychwyn neges f'erthygl mhapur yw y dylid pennu'r Gymraeg yn iaith swyddogol yng Nghymru a'r un breintiau â'r Saesneg. Gweithred i sicrhau statws, yn hytrach nag ysgogi defnydd uniongyrchol, fyddai hon. Serch hynny, byddai'n ddatganiad symbolaidd pwysig iawn i'r Gymraeg ac yn fodd i bwysleisio amcanion Llywodraeth y Cynulliad ar gyfer y Gymraeg. Ond yn ogystal â chefnogi'r elfen symbolaidd, mae cyfiawnhad mwy ymarferol o lawer dros gefnogi 'Deddfwriaeth Newydd a'r Gymraeg'. Dyma chwe rheswm dros hyn:

1. yr angen – mae'n bryd i ni roi sail statudol i elfennau o'n hawliau ieithyddol;
2. mae'r iaith yn rhan o'r agenda cydraddoldeb ac mae angen datblygu ein hawliau ar yr un ffurf â'r hawliau sydd eisoes yn bodoli ym maes polisïau gwrth-hiliol, cydraddoldeb rhywiol, anabledd ac yn y blaen;
3. mae nifer o dueddiadau Ewropeaidd yn arwain at ddiffiniadau mwy cynhwys-fawr o'n hawliau dinesig, cymdeithasol ac economaidd. Mae hyn yn ymateb i nifer o dueddiadau amrywiol, er enghraifft globaleiddio ac esblygiad y genedl-wladwriaeth ymatebol â chonsýrn am athrawiaeth y farchnad gymdeithasol;
4. ac yn fwy ymarferol ac amserol credaf fod diddymu/integreiddio Bwrdd yr Iaith Gymraeg fel rhan o gyfundrefn normal Cynulliad Cenedlaethol Cymru yn golygu fod yna wagle statudol posib. Mae hyn yn codi'r cwestiwn pa gorff fydd yn cymeradwyo a monitro'r cynlluniau iaith statudol, ac yn arbennig cynllun iaith y Cynulliad ei hunan;
5. mae'n bosibl y cawn swyddog, un ai dyfarnydd neu gomisiynydd iaith, fydd yn delio â chwynion gan y cyhoedd neu fydd o leiaf yn archwilio sut mae adrannau'r llywodraeth yn glynu wrth eu cynlluniau iaith statudol. Felly mae'n briodol ein bod yn pwyso am ragor o ddeddfwriaeth a fydd yn ein galluogi i ddewis defnyd-dio'r Gymraeg mewn sefyllfaoedd amrywiol. O dan y ddeddfwriaethol bresennol, bydd angen deddfwriaeth gynradd i sefydlu'r rheoleiddiwr newydd. Wedi dweud hynny, mae Papur Gwyn Llywodraeth y Deyrnas Gyfunol, *Trefn Lywodraethu Well i Gymru* (2005), yn cynnig dulliau newydd o gyflwyno deddfwriaeth o'r fath ac mae hwn yn debyg o fod yn gam allweddol ymlaen, nid yn unig yn hanes yr iaith ond hefyd yn nhermau aeddfedrwydd democrataidd ein cymdeithas;
6. mae angen mireinio rhai agweddau ar y ddeddf bresennol ac angen cymryd camau pellach mewn meysydd eraill. Yn benodol, credaf fod angen datblygu mesurau pellach yn ymwneud â hawliau ieithyddol; datblygu gweinyddu dwy-ieithog o fewn cyrff cyhoeddus; a normaleiddio'r defnydd o'r Gymraeg. Ac yn greiddiol credaf taw Llywodraeth y Cynulliad Cenedlaethol ddylai fod yn gyfrifol am bob agwedd o'r ddeddfwriaeth yn ymwneud â'r Gymraeg. Felly sut y mae deddfwriaeth newydd, datganoli a dyfodol yr iaith yn cydblethu? Beth yw'r ystyriaethau hanfodol wrth drafod rhai o'r cwestiynau allweddol yn y maes?

CWESTIYNAU ALLWEDDOL

Pa fath o ddeddfwriaeth?

1. Un ddeddf gynhwysfawr a/neu nifer o fesurau strategol wrth i ddatganoli datblygu?
2. Beth fydd perthynas deddfwriaeth San Steffan â rôl gynyddol y Cynulliad i

ddeddfu ar y Gymraeg ac i weithredu ar raddfa ehangach yn y maes arbennig hwn?

3. Sut mae deddfwriaeth a phatrymau newydd o gydweithio yn mynd i achosi newid yn ein defnydd ieithyddol fel dinasyddion, cwsmeriaid a gweithwyr? Mae'n amlwg fod cyfle ac arfer yn gysylltiedig â'i gilydd yn hyn o beth.

Ar hyn o bryd mae bwrlwm o weithgaredd yn y maes gan gynnwys papur strategaeth Cymdeithas yr Iaith, 'Deddf iaith newydd: dyma'r cyfle' a gyhoeddwyd ym mis Mai 2005; mesur seneddol arfaethedig a baratowyd gan Hywel Williams, A.S.; pwyllgor arbennig y Cynulliad sy'n trafod tystiolaeth ynglŷn â'r ddogfen 'Trefn lywodraethu well i Gymru'; gwaith arbenigwyr cyfreithiol David Lambert a Marie Navarro o Brifysgol Caerdydd, a'i wefan 'Wales legislation online' a nifer o gyfraniadau eraill.

Ac ar lefel ryngwladol mae ail rownd 'Yr ymgynghoriad ar siarter Ewrop ar gyfer ieithoedd rhanbarthol neu leiafrifol'. Mae Llywodraeth y Deyrnas Gyfunol eisoes wedi cyflwyno tystiolaeth i Gyngor Ewrop ar weithredu'r siarter, ac mae cyfle pwysig yn awr i grwpiau a chyrff amrywiol gyflwyno tystiolaeth i Gyngor Ewrop ac i Bwyllgor yr Arbenigwyr.[1] Mae hon yn drafodaeth bwysig ar lefel Ewropeaidd ynglŷn â pholisi iaith yma yng Nghymru.

HAWLIAU IEITHYDDOL

Mae'r Ddeddf Hawliau Dynol (1998) wedi datblygu ein dealltwriaeth o'r cysyniad o hawliau sylfaenol unigolion.[2] Mae'r Gymraeg eisoes yn rhan o'r agenda cydraddoldeb yma yng Nghymru ond dylem fod yr un mor uchelgeisiol yn achos y Gymraeg ag yn achos y cydraddoldebau eraill. Ar ôl degawd o weithredu cynlluniau iaith, mae'r tir wedi'i fraenaru i gymryd y camau nesaf o ran sefydlu hawliau ieithyddol penodol i unigolion a gwneud y Gymraeg yn rhan o'r agenda deddfwriaethol ar sail gwrth-wahaniaethu. Mae cam o'r fath yn angenrheidiol er mwyn dangos ein bod o ddifrif ynglŷn â diogelu'r Gymraeg.

Mae Deddf yr Iaith Gymraeg (1993) yn gosod dyletswydd ar gyrff cyhoeddus i drin y Gymraeg a'r Saesneg yn gyfartal wrth iddynt ddarparu gwasanaethau i'r cyhoedd.[3] Gwneir hynny ar sail eu cynlluniau iaith a gytunir gan Fwrdd yr Iaith Gymraeg. Anghyson yw gweithredu'r cynlluniau iaith, ac nid yw'n glir i'r cyhoedd beth allant ei ddisgwyl o ran gwasanaethau Cymraeg. Credaf ei bod yn bwysig fod y gwasanaethau a ddarperir yn cyd-fynd â'r hawl i'w derbyn. Dyma'r egwyddor sy'n sylfaen i gynllunio ieithyddol mewn nifer o wledydd ond sydd bron yn llwyr absennol yma yng Nghymru. Yr eithriad i'r sefyllfa yma yw'r hawl i gael gwrandawiad drwy'r Gymraeg mewn llys barn. Mae'r cyrff hynny sy'n gyfrifol am ddarparu'r gwasanaeth penodol hwn wedi cynllunio i gwrdd â gofynion y Ddeddf. Mae'r ddeddfwriaeth yn ei gwneud yn glir bod dyletswydd arnynt i ddarparu'r gwasanaeth a bod gan unigolion yr hawl i'w dderbyn.

Mae'n bryd inni adeiladu ar y sylfeini hyn, a sefydlu hawliau deddfwriaethol eraill i siaradwyr Cymraeg, wrth ddarparu gwasanaethau i'r cyhoedd. Byddai'n amserol, er enghraifft, sefydlu'n statudol bod gan unigolion yr hawl i dderbyn addysg gyfrwng Cymraeg, yr hawl i ddefnyddio'r Gymraeg mewn nifer o achosion wrth ymwneud â'r Gwasanaeth Iechyd, neu yn y gweithle, yr hawl i ohebu yn Gymraeg â chyrff sy'n dod o dan y ddeddf, ac i dderbyn gohebiaeth neu wybodaeth ganddynt drwy gyfrwng y Gymraeg. Cymeradwyaf hefyd y cysyniad o integreiddio'r Gymraeg fel rhan anhepgor o'r agenda deddfwriaethol ar sail gwrth-wahaniaethu. Mae strategaeth Cymdeithas yr Iaith (2005) yn pwysleisio'r egwyddor sylfaenol hon, sydd yn egwyddor gadarn, gydnabyddedig a theg i'r mwyafrif – ac felly yn fwy tebyg o gael ei derbyn a'i gweithredu. Fyddai'r Gymraeg ddim yn cael ei hystyried yn 'cause célèbre' neu yn 'ffetish'. Mae hwn yn ffordd resymegol o dacluso deddfwriaeth sy'n ymateb i anghyfartaledd hanesyddol a diffyg gweithredu yn y gorffennol. Dyma, rwy'n cymryd, yw rhan o'r cysyniad o normaleiddio'r Gymraeg.

Y dasg yw cryfhau'r union hawliau unigolyddol hyn drwy geisio darbwyllo llunwyr polisi nad yw cydnabod hawliau 'pobl' yn fater o dra-arglwyddiaethu hawliau'r unigolyn dros hawliau torfol, neu i'r gwrthwyneb. Yn hytrach maent yn llwyr ddibynnol y naill ar y llall ar y sail eu bod yn 'ddynol' ddibynnol (Carlin 2005).[4] Yn ddi-os, mae agenda enfawr deddfu/polisïau cydraddoldeb yn rhan ddi-droi'n-ôl o offerynnau rhyddfreinio sydd wedi cyflymu yn ddiweddar, ac mae cynnwys y Gymraeg yn y rhyddfreiniad cyffredinol hwn yn gwneud synnwyr. Mae hefyd yn gyfle ymarferol i gynnwys camau pwrpasol dros y Gymraeg.

Mae Carlin (2005) yn cydsynio fod gosod y Gymraeg o fewn terfynau cydraddoldeb yn beth doeth ac yn strategol werthfawr: mae hyn yn galluogi'r gwaith o hybu'r Gymraeg ar lefel arferion da, yn hytrach na deddfu yn y maes hwn. Ac, os bydd deddf iaith newydd, ac egwyddor 'swyddogoldeb' yn cael ei dderbyn, gall arferion da yn deillio o'r agenda cydraddoldeb weithio'n gytûn a'r ddeddf iaith newydd. Ond, mae Carlin yn rhybuddio y byddai'n rhaid i ddeddf iaith newydd fod yn ddigon cryf i wrthsefyll 'cleddyf daufiniog' agenda'r cydraddoldebau. Hynny yw, yn ymarferol gall gweithredu cydraddoldeb brydiau gyfiawnhau hegemoni'r Saesneg yn unig. Oni cheir gwrthbwys ar ffurf swyddogoldeb neu briod iaith mewn deddf iaith newydd, gall cydraddoldeb, sydd ar yr olwg gyntaf yn ymddangos yn arf ychwanegol i'w ddefnyddio o blaid y defnydd o'r Gymraeg, weithio yn ei herbyn.

GWENDIDAU'R SYSTEM BRESENNOL

Hawliau sefydliadol sydd gennym ac nid hawliau fel unigolion. Mae'r gyfundrefn bresennol yn arbennig o dda wrth hybu paratoi cynlluniau iaith, ond nid yw mor effeithiol o ran arolygu a sicrhau gweithredu'r cynlluniau. Un maes lle y gellid cryfhau'r ddeddfwriaeth yw gosod dyletswydd ar gyrff i ddarparu gwybodaeth i'r Bwrdd yn ôl y gofyn fel rhan o unrhyw ymchwiliad statudol o dan adran 17 y ddeddf i ddiffyg gweithrediad cynllun iaith. Mae cyrff wedi manteisio ar hyn ac wedi gwrthod cydweithio a gwrthod darparu gwybodaeth sylfaenol i'r Bwrdd. I'r perwyl hwn, dylid cryfhau'r pwerau statudol. Enghraifft benodol arall o wendid y ddeddfwriaeth bresennol yw adrannau Deddf 1993 yn ymwneud â chyrff y Goron, megis adrannau llywodraethol y Deyrnas Gyfunol (gan gynnwys Llywodraeth y Cynulliad) a nifer o'u hasiantaethau. Nid yw pwerau'r Bwrdd o ran gofyn i gyrff baratoi ac, yna gymeradwyo, cynlluniau iaith, yn berthnasol i gyrff y Goron. Gwelwn ddiffygion tebyg o ran gallu'r Bwrdd i adolygu cynnwys cynlluniau ac, yn achos y Llywodraeth, y pŵer i orfodi gweithredu cynlluniau.[5] Yn hytrach, rhaid dibynnu ar ewyllys da cyrff y Goron. Mae'r ewyllys da yma wedi dod i'r amlwg yn y ffaith fod cyrff y Goron, ar gyfartaledd, yn cymryd dwywaith yn hwy na chyrff eraill i baratoi cynlluniau iaith. Ar achlysuron eraill, mae cyrff y Goron wedi gwrthod gweithredu cynnwys eu cynlluniau iaith – a rhaid oedd ymyrryd yn wleidyddol ar y lefel uchaf i unioni'r sefyllfa.

Nid yw hyn yn dderbyniol nac yn rhesymol. Mae angen cysondeb ac eglurder, a dylid gosod yr un disgwyliadau a safonau ar gyrff y Goron ag ar gyrff cyhoeddus eraill. Darparodd Llywodraeth y Cynulliad dystiolaeth i Gomisiwn Richard yn nodi ei bod hi'n bosibl dod â chyrff y Goron yn llwyr o dan gwmpas y Ddeddf 1993.[6] Mae'n bwysig fod y Llywodraeth yn ceisio unioni'r sefyllfa annerbyniol hon cyn ystyried trosglwyddo unrhyw bwerau i reoleiddiwr newydd. O dan adran 10 Deddf 1993, mae gofyn i'r Cynulliad gael sêl bendith Senedd San Steffan i unrhyw ddiwygiadau i ganllawiau statudol y Bwrdd ar baratoi cynlluniau iaith. Yn sgîl datganoli, ac o gofio taw'r Cynulliad Cenedlaethol sydd yn arwain yn y maes polisi hwn, credaf y byddai'n briodol ac amserol i'r Cynulliad gael y pŵer i gymeradwyo unrhyw newid i ganllawiau statudol ar baratoi cynlluniau iaith.

Mae Deddf 1993 hefyd yn sefydlu'r egwyddor y dylid trin y Gymraeg a'r Saesneg ar y sail eu bod yn gyfartal, cyn belled ag y bo'n briodol o dan yr amgylchiadau ac yn rhesymol ymarferol. Mae yna densiwn amlwg yn bodoli rhwng y ddau gymal uchod. Ar lefel ymarferol, cynllun iaith corff yw'r modd i ddatrys y tensiwn hwn. Serch hynny, mae'n deg dweud bod cyrff yn aml yn defnyddio'r cymal yn ymwneud â phriodoldeb a rhesymoldeb yn fympwyol, er mwyn osgoi cyfrifoldeb a gweithredu mewn dull sy'n trin y ddwy iaith yn gyfartal. Mae'n amserol nawr i hepgor y cymal yn ymwneud â phriodoldeb a rhesymoldeb. Byddai cymryd y cam hwn, ynghyd â phennu'r Gymraeg yn iaith swyddogol yng Nghymru a rhoi iddi'r un breintiau â'r Saesneg, yn hwb sylweddol i atgyfnerthu statws y Gymraeg ac yn dangos ymrwymiad Llywodraeth y Cynulliad a'r Deyrnas Gyfunol i'w hybu a'i diogelu.

Un o wendidau mwyaf y ddeddfwriaeth bresennol yw nad yw'n cwmpasu'r defnydd mewnol o'r Gymraeg. Mae diffyg mesurau o'r fath yn arafu twf defnydd o'r Gymraeg mewn cyrff cyhoeddus ac mae'n aml yn llesteirio datblygu ddarparu gwasanaethau cyfrwng Cymraeg. Gallai gweithredu ymarferol mesurau o'r fath fod yn rhan o gynlluniau iaith cyrff, gyda'r nod o sicrhau cynnydd yng ngallu ieithyddol gweithluoedd dros gyfnod o amser. Mae mesurau i gefnogi'r Gymraeg yn y gweithle yn greiddiol i ddatblygiad gwasanaethau cyhoeddus o'r radd flaenaf yng Nghymru.

Cefnogaf gysyniad Cymdeithas yr Iaith o ganiatáu hawliau i ddefnyddio'r Gymraeg neu'r Saesneg ar sail natur y nwyddau, cyfleusterau a'r gwasanaethau a gynigir yn y farchnad ac nid ar sail statws y darparwr. Dyma gysyniad sydd yn debyg i'r cyfiawnhad am angen ac nid galw fel sail darpariaeth, hynny yw nid ildio yn llwyr i ofynion y farchnad. Mae dau beth yn ein rhwystro yn y farchnad lled rydd, sef 1) hegemoni'r Saesneg – a ninnau mor fychan, a 2) treigl amser – mae'n cymryd o leiaf genhedlaeth cyn bod ymddygiad ac arferion yn newid. Am resymau digon dealladwy, pan fo dewis rhwng y Gymraeg a'r Saesneg wrth dderbyn gwasanaethau, mae'r mwyafrif sydd yn siarad Cymraeg yn fy marn i yn mynd i ddal i ddefnyddio'r Saesneg am gyfnod hir iawn. Ofer i ni weld bai ar ein cymdogion am wneud hyn; mae'n cymryd amser hir i newid arferion. Dyna pam mae angen grym deddf gwlad i sicrhau fod dewis ar gael am gyfnod hir iawn, yn barhaol felly, i ganiatáu i bobl ymgyfarwyddo ac ymgartrefu yng nghyd-destun dulliau newydd o gyfathrebu a chydweithio.

Mae'r pwnc hwn yn holl bwysig am ddau reswm. Mae'r siarad am ymestyn y ddeddf iaith o'r sector gyhoeddus i'r sector breifat yn ddealladwy. Ond yn amlach na pheidio mae hyn yn awgrymu bygythiad ac nid cyfle ychwanegol i'r cyhoedd, sef disgwrs negyddol o orfodaeth sydd ynghlwm wrth hyn. Mae canolbwyntio ar orfodi a chydymffurfio yn cynnig deunydd parod i wrthwynebwyr y Gymraeg sy'n dadlau, er enghraifft, fod cyfundrefn ddwyieithog yn rhwystr i ddenu buddsoddiadau economaidd ychwanegol; bod defnyddio'r iaith yn esbonio ein tlodi cymharol fel cenedl; yn gost ychwanegol annerbyniol i fusnesau. Nid oes neb mewn gwirionedd wedi mesur hyn am nad ydym yn gwybod eto beth fyddai natur y newidiadau. Felly mae angen casglu tystiolaeth i ymateb i'r fath honiadau. Mae angen trafodaeth sy'n grymuso, ac yn rhoi pŵer i'r dinasyddion sydd am ddewis y Gymraeg.

Ond y rheswm pennaf yw cymhlethdod natur economaidd ein sefyllfa. Mae cydymdreiddiad y gwahanol sectorau erbyn hyn yn ei gwneud hi'n anodd iawn i ddiffinio ffin a therfyn gwasanaeth arbennig, ar wahân efallai i bethau lled syml fel cyfathrach fasnachol wyneb yn wyneb mewn siop neu dafarn. Mae hyn yn datblygu'n fwy fwy cymhleth wrth i'r farchnad gymysg a thelegyfathrebu gynyddu, ac wrth i ymddygiad unigolion, yn hytrach na thorfol neu gymunedol, gynyddu fel norm. Felly mae'n briodol ganolbwyntio fwy ar themâu yn hytrach nag ar sectorau, ac ystyried natur y gwasanaethau a ddarperir i'r cyhoedd. Mae Llywodraeth y Cynulliad eisoes wedi mabwysiadu'r polisi hwn drwy ddod â chwmnïau dŵr o dan gwmpas y ddeddf bresennol. Wedi i'r Llywodraeth gwblhau ei gwaith ym maes y cyfleustodau, byddai'n briodol trafod a ddylid ymestyn y ddeddf i feysydd eraill, megis banciau a chwmnïau yswiriant. Credaf y dylai Llywodraeth y Cynulliad Cenedlaethol gael y pŵer i gynnwys grwpiau o gyrff penodol o fewn y ddeddfwriaeth ieithyddol, fel y gwnaed yn achos y darparwyr dŵr. Mater i'r Cynulliad Cenedlaethol ddylai hyn fod – ac yno felly y dylai'r pŵer i ddeddfu orwedd.

RHEOLEIDDIWR NEU GOMISIYNYDD IAITH?

Rwyf wedi cefnogi'r syniad o sefydlu comisiynydd iaith ers 1973 pan wnes i fy ngwaith ymchwil cyntaf yng Nghanada ar gynllunio ieithyddol ac ar frwydr yr iaith yn Quebec (Williams, 1994, 1995; Cartwright a Williams, 1982). Ond ai comisiynydd y Gymraeg neu gomisiynydd iaith sydd angen arnom yng Nghymru? (Williams, 1989). Nid yr un swyddogaeth sydd yn perthyn i'r naill a'r llall, ac os am gomisiynydd y Gymraeg, a fydd y person hwn hefyd yn lladmerydd sy'n hyrwyddo ac yn herio, neu a fydd yn bennaf yn archwilio ac yn adrodd am ffaeleddau'r system?

Ar hyn o bryd mae'r Llywodraeth yn ffafrio'r term 'dyfarnydd' am y rheoleiddiwr, a fydd yn ymyrryd pan fo anghydfod sylweddol yn codi. Mae yna berygl wrth gwrs na fyddai'r dyfarnydd ond yn canolbwyntio ar y pethau hanfodol o dan y ddeddfwriaeth bresennol, sef gweithredu'r cynlluniau iaith ac y byddai rhannau eraill o'r gwaith, ysgogi a hyrwyddo'r Gymraeg, yn cael eu colli oddi fewn i swyddfa ombwdsman gweinyddol y Cynulliad. Ond gan fod Llywodraeth y Cynulliad wedi sefydlu comisiynwyr annibynnol dros blant a'r henoed, dylid sicrhau'r un annibyniaeth, yr un gorolwg strategol a'r un statws i'r rheoleiddiwr arfaethedig ar gyfer y Gymraeg. Felly, mae'n hollbwysig bod gan y rheoleiddiwr arfaethedig lais annibynnol dros weithredu'r ddeddf. Dylai'r penodiad fod am gyfnod penodol, a dylai fod yn benodiad gan y Cynulliad Cenedlaethol yn hytrach na Llywodraeth y Cynulliad. Byddai hyn yn dilyn y patrwm a grybwyllir ym Mhapur Gwyn y Llywodraeth, *Trefn Lywodraethu Well i Gymru*, ar gyfer yr ombwdsman gwasanaethau cyhoeddus a'r archwiliwr cyffredinol. Dylid sicrhau bod gan y rheoleiddiwr arfaethedig y pwerau a'r adnoddau priodol i ymgymryd â'i ddyletswyddau yn effeithiol.

Credaf ei bod hi'n hollbwysig bod gan y rheoleiddiwr y swyddogaeth o oruchwylio'r ddeddfwriaeth ieithyddol a'i gweithredu, yn union fel y cyfrifoldebau eraill, megis hil ac anabledd. Mewn amser wrth gwrs, gellir dychmygu rhwydwaith o gomisiynwyr iaith o Ganada, Iwerddon, Cymru, Gogledd Iwerddon a rhannau eraill o'r byd yn cydweithio ac yn rhannu profiadau â chomisiynwyr mewn meysydd eraill, megis gweinyddiaeth, plant, yr henoed, lles, iechyd ac yn y blaen.

PA FATH O HAWLIAU FYDDAI'R DDEDDFWRIAETH NEWYDD YN EU CYNNIG?

Mater o drafod yw hwn rhwng y cyhoedd, grwpiau gwleidyddol a'r arbenigwyr, er fy mod i'n gwybod o brofiad mai gweision sifil fydd yn llywio'r camau awdurdodol fel a wnaed gyda Deddf Iaith 1993. Rwyf eisoes wedi nodi rhai o'r prif ystyriaethau, sef sefydlu'n statudol bod gan unigolion yr hawl i dderbyn addysg gyfrwng Cymraeg,[7] yr hawl i ddefnyddio'r Gymraeg mewn nifer o achosion wrth ymwneud â'r gwasanaeth iechyd, neu yn y gweithle, yr hawl i ohebu yn Gymraeg â chyrff sy'n dod o dan gwmpas y ddeddf, ac i dderbyn gohebiaeth neu wybodaeth drwy gyfrwng y Gymraeg. Ond mae ymgyrchwyr yn poeni hefyd am yr economi, ein cymunedau bregus, dylanwad globaleiddio, y cyfryngau, gwerthiant tai a thir ac yn y blaen. Yn hyn o beth mae papur strategaeth Cymdeithas yr Iaith (2005) yn addawol iawn ac yn rhoi pwyslais ar hawliau'r unigolyn ac ar hawliau cymunedau.

Ond oherwydd 'rheol y canlyniadau annisgwyl', mae angen llawer mwy o waith ar nifer o gasgliadau eraill sydd ym mhapur y Gymdeithas. Yn bennaf, credaf fod yna fyd o wahaniaeth rhwng galw am hawliau'r unigolyn a galw am hawliau cymunedau. Wrth gwrs mae yna lenyddiaeth eang ar wahanol fathau o hawliau ym myd y gyfraith, athroniaeth wleidyddol a'r gwyddorau cymdeithasol, ond mae angen bod yn fwy manwl o ran diffinio beth yn union fyddai hawliau cymunedol, a phwy yw'r gymuned. Pwy fyddai'n cael cam, a phwy fyddai'n elwa o'r hawliau hyn?

Rwy'n awgrymu ei bod hi'n anodd iawn gweithredu'r cymalau hyn sef:

- yr hawl i'r Gymraeg oroesi fel iaith gymunedol;
- yr hawl i gael ei hadfywio fel rhan integral a sylfaenol o fywyd pob Cymuned yng Nghymru (Cymdeithas yr Iaith, 2005, t. 4).

Mae angen gofyn beth yn union fyddai statws gweithredol cydnabod hawliau o'r fath. Mae'r rhain yn dra gwahanol eu natur i hawl yr unigolyn i dderbyn gwasanaeth Cymraeg fel cwsmer ac fel gweithiwr, neu addysg gyfrwng Cymraeg fel disgybl. Wrth gwrs nid yw'r ffaith ein bod yn cydnabod eu bod yn hawliau cymhleth yn rheswm digonol dros eu hanwybyddu; mae'n rhaid i'r gyfraith drosglwyddo pŵer, er mwyn gweithredu a newid arfer. Nid oes rôl amlwg a ffurfiol gan y gyfraith i wneud gosodiadau gwleidyddol.

Byddai diffinio ein hawliau'r unigolyn, fel dinesydd, yn mynd law yn llaw â sefydlu comisiynydd iaith: mae'r ddau yn dibynnu ar ei gilydd. Ar hyn o bryd rwy'n gwneud astudiaeth o rôl comisiynydd iaith yng Nghanada, Iwerddon ac mewn nifer o gyd-destunau eraill lle mae yna ombwdsman ar gyfer hawliau arbennig.[8] Un casgliad amlwg yw bod hawliau'r unigolion yn cael eu cymryd o ddifrif gan asiantaethau a chyrff oherwydd bodolaeth y comisiynydd, ond bod polisi yn fwy debyg o gael ei lunio gan y llysoedd a'r gyfundrefn gyfreithiol. Casgliad arall yw pe na fyddai Llywodraeth y Cynulliad am sefydlu swyddfa ar gyfer Cymru yn unig, mae'n bosib dwyn perswâd ar Lywodraeth y Deyrnas Gyfunol i sefydlu ombwdsman ieithyddol ar gyfer yr ieithoedd yn y DU a enwir gan 'Siarter Ewrop ar gyfer ieithoedd rhanbarthol neu leiafrifol'. Gall hwn fod naill ai yn gysylltiedig â'r Swyddfa Tramor neu â'r Swyddfa Cartref fel rhan o'r agenda cydraddoldeb.

SIARTER YR IAITH GYMRAEG

Yn ogystal â deddf iaith newydd, mae angen siarter yr iaith Gymraeg arnom fyddai'n datgan ein hawliau mewn meysydd fel addysg, yr economi, gwasanaethau cyhoeddus, y cyfryngau. Yn y meysydd hyn gellir gweithredu ar osodiadau gwleidyddol a chymdeithasol ynglŷn â natur a rôl y Gymraeg. Pa gynsail rhyngwladol sydd i'r fath ddatganiad? Mae Quebec yn rhoi enghraifft i ni ym maes iaith yn y gweithle.[9] Dyma rhan o gyfiawnhad llywodraeth Quebec dros ddeddfu ynghylch beth yn union yw hawliau gweithwyr a chyfrifoldebau cyflogwyr a chwmnïau ym maes iaith: 'mae gan bawb sydd yn gyflogedig yr hawl i weithio trwy gyfrwng y Ffrangeg . . . Os na all y Ffrangeg ddangos ei bod

yn arf anhepgorol yng ngweithle Quebec, bydd yn colli tir i'r Saesneg, yn
enwedig felly ymhlith trigolion sydd yn newydd-ddyfodiaid i Quebec.'

Yn ail, os am hawl, hawl i bawb yng Nghymru ble bynnag maent yn byw. Ni
ddylid gwahaniaethu yn ddeddfwriaethol ar sail ddaearyddol, am ddau reswm.
Yn gyntaf, mae'n gwanhau'r cysyniad o gydraddoldeb o fewn y genedl. Yn ail,
mewn achosion perthnasol fel yr Iwerddon, Gwlad Belg, Y Ffindir, De Affrica,
mae'r pwysau i newid y ffiniau (h.y. eu crebachu ac nid eu hymestyn) tua bob
deng mlynedd. Mae hyn yn tynnu oddi ar lwyddiant unrhyw weithgaredd i
gryfhau'r gymuned. Felly, er fy mod o blaid rhaglenni sydd wedi eu targedu at y
fro Gymraeg, nid wyf am weld diffiniad statudol o'r fro Gymraeg – boed hynny
am resymau hawliau ieithyddol neu wasanaethau economaidd.

Yn drydydd, mae'r Llywodraeth a Cymdeithas yr Iaith yn galw am fforwm
democrataidd i drafod yr iaith ac yn awgrymu sefydlu 'Cyngor ar gyfer y
Gymraeg' sy'n ddemocrataidd a chynhwysol. Cydnabyddaf fod i'r cyngor neu'r
fforwm rôl allweddol yn arbennig i gynnig tystiolaeth a chaniatáu llais i'r rheiny
sydd yn amhleidiol. Ond oes rôl fwy na hynny i'r cyngor hwn? Beth fyddai
union swyddogaeth a chyfrifoldebau'r cyngor? Ai Bwrdd yr Iaith estynedig
newydd heb weision sifil? Beth sydd wir ei angen yw pwyllgor cryf o
arbenigwyr i gymryd rhai o'r cynigion doethaf, gan gynnwys rhai fydd yn deillio
o'r cyngor, a'u troi yn gynigion ymarferol y gall y gwleidyddion eu deall a
gweithredu arnynt.

Y PAPUR GWYN AR DDATGANOLI I GYMRU

Y newidiadau gwleidyddol arfaethedig wrth i ddatganoli ddatblygu sydd y
bwysicaf oll. Fis Mehefin 2005, gyhoeddwyd y Papur Gwyn ar ddatganoli i
Gymru. Mae'r Papur Gwyn, *Trefn Lywodraethu Well i Gymru*, yn cyflwyno
cynigion ar ddiwygio deddf Llywodraeth Cymru ac ymateb y Llywodraeth i
argymhellion Comisiwn Richard. Nododd y papur sut y gellid cynyddu pwerau'r
Cynulliad, gan roi iddo fwy o ryddid oddi wrth ddeddfwriaeth San Steffan.
Mae'n trafod ailffurfio strwythur y Cynulliad, gwahanu'r ochr ddeddfwriaethol
oddi wrth Lywodraeth y Cynulliad, a newid trefniadau etholiadol y Cynulliad.
Mae'r Papur Gwyn yn cynnig y cyfle, maes o law, i drosglwyddo rhagor o
gyfrifoldebau i'r Cynulliad i ddeddfu mewn meysydd penodol.

Un maes amlwg, unigryw lle y gellid manteisio ar y pwerau newydd yw ym
myd polisi iaith ac addysg Cymru. Wrth gwrs, mae popeth yn dibynnu ar sut yn
union mae'r llywodraeth yn Llundain ac yng Nghaerdydd yn dehongli'r
berthynas newydd sydd rhwng y lefelau gwahanol o lywodraeth. Pe bai'r

drafodaeth sydd yn dilyn y Papur Gwyn yn awgrymu dwyieithrwydd fel maes polisi arbennig o dan ofal Llywodraeth Cymru, gallai hynny roi hwb sylweddol, nid yn unig i ddeddf iaith newydd ond i ddeddfwriaeth hollol unigryw ym maes dwyieithrwydd. Yr allwedd i hyn yw'r Gorchmynion yn y Cyngor. Mesurau ac nid deddfau fel y cyfryw yw'r Gorchmynion yn y Cyngor (*Orders in Councils*), ac mae'n bosib nodi pa faterion penodol y byddai'r Cynulliad yn derbyn cyfrifoldeb statudol trostynt wrth ddyfarnu, dyweder, ar faterion ieithyddol, neu addysg. Wedi trosglwyddo'r cyfrifoldeb, o hynny ymlaen, ni fyddai'n rhaid i bob rhan o ddeddfwriaeth ddod ger bron San Steffan, dim ond yr elfennau a neilltuwyd naill ai i'r Senedd neu i'r Ysgrifennydd Gwladol.[10]

Credaf y dylai Llywodraeth y Cynulliad sicrhau fod trosglwyddo pwerau yn ymwneud â'r Gymraeg yn flaenoriaeth. Proses fydd yn digwydd dros gyfnod hir o amser yw adfywio'r Gymraeg a chreu Cymru ddwyieithog a bydd gofyn diwygio'r ddeddfwriaeth berthnasol yn rheolaidd. O gofio bod gan y Cynulliad swyddogaethau gweithredol yn ymwneud â'r Gymraeg, mae'n gwneud synnwyr bod y Cynulliad yn cael y pŵer i newid y ddeddfwriaeth yn hytrach na gorfod cystadlu am amser deddfu yn San Steffan. Dylai unrhyw drosglwyddo pwerau deddfwriaethol fod yn ddigon eang i ddelio ag amrywiaeth o sefyllfaoedd a meysydd polisi yn ymwneud â'r Gymraeg.

TREFN WEINYDDOL 'GORCHMYNION YN Y CYNGOR'

* Llywodraeth y Cynulliad a'r Cynulliad yn cynnig 'gorchymyn' i'r Ysgrifennydd Gwladol;
* yr Ysgrifennydd Gwladol yn cyflwyno'r gorchymyn ger bron y Senedd;
* pwyllgorau Tŷ'r Cyffredin a Thŷ'r Arglwyddi yn archwilio'r dystiolaeth a'r cyfiawnhad drostynt;
* dadl hyd at 90 munud yn y ddwy siambr;
* sêl bendith y Frenhines a'r Cyfrin Gyngor;
* y gorchmynion yn ddarostyngedig i benderfyniad cadarnhaol (*affirmative resolution*) ond nid i ddeddfwriaeth y Cynulliad;
* mae'r gorchmynion yn cynnwys amodau galluogi er mwyn i'r Cynulliad baratoi deddfwriaeth.[11]

Yn ymarferol, golyga hyn y gall y Cynulliad fod yn senedd anffurfiol, yn datblygu grym mewn meysydd priodol heb orfod mynd yn ôl ac ymlaen i San Steffan. Yn achos y Gymraeg mae'n bosib i'r Cynulliad hawlio fod ganddo'r cyfrifoldeb a'r arbenigedd i weithredu drosti. Felly, yn ôl fy nehongliad i o oblygiadau'r Papur Gwyn, gallai'r Cynulliad ofyn bron am fonopoli ym myd datblygu polisi ar ddwyieithrwydd. Ofer yw cael y polisi heb y pŵer.[12]

Er mwyn gwireddu hyn y cymal i'w gynnwys fel gorchymyn yn y Cyngor fyddai 'i ddiogelu ac i hyrwyddo'r Gymraeg'. Byddai hwn yn cydsynio gyda chymal 32 Deddf Llywodraethu Cymru, 1998.[13] Er mwyn i'r Cynulliad argyhoeddi'r Ysgrifennydd Gwladol, mae'n ofynnol i'r Cynulliad ddibynnu ar gymdeithas sifil Cymru cyn y fath ddeddfwriaeth, yn ystod y cyfnod ac ar ôl hynny. Fel canlyniad, byddai hyn yn creu ddemocratiaeth fwy cynhwysfawr ac adeiladol na nifer o wledydd eraill Ewrop gan y byddai'r Cynulliad yn fwy dibynnol ar y cyhoedd o hynny ymlaen. Ni fyddai'n gallu troi at Lundain am gymorth, na beio San Steffan ychwaith. Ein cyfrifoldeb ni, yma yng Nghymru, fyddai'r ddeddfwriaeth a'r polisïau fyddai'n deillio o'r ddeddfwriaeth newydd.

Canlyniad arall fyddai rhoi mwy o waith a chyfrifoldeb i Aelodau'r Cynulliad. Mae'n wir na fyddai aelodau'r gwrthbleidiau yn llywio cymaint ar bolisi o ddydd i ddydd, ond yn sicr byddent yn ymwneud llawer mwy â pharatoi deddfwriaeth o hynny ymlaen, a thrwy hynny yn gallu llunio siâp a chymeriad natur unigryw ein Cynulliad a'r gymdeithas. Elfen arall amlwg wrth gwrs yw y byddai pob darn o ddeddfwriaeth yn gorfod bod yn ddwyieithog; mae hyn hefyd yn ategu at natur unigryw ein cyfansoddiad anffurfiol a'n gweithgaredd wrth ddefnyddio'r Gymraeg mewn meysydd newydd am y tro cyntaf. Yn naturiol, mae hyn oll yn codi cwestiynau sylfaenol ynglŷn â datganoli. Byddai angen ystyried goblygiadau llwyr ddatganoli pŵer deddfu ar y Gymraeg ar gyrff y Deyrnas Gyfunol sy'n darparu gwasanaethau yng Nghymru. Serch hynny, rwyf o'r farn taw'r Cynulliad ddylai fod yn gyfrifol am osod cyfeiriad a phennu cynnwys polisïau sydd yn ymwneud â'r Gymraeg, ac y dylai gael y pwerau priodol i wneud hynny.

Pen draw hyn oll fyddai ailstrwythuro'r ymgyrch dros ddeddfwriaeth, sef cadw'r pwysau ar ddeddfwriaeth iaith newydd a gweithredu trwy'r gorchmynion yn y cyngor. Byddai'r rhain yn gorfod cael sêl bendith San Steffan, ond gellid mynnu llawer mwy o fesurau yng Nghaerdydd yn sgil grymuso'r llywodraeth yma; rwy'n cymryd y byddai'r ail yn haws i'w gwneud na'r cyntaf am nifer o resymau eithaf amlwg. Yn sicr, bydd yr adrefnu arfaethedig yn llwyr weddnewid y dull o ddatblygu a gweithredu polisïau iaith yng Nghymru. Un o'r cwestiynau allweddol a ofynnais uchod oedd 'un ddeddf gynhwysfawr a/neu nifer o fesurau strategol wrth i ddatganoli datblygu'. Yn sicr, mae'n bosib rhagweld sut gallai Gorchmynion yn y Cyngor osod rhaglen o is-ddeddfau ar waith, a bwrw bod yr ewyllys gwleidyddol yn bodoli. Mae'r mwyafrif o sylwebyddion, yn dilyn dehongliad John Osmond (2005), yn amau ymarferoldeb gwleidyddol y ffordd yma o weithredu. Ond rwyf am fod ychydig yn fwy greadigol. Mae Papur Gwyn gan amlaf yn arwain at ddeddfwriaeth, felly mae'r cynigion a geir yma yn fwy debyg o weld golau dydd na nifer o gynigion eraill. Yn ail, mae'r Senedd yn San Steffan yn debyg o orffen y Ddarlleniad Cyntaf cyn diwedd 2005 ac mae'n bosib i'r Ail Ddarlleniad ddilyn yn fuan wedi hynny, ac o ganlyniad bydd y mesurau yn bodoli o fewn deunaw mis. Golyga hyn y bydd y Cynulliad yn gorff ddeddfwriaethol, y bydd yna gyfle i dacluso a chywiro nifer o wendidau y gyfundrefn bresennol, yn arbennig felly y grymoedd gwasgaredig neu amhendant, ac y bydd gan Lywodraeth y Cynulliad y grym i ddatblygu rheoliadau mewn nifer o feysydd ychwanegol.

Felly i gloi, dyma un agenda bosib ar sut i fanteisio ar y cyfleoedd newydd. Nid wyf o anghenraid yn hawlio mai dyma'r unig ffordd ymlaen, ond yn sicr y mae'n cynnig ffordd ddyfeisgar ymlaen:

- deddfwriaeth iaith newydd trwy ddyfais Gorchymyn yn y Cyngor;
- prif-ffrydio'r Gymraeg fel ystyriaeth ac fel iaith gyfansoddiadol wrth baratoi deddfwriaeth eilaidd yn y Cynulliad ac fel rhan o raglen ddeddfwriaethol San Steffan;[14]
- sefydlu swydd comisiynydd y Gymraeg;
- cryfhau pwerau'r Cynulliad;
- democrateiddio cyfraniad cymdeithas sifil trwy gynnig fforwm iaith neu gyngor y Gymraeg wirioneddol werthfawr;
- integreiddio gwaith y Bwrdd i ganol y Llywodraeth ac nid yn adran ymylol;[15]
- ceisio argyhoeddi'r cyhoedd a'r darparwyr i newid eu hymddygiad fel ymateb i gyfuniad o ddeddfwriaeth, ideoleg wleidyddol ac effaith y system addysg wrth greu mwy o ymwybyddiaeth ieithyddol.

Mae'r gyfraith yn creu cyfle, ond profiad bob dydd fel dinesydd sy'n creu'r awydd i'w ddefnyddio.

CYDNABYDDIAETH

Fersiwn diwygiedig o ddarlith a draddodwyd yn Eisteddfod Eryri ar 4 Awst 2005. Pleser yw cael diolch yn ddidwyll i bawb a gytunodd i gael eu cyfweld ar gyfer yr ymchwil hwn. Diolch arbennig iawn i Prys Davies, Bwrdd yr Iaith Gymraeg, David Lambert, Marie Navarro, Wyn James a Huw Thomas, Prifysgol Caerdydd, Patrick Carlin, Prifysgol Cymru, Aberystwyth, Catrin Dafydd, Cymdeithas yr Iaith Gymraeg, Gerard Finn, Swyddfa Comisiynydd Iaith Canada am eu parodrwydd i'm helpu deall agweddau o'r gwaith. Cefais adborth adeiladol ar fy syniadau wrth i mi gyflwyno seminar ar 'Hawliau dinesig a chomisiynydd iaith', sef seminar agoriadol cyfres Gwleidydd IAITH, Prifysgol Cymru, Aberystwyth. Diolch i Richard Wyn Jones, Adran Gwleidyddiaeth Rhyngwladol, am fy ngwahodd i siarad ar 4 Hydref 2005. Diolch hefyd i ddarllenydd anhysbys y wasg am nifer o sylwadau gwerthfawr.

NODIADAU

1   Gweler *www.coe.int/T/E/Legal_Affairs/Local_and_ regional_Democracy/Regional_ or_ Minority_languages.*
2   Gweler *www.opsi.gov.uk/acts/acts 1998/19980042.htm.*
3   Mae hanes datblygiad deddfwriaethol y Gymraeg yn dangos sut y dysgwyd o brofiad er mwyn dileu achosion o anghyfartaledd ieithyddol yn y sffêr gyhoeddus a chryfhau statws y Gymraeg dros gyfnod o amser. Caniataodd Deddf Llysoedd Cymru 1942 y defnydd o'r Gymraeg mewn llysoedd barn gan unigolion a fyddai o dan anfantais pe defnyddient y Saesneg. Fe gynyddodd Deddf Iaith 1967 statws y Gymraeg yn y llysoedd, a rhoi'r pŵer i weinidogion bennu fersiynau dwyieithog o ffurflenni swyddogol. Serch hynny, nid oedd y Gymraeg yn cael ei thrin yn gyfartal mewn bywyd cyhoeddus – a phrif amcan Deddf Iaith 1993 oedd unioni'r anghyfartaledd hwn (gweler Williams, 1989).
4   Serch hynny, mae Patrick Carlin wedi cynnig y sylw ei fod yn 'cytuno ei bod yn well pe bai pracsis y dydd yn gofyn am gychwyn unrhyw ddeddfu ar y Gymraeg drwy dorri cwys deddfu ar sail yr unigolyn, ond bod llunwyr rywsut yn dod yn fwyfwy ymwybodol o wedd fwy cyfannol i wead "pobl" a bod continwwm rhwng yr unigolyn a'r "gymuned". O gydnabod hyn, dw i'n cyfadde na fyddai'n fawr o dro nes i fater "tiriogaeth" frigo i'r wyneb ond dylid, dw i'n cytuno, ddadlau'n gryf yn erbyn hynny am y rheswm syml nad yw'n opsiwn synhwyrol, waeth beth yw barn y dydd am hyd a lled y "Fro Gymraeg". O ran cael y maen i'r wal a darbwyllo llunwyr, dw i ddim yn meddwl y byddai'n sut gymaint o naid ffydd iddyn nhw ymrafael â chyd-ddibyniaeth yr unigolyn a'r torfol. Oni fyddai hyn yn ei gwneud yn haws i "gyfateb y ddyletswydd o ddarparu gwasanaeth â'r hawl i dderbyn", drwy ddefnyddio dadl y "torfol sy'n amddiffyn yr unigolyn" yn yr union ieithwedd honno sydd mor hegemonig y dwthyn hwn.' (Carlin 2005, cyfathrebiad personol).
5   Yn dilyn penderfyniad y Llywodraeth i ohirio integreiddio'r Bwrdd ar ôl Ebrill 2007, bydd angen eglurhad ar sut yn union y bydd y Cynulliad a'r Bwrdd yn datrys yr amwyster a fydd yn perthyn i'r pŵerau hyn.
6   Papur gan y Bwrdd i Comisiwn Richard, gweler *www.bwrdd-yr iaith.org.uk/cy/ cynnwys.php?cID=1&pID=109&nID=109.*
7   Yn hyn o beth fyddai'n werthfawr iawn drafod 'iawnderau' rhieni sydd am i'w plant dderbyn addysg cyfrwng Cymraeg er mwyn iddynt gwybod beth yn union pa fath o ddarpariaeth fyddai pob awdurdod addysg yn cynnig iddynt.
8   Am y sefyllfa yng Nghanada gweler *www.ocol-clo.gc.ca*, ac am Iwerddon gweler *www.pobail.ie/en/Irish Language/Official Languages Act 2003/.* Bydd ymdriniaeth o Ganada, Iwerddon a Chymru yn ymddangos yn fy llyfr *Language and Governance* a gyhoeddir gan Wasg Prifysgol Cymru yn 2007.

9   Rwy'n deall, wrth gwrs, fod Quebec yn dra wahanol i Gymru, ond yr egwyddor sydd yn bwysig yma a'r cyfiawnhad dros warchod gan ddefnyddio'r gyfraith i sicrhau hawliau statudol. 'Every employee has the right to work in French. Enterprises having 50 or more employees must register with the Office québécois de la langue française and must produce an assessment of their linguistic situation. If French is not used at all hierarchical levels, the enterprise must implement a francization programme to make French the language for its operations and internal communication. In order that French be seen as important and valuable to learn, it must not be confined to private life or to low-level jobs within the hierarchies of Quebec enterprises. In other words knowledge of French must lead to well-paying jobs, including those in senior positions. If French cannot show that it is an indispensable tool in the workplace of Quebec, its ability to show its usefulness will decline rapidly to the benefit of English, particularly so among people who take up permanent residency in Quebec.' (*About Quebec's Language Policy*, 2003).

10 Fel ag y mae Patrick Carlin (2005) wedi nodi nid yw hyn yn ymddangos yn bell iawn o'r sefyllfa ym mhob un o ranbarthau ymreolus Sbaen lle mae angen 'Orden' oddi fry yn Cortes Madrid cyn bod trosglwyddo cymhwysedd arbennig i'r rhanbarth dan sylw. Yna, mae gweithrediadau'r rhanbarthau yn gallu cynhyrchu rheoliadau rif y gwlith fel y mynnan nhw, ar gefn yr 'Orden' cychwynnol. Gweler Gardner et al. (2000).

11 Carwn ddiolch wrth David Lambert am ei gymorth wrth fy nhywys trwy'r broses.

12 Wrth gwrs rwy'n derbyn mai Llywodraeth y Cynulliad, ac nid y Cynulliad, sydd yn gyfrifol am lunio polisi. Mae'n debyg y fydd y Cynulliad fel y cyfryw yn ymwneud yn fwy gyda deddfu yn y dyfodol, ac o ganlyniad yn debycach i Senedd yr Alban o ran rhaniad y cyfrifoldebau rhwng Senedd a chorff gweithredol (sef yr executive).

13 Sef y cymal sydd yn annog y Llywodraeth i hyrwyddo'r Gymraeg; gweler *www.wales-legislation.org.uk/scripts/format.php?lang=W*.

14 Er enghraifft, deddfwriaeth 'Deddf galluedd meddyliol' (2004). Mae'r Ddeddf Galluedd Meddyliol yn darparu fframwaith statudol i rymuso a gwarchod pobl ddiymgeledd na allant wneud penderfyniadau drostynt eu hunain. Mae'n nodi'n glir pwy sydd â'r hawl i wneud penderfyniadau, ym mha sefyllfaoedd a sut y dylent wneud hynny. Mae'n galluogi pobl i gynllunio ar gyfer cyfnod yn y dyfodol pan na fyddant o bosibl yn gallu gwneud penderfyniadau drostynt eu hunain. Yn ogystal mae'r ddeddf yn cwmpasu'r ystyriaethau canlynol: rhagdybiaeth ynghylch galluedd – mae gan bob oedolyn hawl i wneud ei benderfyniadau ei hun, a rhaid cymryd yn ganiataol ei fod yn gallu gwneud penderfyniadau drosto'i hun oni phrofir yn wahanol; hawl unigolion i gael cefnogaeth i wneud eu penderfyniadau eu hunain – rhaid i bobl gael pob cymorth priodol cyn i unrhyw un ddod i'r casgliad na allant wneud penderfyniadau drostynt eu hunain; bod rhaid i unigolion gadw'r hawl i wneud penderfyniadau a allai gael eu hystyried yn rhai ecsentrig neu annoeth; lles pennaf – rhaid i unrhyw beth a wneir ar ran pobl sydd wedi colli'r gallu i wneud penderfyniadau drostynt eu hunain fod er pennaf les iddynt; ac ymyriad lleiaf cyfyngol – dylai unrhyw ymyriad ar ran pobl nad ydynt yn gallu gwneud penderfyniadau drostynt eu hunain gyfyngu cyn lleied ag sy'n bosibl ar eu hawliau a'u rhyddid sylfaenol. Beth mae'r ddeddf yn ei wneud? 'Mae'r Ddeddf yn cynnwys mewn statud yr arferion gorau presennol ac egwyddorion cyfraith gwlad sy'n ymwneud â phobl nad ydynt yn gallu gwneud penderfyniadau drostynt eu hunain a'r rheini sy'n gwneud penderfyniadau ar eu rhan. Mae'n disodli'r cynlluniau statudol cyfredol ar gyfer atwrneiaethau parhaus

a derbynyddion y Llys Nodded gan roi cynlluniau sydd wedi'u diweddaru a'u diwygio yn eu lle. Mae'r Ddeddf yn ymdrin â sut mae'r sawl sy'n gofalu am bobl nad ydynt yn gallu gwneud penderfyniadau drostynt eu hunain, yn asesu eu galluedd ac Asesu diffyg galluedd meddyliol. Mae'r Ddeddf yn nodi un prawf clir er mwyn asesu a yw person yn abl i wneud penderfyniad penodol ar adeg benodol. Mae'n brawf sy'n seiliedig ar "benderfyniad penodol". Ni ellir rhoi'r label "analluog" ar unrhyw un o ganlyniad i gyflwr neu ddiagnosis meddygol penodol.' Awgryma fy nghyfaill Dr Wyn Bellin o Brifysgol Caerdydd fod hwn yn cynnwys y gallu i ddefnyddio'r Gymraeg o dan y fath amgylchiadau. Mae'n dilyn felly fod yna doraith o fesurau tebyg sydd yn ceisio grymuso'r unigolyn. Mater o ddehongliad, hyrwyddo ac wedyn ffurfioli'r broses o gynnwys y Gymraeg fel rhan annatod o'r fath ddeddfwriaeth yw hi.

15   Yr wyf yn ymwybodol fod llwyddiant cynnig yr wrth blaid bod y Cynulliad Cenedlaethol 'yn cyfarwyddo Llywodraeth Cynulliad Cymru i ohirio'r broses o uno Bwrdd yr Iaith Gymraeg â'r Cynulliad hyd nes bydd y Cynulliad yn cymeradwyo cynnig sy'n ymdrin yn foddhaol â gweithrediad swyddogaethau rheoliadol y Bwrdd a phwerau monitro cynlluniau awdurdodau addysg lleol ar gyfer hybu'r iaith' wedi creu cryn dipyn o ansicrwydd ynghylch yr achos hon. Gweler dadl plaid leiafrifol NDM2613 Jocelyn Davies (dwyrain de Cymru), Y Cynulliad Genedlaethol, 11 Hydref 2005. Diwedd Gorffennaf 2006 penderfynodd y Llywodraeth ohirio'r broses o uno.

CYFEIRIADAU

Carlin, P. (2005). Cyfathrebiad personol, 8 Hydref.

Cartwright, D. a Williams, C. H. (1982). 'Bilingual districts as an instrument in Canadian language policy', *Transactions of the Institutue of British Geographers*, 7, 474–93.

Commissioner of Official Languages (2005). *Annual Report 2004–5*, Ottawa: Office of the Commissioner of Official Languages.

Cymdeithas yr Iaith Gymraeg (2005). *Deddf Iaith Newydd: Dyma'r Cyfle*, Aberystwyth: Cymdeithas yr Iaith Gymraeg.

Gardner, N., Puigdevall i Serralvo, M. a Williams, C. H. (2000). 'Language revitalization in comparative context: Ireland, the Basque Country and Catalonia', yn C. H. Williams, (gol.) *Language Revitalization: Policy and Planning in Wales*, Caerdydd: Gwasg Prifysgol Cymru, tt. 311–61.

Gouvernment de Québec (2003). *About Quebec's Language Policy*, Dinas Quebec: Gouvernment de Québec.

Llywodraeth Cynulliad Cymru (2003). *Iaith Pawb: Cynllun Gweithredu Cenedlaethol ar gyfer Cymru Ddwyieithog*, Caerdydd: Llywodraeth Cynulliad Cymru.

Morgan, K. J. a Upton, S. (2005). 'The new centralism', *Agenda*, haf, tt. 29–31.

Osmond, J. (2005). 'Virtual parliament', *Agenda*, haf, tt. 25–8.

Swyddfa Cymru (1993). *Deddf yr Iaith Gymraeg 1993*, Caerdydd a Llundain: Swyddfa Cymru, gellir ei weld ar *www.swyddfa.cymru.gov.uk/languagescheme*, wedi'i gyrchu 5 Mai 1995.

Swyddfa Cymru (2005). *Papur Gwyn 'Gwell Trefn Lywodraethu Well i Gymru'*, gan Swyddfa Cymru, rhan o Lywodraeth y Deyrnas Gyfunol, 15 Mehefin, Caerdydd a Llundain: Swyddfa Cymru, gellir ei weld ar *www.swyddfa.cymru.gov.uk/ 2005/trefn_ lywodraethu_well_i_gymru*, wedi'i gyrchu 12 Tachwedd 2005.

Williams, C. H. (1989). 'New domains of the Welsh language: education, planning and the law', *Contemporary Wales*, 3, 41–76.

Williams, C. H. (1995). 'A requiem for Canada?', yn G. Smith (gol.), *Federalism: The Multiethnic Challenge*, Llundain: Longman, tt. 31–72.

Williams, C. H. (1996), 'Citizenship and minority cultures: virile participants or dependent supplicants?', yn A. Lapierre, P. Smart a P. Savard (goln), *Langauge, Culture and Values in Canada at the Dawn of the 21st Century*, Ottawa: International Council for Canadian Studies, tt. 155–84.

Williams, C. H. (2004a). *'Iaith Pawb: Iaith Braidd Neb'*, darlith gyhoeddus y sefydliad Cymreig ar faterion cymdeithasol a diwylliannol, Prifysgol Cymru, Bangor, 15 Mawrth. Gweler safle we y sefydliad am gopi o'r papur gellir ei weld ar *www.bangor.ac.uk/ wisca/site_english/conf_sem/wisca_essays/lecture_trans/January%202004%20Short% 20Contemporary%20Wales%20version.pdf*.

Williams, C. H. (2004b). 'Iaith pawb: the doctrine of plenary inclusion', *Contemporary Wales*, 17, 1–27.

Williams, C. H. (2005). *Deddf Iaith Newydd. Dyma'r Cyfle a'r Ymateb*, araith i gyfarfod Cymdeithas yr Iaith, Eisteddfod yr Urdd, Caerdydd, 30 Mai.

14. PERCEPTIONS OF WELSHNESS IN PATAGONIA

Carol Trosset, Jennifer Thornton and Douglas Caulkins

ABSTRACT

Ethnographic research was conducted in 2002 in the Welsh towns of Patagonia. Residents of these communities, with and without Welsh ancestry or language ability, provided insights into their perceptions of Welshness and the cultural identity and characteristics of the Welsh community in Chubut. Formal interviews conducted by the authors provided information about the ways Patagonians perceive both Welshness and their own identities. Cultural exchanges between Welsh speakers in Wales and Argentina create opportunities for Welsh Patagonians to reflect on the similarities and differences between the two groups.

STUDYING WELSH PATAGONIA

Most of the scholarly literature on the Welsh population in Patagonia, Argentina, has been written by researchers from Wales or of Welsh descent. The majority of it focuses on the history of 'The Colony'. From books such as Glyn Williams's *The Desert and the Dream* (1975), we learn of the 1865 arrival of the ship *Mimosa* in the Chubut region, the Welsh settlement of the area and the help the settlers received from the indigenous Tehuelche. There is also a historical literature in Spanish, written by Argentine scholars (some of Welsh descent). A good example would be Clery Evans's *John Daniel Evans: 'El Molinero'* (1994), an account of one of the major figures in the Welsh exploration and settlement of the Andes.

The literature analysing contemporary Welsh-Patagonian society is more limited. Glyn Williams's *The Welsh in Patagonia: The State and the Ethnic Community* (1991) is part history, part rural sociology. There are linguistic analyses of the Welsh spoken in Argentina, such as R. O. Jones (1984). And there are articles by both Welsh and Argentine scholars examining a variety of aspects of the Welsh situation in and influence on Chubut culture (cf. Bowen, 2002; Coronato and Gaviratti, 2003; Davies, 1995). Our study approaches Welshness and ethnicity differently – ours is not an historical study, and does not start with a particular aspect of culture already defined by others as Welsh, or focus on things popularly seen as representative features of either Wales or Welsh-Patagonia. Instead, we are concerned with how people alive today perceive Welsh culture and identity, including certain values and behaviours that we have identified and documented in contemporary Wales (Trosset, 1993; Trosset and Caulkins, 2001). The research presented here is part of our larger study comparing Wales and several Welsh-descended populations and their non-Welsh compatriots in Argentina, Australia and the United States.[1]

Between September and November 2002, Trosset and Thornton lived in Patagonia to observe and participate in the Welsh community there and to conduct interviews. Trosset speaks Welsh and Thornton Spanish. During our stay, we interviewed eighty-five people about their views of Welsh and Argentine culture. About two-thirds of the interviews were conducted in Gaiman, with others in Esquel, Puerto Madryn, Trelew and Trevelin. We spoke with Argentines with and without Welsh ancestry, Welsh speakers and non-Welsh speakers, and a few Welsh citizens living in Patagonia. The people we spoke with also varied with respect to sex, age, education level, occupation and their level of involvement in Welsh cultural pursuits. The formal interviews replicated questions that Trosset and Caulkins had asked in Wales and in other diaspora populations in the United States and Australia. Our understanding of local Chubut culture also came from many informal social interactions and from our participation in the communities we visited.

At the time of the 2001 Argentine census, the province of Chubut (where the Welsh towns are located) had a population of 413,237. Gaiman, with a population of 5,760, is widely considered the 'most Welsh' of the Welsh towns, and it was there that we spent most of our time. We did not obtain any current data on the number of Welsh speakers. However, in 1973 prominent local Welsh speakers who knew everyone on the Gaiman electoral roll calculated that '23 per cent of the Gaiman district were of Welsh extraction but only 15 per cent of the population spoke Welsh regularly' and that 'a third of all Welsh speakers [were] over 60 years of age' (Jones, 1984, p. 240). At the time of our visit in 2002, it was easy to find Welsh speakers but rare to encounter a first-language speaker under forty years of age. There are younger Welsh speakers, partly as a result of special programmes that teach Welsh in Patagonia and that send Patagonians to

Wales for intensive language study. Some learners become fluent and assume prominent roles in the Welsh-speaking community. Welsh speakers in Patagonia often, but not always, choose to speak Welsh together in the absence of non-Welsh speakers.

SCENARIO INTERVIEWS

Our interviews included a battery of twenty-one scenarios or short narratives from lived experience, dealing with the Welsh concepts of egalitarianism, emotionalism, martyrdom, nostalgia, performance (Trosset, 1993; Trosset and Caulkins, 2001) and two American concepts of individualism and achievement (Spindler, Spindler and Williams, 1991). Most of these scenarios were drawn from actual events observed during Trosset's and Caulkins' field experience in Wales. Each of the scenarios was printed on a separate card and the twenty-one cards were shuffled before each interview to avoid order bias. Next, each card was presented to the consultant and three questions asked: first, on a scale of 1 to 5, with 5 being the highest or most intense, how 'Welsh' is the behaviour in this scenario? Next, how 'Argentine' (or American or Australian) is the behaviour? Finally, how 'good or desirable' is the behaviour in the scenario?

Thus, for each scenario there are three ratings: Welshness, Argentineness and desirability. For example, here is a scenario measuring egalitarianism: a university professor has tea in his kitchen with the workers who are repairing his garden wall. A score of 4 or 5 would indicate that the person being interviewed considered this behaviour to be characteristically Welsh (or Argentine) or to be highly desirable, while a score of 1 or 2 would indicate the opposite. Some scenarios present behaviours that contradict the concepts, so that rejecting the scenario would confirm the Welshness or desirability of the concept being illustrated in those cases. Research participants are not asked to articulate the concept that informs a given scenario. Thus, we are not asking to invent or articulate some representation of 'Welshness', only to recognize a pattern that may be incorporated in cultural schema associated with the imagined community (Anderson, 1983) of Welsh people. Appendix A lists all twenty-one scenarios that we have used for interviews in Wales and diaspora populations.

We then use consensus analysis (Romney, Weller and Batchelder, 1986; Romney, Batchelder and Weller, 1987; Caulkins, 1998), a statistical technique that factor analyses the rows (rather than columns) of a person-by-concept matrix and compares the patterns of individual responses and measures the level of agreement or disagreement between them. We can imagine a variety of possible outcomes of consensus analysis for each of the three sets of rating by the Welsh and Welsh diaspora populations. The findings could include random, patternless responses, bimodal distributions, overlapping subcultures or high concordance agreement that we can call cultural patterns (Caulkins, 2004). When there are high levels of agreement, consensus analysis also provides us with a 'culture key' that describes what it is that people have agreed about (Borgatti, 1992; Caulkins et al., 2000).

Our overall results from Argentina are presented in Table 14.1 below, and are compared to results from Wales in Table 14.2. As Table 14.1 shows, we found single-culture agreement (conventionally interpreted as a ratio between the eigenvalues of the first and second factors greater than 3.0) for all three descriptions: Welshness, Argentineness and desirability. Single culture agreement, in other words, means that most of the variance in the data is explained by a single large factor. The rest of the factors are small in comparison. If we had encountered two large factors we would have interpreted this as a multicultural situation. Since we found single-culture agreement, we can examine the perspectives reflected in the composite 'culture key'. Appendix B gives the detailed culture keys for the responses from Argentina, while Table 14.1 shows what that key indicates about the seven concepts being examined.

Table 14.1
Overview of Argentine results

	Welshness	Argentineness	Desirability
Ratio between eigenvalues of factors 1 and 2	4.5	5.7	8.5
Egalitarianism	Mixed	Mixed	Yes
Martyrdom	Mixed	No	No
Emotionalism	Yes	Yes	Yes
Nostalgia	Yes	Yes	Yes
Performance	Mixed	No	Mixed
Individualism	No	Mixed	Yes
Achievement	Mixed	Mixed	Mixed

Egalitarianism is, then, seen as a good thing, but as only somewhat characteristic of either Welsh or Argentine culture. Martyrdom is seen as not good and not Argentine, but as somewhat Welsh. Emotionalism and nostalgia are seen as good, and as characteristic of both groups. The other concepts received mixed responses as described in the table. Differences in age, gender and town or region did not produce interesting or significant differences in perspective.

Table 14.2
Comparison of personhood results in Argentina and Wales

	Welshness as seen in Argentina	Welshness as seen in Wales	Desirability as seen in Argentina	Desirability as seen in Wales
Agreement ratio	4.5	3.8	8.5	4.8
Egalitarianism	Mixed	Yes	Yes	Yes
Martyrdom	Mixed	Yes	No	Yes
Emotionalism	Yes	Yes	Yes	Yes
Nostalgia	Yes	Yes	Yes	Yes
Performance	Mixed	Yes	Mixed	Yes
Individualism	No	Mixed	Yes	Mixed
Achievement	Mixed	Mixed	Mixed	Mixed

When we compare responses given by Argentines to those given by people living in Wales, we find both similarities and differences. Perceptions on emotionalism, martyrdom and achievement were very similar in both locations. However, the groups differed in their perceptions of martyrdom, performance and individualism. The interview results that provided these results will be discussed in more detail below.

Although we do not present them here, our interview data from the United States and Australia compare in interesting ways with results from Argentina and Wales. US, Australian and Welsh populations all have similar perceptions of Welshness. Americans and Australians, however, perceive Welshness as being very different from their own cultures. Argentines, on the other hand, differ more in their perception of Welshness as compared to how it is seen in Wales, but see Welshness and their own Argentine culture as quite similar. The fact that many of our research participants used Welsh Argentines instead of the Welsh in Wales as their reference for Welshness may help explain why Argentines perceived 'Welshness' and 'Argentineness' as being nearly identical. All four perceptions of what is desirable are quite similar overall. These degrees of similarity can be represented by correlation coefficients, as in Table 14.3. If two culture keys were exactly the same, the correlation coefficient would be +1.0, while if the two were exact opposites, the coefficient would be -1.0. (Caulkins, et al., 2005.)

Table 14.3
Correlations among perceptions

	Correlation between own perception of Welshness and of Welshness as seen in Wales	Correlation between own perception of desirability with desirability as seen in Wales	Correlation between own perception of Welshness and own perception of local culture
Argentina	+0.7	+0.92	+0.97
Australia	+0.89	+0.93	+0.25
United States (three sites)	+0.91 to +0.94	+0.88 to +0.93	-0.16 to +0.46

DIFFERENCES ARGENTINES SEE BETWEEN WELSH PATAGONIANS AND THE WELSH IN WALES

Our Argentine respondents did vary with respect to the levels of involvement they had with various aspects of local Welsh culture, including their Welsh-language ability, their ancestry and their participation in activities associated with Welshness. Some of their responses to the scenarios varied with these differences, which raises the issue of what population forms people's 'reference group' for thinking about who is considered 'Welsh'. Many Welsh Patagonians perceive Welshness through direct experience of the Welsh either in or from Wales. Thirteen individuals of the eighty-five we interviewed had sufficient contact with the Welsh in Wales (most by visiting Wales, sometimes to study the Welsh language there) that they explicitly used Wales as their reference group for our questions about Welshness. Some also considered this question by thinking about the visitors from Wales whom they had known in Chubut. Those without such experiences answered questions about Welshness by describing the Welsh-Patagonian community. In addition to our formal interviews, we often asked people in casual conversation about their views of similarities and differences between Welsh Patagonians and the Welsh in Wales.

Most Welsh Patagonians we spoke with felt that the Welsh in Wales and their descendants in Argentina were similar in that they shared some customs and cultural traits, such as drinking tea, the *eisteddfod* and the Welsh language. These similar traits result in a bond that some Argentine Welsh feel toward the Welsh in Wales, despite other cultural and nationalistic differences. It was common for Welsh Patagonians to say that they felt comfortable and 'at home' around Welsh people, and that the reverse was also true, due to basic cultural similarities. At the same time, almost everyone we interviewed described the Argentine Welsh as being identical to other Argentines, and therefore more different than similar to the Welsh in Wales. Some said that many immigrant groups maintain their particular customs, but that aside from certain customs the Argentine Welsh were no different from their fellow citizens. The Welsh in Wales, therefore, were generally seen as being quite distinct from the Welsh descendants in Argentina. While they shared some customs, and some of them shared a language, their nationality and other cultural traits distinguished them. The concepts explored by our interviews do a fairly good job of describing these perceived cultural differences.

Egalitarianism
The Welsh in Wales see themselves as very egalitarian, but the Welsh Patagonians do not see them that way. Those who answered our questions about Welshness by thinking about the Welsh in Wales described Welsh culture as more status-conscious and concerned with public opinion than Argentine culture. Though we heard few detailed anecdotes, we were frequently told that in Wales, people were very class-conscious and thought a lot about how different people were positioned in society.

Martyrdom and achievement
The Welsh Patagonians see themselves as more achievement-oriented than the Welsh in Wales, and tended to think about issues of self-sacrifice from a very pragmatic point of view.

The scenarios that made up our formal interview included a mother who makes personal sacrifices 'so that her not-very-talented daughter can continue her piano lessons'. While on average our respondents approved of mothers sacrificing for their children, Trosset found it far more common in Argentina than in Wales for people to talk in terms of a cost-benefit analysis. Some very culturally involved Welsh speakers remarked that this was 'a stupid thing to do, if the child had no talent', which contrasted sharply with the emotionally charged approval the scenario usually elicited in Wales. Another interview scenario describes a girl who puts little effort into and frequently skips her music lessons. In a similar contrast to our respondents in Wales, who simply expressed disapproval, many young Argentines told us that 'she should talk to her parents, and tell them she doesn't want to take lessons any more'.

The different histories of Wales and Chubut also lend themselves to a difference in emphasis, toward achievement and away from self-sacrifice. Another researcher studying Welsh Patagonia remarked to us that the colonial history of Chubut is unusual in that it presents stories of successful Welsh heroes, among them people who first explored the Andes and settled there. In Wales, many stories of heroic Welshmen from the past centre instead on their eventual failure to achieve their aims.

Emotionalism and nostalgia

Although the Welsh in Wales see themselves as very emotional (especially compared to the English), Patagonians sometimes describe them as 'cold'. As mentioned earlier, almost everyone interviewed considered the Argentine Welsh to be fully Argentine, and therefore *latinos*. The Welsh from Wales, on the other hand, were labelled *británicos*. As *latinos*, the Argentine Welsh were perceived as warm, open, passionate people. Research participants described Argentines generally as emotional, expressive and spontaneous. The two most common adjectives used to describe the Welsh, however, were *cerrados* and *fríos* – closed and cold. This reputation is ironic given that the Welsh see themselves as being emotional and warm people, especially compared to the English. In Argentina, by contrast, the Welsh were seen as much more reserved or even repressed, not so physical or demonstrative of affection. 'We kiss everyone', people said.

A small minority of research participants felt that the Argentine Welsh were just as *cerrados* and *fríos* as were the Welsh in Wales. These attributes were more closely associated with the 'old' generations. One non-Welsh Argentine stated that the old Welsh were cold and closed but the younger generation was indistinguishable from other Argentines. A few research participants, most of non-Welsh descent, thought that the modern Welsh descendants have continued to be less 'warm' than the typical Argentine. One of these stated that Welsh descendants were more serious, traditional and conservative. An Italian-Argentine described Welsh-descended Patagonians as more *cerrados*, guarded, not overly friendly, and 'false'. By false he meant that they would pretend to like someone when they did not, in order to comply with social expectations. Finally, one consultant of Welsh descent remarked that the Argentine Welsh were, like the Welsh in Wales, more reserved and quiet, despite being somewhat 'Latinized'.

Performance and individualism

Both groups see the Welsh in Wales as performance-conscious, while the Welsh Patagonians do not see themselves that way, but rather as more independent and less ruled by social convention. We were told that Welsh people in Wales are more likely to worry about what others think of them, and are therefore more likely than Argentines to obey their parents and to conform to the behaviour of those around them. Many Argentines we spoke with saw – and were somewhat critical of – the Welsh as more rigid and liking to have everything planned out and 'just so'. When describing this phenomenon in Welsh, they used the word '*twt*', a word suggesting neat, tidy, everything in its place – generally a positive notion in Wales. One young Welsh-Argentine who had spent considerable time in Wales was quite critical of what he saw as Welsh formality. He said that while in

Wales he felt that it was never acceptable to say what he really thought. Along similar lines, having lived in both places Trosset found Argentines generally more flexible about the ways in which we lived in and interacted with their communities than was usually the case in Wales.

Another of our interview scenarios describes a family loading their moving van in the back alley behind the house to prevent the neighbors from seeing their belongings. In Wales, many of Trosset's interviewees readily recognized this practice and the attitudes behind it, and one woman gave a lively pantomime of people peeking out from behind their curtains to see the things being moved. In Argentina this scenario was considered quite implausible; we were told that moving is a very public event where all the neighbours come and help and no one would attempt to hide their things from view.

Visiting language teachers from Wales were living in several Chubut towns during our stay. Their participation in local choirs gave us an opportunity to notice some differences between Welsh and Argentine performance practice. Singing and recitation in Wales are typically accompanied by very lively and exaggerated facial expressions. Patagonian members of choirs did not use this style – which resulted in a striking contrast between them and the few visiting Welsh men and women in the groups. One Welsh-Patagonian musician told us she did not like this Welsh style. She added that people in Wales are taught to act in ways that aren't real, and told us a story about a young Welsh singer with tremendous stage presence who turned out after the performance to be terribly shy and hard to talk to.

BEING ARGENTINE AS CENTRAL TO WELSH-PATAGONIAN IDENTITY

There is a Patagonian version of Welsh culture that is inclusive in ways unlike Welsh-language culture in Wales. Of the twenty-seven of our interviewees who were the most involved in local Welsh cultural activities, nine spoke no Welsh, and three of those had no Welsh ancestry at all. Many ethnic groups – even including the indigenous Mapuche – were represented among those taking Welsh lessons, singing in Welsh choirs and competing in the *eisteddfod*. Many prominent *eisteddfod* winners and organizers in Chubut do not speak Welsh, but feel no less involved because of that. Competitions at the Chubut *eisteddfod* include many Welsh-language genres, but also singing, recitation and poetry composition in Spanish and the performance of some regional Argentine dances. At the same time, there are usually visiting competitors (such as choirs) from Wales and the fact that these groups and many Chubut contestants share a common language and have learned the same music makes possible close interactions and joint music-making.

Even those people who were the most involved in Welsh cultural activities stressed that they were Argentine, not Welsh. During previous research in Wales, Trosset had encountered some tendency for Welsh speakers there to describe Welsh Patagonians as 'fully Welsh' and to expect them to feel nostalgia for Wales. Some of our research participants in Patagonia had also heard these views expressed by Welsh visitors, and sometimes experienced this assumption as a source of frustration. One older Welsh speaker expressed exasperation with Wales's lack of understanding of how the descendants of the Welsh colonists were Argentine. She mentioned that visitors from Wales expect her and other descendants to miss Wales, a country most have never even visited. She said that, being Argentine, they do not feel nostalgia for Wales but rather for Argentina; they get emotional when they see the Argentine flag and hear the Argentine national anthem. She explained, 'we like Welsh songs, but we like to hear tango and drink *mate* too!' Despite feeling an affinity for Wales and the Welsh people there, and taking an interest in their Welsh heritage, their identity and their loyalties lie with Argentina.

The older generation was the most insistent that they were not in fact Welsh, but rather Argentine. This is the generation that had to defend its 'Argentine-ness' during the hyper-nationalism and anti-British sentiment of the Peron years and during the Malvinas War. It was very common for older research participants to become confused when Welsh descendants were referred to as Welsh, and they would frequently respond by saying that they have been Argentine for quite some time now. One Welsh descendant in her eighties proudly declared that her grand-parents and parents were born in the Chubut and were true *chubutenses*; not Welshmen 'transplanted' to Patagonia. Another of our older research participants patiently explained to us that he and others of Welsh ancestry should not be referred to as *galeses* (the Spanish word for 'Welsh'), as there are no Welsh in Patagonia and the last immigration wave from Wales occurred a long time ago.

Another source of frustration and some tension occurs when the Welsh assume that Welsh nationalist issues exist in Patagonia as they do in Wales. Patagonians do not discuss the Welsh language in the same emotionally charged way that it often is in Wales. People value it, but no one we met appeared disturbed about its status, except visitors from Wales. While everyone we interviewed supported the younger generation learning Welsh, no one seemed upset if his or her children only spoke Spanish. It was more important to involve as many people as possible in Welsh activities, such as the *eisteddfod*. Most culturally Welsh activities are conducted bilingually and therefore do not exclude non-Welsh speakers. 'We're

Argentine, and Spanish is the language of the country', we were told. Some Welsh speakers showed a stronger emotional attachment to Spanish, such as one older woman who told us that Spanish is a nicer-sounding language than Welsh, characterizing it as more smooth and flowing. Several people expressed their concern that visitors from Wales sometimes emphasize the use of the Welsh language at the expense of open participation. For instance, the Welsh-only restriction on meetings and ceremonies of the *gorsedd* (a branch of the honorary order of poets, singers and other culturally important people in Welsh-speaking Wales, associated with the *eisteddfod*) was seen as problematic. First, many of the people being honoured at *gorsedd* ceremonies do not speak Welsh and thus do not understand what is going on during the ceremony, and the translation required during meetings takes a lot of time and slows down business. Furthermore, several members of the Chubut *gorsedd* worry that the Welsh in Wales do not understand that if the *gorsedd* is going to continue past this generation it needs to be bilingual, as there are almost no first-language Welsh speakers in the younger generation.

In conclusion, there are three major ways in which Welshness differs between Wales and Argentina. First, although their Welsh heritage is important to them and they value their ties with Wales, Welsh Patagonians self-identify as Argentine, not as Welsh. Secondly, although many Patagonians have a well-grounded understanding of Welsh culture due to continued contact between the two populations, they do not always perceive or describe it the same way people in Wales do. And finally, Welsh Patagonians really are different in some ways from the Welsh in Wales and have different priorities – both personally such as being more pragmatic and less performance-conscious, and ethnically, by focusing more on involvement in cultural pursuits than on the Welsh language.

APPENDIX A. THE SCENARIOS USED IN THE INTERVIEWS

Egalitarianism

1. A school teacher, while shopping, modifies her speech in an attempt to avoid sounding more educated than the shop employees.
2. A university professor has tea in his kitchen with the workers who are repairing his garden wall.
3. An employee of a firm is pleased because he wins a promotion that gives him authority over other workers.
4. A child is discovered in tears after receiving third prize in a local competition.

Martyrdom

5. A woman regularly buys gas at the higher of two available local prices, because the owner of that gas station is a member of the same religious denomination.
6. A mother, who needs a winter coat, goes without so that her not-very talented daughter can continue her piano lessons.
7. A person chooses a career and a place to live based on the opportunity they provide for a high salary and job advancement.

Emotionalism

8. A middle-aged man speaks with deep feeling about how moved he is by the words of a song.
9. A published letter from a reader of a newspaper asserts that one should argue social policy from the heart, not from the head.

Nostalgia

10. After five years in Buenos Aires, a bank clerk still feels a bit homesick every Sunday as he thinks about his parents and sister having dinner without him.
11. When an old couple dies, their adult children clear out the house before selling it, and toss old things like family photographs in the dustbin.

Performance

12. A family unloads their removal van after dark to prevent the neighbours from seeing their belongings.
13. At her parents' request, a small child stands on a kitchen stool, smiles at their family guests, and sings a song she recently learned at school.

Individualism

14. The youngest daughter in a family refuses to learn the piano like her older siblings and insists on playing a different instrument.
15. When given the choice, office workers decide to work on a project as a group rather than on their own.
16. Despite her dreams of becoming a lawyer, a young woman attends medical school at her parents' urging.
17. A man purchases an automobile similar to those of his associates at work.

Achievement

18. A young woman whose parents cannot afford to pay for her college education works her way through college with part-time jobs.
19. A primary school teacher rewards children who read the greatest amount of books in the shortest amount of time.
20. A young girl has music lessons every day but rarely puts much effort into them and will sometimes just skip class entirely.
21. A single man decides he doesn't have enough time to himself and quits his steady job for part-time work.

APPENDIX B. CULTURE KEYS FOR INTERVIEWS IN ARGENTINA

	Welshness	Argentineness	Desirability
1. speech	1.6	1.6	2.0
2. professor	3.4	3.4	4.3
3. promotion	3.5	3.9	2.8
4. third prize	2.9	3.2	2.1
5. gas	1.8	1.7	1.6
6. mother	3.7	3.7	4.3
7. career	3.8	4.0	3.6
8. song	3.8	3.6	4.7
9. article	3.4	3.5	3.8
10. homesick	3.8	4.0	4.1
11. photos	1.7	2.0	1.1
12. van	1.9	1.8	1.9
13. stool	3.8	3.5	3.6
14. different instrument	3.7	3.7	4.4
15. group	3.7	3.5	3.9
16. parents	2.4	2.8	1.2
17. auto	3.0	3.3	2.0
18. work	4.2	4.4	4.6
19. books	2.7	2.6	3.0
20. lessons	3.2	3.4	1.8
21. part-time	1.9	1.7	2.9

NOTE

[1] The field research for this project was carried out with the support of National Science Foundation grant BCS-0217156. We are grateful for the additional support of the Committee for the Support of Faculty Scholarship of Grinnell College, chaired by Dean Jim Swartz. We also wish to thank the many people who assisted and befriended us in Chubut.

REFERENCES

Anderson, B. (1983). *Imagined Communities: Reflections on the Origin and Spread of Nationalism*, London: Verso.

Borgatti, S. (1992). *Anthropac 4.0.*, Natick, Mass.: Analytic Technologies.

Bowen, G. (2002). 'Gorsedd y beirdd yn y Wladfa', *Cylchgrawn Llyfrgell Genedlaethol Cymru*, XXXII, Haf, 3, 317–36.

Caulkins, D. (1998). 'Consensus analysis: do Scottish business advisers agree on models of success?', in J. de Munck and P. Sobo (eds), *Using Methods in the Field: A Practical Introduction and Case Book*, Walnut Creek, Calif.: Altamira, pp. 175–95.

Caulkins, D. (2004). 'Identifying culture as a threshold of shared knowledge: a consensus analysis method', *International Journal of Cross Cultural Management*, 4, 3, 317–33.

Caulkins, D., Trosset C., Painter A. and Good, M. (2000). 'Using scenarios to construct models of identity in multi-ethnic settings', *Field Methods*, 12, 4, 267–81.

Caulkins, D., Offer-Westort, M. and Trosset, C. (2005). 'Perceiving ethnic differences: consensus analysis and personhood in Welsh-American populations', *Mathematical Anthropology and Cultural Theory*, November, *www.mathematicalanthropology.org/pdf/Caulkinsetal1005*.pdf, accessed 17 July 2004.

Coronato, F. and Gaviratti, M. (2003). 'New flag of the old dragon: the Welsh-Patagonian flag', *Flagmaster*, 110, Autumn, 14–15.

Davies, G. A. (1995). 'Wales, Patagonia, and the printed word: the missionary role of the press', *Llafur*, 64, 44–59.

Evans, C. A. (1994). *John Daniel Evans: 'El Molinero'*, Buenos Aires.

Jones, R. O. (1984). 'Change and variation in the Welsh of Gaiman, Chubut', in M. Ball and G. Jones (eds), *Welsh Phonology*, Cardiff: University of Wales Press.

Neumann, D. B. (2002). *Eisteddfod del Chubut: Cultura Galesa E Identidad Regional*, International Forum on the Welsh in Patagonia, Toronto, Canada.

Romney, A. K., Weller, S. and Batchelder, W. (1986). 'Culture as consensus: a theory of culture and informant accuracy', *American Anthropologist*, 88, 2, 313–38.

Romney, A. K., Batchelder, W. H. and Weller, S. C. (1987). 'Recent applications of cultural consensus theory', *American Behavioural Scientist*, 31, 2, 163–77.

Spindler, G., Spindler, L. and Williams, M. D. (1991). *The American Cultural Dialogue and its Transmission*, Bristol, Pa: Falmer.

Trosset, C. (1993). *Welshness Performed: Welsh Concepts of Person and Society*, Tucson: University of Arizona Press.

Trosset, C. and Caulkins, D. (2001). 'Triangulation and confirmation in the study of Welsh concepts of personhood', *Journal of Anthropological Research*, 57, 61–81.

Trosset, C. and Caulkins, D. (2002). 'Cultural values and social organization in Wales: is ethnicity the locus of culture?', in N. Rapport (ed.), *British Subjects: The Anthropology of Britain*, Oxford: Berg Publishers, pp. 239–56.

Williams, G. (1975). *The Desert and the Dream: A Study of Welsh Colonization in Chubut, 1865–1915*, Cardiff: University of Wales Press.

Williams, G. (1991). *The Welsh in Patagonia: The State and the Ethnic Community*, Cardiff: University of Wales Press.

15. THE WELSH ECONOMY: A STATISTICAL PROFILE

Jane Bryan, Max Munday and Neil Roche

INTRODUCTION

This article is the annual profile of the Welsh economy, and is in a similar format to the profiles in volumes 9–18 of *Contemporary Wales*. The analysis of the regional economy proceeds under the following headings: output, income and expenditure; labour markets, that is employment, unemployment and earnings; housing markets; and regional competitiveness. The table and figures presented in the article reflect information available to the end of 2005. In several of the statistical series examined there are lags brought about by ongoing methodological problems, and delays caused by survey requirements and compilation. For these reasons the commentary written in early 2006 often reflects data for 2003–4 or even earlier.

The review is undertaken at an interesting time. The institutional landscape of the region is changing with organizations such as Education and Learning Wales (ELWa), the Welsh Development Agency and Wales Tourist Board coming under direct Assembly Government control from April 2006. The period 2004–5 has also seen continuing pressure on the region's manufacturing sector with a string of large closures, particularly amongst inwardly investing companies from overseas. Despite problems in local manufacturing, the services sector has been more buoyant, with selected sectors seeing strong employment growth. Another key issue for 2006 is the scheduled end of the current programming period for European Union Objective 1 and Objective 3 economic aid funding, and with continuing uncertainty on the scope and scale of funding available for the 2007–13 period. Recent mid-term evaluations of the structural fund frameworks, coupled with continuing evidence of large gaps in access to economic opportunity across the region, point to important developmental challenges remaining. This is a theme that is picked up in several of the statistical series that are reviewed.

Where possible and appropriate, this review compares information for Wales with that from other Government Office Regions of the UK. Selected data are also reported at the Unitary Authority, or in some cases (output) at the NUTS3 level.[1] Readers should be aware that with greater disaggregation of statistical data there are greater problems of confidence in the data.

OUTPUT, INCOME AND EXPENDITURE

Gross value added (GVA) is an indicator of the economic activity being undertaken in a region, and is an important means of comparing the economic performance of one region with another. There are a number of problems with this measure of economic progress. Interestingly the Welsh Assembly Government acknowledges in recent strategic and consultation documents (for example, *A Winning Wales* and *Wales: A Vibrant Economy*) that there are problems with conventional measures of economic progress such as GVA, particularly in its failure to accommodate key elements of welfare. Notwithstanding these problems GVA continues to be the most important indicator of economic progress.

In 2004, Welsh GVA was £39.2bn or around 3.9 per cent of UK GVA, slightly less than Wales's population share of the UK. Welsh GVA grew by an estimated 4.5 per cent between 2003 and 2004 in nominal terms. The absence of regional deflators means that it is difficult to estimate real growth in regional GVA. Table 15.1 provides provisional information on GVA per head of the population for 2003 for Wales and other UK regions. Table 15.2 provides a further interesting perspective revealing differences in GVA per head across Wales. GVA per head in Wales was an estimated £13,292 in 2004. This was 21 per cent below the UK average. In terms of GVA per head, Wales is well below not only London and the south-east, but also below other regions. Low GVA per head levels in Wales compared to the UK average reflect factors such as relatively low economic activity rates, lower earnings (particularly in services sectors), and a relatively large number of employees in industries that are growing slowly at national and international levels. Of equal concern is how GVA per head levels vary within the region. Whilst GVA per head in Cardiff and the Vale of Glamorgan exceed average UK levels, in areas such as West Wales and the Valleys (the area currently qualifying for Objective 1 funding) GVA per head is around 34 per cent below the UK average.

Table 15.1

Regional accounts

	GVA per head 2004[1]		Household disposable income per head 2003		Individual expenditure per head[2] 2001–2/2003–4	
	£	% of UK	£	% of UK	£	% of UK
London	22,204	132.2	15,235	120.8	10,104	113.3
South-east	19,505	116.1	14,265	113.1	10,592	118.8
East	18,267	108.7	13,685	108.5	9,464	106.1
South-west	15,611	92.9	12,704	100.7	9,053	101.5
East Midlands	15,368	91.5	11,612	92.1	8,530	95.7
West Midlands	15,325	91.2	11,552	91.6	7,987	89.6
North-west	14,940	88.9	11,559	91.7	8,497	95.3
Yorkshire and Humber	14,928	88.8	11,462	90.9	8,263	92.7
North-east	13,433	79.9	10,787	85.5	7,363	82.6
England	17,188	102.3	12,952	102.7	9,105	102.1
Scotland	16,157	96.2	11,753	93.2	8,237	92.4
Northern Ireland	13,482	80.2	10,809	85.7	7,665	85.9
Wales	13,292	79.1	11,137	88.3	7,758	87.0
United Kingdom	16,802	100.0	12,610	100.0	8,918	100.0

Source: ONS see www.statistics.gov.uk/downloads/theme_social/Family_Spending_2003–04/
FamilySpending2003–04.pdf.
Note 1: Figures for GVA 2004 are provisional.
Note 2: Figures from the ONS *Family Spending Report* 2003/4, three-year average.

Table 15.2

Sub-regional accounts

	GVA per head 2003[1]		Household disposable income per head 2003	
	£	% of UK	£	% of UK
West Wales and the Valleys	10,578	66	10,929	86.7
Isle of Anglesey	8,747	54	10,944	86.8
Gwynedd	11,820	73	10,571	83.8
Conwy and Denbighshire	10,071	62	12,143	96.3
South-west Wales	9,659	60	10,526	83.5
Swansea	13,507	84	11,669	92.5
Bridgend and Neath-Port Talbot	11,094	69	11,196	88.8
Central Valleys	10,486	65	10,179	80.7
Gwent Valleys	9,531	59	10,684	84.7
East Wales	16,446	102	11,499	91.2
Flintshire and Wrexham	15,384	95	11,404	90.4
Powys	12,459	77	11,406	90.5
Cardiff and the Vale of Glamorgan	18,794	116	11,394	90.4
Monmouthshire and Newport	15,503	96	11,874	94.2
Wales	12,716	79	11,137	88.3

Source: Office for National Statistics/National Assembly for Wales.
Note 1: Figures for GVA 2003 (sub-regional areas) are provisional.

Differences in GVA per head link through to differences between Wales and other regions in household disposable income and spending. Clearly the difference between Wales and UK household income per head is smaller than that for GVA because social security and other transfer payments assist a large number of Welsh households. In 2003, household disposable income in Wales was £11,137 per head which was around 12 per cent below average UK levels, and close to levels in adjacent regions. Individual spending per head is based on a three-year average (2001–2/2003–4) and was £7,758, some 13 per cent below the UK average.

Figure 15.1 Recent trends in the Welsh and UK indices of production.

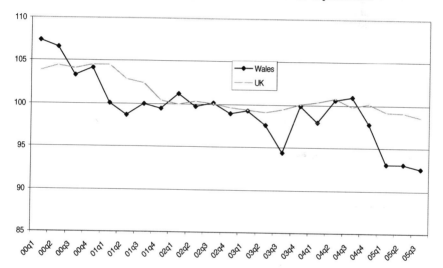

Source: Statistical Directorate, National Assembly for Wales.

The Index of Production for Wales provides one measure of movements in industrial output, and is one of the ways in which the strength of the regional economy can be assessed. The index of production includes information on manufacturing, mining and quarrying, and electricity, gas and water supply. Figure 15.1 shows the index of production for Wales, and then for the UK as a whole, for the period 2000 until the third quarter of 2005. The index of production for Wales fell by 8 per cent in the year to the third quarter of 2005. Of particular concern is how the recent performance of Wales has compared to the UK since the early part of 2004, with the region showing a sharp fall in industrial production, and with this fall almost wholly down to problems in manufacturing as opposed to other elements of the index. Then towards the end of 2005 the level of industrial production in the region was around 7 per cent below levels in 2002 (the index base year). The largest losses in manufacturing output in the year to 2005Q3 have been in sectors such as textiles, pulp and paper, machinery, electrical and general engineering. Of particular concern have been output losses in the inward investing sector with firms seeking to restructure and rationalize operations. In many cases this has led to production being moved to central and eastern Europe to take advantage of cheaper factor costs, particularly in sectors such as automotive components and electronic engineering. At the same time it has become far more difficult for Wales to attract new inward investment in an environment of increasingly tight competition from an enlarged European Union.

Table 15.3 shows that identifiable general government spending per head of the population for Wales was £6,901 in 2003–4. This was around 16 per cent above average English levels of government spending per head but below comparable figures for Scotland (£7,347) and Northern Ireland (£7,946). In comparison to England, Wales features relatively high levels of government spending per capita on general government services, enterprise and economic development, agriculture, forestry and fishing, environmental protection, and on recreation, culture and religion. Indeed spending per capita in Wales is only lower than in England on one category and this is science and technology related spending. This is an area of real concern as this potentially links through to very low levels of R&D spending in the region (see below).

EMPLOYMENT

This section focuses on comparative employment indicators and outlines particular concerns in areas such as participation rates. The focus then moves to factors that will influence future trends in employment.

Table 15.4 shows *Labour Force Survey* (LFS) data for employment by Government Office Regions. These figures are four-quarterly averages, seasonally adjusted, for the periods June 2003 to May 2004, and June 2004 to May 2005. Table 15.4 shows that the employment level in Great Britain remained stable over the year, rising by a modest 0.5 per cent to 26.5 million. The employment level for Wales fell slightly during this period by 0.9 per cent to 1.25 million.

Table 15.3

Identifiable general government expenditure on services by function: 2003–4

	£ per head				Index (UK identifiable expenditure = 100)			
	England	Scotland	Wales	N. Ireland	England	Scotland	Wales	N. Ireland
General public services	70	166	158	196	81	192	183	228
International services	0	–	–	–	119	0	0	0
Defence	0	0	–	1	117	–35	0	186
Public order and safety	356	360	367	692	97	98	100	189
Enterprise and economic development	85	109	269	222	85	108	268	221
Science and technology	25	32	14	10	102	128	57	42
Employment policies	65	181	73	21	88	245	99	29
Agriculture, fishes and forestry	74	145	106	258	85	166	121	296
Transport	271	341	220	210	99	125	81	77
Environment protection	88	220	119	274	83	207	112	258
Housing and community amenities	90	179	91	204	89	178	91	203
Health	1,225	1,456	1,345	1,367	98	116	107	109
Recreation, culture and religion	100	182	171	66	91	167	156	61
Education and training	1,013	1,102	1,047	1,322	98	107	102	128
Social protection	2,476	2,874	2,921	3,103	97	113	115	122
Total	5,938	7,347	6,901	7,946	96	119	112	129

Source: HM Treasury Public Expenditure Statistical Analysis 2005, www.hm-treasury.gov.uk/media/172/83/pesa2005 chapter8.pdf (pages 22–25).

Table 15.4
Employment: Wales, Great Britain and regions, labour force survey employment (thousands and rate[1])

	June 2003–May 2004						Jun 2004–May 2005					
	Male	Rate (%)	Female	Rate (%)	Total	Rate (%)	Male	Rate (%)	Female	Rate (%)	Total	Rate (%)
London	1873	76.6	1457	63.1	3330	70.1	1863	75.6	1464	62.8	3327	69.4
South-east	2107	84.0	1754	73.1	3861	78.7	2119	83.9	1774	73.5	3894	78.8
East	1419	84.1	1182	73.4	2601	78.9	1425	84.0	1191	73.5	2616	78.9
South-west	1249	82.6	1071	74.9	2320	78.8	1261	82.9	1070	74.5	2332	78.8
West Midlands	1294	78.4	1060	68.7	2354	73.7	1315	79.6	1073	69.5	2388	74.7
East Midlands	1067	80.6	891	71.2	1958	76.1	1069	80.5	896	71.4	1965	76.1
Yorkshire and the Humber	1228	78.4	1028	70.1	2256	74.4	1236	78.7	1031	70.1	2267	74.6
North-west	1626	77.3	1385	69.7	3010	73.6	1621	77.0	1389	69.8	3010	73.5
North-east	563	72.2	493	66.0	1056	69.2	566	72.7	504	67.5	1070	70.2
Scotland	1233	77.3	1091	71.2	2323	74.3	1242	77.9	1104	72.1	2346	75.1
Wales	678	75.9	586	69.1	1264	72.5	669	74.6	584	68.7	1253	71.7
Great Britain	14335	79.4	11997	70.1	26332	74.8	14387	79.3	12081	70.3	26468	74.9

Source: Office for National Statistics *Labour Force Survey* (from NOMIS).
Note 1: Denominator is all persons of working age.

Of particular interest, given the discussion on GVA per head figures in the second section, is the *employment rate*. This is the number of people in employment of working age as a percentage of all people of working age. Whereas in Great Britain the employment rate has remained steady over the year, rising only slightly from 74.8 per cent to 74.9 per cent, in Wales it fell from 72.5 per cent to 71.7 per cent. This means that compared to Great Britain as a whole, relatively fewer people in Wales are in, or seeking, work and this difference in participation has been widening. Underlying this participation (or *activity*) gap are such factors as higher levels of long-term sickness and early retirement, mainly in males, the latter resulting largely from a scarcity of opportunities in certain regions. Table 15.5 highlights the employment rates for males in Welsh unitary authorities (UAs). The lowest rates were found in Merthyr Tydfil (51.6 per cent), Blaenau Gwent (53.2 per cent) and Caerphilly (66.7 per cent). Schemes such as *Pathways to Work* and the £21 million *Want2Work* initiative have been put in place to target these problems. However, low participation rates in Wales compared to other UK regions remain a key ingredient of GVA per head differentials, and therefore will also remain a policy imperative.

Table 15.5
Male employment rate[1], Wales unitary authority, June 2004–May 2005

	%		%		%
Anglesey	75.0	Denbighshire	74.9	Powys	85.9
Blaenau Gwent	53.2	Flintshire	84.3	Rhondda Cynon Taff	71.7
Bridgend	74.5	Gwynedd	72.3	Swansea	72.0
Caerphilly	66.7	Merthyr Tydfil	51.6	Torfaen	73.9
Cardiff	79.1	Monmouthshire	79.9	Vale of Glamorgan	78.2
Carmarthenshire	79.3	Neath-Port Talbot	72.8	Wrexham	74.3
Ceredigion	72.4	Newport	74.5		
Conwy	76.1	Pembrokeshire	76.8		

Source: Office for National Statistics *Labour Force Survey* (from NOMIS).
Note 1: Denominator is male persons of working age.

The Welsh Development Agency (WDA) surpassed its overall job target for the financial year 2004–5 as set out in the Assembly Government's economic development strategy document *A Winning Wales*. A total of 41,550 jobs were claimed as created or safeguarded by the agency, which, through its business starts programme, helped to create 4,523 new enterprises during the year.

Table 15.6 shows the employment breakdown by industry sector in Wales and Great Britain for December 2003 and December 2004. These data are from the

Annual Business Inquiry (ABI). This survey was launched in April 2001 to supersede the *Annual Employment Survey* referenced in previous editions of *Contemporary Wales*. The table shows that there was a total of 26.0 million employee jobs in Great Britain in December 2004, an increase of 1.2 per cent from the previous December. Wales had a total of 1.16 million employees, a rise of 3.9 per cent in the year, the highest in any region. A relatively large proportion of the rise in Welsh jobs was in part-time work where male jobs increased by 10.2 per cent and female by 4.8 per cent. The equivalent increases in Great Britain as a whole were only 2.5 per cent and 1.3 per cent respectively. Workers in part-time jobs naturally tend to earn lower incomes and with Wales having a greater proportion of its employees only working part-time (34.5 per cent) compared to Great Britain (32.0 per cent), this is also a contributing factor to the relatively low levels of GVA per head described earlier.

Table 15.6
Employee jobs (000s) in Great Britain and Wales, by industry, 2003 and 2004

	Great Britain			Wales		
	2003	**2004**	**% change**	**2003**	**2004**	**% change**
Agriculture and fishing (SIC A, B)	226	233	3.0	13	14	9.8
Energy and water (C, E)	172	155	−9.8	8	7	−8.0
Manufacturing (D)	3,230	3,092	−4.3	179	177	−1.1
Construction (F)	1,138	1,178	3.5	47	53	12.7
Distribution and restaurants (G, H)	6,333	6,419	1.4	261	277	6.1
Transport and communications (I)	1,541	1,544	0.2	53	54	0.5
Banking, finance and insurance, etc (J, K)	5,054	5,193	2.7	132	136	3.0
Public administration, education and health (L, M, N)	6,681	6,872	2.9	368	381	3.4
Other services (O, P, Q)	1,336	1,338	0.1	56	62	11.6
Total	25,711	26,024	1.2	1,117	1,161	3.9
Total male	12,972	13,077	0.8	540	565	4.6
Male part time	2,028	2,079	2.5	88	97	10.2
Total female	12,739	12,947	1.6	577	596	3.3
Female part time	6,181	6,262	1.3	289	303	4.8

Source: ONS *Annual Business Inquiry* (from NOMIS).

Over the year to December 2004, male employment increased by 0.8 per cent in Great Britain and by 4.6 per cent in Wales, continuing the trend seen in previous reviews. Conversely, female employee jobs rose by 1.6 per cent nationally and 3.3 per cent in Wales. Table 15.6 also illustrates that employment in Welsh manufacturing fell by 2,000 jobs (1.1 per cent) between 2003 and 2004. This fall was not as severe as that experienced by Great Britain as a whole (where a 4.3 per cent fall in employment occurred over the year). In 2004 around 15.2 per cent of all jobs in Wales were in manufacturing compared to 11.9 per cent in Great Britain, making the region more vulnerable to any shocks in this sector.

Linking these figures to those reported in the index of production in Figure 15.1 would suggest that Wales will have lost a great deal of manufacturing employment when ABI data for 2005 become available. The summer of 2005 saw job losses at furniture manufacturer Christie-Tyler in Bridgend attributed to the greater availability of low cost imports into the UK. Another factor presently causing concern for domestic producers is escalating energy costs. Walkers Crisps cited the high price of fuel in 2005 as a major factor in the decision to close its Swansea plant with the loss of some 250 jobs. Impacts of rising fuel prices are likely to be stronger amongst areas on the geographic periphery, which also tend to be some of the less prosperous parts of Wales.

According to Table 15.6 nearly one-third (32.8 per cent) of employment in Wales in 2005 was in the non-market sector. This compares to just over a quarter (26.4 per cent) of all employment in Great Britain within this sector. The construction industry in Wales saw the highest proportionate increase in employment with a 12 per cent rise in the workforce between 2003 and 2004. Jobs in the distribution, retail and restaurant/hotel sector grew by 6 per cent, or some 16,000 jobs, over the same time period, whilst the banking, finance and insurance sector in Wales experienced growth of 3 per cent, or 4,000 jobs.

A cause for concern regarding the quality of Welsh employment growth is the relatively low levels of research and development (R&D) spending in the region compared to the rest of the UK. While observers have stressed the importance of innovation and producing niche products to increase Welsh competitiveness, the latest published ONS figures (for 2003) show that R&D investment in Wales amounted to £482m, or just 2.4 per cent of the UK total,[2] despite the region accounting for around 5 per cent of the UK population.

Attracting foreign direct investment (FDI) became an important policy objective in Wales as a panacea to job losses in older manufacturing and resource-based industries. With the recent growth in the location competitiveness of eastern European nations, the impact and future role of FDI in Wales has again been brought to the fore. Table 15.7 shows employment numbers in foreign-owned manufacturing from the *Welsh Register of Manufacturing Employment*. This shows that there were 61,900 workers employed in some 312 overseas-owned manufacturing plants in Wales in 2003, and represents a drop in employment of 6,100 workers and 8 plants from figures published for 2001. Wrexham accounted for 9.7 per cent of all foreign-owned manufacturing company jobs in Wales, Flintshire 9.2 per cent and Rhondda Cynon Taff 9.0 per cent. Since 2003, Wales has experienced further job cuts by foreign investors producing goods at the twilight stage of their product life. For example, Sony and Panasonic ceased to manufacture traditional cathode-ray tube televisions in south Wales, which had the knock-on effect of the closure of operations for their supplier, Nippon Electric Glass, in Cardiff. This latter event was a reminder that, in addition to the figures shown in Table 15.7, a number of extra jobs are dependent on the existence of FDI in Wales through the supply chain.

Table 15.7
Foreign-owned manufacturing companies in Wales: enterprises and employment

	1981	1988	1996	2001	2003
Number of enterprises	144	236	314	320	312
Employment (000s)	45.4	51.3	75.4	68.0	61.9

Source: Welsh Register of Manufacturing Employment.

Welcome news for Wales came with the announcement by Irish conglomerate the Quinn Group that it was to base its European radiator manufacturing site in Newport at the former LG Philips location, and with the continuing success story of Airbus in Broughton, which revealed in January 2006 plans to create a further 650 jobs.

Future employment prospects for the Welsh economy should be improved as the impact of European Objective 1 funding continues to filter through. Since being awarded Objective 1 status for the period 2000–6 a total of 1,628 projects have been approved for the West Wales and the Valleys area. This is associated with a total of £1.26bn being approved in grants as of January 2006, and includes spending on schemes to carry out infrastructure improvements, raise the skill levels of the workforce and engender greater entrepreneurship. Employment in the Objective 1 qualifying area (West Wales and the Valleys) increased by 20,000, or 3.1 per cent, from 2003 to 2004.

UNEMPLOYMENT

In historical terms unemployment rates in Wales during 2004–5 have been very low, with the region succeeding in closing the unemployment gap with the rest of the UK. However, disparities still exist in some areas of Wales along with persistent high rates of inactivity, or hidden unemployment.

Table 15.8 shows regional unemployment rates. These are claimant count rates, calculated by expressing the total number of unemployment related benefit claimants of an area as a percentage of workforce jobs plus the claimant count. The workforce denominators have recently been updated using the mid 2004 population estimates published by ONS to improve the accuracy of the calculated rates. Following the relatively high unemployment figures experienced in the UK at the start of the 1990s (where average yearly rates of over 9 per cent were seen), a sustained fall in claimant count rates were observed up until 2004. Table 15.8 highlights that in the period 1995 to 2004 the average unemployment rate for the UK dropped from 7.6 per cent to 2.7 per cent, with this pattern being mirrored in each of the regions.

The differential between the Wales and UK jobless percentages gradually diminished in the period after 1999. In Wales, the average annual unemployment rate fell to 3.0 per cent in 2004, close to the UK average. A mark of the relative success of Wales in curbing unemployment over this period can be seen in the fact that in 1995, only three regions had higher average rates than Wales, whereas by 2004 this had increased to five regions.

There was a slowdown in the UK economy during 2005 partly a result of a fall in consumer spending in the face of higher levels of household debt and pension worries, and more importantly a slowdown in some of the UK's main trading partners, particularly in the Euro-zone. Inevitably this has started to impact upon the regional jobs market, and Table 15.9 reveals a rise in claimants in nearly all regions over the year to December 2005. For example, in the North West claimant numbers grew by 12,500 whilst the highest proportionate increases in unemployment were experienced in Yorkshire and Humber, the West Midlands (both up nearly 20 per cent), and the East Midlands (up 15 per cent). Wales experienced an increase in claimants of 5,200 (a leap of 13 per cent) over the year. By gender, unemployed males in the UK increased by 61,100 to 665,100 over the year, with females rising by 21,800 to 227,800. The proportion of females in the total number unemployed increased in the UK (to 25.5 per cent of the total) but decreased in Wales (to 23.6 per cent).

When examining comparative unemployment levels it is important to study the relative length of time claimants have spent out of work. Structural changes in the Welsh economy, such as the decline of traditional industries, have given rise to persistent pockets of high long-term unemployment, particularly amongst males. Table 15.10 shows the duration of male unemployment experienced throughout the UK regions in December 2005.

Table 15.8

**Annual average unemployment rates, Wales, United Kingdom and regions
All persons, claimant count seasonally adjusted 1993–2004**

	1995	1996	1997	1998	1999	2000	2001	2002	2003	2004
South-east	5.6	4.9	3.3	2.6	2.3	1.9	1.6	1.6	1.7	1.6
Eastern	6.2	5.7	4.0	3.2	2.9	2.4	2.0	2.1	2.1	2.0
London	8.9	8.3	6.3	5.1	4.5	3.7	3.3	3.6	3.7	3.5
South-west	6.5	5.8	4.1	3.4	3.0	2.5	2.1	1.9	1.9	1.6
West Midlands	7.7	6.8	5.2	4.5	4.4	4.0	3.7	3.5	3.5	3.3
East Midlands	7.1	6.4	4.7	3.9	3.6	3.4	3.1	2.8	2.8	2.5
Yorkshire and the Humber	8.1	7.4	6.0	5.4	5.0	4.3	3.9	3.6	3.4	2.9
North-west	8.1	7.4	5.8	5.1	4.6	4.1	3.7	3.5	3.2	2.9
North-east	10.8	9.6	7.7	7.0	7.0	6.3	5.6	5.1	4.5	4.0
Scotland	7.5	7.2	6.0	5.4	5.0	4.5	4.0	3.9	3.8	3.5
Northern Ireland	11.2	10.6	8.0	7.3	6.3	5.3	4.9	4.4	4.2	3.6
Wales	8.1	7.6	6.1	5.4	5.0	4.4	4.0	3.6	3.3	3.0
United Kingdom	7.6	7.0	5.3	4.5	4.1	3.6	3.2	3.1	3.0	2.7

Source: Office for National Statistics, *Labour Market Trends.*

Table 15.9
Unemployment Wales, United Kingdom and regions, claimants, thousands, not seasonally adjusted, December 2004 and December 2005

	December 2004			December 2005		
	Male	Female	Total	Male	Female	Total
South-east	49.3	17.8	67.1	56.1	20.1	76.2
East	39.0	14.8	53.8	43.9	16.4	60.3
London	112.7	44.6	157.3	117.4	48.6	166.0
South-west	29.3	11.0	40.3	31.8	11.5	43.3
West Midlands	62.5	20.7	83.2	75.7	24.0	99.7
East Midlands	36.2	13.4	49.6	42.1	15.3	57.4
Yorkshire and the Humber	52.3	16.4	68.7	62.7	19.9	82.6
North-west	71.7	21.7	93.4	80.9	25.0	105.9
North-east	34.5	9.8	44.3	36.4	10.5	46.9
Scotland	65.7	20.3	86.0	63.8	19.9	83.7
Northern Ireland	21.5	6.3	27.8	20.9	6.3	27.2
Wales	29.3	9.2	38.5	33.4	10.3	43.7
United Kingdom	604.0	206.0	810.0	665.1	227.8	892.9

Source: Office for National Statistics (from NOMIS).

Table 15.10
Male unemployment by duration: Wales, United Kingdom and regions, December 2005

	Unemployed for over 52 and up to 104 weeks	Unemployed for over 104 weeks	Percentage claiming over 1 year
South-east	5,220	2,225	13.3
East	4,290	1,765	13.9
London	15,365	7,325	19.5
South-west	2,480	1,060	11.2
West Midlands	8,370	4,615	17.2
East Midlands	4,340	1,935	14.9
Yorkshire and the Humber	5,440	2,080	12.1
North-west	7,620	3,580	13.9
North-east	3,645	1,630	14.6
Scotland	6,430	3,460	15.6
Northern Ireland	3,065	1,740	23.3
Wales	2,800	1,545	13.1
United Kingdom	69,065	32,960	15.4

Source: Office for National Statistics (from NOMIS).

In Wales, the proportion of claimants who had been out of work for more than one year was 13.1 per cent, below the level found in the UK as a whole (15.4 per cent). For most regions the amounts of long-term unemployed had dropped year on year from December 2004. The UK percentage of those claiming unemployment related benefits for more than one year in December 2004 had been 16.7 per cent, and in Wales 15.0 per cent. The only two regions that had experienced an increase in the proportion of long-term claimants were the East (from 13.8 per cent in December 2004 to 13.9 per cent in December 2005) and the North East (13.9 per cent to 14.6 per cent). In December 2005 the highest proportions of long-term unemployed were found in Northern Ireland (23.3 per cent) and London (19.5 per cent).

The figures examined so far would seem to suggest that Wales has overcome most of its past difficulties with joblessness. However, serious disparities remain at the sub-regional level. Table 15.11 shows the claimant count numbers and rates for UAs. To prevent distortions caused by commuting patterns the rates here are the claimant count expressed as a proportion of the local resident (not workforce) population of working age.

Table 15.11

Unemployment by unitary authority and Wales, unadjusted, resident base, December 2005

	Male Number	Rate	Female Number	Rate	All Number	Rate
Anglesey	976	4.6	314	1.6	1,290	3.2
Blaenau Gwent	1,346	6.3	391	2.0	1,737	4.2
Bridgend	1,498	3.7	477	1.3	1,975	2.5
Caerphilly	2,354	4.4	750	1.5	3,104	3.0
Cardiff	3,897	3.7	1,028	1.0	4,925	2.4
Carmarthenshire	1,637	3.1	515	1.0	2,152	2.1
Ceredigion	492	2.0	200	0.9	692	1.4
Conwy	1,165	3.6	337	1.1	1,502	2.4
Denbighshire	988	3.5	333	1.3	1,321	2.4
Flintshire	1,357	2.8	503	1.1	1,860	2.0
Gwynedd	1,356	3.7	422	1.3	1,778	2.6
Merthyr Tydfil	960	5.6	245	1.5	1,205	3.6
Monmouthshire	513	1.9	216	0.9	729	1.4
Neath-Port Talbot	1,718	4.1	507	1.3	2,225	2.7
Newport	1,882	4.4	558	1.4	2,440	2.9
Pembrokeshire	1,209	3.5	464	1.4	1,673	2.5
Powys	922	2.3	362	1.0	1,284	1.7
Rhondda Cynon Taff	2,814	3.9	876	1.3	3,690	2.6
Swansea	2,821	4.0	796	1.2	3,617	2.6
Torfaen	972	3.5	282	1.1	1,254	2.3
Vale of Glamorgan	1,252	3.4	327	0.9	1,579	2.2
Wrexham	1,236	2.9	398	1.0	1,634	2.0
Wales	33,365	3.6	10,301	1.2	43,666	2.5

Source: Office for National Statistics (from NOMIS).

Unemployment amongst the Welsh UAs was highest in Blaenau Gwent, where 4.2 per cent of the resident population of working age were claimants, and Merthyr Tydfil, where the proportion was 3.6 per cent. When comparing changes in unemployment over the year only three UAs in Wales saw a fall in the rate: Anglesey (from 3.4 per cent in December 2004 to 3.2 per cent in December 2005); Gwynedd (2.7 per cent to 2.6 per cent); and Pembrokeshire where developments in the energy sector (Dragon LNG at Milford Haven) were seen as making an important contribution to the rate falling from 2.8 per cent to 2.5 per cent. Unemployment rates increased in the majority of UA areas in the year to December 2005. In Cardiff the rate rose from 2.1 per cent to 2.4 per cent, Swansea saw a climb from 2.2 per cent to 2.6 per cent, Wrexham 1.6 per cent to 2.0 per cent, and Newport an increase from 2.4 per cent to 2.9 per cent.

The figures examined in this section so far have not taken into account those people who were *economically inactive*, that is those who are neither in employment or unemployed such as persons with a long-term sickness. The economic inactivity rate (working age) is the number of people who are economically inactive aged 16 to 59/64, expressed as a percentage of all working age people. Table 15.12 shows economic inactivity rates for regions and then Welsh UAs. These figures give an indication of the extent of 'hidden' unemployment existing within the areas. A higher rate of inactivity was found in Wales (24.8 per cent) when compared to Great Britain (21.3 per cent), with only the north-east and London experiencing higher average rates over the reference time period (both at 25.3 per cent).

Closer to home and of particular concern were high proportions of inactivity found in the Welsh UAs of Merthyr Tydfil and Blaenau Gwent. For both of these areas the four-quarter average economic inactivity rates for June 2004 to May 2005 were above 40 per cent. Worryingly, the likelihood that such high rates may prove difficult to reverse was given credibility by Labour Force Survey results published by ONS in April 2005. These showed that the majority of the economically inactive in Wales had no desire to work and that only Northern Ireland and the North West of England had a higher proportion of economically inactive not wishing to join the workforce.

With the economic conditions still fragile in the UK, some commentators are predicting an increase in unemployment to around the one million mark nationally in 2006. Restraining unemployment levels in Wales during the near future may prove a difficult objective to achieve.

Table 15.12

Economic inactivity rates Great Britain, regions and Wales unitary authorities, combined males and females, June 2004–May 2005

Government office region	Rate	Unitary authority	Rate
South-east	18.1	Anglesey	22.5
East	18.0	Blaenau Gwent	41.0
London	25.3	Bridgend	24.1
South-west	18.4	Caerphilly	32.3
West Midlands	21.4	Cardiff	21.4
East Midlands	20.5	Carmarthenshire	22.1
Yorkshire and the Humber	21.8	Ceredigion	27.4
North-west	23.0	Conwy	24.1
North-east	25.3	Denbighshire	17.7
Scotland	20.3	Flintshire	20.5
Wales	24.8	Gwynedd	23.9
Great Britain	21.3	Merthyr Tydfil	41.9
		Monmouthshire	21.3
		Neath-Port Talbot	23.6
		Newport	25.7
		Pembrokeshire	27.4
		Powys	14.9
		Rhondda Cynon Taff	25.3
		Swansea	30.2
		Torfaen	24.5
		Vale of Glamorgan	21.5
		Wrexham	25.9

Source: ONS *Labour Force Survey* quarterly, four quarter averages (NOMIS).

EARNINGS

In October 2004, the Office of National Statistics (ONS) replaced the *New Earnings Survey* (NES) with the *Annual Survey of Hours and Earnings* (ASHE). The new methodology has been designed to reduce biased estimates by weighting the responses to the population of employees, and through handling more accurately the effect of job changes occurring between sample selection and survey. Unfortunately, these alterations have resulted in discontinuities in earnings statistics, which means that no direct comparisons can readily be made between earnings data published in previous profiles of the Welsh economy and the data referred to in the current review.

Changes to the typical occupational structure of regions also tend to make historical comparisons more difficult. ASHE 2005 data for occupation is coded to Standard Occupational Classification (SOC) 2000 which was introduced in 2002 (ONS, 2005), and this is used in this review.

In Wales the established policy challenge of recent decades has been to halt the decline of incomes relative to the UK average. It has been Wales's poor earnings performance coupled with low activity rates that contributed in large measure to much of the region's qualification for the top level European structural funding (Objective 1). The previous earnings profile in *Contemporary Wales* used 2002 NES figures and showed that Wales lagged behind most regions, and with few signs of pay gaps narrowing. According to those figures Wales had the highest shares of male employees in low-paid jobs, while the earnings of manual male workers were below the Great Britain average. Alarmingly, up until then, male manufacturing workers' earnings in Wales had been on a par with other parts of Great Britain – partly held up by relatively high pay in the steel, automotive and chemicals sectors. The 'positive' effect of these sectors is now much reduced with previous sections of this review demonstrating falling employment in precisely those sectors where regional pay levels are closer to national averages.

The ASHE shows that average gross weekly earnings in the UK[3] are now £431 for full-time employees, up 2.8 per cent in the year to April 2005. Gross weekly earnings for full-time women increased by 4.2 per cent compared to a 2.5 per cent rise for men. In Wales, average gross weekly earnings increased by only 2.1 per cent in the year to April 2005; male earnings rose by 1.9 per cent from £418 to £426, and female earnings rose by 4.4 per cent from £321 to £335. Hence, while the earnings gap between Wales and the UK widened, the gender gap narrowed over the year *within* Wales.

The employment section of this review demonstrated that part-time male employment in Wales had risen by around 10 per cent between 2003 and 2004, with female part-time employment rising by just under 5 per cent, these being amongst the largest rises in the UK. The relative contribution of part-time opportunities has then increased. The ONS observe that the ratio of part-time to full time earnings has been steady in the country since the late 1990s (ONS, 2005). However, the female ratio is 67.8 per cent compared to 57.5 per cent for men, so a relative gain in male part-time employment at the expense of full-time male employment (as opposed to unemployment) could be disadvantageous to Wales in terms of pay differentials with other regions. However, the 2005 ASHE figures suggest that over the year part-time males in Wales experienced an increase of just under 20 per cent representing a significant catch-up from a low base by UK standards.

An occupational breakdown for earnings for Wales and UK is given in Table 15.13. The table reveals that Wales performs better in some occupations than others, relative to the rest of the UK. For example, in professional occupations, and skilled trade occupations, Welsh pay is close to the UK average. However, managers and senior officials are only paid around 86 per cent of the UK average. Relatively low earnings in administration and secretarial (90.7 per cent of the UK average) and process plant and machine operatives (96 per cent of the UK average) are also in evidence, particularly as the latter category was one where pay levels were close to UK averages.

Table 15.13
Average (median) weekly earnings: Wales and UK, £s, all industries and services. Full-time males and females adult rates, April 2005

| | United Kingdom | | | Wales | | |
	All	Male	Female	All	Male	Female
All	431.2	471.5	371.8	389.9	425.7	334.8
Managers and senior officials	632.4	687.1	528.2	543.8	580.7	469.9
Professional occupations	633.4	670.8	598.6	625.2	637.3	616.8
Associate professional and technical	498.3	525.7	468.9	477.9	490.6	458.7
Administrative and secretarial	325.7	351.0	316.9	295.5	327.0	291.0
Skilled trades occupations	402.5	411.2	276.0	397.4	403.2	316.6
Personal service occupations	283.6	312.2	275.0	263.3	287.5	257.9
Sales and customer service	256.8	275.9	245.1	241.9	249.7	236.2
Process, plant and machine operatives	370.6	382.0	269.9	355.7	374.0	271.1
Elementary occupations	289.5	311.0	237.0	278.7	293.0	236.5

Source: Annual Survey of Hours and Earnings (ASHE) 2005 ONS.

Table 15.13 also focuses on gender differences in earnings by occupation. The first row shows that the *all occupation* earnings for both males and females in Wales at £389.9 is around 90 per cent of the UK average. The table allows analysis of where male and female earnings diverge as a result of occupation. Female professionals in Wales are achieving above UK average earnings for their gender, while male professionals earned below the UK average. The limited presence of females in the professions and indeed skilled trades occupations in Wales, where females also fare relatively well, means that their good relative earnings will impact little on overall averages. A key need for the regional economy is more employment in the higher paid occupations.

Male earnings in Wales are lower than the UK average for every occupation, being the closest in skilled trades (98 per cent of UK), and process plant and machine operatives (97 per cent of UK), but sadly well adrift in the higher paid managerial and senior occupations (only 85 per cent of the UK average). Table 15.14 uses data from the *Labour Force Survey* (four-quarter average June 2004 to May 2005) to calculate employment shares in each occupation category. Note the relatively high proportion of employment in Wales found in low-skilled 'elementary' occupations (13.5 per cent of all jobs), compared to the UK as a whole (where the figure was 11.6 per cent). Meanwhile, a relatively low proportion of employment in Wales is to be found in managerial, professional and technical occupations for which the rewards are much higher.

Table 15.14
Average gross weekly earnings and employment breakdown by occupation, Wales and UK

Occupation	UK Average gross weekly earnings £	% of all employment	Wales Average gross weekly earnings £	% of all employment
Managers and senior officials	632.4	15.0	543.8	13.5
Professional occupations	633.4	12.4	625.2	10.8
Associate professional and technical	498.3	13.9	477.9	12.0
Administrative and secretarial	325.7	12.6	295.5	12.0
Skilled trades occupations	402.5	11.4	397.4	12.8
Personal service occupations	283.6	7.7	263.3	7.8
Sales and customer services	256.8	8.0	241.9	8.8
Process plant and machine operatives	370.6	7.4	355.7	8.8
Elementary occupations	289.5	11.6	278.7	13.5
All occupations	431.2	100.0	389.9	100.0

Source: Earnings: *Annual Survey of Hours and Earnings* (ASHE) 2005, ONS. Employment: Labour Force Survey, quarterly: four quarter averages: June 2004 to May 2005, ONS (from NOMIS).

Table 15.15 gives earnings data for males and females by broad industry groupings for the UK and Wales. In 2002 it was reported in *Contemporary Wales* that the relative fortunes of both manual and non-manual male Welsh workers had deteriorated. It was of particular concern that Welsh male production workers were no longer being paid close to the national average, where previous reviews had been able to report slightly higher than average earnings. While direct comparisons cannot be made, Table 15.15 demonstrates that for *all industries and services* male earnings in Wales were 90.3 per cent of the UK average. While the difference is smallest with respect to manufacturing (96.7 per cent) it does nonetheless suggest that the region appears to have lost some of the contribution made by well-paid male manufacturing employment to creating wages parity. Given the increasing share of employment in services at the expense of manufacturing activities it is alarming that male earnings in Wales are only 87.6 per cent of the UK in this (fastest growing) sector. Moreover, the same earnings disadvantage applies to female employment in services.

Table 15.15
Average (median) gross weekly pay (£) by broad industry groupings, full-time employees[1],
United Kingdom and Wales, 2005

	Males			Females			All		
	UK	Wales	%UK	UK	Wales	%UK	UK	Wales	%UK
All industries and services	471.5	425.6	90.3	371.8	334.8	90.0	431.2	389.8	90.4
All index of production industries	464.3	446.6	96.2	339.6	324.9	95.7	437.9	419.3	95.8
All manufacturing	460.0	444.8	96.7	336.0	322.0	95.8	434.1	418.4	96.4
All service industries	476.7	417.8	87.6	376.7	335.9	89.2	427.6	376.8	88.1

Source: *Annual Survey of Hours and Earnings* (ASHE) 2005.
Note 1: Employees on adult rates whose pay for the survey pay-period was not affected by absence.

Table 15.16 provides average (median) gross weekly earnings by local authority for 2005. This table is included with some concerns because data becomes statistically less reliable for small areas. This noted the table confirms expectations that differences in earnings *within* Wales remain as established as those *between* Wales and other UK regions. Higher average weekly earnings (above the Welsh average) occur in Flintshire, Vale of Glamorgan, Neath-Port Talbot, Monmouthshire and Bridgend. Towards the bottom of the (all) earnings rankings are Pembrokeshire and Powys. Earnings by gender show no consistent pattern with, for example, female earnings in Powys being 88 per cent of the Welsh average while male earnings there are 94 per cent of the Welsh male average. Meanwhile in Cardiff female wages are 6 per cent above the Welsh female average, whilst male earnings only just exceed the Welsh male average. Females in Newport are faring best, earning £403 per week, and up 10 per cent on 2004.

Clearly our appreciation of Welsh earnings is hampered in the short term by discontinuities arising from the introduction of a new survey and methodology. A number of revisions have been made to the ASHE data since it was first published and more are likely. However, in the longer term, ASHE promises greater consistency and accuracy, while still having weaknesses with respect to reporting the earnings of the lowest paid, and the self-employed. Despite the data issues, it can be concluded that Wales, the North East and Northern Ireland are positioned along the bottom of the UK regional earnings rankings, with earnings in Wales around 90 per cent of the UK. There are several factors expected to influence the earnings gap between Wales and the UK including: the growth of part-time employment, particularly for men; an occupational structure that compares unfavourably with rest of the UK; and the growth of employment in

Welsh services where pay differentials with respect to other UK regions are greatest. Against this it must be remembered that these earnings comparisons do not consider the different price levels that prevail between regions.

Table 15.16
Average (Median) gross weekly earnings £s, Wales and Unitary authorities, all, male and female full-time employees on adult rates, 2005, workplace based

	All full-time	Male full-time	Female full-time
Blaenau Gwent	368.9	478.1	305.7
Bridgend	426.9	455.7	380.4
Caerphilly	367.6	431.5	310.0
Cardiff	396.0	426.3	357.5
Carmarthenshire	363.0	403.8	340.7
Ceredigion	339.6	348.5	306.6
Conwy	396.5	416.3	361.1
Denbighshire	354.9	395.7	305.8
Flintshire	457.1	482.0	314.9
Gwynedd	358.7	375.4	321.3
Isle of Anglesey	401.2	439.2	329.3
Merthyr Tydfil	385.5	406.1	344.9
Monmouthshire	434.4	478.9	361.4
Neath-Port Talbot	435.1	483.6	307.2
Newport	418.2	419.1	403.1
Pembrokeshire	341.6	349.8	–
Powys	348.0	400.0	295.3
Rhondda Cynon Taff	357.5	374.1	326.5
Swansea	362.1	401.9	330.8
Torfaen	443.4	458.6	330.3
Vale of Glamorgan	401.6	441.4	313.3
Wrexham	381.7	428.3	308.9
Wales	389.9	425.7	334.8

Source: *Annual Survey of Hours and Earnings* (ASHE) 2005.
Note: – denotes not available as sample requirements were not met. Employees on adult rates whose pay for the survey pay-period was not affected by absence.

HOUSING MARKETS

The rapid rise in house prices in Wales over recent years was fuelled by confidence in the low cost of borrowing, and a poorly performing stock market provoking many to enter the buy-to-let market. Much of the steam has now been taken out of the Welsh housing market with lower levels of house price inflation in 2005, compared to 2003 and 2004. According to the Halifax, all house prices rose in Wales by 5.6 per cent in 2005, slightly above the average price increase for the whole of the UK. It is expected that further stabilization in Welsh house prices will occur in 2006 in line with expected trends in national house prices. The Halifax is predicting house price inflation of the order of 3 per cent in the UK for 2006.

Table 15.17 provides seasonally adjusted regional house prices for the UK regions for the fourth quarter of 2005. The annual percentage changes (based on quarterly year on year figures) reveal the very familiar north–south divide. The statistical profile of Wales appearing in *Contemporary Wales* in 2003 showed that Northern Ireland was experiencing negative annual growth in the first quarter of 2003, while house prices in each of the other UK regions were growing at annual rates well in advance of 20 per cent. Now, the peripheral regions are experiencing the last throws of a catch-up process even as the UK core regions begin to enter a phase of more subdued growth. Indeed, the table shows East Anglia and the South West registering negative growth for the first time in many years, although with Greater London so far maintaining a stronger position. Overall, the latest quarterly figures indicate that this market slow-down is creeping outwards, and with house prices growing by less than 10 per cent in all but two regions.

Table 15.17
Average house prices[1], fourth quarter 2005, United Kingdom, regions and former Welsh counties

Regions of the UK	£	Annual % Change	Welsh counties and cities[2]	£	Annual % change
South-east	221,328	2.7	Clwyd	143,950	–1.0
East Anglia	161,352	–1.0	Dyfed	156,400	9.1
South-west	181,257	–1.9	Gwent	134,539	–2.8
West Midlands	160,832	2.0	Gwynedd	153,122	8.9
East Midlands	148,609	1.8	Mid Glamorgan	122,262	5.9
Yorkshire and Humberside	131,064	8.4	Powys	175,173	–4.8
North-west	138,356	7.2	South Glamorgan	160,981	–4.3
North	142,070	9.1	West Glamorgan	129,953	1.4
Greater London	257,120	6.7	Cardiff	160,248	–3.6
Scotland	113,169	14.8	Newport	133,295	–2.0
Northern Ireland	129,447	14.1	Swansea	136,302	–0.7
Wales	143,477	5.6	Wrexham	137,102	–7.9
United Kingdom	169,901	5.1			

Source: HBOS house price index.
Note 1: figures are for standardized average house prices.
Note 2: twelve-month average prices to December 2005 for Welsh counties and cities.

The general ranking of regions by house values has changed very little over time. The South East and Greater London show the highest average values at the end of 2005, with average house prices in Wales only a little over half the value of an average home in Greater London. In Wales, the average (standardized) house is now worth £143,477, having increased in value by just over 5.6 per cent over the year to the final quarter of 2005. However, housing is currently less affordable in Wales than in the UK as a whole. House price/earnings ratios show the ratio of standardized average price of *all houses* to the average earnings of full-time males. At the end of 2005 the ratio was 5.8 in Wales compared to 5.5 for the UK as a whole.

There are considerable variations in house prices within Wales. The most expensive locations are Chepstow (average price in the final quarter of 2005, £225,200) and Penarth (£207,976). The city of Cardiff is also a persistent property hotspot, with demand for property reflecting the strong local labour market and, as a result, house buyers, particularly first-timers, are now buying further afield and driving up prices in the Welsh valleys. Those towns in Wales experiencing large house price gains by UK standards include Holyhead with an annual rise in 2005 of 30 per cent and Port Talbot (22 per cent); both of these towns appeared in the UK top 20 for house price inflation during 2005. Other hotspots included Deeside, Haverfordwest, Aberdare, Abergavenny, Blackwood and Penarth.

Favourable economic indicators including low interest rates, employment and steady earnings growth are likely to fuel housing demand in Wales over the following year. However, against these causes of optimism must be offset the dulling effect of rising fuel prices and council taxes, and declining affordability indices which will likely prevent a return to the near-boom conditions of the early nineties, and hence yield the much more modest but healthy predictions with which this section began.

REGIONAL COMPETITIVENESS

This section considers the regional competitiveness indicators produced by the DTI. As Table 15.18 reveals these indicators cover some of the ground covered earlier in this review. In comparison to other regions gross disposable household income in Wales is low being in 2003 some 12 per cent below the UK average, and with GVA per head figures well adrift of those for England and Scotland. Wales does slightly better in terms of proportions of income support claimants in the total population. In Wales this figure stood at 7.6 per cent in August 2004, a little below figures for the North East, North West and London.

Table 15.18

Regional competitiveness indicators

Region	Gross disposable household income per head (UK=100) 2003	Gross value added (workplace basis) per head (UK=100) 2004	Proportion of income support claimants (in population over 16) August 2004	Manufacturing investment by foreign and UK-owned companies (£m) 2001**		Manufacturing investment by foreign and UK-owned companies (£m) 2002[1]	
				Foreign	UK	Foreign	UK
London	120.8	132.2	7.7	196	934	172	875
South-east	113.1	116.1	4.1	883	1,093	651	1046
Eastern	108.5	108.7	4.5	398	1,012	289	794
South-west	100.7	92.9	4.9	638	754	321	818
West Midlands	91.6	91.2	6.4	888	923	466	858
East Midlands	92.1	91.5	5.2	341	940	307	753
Yorkshire and the Humber	90.9	88.8	6.4	440	969	409	946
North-west	91.7	88.9	8.0	421	1,561	494	1,452
North-east	85.6	79.9	8.1	633	507	421	393
England	102.7	102.3	6.1	4,837	8,693	3,529	7,936
Scotland	93.2	96.2	7.7	497	960	273	786
Northern Ireland	85.7	80.2	10.0	169	282	–	–
Wales	88.3	79.1	7.6	354	501	283	634

Source: DTI *Regional Competitiveness & State of the Regions*, April 2005/National Assembly for Wales.
Note 1: 2002 figs are available for every region except NI (and therefore UK).

The manufacturing investment figures tell us something of the location competitiveness of Wales. Unfortunately the published figures in the DTI indicators set are very dated, and there is a strong expectation, following conclusions earlier in this review, that manufacturing investment levels have fallen sharply since 2002. Manufacturing investment by foreign-owned firms in Wales in 2002 was an estimated £283m, down from £354m in 2001, and with the investment by UK companies at £634m, up from £501m in 2001. This series at regional level can be influenced strongly by one-off investments. In overall terms in 2002, Wales attracted around 6–7 per cent of UK manufacturing investments. Compared to other regions this is a good performance given the small size of Wales.

The indicators produced by the DTI say little about regional export performance, which is a critical indicator of competitiveness. Information from HM Customs and Excise reveals that the value of exports for Wales for 2004 was £8.316bn and up nearly 16 per cent on figures for 2003. Of this total around 66 per cent represented exports to the European Union. Taking the very latest information and the four quarters to the third quarter of 2005 showed exports rising by 9.3 per cent (or £727m) compared to the previous four quarters, whereas the value of exports for the UK over this same period rose by 7.3 per cent. Growth in exports from Wales between the four quarters up to and including the third quarter of 2005 and 1999 was almost 34 per cent compared to 22 per cent for the UK as a whole.

The divergence between the index of manufacturing reported earlier in this section and export performance is difficult to explain. In part the strong exports performance can link to changes in overseas sales of just a few large plants in Wales. Moreover, the index of manufacturing is also picking up on limited growth in domestic sales such that some firms may be seeing stronger trends on overseas trade compared to sales at home.

OVERVIEW

This review was written during the early part of 2006. The increasing number of manufacturing job losses is undoubtedly shaking overall confidence levels in the region. Moreover, fragile confidence is becoming a theme in the main business surveys. For example, the most recent CBI and Experian *Regional Trends Survey* in November 2005 reported falling business confidence in Wales, and with the CBI *Distributive Trades Survey* in the same month also showing falling levels of regional sales in the run up to Christmas. Then in overall terms the employment outlook for 2006–7 is not particularly good, and with employment growth expected to be largely restricted to selected services industries.

The Welsh Assembly Government in November 2005 set out its strategic development plan in the consultation document *Wales: A Vibrant Economy*. The Assembly Government claims that success in reducing unemployment will allow a focus on issues such as improving employment quality and competing internationally with the newly emerging industrial economies. Key themes addressed also include the reduction of economic inactivity, raising earnings and creating an attractive business support environment. Interestingly, in assessing future progress the Welsh Assembly Government has decided to focus on improvement in employment rates and jobs quality. The key aspiration in the earlier *A Winning Wales* was improvements in GVA per capita. The earlier part of this review shows the continued poor showing of Wales on this indicator.

The progress of the Welsh economy into 2006–7 links closely to global and UK economic prospects. However, local factors are also expected to strongly influence prospects. Key issues include: first, the extent to which Welsh Assembly Government expenditure in areas such as economic development, health and education has to be trimmed in line with public efficiency reviews. Secondly, the end of the current structural funding programmes after 2006. It is unlikely that the region will attract similar levels of funding from Europe post 2006, and with the findings from the mid-term evaluations of the extant funding only pointing to moderate additionality in terms of genuine new SME and employment creation.[4] Thirdly, the extent of recovery in manufacturing output. The sharp fall in levels of manufacturing output reported in this review are of real concern. Manufacturing closures have become widespread and there are few signs that the rate of closures and employment losses are slowing. The closures in the foreign manufacturing sector are of particular concern given the reported higher productivity and earnings in the sector. Fourth, the extent to which the Welsh Assembly Government can successfully merge the activities of organizations such as the WDA, Wales Tourist Board and Education and Learning Wales to produce a coherent developmental focus.

The underlying economic development challenges facing the regional economy change little. There remains a gap in prosperity in terms of GVA per capita between Wales and other UK regions. Indeed evidence suggests these gaps are widening through time, partly as a result of the persistence of economic inactivity, coupled to the more recent losses of manufacturing jobs, and employment increases in lower productivity sectors.

NOTES

1. NUTS (Nomenclature des Unites Territoriales Statistiques) was established by the Statistical Office of the European Union (EUROSTAT) to provide a uniform breakdown of territorial units for the production of regional statistics.
2. See *Economic Trends*, 621, 2005.
3. Note ASHE covers Northern Ireland hence the UK comparator here.
4. [Editors' note: after this paper was written, at the first National Assembly Economic Development and Transport Committee meeting of 2006 the Assembly Government Minister told AMs that post 2006 EU economic aid funding for west Wales and the Valleys ('convergence funding') 'is likely to be at a similar level to the current programme, which is approximately £1.3 billion over 7 years'. *Source*: Transcript of Proceedings, Papers of the EDT Committee, 11 January 2006.]

REFERENCES

ONS (2005). *Patterns of Pay: Results of the Annual Survey of Hours and Earnings 1997–2005*, report by Clive Dobbs, Employment, Earnings and Productivity Division, London: ONS.

National Assembly for Wales (2001). *A Winning Wales*, Cardiff: National Assembly for Wales.

Welsh Assembly Government (2005). *Wales: A Vibrant Economy*, Cardiff: Welsh Assembly Government.

16. REVIEW SYMPOSIUM: *POSTCOLONIAL WALES*

The following review symposium offers critical perspectives on the volume *Postcolonial Wales*, edited by Jane Aaron and Chris Williams (Cardiff: University of Wales Press, 2005, ISBN 0-7083-1856-8, 257 pp.). *Postcolonial Wales* is an important contribution to academic debates about problematizing the notion of Wales. It presents a series of essays organized around three sections: the political and socio-historical; contemporary Wales and the impact of devolution; and, Welsh culture. As such it explores aspects of the contemporary cultural and political life of Wales from perspectives informed to a greater or lesser degree by postcolonial theory.

WALES: POST IN PARENTHESIS

A review by Dai Smith

It is difficult to agree with any overall proposition arising from this volume of essays since any such possible engagement is defused by the joint editors' early disclaimer that, like the thirteen essays they have assembled in three separate sections (on history and politics, the currents of devolution, culture), the book 'as a whole' aims 'not so much to produce a blueprint for the application of postcolonial theory to Wales, but rather to stimulate ideas and suggest further avenues for investigation'. Confronted by such a bland bill of fare a ravenous reviewer might well consider removing any remaining critical teeth and wisely gumming assent to the inoffensive ambitions of academic gut-thinking, if it were not for the fact that individual essays actually dish out rather more than flexible diversity: they are often mutually contradictory and occasionally deeply antagonistic the one to the other. It seems we still cannot trust a book by its title. The interesting question, since these authors only unite in the assertion that some of the insights to be derived from a postcolonial theoretical perspective may or may not be useful to the study of Wales, is why use this title in the first place? And therein lies the clue to the book's genuine interest: its salon title and its softly delivered intent are both by-products of the underlying intellectual crisis afflicting Wales, a compound of derivative thought and cultural despair that has its observable roots in the material and social fragmentation that has been undermining for over twenty years various long-standing concepts of Welshness even as the concept of Wales arises, in Cardiff Bay, as a hologram from the ashes.

Postcolonial, as an epithet, is meant to suggest the ambivalent, plural, hybrid, questing society which might serve to turn the key in the closed noun of Wales itself. One of the editors, Chris Williams, openly embraces the idea of a 'post-national' Wales as a liberating means of creating a civic society in which 'a postnational citizenship crosses existing political borders and cultural boundaries' (p. xix). To get there he spins heroically around the distinction between a 'post-colonial Wales' as actual legatee of an actual colonial legacy (no, he avers) and a 'postcolonial' theory (yes, he says) that can illuminate contemporary Wales. His survey concludes that Wales, certainly after the medieval era, was not a colony as such but that complex issues of dependency and inter-relationship with England or Empire gives the theoretical perspective a certain leverage. That may well be since it is defined with such looseness, by him and everyone else, that he declares candidly 'my approach is confessedly eclectic' (p. 16). So much so that when he turns to 'post-nationality' we not only learn (surprise, surprise) that it is 'not exclusively an idea generated by postcolonial thought' (p. 15) but also that, in arguing against holistic accounts of national experience, it seeks out the marginal, whether ethnic or economic or exceptional, to probe overriding narratives of assumption. But that has been a commonplace of social historical scholarship across the globe since at least the 1960s and, arguably, earlier. His understanding of what that kind of historical analysis reveals causes him to warn of 'the ambiguities and complexities that render the national project so problematic' (p. 12). He is, in turn, challenged directly by co-editor Jane Aaron, in her lively account of bardic 'anti-colonialism' as evidenced by successive Welsh-language and English-language writers. Her ultimate stance is that these voices cannot, by their nature and no matter any universal idealism they might wish to promote, be 'post-national' since this would, in any recognizable current situation, mean categorization as 'British' and 'an unexamined English cultural identity' (p. 17). So, she asserts, 'for contemporary Wales to give up its aspirations to nationhood' (p. 137) would be no help in creating the culturally diverse, democratically participating post-national Wales for which Chris Williams yearns. But, though her practical objections to the utopian projection seem sound, they take no account of the manner in which the Welsh see themselves as British and Welsh, in various orders and with various strength form time to time. Nor can we simply nod to the assertion that Wales, here and now, just has this grand national aspiration. As if it was a way of growing up, of maturing, of putting its inadequate past behind it. Of course numbers of people in Wales have thought all of that yet we do not need to go to Williams's sharp comment that, at 590,000 strong, English-born people are the largest ethnic group in Wales and only 75 per cent of the Welsh are native born, to remember that, for whatever reason you may wish to conjure up, the aspirers are a minority who, crucially perhaps, do not accept that aspirations to (diverse) Welsh nationality (short of nationhood if that means institutionalized independence) have been met to the satisfaction of most of the Welsh most of the time. Either way the wedge between the editors is rather more than a hyphen thin.

When we turn to the contributors the parenthesis often becomes positively abyss-like. The late Robert Phillips in a deeply informative essay on history teaching in the school curriculum even-handedly stresses that Wales 'is experiencing a degree of post-colonialism but also post-collectivism' (p. 50) and Dai Griffiths and Sarah Hill in their sassy piece on 'Music in postcolonial Wales' are so subtle in their evocation of the 1990s and onwards explosion of sound that they bravely conclude: 'Whether postcolonial theory offers suitable clues for the pop music of the period is debatable. Welsh pop music was by this time a complex thing . . . If anything, theoretically, one ought at least to acknowledge the possibility of two other "posts": the postmodern . . . and a phrase such as "post-industrial"'(p. 230). Iwan Bala gives us a spirited overview of the way 'cultural colonialism' has afflicted the visual arts in Wales but, again, his scrupulous mind takes him on to consider whether 'post-provincial' is not a more accurate description whilst 'postcolonial' would be a state which we might yet attain when deep social structures have truly changed. David Barlow on 'media' and Steve Blandford on 'dramatic fictions' move through their descriptive surveys adequately enough but only to rest their cases on a sense of potential as they shuffle between a 'colonial, or quasi-colonial, situation' (Blandford, p. 181) to 'the idea of postcolonial as a period of "in-betweeness" ' (Barlow, p. 197). Stephen Knight provides a vigorous summation of his contention that Welsh writers in English, in using the language of the colonizer under the impact of 'colonial capitalism', have had to fight through imposed confusions to reach the energy of fiction in English at the moment, a stage in postcolonial development where the formerly colonized country is, through its culture, determinedly considering its options. However, Alys Thomas, in a cool and measured look at the governance of 'post-devolution Wales' gently reminds us: 'It remains debatable . . . whether the relationship between dominant England [and the other home nations] can be described as colonial. It is a question of perception and identity' (p. 87) whilst, for any foreseeable future, the question 'Is Wales postcolonial?' is neatly sidestepped by the unexceptionable statement that it 'is certainly undergoing a period of constitutional transformation within its borders' (p. 97) and 'exists in the wider political context of the UK, the European Union and a globalized world' (p. 98). With which empirical douche we can clear our head of the confusion of this plethora of post-somethings to turn, with some relief, to the real, unashamed thing.

And that is, of course, the original core of 'post-colonialism' from which postcolonial theory has, in all its ramifications, sprung. It is, or was, about analysis leading to action and change when any undeniable colony sloughs off – in every sense – the colonizer. Whether Paul Chaney is right, in his lucid chapter on women's political participation in devolutionary politics, to argue that their unprecedented, if relative, success is properly linked to the thinking about the 'history of colonialism in Wales', he is indubitably right to point up the rhetoric and imagery employed to imply it was so. More centrally Richard Wyn Jones, though considerably less controversial than he claims to be, delivers a rare (for Wales that is) sketch 'in the form of historical sociology' which proposes that the colonization of Wales in the Middle Ages lingered on, in a multi-fashioned if not formal manner, after the Tudor incorporation. Then, and it is crucial to his argument, he develops the point that an economy based largely on primary extraction of materials, however buoyant in the long cycle of Victorian and Edwardian boom years, also meant that a work-force, growing and increasingly immigrant, though he skips over that lightly, was at direct risk in a non-diversified, non-manufacturing Wales. Intriguingly, he prefaces the main body of his chapter by, disarmingly it must be said, deliberately eschewing the discourse of 'postcolonial studies' since he thinks other methodologies more effective in clarifying 'this particular [Welsh–English] postcolonial relationship'. Yet not, perhaps, if the questions that are evaded would ask why it was to the concept of an interventionist British state that collectivist policies and politics both looked in the interwar years, and not exclusively in Wales of course, and found respite through such a state and government after 1945. He does not ask because he conflates 'British economic policy' in 'the Great Depression' (he means here the 1930s though the term is usually applied to the years 1873–96) with the abiding British values of commercial/financial capitalism through linear British governments as if all such phenomena are transparently identifiable. (It is as if K. O. Morgan had never written a word.) For Wyn Jones the key 'post-' word is, then, 'post-imperial', since it follows, from the end of the sustaining power of the

Empire, that the induced dream is over and the day of the (Welsh) nation-state as political legitimizer of the Welsh nation is still to come as devolution opens the door 'to the animating potential of a Welsh national discourse . . . Wales may be walking backwards . . . towards a much more conventional post-colonial future – a national future' (p. 101). Llew Smith, Blaenau Gwent's former tribune, could not have put it better, though he would have substituted horror for hurrahs. Readers of this review critique will have gathered, by now, that we are on very familiar ground though we have had some enticing turns on the theoretical whirligig. Those authors who wish to utilize the postcolonial literature to illuminate further their own work all use or seek more detailed levels of information and analysis. For others, buttressed of course by scholarship and solidity, the whole terminology offers a more direct route to desired outcome. They are the true believers in this broad, sceptical church. The familiar sound here is of genuine surprise that there could be any dissent or even doubt. The veil is lifted in Dylan Phillips's careful and hopeful assessment of the health of the Welsh language in the light of the Assembly's declared policy to create and sustain a future Wales that is recognizably bilingual in a wide sense. He tells it, as they say, as some think it really is:

> Elsewhere in this volume it is evident that there are conflicting opinions as to in what context Wales can, or even should, be considered a 'postcolonial' country. Many dispute the use of such a term as 'postcolonial' to describe the Welsh experience, and much uncertainty remains as to its actual meaning. However, within Welsh-language political discourse it would appear that terms such as 'colonial' and 'postcolonial' hold no such uncertainties. The idea that Wales has been colonized has been a central theme in Welsh-language politics for many years. The semantics of the 'language struggle' discourse has been particularly loaded with references to colonization, from the description of Whitehall policy in Wales as 'colonial policy', to the ironic labelling of the secretary of state for Wales as the 'governor general'. After generations of common usage, this type of discourse holds very strong connotations for Welsh speakers today. It is hardly surprising, therefore, that the advent of devolution was frequently hailed as a watershed between the 'colonial' and 'postcolonial' periods in Welsh history; this was a recurring theme in Welsh-language political discourse following the success of the 'Yes' vote in the 1997 referendum . . . To many Welsh speakers in particular, therefore, the terms 'post-devolution Wales' and 'postcolonial Wales' are synonymous. (p. 101)

All of which returns us to the editors' oscillating preface where we have read that 'Given the degree of disagreement between the two of us on some of these issues it would have been impossible for us to have arrived at any one agreed view' (p. xvii).

A bit of a pantomime horse then. But at least acknowledged as such. And then, as it kicks out, 'apart, that is, from the view that there are questions that contemporary Wales needs to debate' (p. xvii). To which we must ask, in a group of essays that swell with portentous biographical and bibliographical afflatus, which exact questions – beyond those that pirouette around this contentious terminology – are being addressed? And how, precisely, does a literature review, reverentially, even exhaustively referenced, take us further than the familiar assemblages of fact and event and process to which the essays largely refer? One answer may lie in the single best essay in the volume: Glenn Jordan's extraordinarily rich 'Post-colonialist reflections on immigrants and minorities in Wales' (p. 56).

For here, at last, is work which perceptively but lightly garners insights from 'postcolonial theory' (p. 57), avoids the baggage of discussing whether Wales is 'a postcolonial nation' (in the manner, say, of India or Nigeria) and decides 'At the risk of displeasing positivists and grand theorists' (p. 59) to engage 'with fragments, with bits of lives revealed via photographic images and personal narratives' (p. 59) his concentration on the 'sameness' of 'others' is individually detailed, and moving, yet never removed, as Stuart Hall had sternly warned post-colonial intellectuals in 1996, from both the impact of an overseas Empire *and* the transition to global capitalism. This essay, full of startling material modestly interpreted, is, in itself, a vindication of Chris Williams's sense that a postcolonial perspective can indeed open up issues of Welsh identity. It is the marginalized, here, who truly ask questions of the dominant, both within and outside Wales. Glenn Jordan's approach really is flexible (in its use of theoretical discourse) and diverse (in the nature of the evidence adduced). His concluding reflections are two devastating questions that ought to take us beyond the lamented binary divisions of language, geography and regional typography. He asks, with all the force of actual lives lived and real rejection encountered: 'Can we reimagine Wales as consisting of a plurality of experiences, cultures and identities? Can we rethink Welshness as heterogeneous, as inclusive of difference?' (p. 60). To which I would add that if we choose to do so it will need to be rather more than by offering the piously raised arms of the 'anyone can be Welsh if they want to be' variety so beloved of politicians, largely white and recent middle-class incomers and subscribers to Dylan Phillips's outmoded mantra of belief that: 'What the Assembly needs to bear in mind is the fact that although 2.2 million people in Wales . . . are unable to speak the language, they remain Welsh [grateful thanks]. The very existence of Welsh . . . is the one remaining factor that identifies them as such – a people [mmm]' (p. 78). On the contrary, we should open up the editors' plea for 'further avenues of investigation' by removing the shackle of a fixed Wales – which almost demands a theoretically derived methodology to make sense of it – and embrace the release that the human specificity involved in Welshness offers – where the detail and the perspective require both empirical investigation and the framework of explanation which intermeshes rather than pre-dates or post-stamps. Intellectual leadership in Wales too readily retreats nowadays into servicing power or promoting the pomp of scholarly discourse. The times are too harsh for that since it is not the integument of Wales with which we need to be urgently concerned but the interstices of a Welsh society deprived of the means of common purpose by corporate and professional take-over of what was once local and lively with endeavour.

There is scant reference in *Postcolonial Wales* to the demographic swirl – with and from without – which will directly mark any future Welsh identity. Pause to think of a north-east region where over 60 per cent are not native-born and of the still populous south Wales valleys where 90 per cent are rooted by three generations and more. Throw in the scarcely whispered issue of the emergence of real, socially marginalized groups within existing communities, as Dave Adamson has consistently uncovered, and persistent patterns of poverty where travel-to-work is a joke and travel-to-town a fantasy. When you do that you begin to consider the residual characteristics of the cultural power struggle that has been occurring in Welsh life and the list of winners and losers. In any happy racing card of runners and riders in our knee-jerk entrepreneurial promoting press, we do not identify the élites, self-appointed or meritocratic, who shape so much through social cliques or economic controls. We whitewash so much with the homogenous cover-up of Team Wales that we have no political economy or sociology or even fiction which can be said to go into the deep structures of our existence. Our architecture, for what it is, speaks the mute language of class and wealth. The streets and back lanes of our towns and cities are clogged with the plastic and cardboard detritus of a society which has neglected its public services whilst it prates of can-do initiative to those it trains to the imprisonment of the keyboard in the interest of 'upskilling'. Meanwhile, in a wonderful exemplum of real postcolonial fantasy we erect the Kyffin Williams Memorial Sheepfold, in indigenous materials naturally, and pretend it is an architectural glory. It is the pretence which is the significance.

Only close-ups – of street life, of diet, of accent, of dress, of leisure, of landscape's effect on social psychology, of apathy, or surging violence, of gradations of hope and ambition – will allow a contemporary Wales to claim validity for things and people in and for themselves and not just against other validities. The most self-defining process for an emerging Wales then will, in due course, be seen not to be 1997 or even 1984 but the relationship between the end of one social dynamic and the still evolving institutional riposte that was half-heartedly substituted, as a salve to the bewilderment caused by disappearing certitudes. You would be hard pushed to find much of anything of this or how to make sense of it in the grandiose sweep of *Postcolonial Wales*. That is because it is another symptom of the crisis it seeks to dissect. Perhaps the editors were right all along and their purpose was only to erect signposts even if they do turn, somewhat disconcertingly in the passing wind of the new, and surely as yet unforeseeable, century in Wales.

We have to hope that a different Welsh life will indeed be eventually discernible beyond the lineaments of this shrouded present. We may be puzzled a while yet by the (re-)emergence of conservatism in Welsh politics as the standard bearer for both local politics and elected officials with power to connect to regional needs within Wales. Certainly the running crisis within Plaid Cymru is directly traceable to their wayward GPS finder where a political mapping – according to Dafydd Iwan at their September 2005 conference the 'nation' had been 'on its knees for centuries' before 1997 – will take them nowhere if they still insist, despite the advice of people at ground level, of starting from there and not some point nearer to reality, then and now. As for the Labour Party, whether Welsh or New, it has only survived its lack of direction in Wales by staying rooted to the spot. Its MPs in Westminster cannot lead it where they themselves will never choose to go and its AMs, hamstrung by the fudged outcome of Labour's devolution settlement and hog-tied by related electoral indifference, wait sullenly for the crisis that will disrupt an uneasy consensus. When that happens, as it decidedly will, it will not only be a generational change we might welcome, for the right of any identifiable Wales to continue its national existence will then be firmly on the agenda *only* under the aegis of a Welshness that has sloughed off the traces of any 'colonial' or 'postcolonial' confusion, real or projected, in favour of the clear acceptance of a plural Welsh existence that is inclusive in all of its plurality because it has finally chosen not to be a young country in any other way.

Review by Mark Leslie Woods

Welsh historian Geraint H. Jenkins tells us,

> Some historians have simply presumed that the political assimilation of Wales by England necessarily meant that the history of this 'internal colony' was no more than a tranquil and uneventful interlude between the rebellions of the fifteenth century and the epoch-making industrial revolution. (Morgan, 1981)

Describing Wales as an 'internal colony' of England during this or any period, or variously describing Wales as colony/former colony/neo-colony, etc. of England, raises the question as to whether postcolonial theory is applicable in the case of Wales, which is not without controversy. *Postcolonial Wales* is a collection of edited essays derived from a one-day conference 'exploring aspects of contemporary Welsh cultural and political life from "postcolonial" theoretical and critical perspectives' that considered this question on 13 July 2002 at the University of Glamorgan (*Postcolonial Wales*, conference programme, University of Glamorgan, 17 July 2003).

Postcolonial theory has emerged as a pan-disciplinary movement which has the potential to refract history's cultural quandaries within a prism of both perceived and projected possibilities: irreverent and iconoclastic, postcolonial theorists thumb their noses at the 'old guard' and, like the overlooked innocent in Anderson's fable, blurt out the historically ignored, but cloyingly evident, 'but the Emperor is not wearing any clothes'. Postcolonial theory has quickly won world-wide academic credibility and because of the nature of its underlying inclinations toward the qualities of 'expansiveness' and 'inclusiveness', it has been appropriated by many diverse and unrelated disciplines (often to the dismay of critical purists). Within the discussions of postcolonial theory, some of its assertions are historically provable while others seem culled from an intuitive-hunch on behalf of a formerly subjugated group's collective consciousness and from folklore, urban legends, Jungian dreams, wives' tales, rumours and so on. Postcolonial theorists (along with feminism theorists) claim that history has too long been the purview of the powerful, that is a male-dominated elite, and that it is time that 'tales of the hearth' are at least considered in the marketplace of ideas. It is this employment of fuzzy storytelling about the impossible-to-substantiate within postcolonial theory that bothers some historians because, while it has captivated the minds of the formerly marginalized, offering the ability to recall and narrate to the ignored or erased identities of thousands of categories and classes of individuals, those disenfranchised by earlier systems, for example, cultural, religious and political, etc., the 'stuff' of its discourses occasionally seems to echo tones of touchy-feely pop psychology of the 1970s. Within Wales, some notable historians including Chris Williams (Aaron and Williams, 2005) seem to think that postcolonial theory lacks the methodology of earlier theoretical systems (which appeared reliable to them, because of some perceived, rigid accuracy).

It is not surprising that Williams would take this position for two reasons: first, one might picture postcolonial theory as a ruthless turn-coat which points the finger at anyone who has officially told the story before, that is, all historians, since postcolonial theory always suspects that tellers of history are somehow in league with the imperial powers of history. In other words, even those who tell a different story, if it is still the colonized (think gendered) story of *any* establishment, that is, the patriarchy, it is really the story of Empire; as postcolonial writers might say, it remains *his-* 'imperial' story and not *her*-story (Gittings, 1996). Consequently, application of postcolonial theory to Wales must seem like an ungrateful, revisionist attack on those Welsh historians who have already composed an independent narration for Wales, for example, the proudly industrial, left-leaning, 'junior partner' in the 'formerly expanding British empire' (Aaron and Williams, 2005), which goes beyond the British imperial 'party-line', that is, exceeding the confines of 'England writ-large'. However respectful one can be for the constructs of these fine but evanescent Welsh historians, or what Jane Aaron has elsewhere described as the 'last gasp of the voice of Old Labour',[1] it is no less, an attack. Accordingly, it is little wonder Williams has exited the pit with his post-industrial fists up. Secondly, there is a prevailing notion within postcolonial theory that individuals within nations long-subjugated under colonialism are inclined to develop coping mechanisms for co-existence with oppression. For example, it is posited that the male members of an emasculated, colonial society seem inclined to displace their anger about chronic deprivation of self-determination, since these individual males within the oppressed groups must still construct their personal and collective constructs of masculinity in order to have functional psychological/social existences (Gittings, 1996). Social scientists embracing postcolonial readings of these groups note that the choices for males under colonialism are limited (Loomba, 1998; McLeod, 2000). A general inclination among males within oppressed classes could be characterized as macho and hyper-masculine, effectively, the othered male with no real power struts as if he has power, in a desperate attempt to protect what is left of his dignity. Imagine please, tales of the demoralized miner made redundant by decisions of his post-imperial superiors, getting drunk with his mates, then going home and attempting to shore up the shreds of his male dominance by abusing his wife. A stereotypically postcolonial reading of this domestic scenario might say that with coal-blackened-face, the working-class Welshman needs to assert his power somewhere, so he abusively does so by lambasting his spouse. His clumsy mimicry of patriarchy, however, is a quasi-negritudinal mockery, and he becomes a parody of himself as the Empire continues to rule his life by insinuating its hierarchy into all his affairs, even into the intimacy of marriage (Ashcroft, Griffiths and Tiffin, 2000).

How does this sad miner's tale relate to *Postcolonial Wales*? Well, what Aaron typifies as the 'last gasp of Old Labour' has the remarkably similar *machismo* flailing and stomping of the demoralized male ego described above. One is compelled to assume Aaron, co-editor of *Postcolonial Wales* with Williams, was also reacting to the arguments of Williams in his introductory article in *Postcolonial Wales*, titled 'Problematizing Wales'. In his discussion of the application of postcolonial theory to Wales, Williams dissipates his opportunity to expand postcolonial theory for the benefit of a world-wide audience while using Wales as a case study. Instead, he makes every effort to discredit postcolonial theory. It is embarrassing that Williams rehashes arguments long ago settled within the methodology of postcolonial theory, especially when he seems to insist that there needs to be a linear historical prerequisite for the application of postcolonial theory to a nation. Williams limits his discussion to early inventors of postcolonial precepts, but ignores the evolved answers of later scholarship (Loomba, 1998; McLeod, 2000; Ashcroft, Griffiths and Tiffin, 2000; Gittings, 1996, etc.) One might conclude that either Williams has a prior agenda or he has selectively read the theory he purports to discredit or, not unlike the fractured male ego mentioned above, Williams is unable to separate his personal constructs of collective masculinity from their scholarship and hence Williams's apology for dismissing postcolonial theory comes just short of name-calling, that is, 'postcolonial gurus'. One ponders why a co-editor, a role which assumes some balanced consideration of the contributors' arguments he is effectively introducing, chooses to stab at the credibility of the critical idiom they utilize in their articles. Williams's article is clearly written and makes some important points about post-imperialism, etc., but does not provide the most positive climate possible for what follows. Williams rightly names 'utopian' his call for 'leaving behind Welshness' in favour of some amorphous identity within a Welsh state of never anything more than 'partial autonomy'. In fairness, Williams's sensitivity to overlooked issues of class and economics, etc., in Welsh society deserves a fuller airing, as Adamson has previously begun (Adamson, 1991, 1996).

Postcolonial Wales does not significantly expand the theoretical base of postcolonial theory. On the contrary, one of its editors is its antagonist. Neither do the contributors offer theoretical interpretations of modern Wales, which might augment critical concepts. Their articles employ terminology of the theory but are effectively more anecdotal, providing a rich wealth of evidence that Wales is indeed in some condition which is well served by postcolonial theory.

As I have described, Chris Williams delivers as anticipated the essay 'Problematizing Wales' but he spends much time qualifying (or correctly, disqualifying) postcolonial theory. Williams might have used as a more academically pluralistic starting-off point, a succinct simplification of 'postcolonialism', for example: 'Postcolonialism describes a critical practice dedicated to addressing the types of cultural marginalization propagated by imperialism' (Gittings, 1996). Richard Wyn Jones balances co-editor Chris Williams's assertions in his article where Jones tell us, 'What gives Wales its distinctiveness is, in many ways, the distinctiveness of England' (p. 27). Compared to Williams, who envisions a 'post-national' Wales as preferable to postcolonial, Jones sees a 'national' Wales 'full of possibilities' (p. 34). Jones's article challenges Williams's ending argument against Welsh nationalism by pointing out how present realities demonstrate at least a de facto Welsh national revival.

Perhaps the most readable essay in *Postcolonial Wales* is by Glenn Jordan, in his 'Reflections on immigrants and minorities in Wales'. Jordan's 'collage' style is a postmodern 'intervention' approaching a bricolage of anecdotal storytelling blended with commentary about the 'invisible' Welsh, that is, non-white minorities. Jordan gives voice to persons-of-colour excluded from what is typically deemed part of the historical record in Wales. His chapter flows with the structure of a documentary film, leaving space for the reader to bring their own conclusions.

Robert Phillips's article considers education in a post-devolutionary context. He emphasizes 'why it is important to place distinctive Welsh experiences within the wider British, European, and world contexts' (p. 51) within the curricula, arguing for a post-devolutionary context, as well, and even for a 'border pedagogy' (p. 51). Phillips's report on education in Wales shows how some arenas of Welsh life are more fully devolved than others, as compared to later chapters by Blandford and Barlow (Aaron and Williams, 2005).

For Alys Thomas, the debate turns on political science, with the concept of 'post-colonial' or 'post-independence' reckoning explicit meaning in this field, 'The colonial state had the hybridity of "an alien executive instrument of a culturally different community"' (p. 96). Thomas's discussion is refreshingly outward-looking for Wales, maybe a reflection of a growing national self-confidence, not solely dependent upon comparisons to England for self-definition. Thomas's comparisons to the 'Quiet Revolution' in Québec are especially insightful.

Dylan Phillips makes the point in his article on the 'Welsh language in Wales' that in Welsh-speaking circles there has never been any debate: Wales and Welsh culture were and continue to be the subject of English conquest. Phillips sees devolution as pivotal: 'To many Welsh speakers in particular, therefore, the terms "post-devolution Wales" and "postcolonial Wales" are synonymous' (p. 109).

In his book on *Imperialism and Gender: Constructions of Masculinities*, Christopher E. Gittings tells us, 'Western European imperial projects were predicated on the dominant white patriarchal construction of difference to itself as inferiority. This type of alterity or othering is sexual, gendered, racial and cultural' (Gittings, 1996, p. 156). To follow Gittings's logic, a reversal of the gendered prejudices of the imperial project might constitute a reasonable measure of decolonization. The article authored by Paul Chaney renders a refreshing account of the political successes of the pro-devolution group Women Say Yes in the structuring of the Welsh Assembly Government and its implied decolonization. This might be the most important article in the collection because of its far-reaching relevance to feminist movements worldwide. While Chaney does not extend postcolonial theory with his article, he offers rich evidence of a Welsh postcolonial exception regarding the rights of women and the use of consensus (versus the traditionally machismo, winner-takes-all politics of 'white men in grey suits') which Chaney implies will attract international attention to Wales. The only other comparable example of a postcolonial government empowering by statute the formerly gender-marginalized might be when post-apartheid South Africa placed equality for gays and lesbians in their new constitution.

In *Postcolonial Wales* co-editor Williams decries some of the twentieth-century Welsh writer Emyr Humphreys's ideas as 'bizarre', and while Humphreys's *The Taliesin Tradition* has its fanciful moments, its central theme is echoed and given concrete structure in co-editor Jane Aaron's chapter in *Postcolonial Wales*, 'Bardic anti-colonialism', recognizing the place in Welsh history, culture and politics held by poetry, a distinction among world cultures which is almost, if not entirely, unique. Stephen Knight's article on 'Welsh fiction in English as postcolonial literature' is a brief distillation of his recent ground-breaking work, *One Hundred Years of Fiction*. Knight's careful reading of a century of Anglo-Welsh writing raises milestones which easily differentiate into 'colonial' 'anti-colonial/ industrial' and 'post-colonial'.[2] Film and theatre scholar Steve Blandford discusses whether the hereunto non-devolved area of film can even be described as 'postcolonial', which seems to assume that 'postcolonial' could be applied to other already devolved arenas in Welsh culture and politics:

> In terms of institutions and public policy, neither film nor television in Wales is postcolonial to even the same limited degree as theatre might be said to be. Broadcasting in Wales remains under the direct control of the UK Department of Culture, Media and Sport. There has been talk of an Assembly-controlled Film Fund for Wales, but, for now, policy-making remains in London. (Blandford, 2000, p. 42).

And, if Blandford's view is pragmatic but bleak, then David M. Barlow's is bleaker still:

That the vast majority of the media in Wales – press, television and radio – is owned, controlled and accountable to bodies beyond its borders is indisputable. As a result of such arrangements, it is not surprising to find doubts being raised about the media's ability to represent and fully reflect the nation's cultural diversity. (Barlow et al., 2005, p. 127)

The final articles by Dai Griffiths and Sarah Hill, 'Music in postcolonial Wales', and by Iwan Bala, 'Horizon Wales: visual art and the postcolonial', raise interesting questions about the interplay of commercially marketed art objects and entertainment products with globalization, and about Welsh branding, which will be of interest even to those not specifically interested in these fields. The article by Griffiths and Hill has pop culture appeal and demonstrates how nationalism[3] is realized simply by the invention of independent distribution labels not beholden to London or New York. Bala's erudite discussion raises the question, 'Is there anything this acclaimed artist and "renaissance man" doesn't do well?' Bala discusses the role of art in the decolonization of Wales while asking the poignant question, 'Can Wales become post-provincial?'

Kenneth O. Morgan tells us that, 'A sense of nationality is as old as the Welsh themselves' (Morgan, 1981), but John Edward Lloyd's early assessment of the Welsh, (whom Morgan quotes and calls 'the pioneer of . . . the writing of Welsh history', Morgan, 1981, p. 5) outlines the history of a nation (but not necessarily of a nationalism) forever altered by the invasion led by Edward I: 'Edwardian conquest was a massive tragedy, an imperialist invasion of a small, vigorous, self-conscious nation' (Morgan, 1981, p. 32). Morgan's book is titled *Rebirth of a Nation*, and in the chapter called 'The national revival', Morgan tells us how John Edward Lloyd was Wales's first historian, and a scholar who dedicated forty years of his life to his college at Bangor. Morgan explains how the writings of historians, poets and scholars, with the aid of chapels, *eisteddfodau*, and popular publishing created an educated elite in Wales in the decades leading up to the beginning of the twentieth century, which resulted in a sense of national consciousness, which eventually resulted in the establishment of Wales's first national institutions. Geraint H. Jenkins and Kenneth Morgan agree that for much of its history, Wales lacked national institutions. It was during this 'national revival' that the Welsh elevated the *eisteddfod* to a level of national awareness, they developed a rationale for support of the Welsh language and they established a national university, national library and national museum, all typical hallmarks of a nation attempting to asserting its self-conscious nationhood. Morgan says that the momentum created by this 'national revival' carries into the 1980s and laid the foundation of the political movement which resulted in the passing of the Devolution Act (Morgan, 1981). There is a need for current Welsh scholars not only to engage in self-reflective discourses but also to develop models for policy-making which manifest the goals of this new national self-awareness. Most importantly, it is hoped that *y werin* in the once proud valleys, those laid-off masses left to malinger in slums of Merthyr Tudful – but lately deserted by the industries which permitted their brief complicity in the imperial project – will not be overlooked. One has to believe that as these modern Welsh scholars in *Postcolonial Wales* take up the self-reflective debate about the Welsh nation, it might again foretell a true and enduring national revival, maybe beyond the success of the first.

Response by Chris Williams

> To the question when was [postcolonial] Wales, it is possible to return several answers. One could say, with a measure of truth within narrow limits, that [postcolonial] Wales never was. It is equally possible to say, with equal truth within equally narrow limits, that [postcolonial] Wales always was.[4]

I am grateful to the editors of *Contemporary Wales* for inviting me to respond to the reviews of *Postcolonial Wales* by Dai Smith and Mark Leslie Woods. However, I am disappointed that the editors were not able to find two reviewers better equipped to debate the merits and demerits of the volume. Whatever their strengths as scholars in other fields, neither Smith nor Woods appears to have anything more than a passing acquaintance with postcolonial scholarship. Smith's views on some applications of postcolonialism to modern and contemporary Wales have already been made public at length in *New Welsh Review*: I am not sure that the debate is moved on significantly by his contribution here. And whilst I welcome what I believe is Woods's first academic publication, I trust that his doctoral thesis, when submitted, will be more accurate and scrupulous. Interested readers will find far more incisive, well-informed and more measured (though not necessarily less critical) reviews elsewhere by Kirsti Bohata[5] and Daniel Williams[6]. Both Smith and Woods nonetheless raise important points that require further discussion. Some relate to the volume as a whole, some only to my contribution to the volume, and I will deal with these first.

Mark Leslie Woods is obviously not enamoured with my views of Wales nor with my interpretation of postcolonial theory. He is entitled to his interpretations, although I believe him mistaken on both counts, as I shall demonstrate below. Whether he is qualified to pronounce on the health of my 'male ego' I am less certain, and I suspect that in future years Woods will look back on his sad miner's tale with some embarrassment. If *Contemporary Wales* wishes to be treated as a serious academic journal then greater editorial control would have been sensible here.

To move from the tabloid to the middlebrow criticisms, I believe Woods's critique to be flawed on several grounds. First, he claims that I think that postcolonial theory 'lacks the methodology of earlier theoretical systems'. What I actually wrote was that 'there is no single body of theory, no common set of assumptions, that constitutes postcolonialism' (p. 11), and I believe that to be the case. Indeed, I cited Robert Young, editor of *Interventions* and author of many volumes on the subject, to the effect that 'there is no such thing as postcolonial theory as such' (p. 12). To argue this is not particularly novel, but its purpose is rather to explain that to adopt and utilize postcolonial concepts does not automatically commit one to a nationalist position. Woods, however, operates with a simplistic, monolithic understanding of postcolonial theory and its impact. I would suggest he returns to volumes such as *Colonialism/Postcolonialism* by Ania Loomba,[7] and takes note of the following passage (p. 2):

> we cannot dismiss the critiques that postcolonial theory can be often written in a confusing manner, is marked by infighting among the critics who all accuse each other of complicity with colonial structures of thought, and although its declared intentions are to allow the voices of once colonised peoples and their descendants to be heard, it in fact closes off both their voices and any legitimate place from which critics can speak . . . It is also true that . . . the term 'postcolonialism' has become so heterogeneous and diffuse that it is impossible to describe satisfactorily what its study might entail.

Woods appears to argue that postcolonialism and historical scholarship are antithetical but this is surely contradicted, to give just one example, by the substantial body of work associated with the 'Subaltern Studies' collective of Indian historians. I do not see my status as a historian undermined by post-colonialism. On the contrary, as someone who has taught not only the histories of Wales and of Britain but also those of Indonesia, Malaysia, the Philippines and Vietnam I see much to be gained from an appreciation of Wales in a global and multi-disciplinary context. Certainly, the *Postcolonial Wales* project, not in spite of, but precisely because of, the differences that existed between editors and contributors, was one of the most enjoyable and intellectually stimulating I have been involved with.

Secondly, Woods suggests that I am concerned to 'discredit' postcolonial theory, that I am its 'antagonist', and that I merely rehash 'arguments long ago settled'. I fail to recognize either claim as bearing any relationship to reality.

What I sought to do was to indicate the enormous diversity of postcolonial theory and the fact that it is not reducible to a single meaning. As far as I am aware, 'guru' is not a term of abuse (my copy of the *OED* defines it as a 'teacher' or 'priest', 'weighty, grave, dignified'), and Woods is simply wrong to suggest that I ignored 'the evolved answers of later scholarship' (as if these were settled), preferring to concentrate on the 'early inventors of postcolonial precepts'. Two of the four works he cites as examples of the former are directly quoted in my essay (pp. 4, 13), sitting alongside many other references to interpretative and theoretical work published in the last decade.

Where Woods is right is to suggest that I had a prior agenda and that I have read postcolonial theory 'selectively'. Guilty on both counts. My prior agenda was one, that I was not born yesterday, and two, that I happened to know enough about the history of Wales, of Britain and of empire and imperialism generally to feel that I could make a judgement as to how helpful postcolonial theory could be in understanding that past. As for selective reading, given the self-contradictory nature of much postcolonial scholarship this was absolutely necessary. I frankly confessed (p. 12) to eclecticism and to deliberate inversion and reading against the grain of postcolonial concepts: a technique I felt could be helpful in opening up new avenues of scholarly enquiry and political possibility, and one that is very much in tune with the approach of many postcolonial scholars. I would have thought this is precisely the 'irreverent and iconoclastic' attitude, the exploration of 'perceived and projected possibilities' that Woods himself endorses.

Woods also finds fault with my criticism of the 'credibility of the critical idiom' used by other contributors to the volume. Given the manifold variations in the positions adopted by the other contributors, which range from enthusiastic endorsements of the relevance of postcolonial theory to outright dismissal of its appropriateness in the Welsh context, one wonders whether he has read the same book. In his assessments of the essays by Glenn Jordan, Robert Phillips and Alys Thomas, to name just the most obvious, he appears oblivious to the serious objections they raise either to his preferred unilinear reading of postcolonial theory or to his enthusiasm for a 'Welsh national revival'. And I suggest that when he is next tempted to spout about '*y werin* in the once proud valleys, those laid-off masses left to malinger in the slums of Merthyr Tudful', he should take a deep breath and reconsider.

Dai Smith's critique of *Postcolonial Wales* is of a wholly different character from that of Mark Woods. Politically, ideologically, he and I are evidently much closer, and his grasp of historical scholarship and of the nature of contemporary Wales is much firmer than that of Woods. As my former doctoral supervisor and as an erstwhile colleague at both Cardiff University and the University of

Glamorgan, as well as currently one at the University of Wales Swansea, Dai Smith is someone who has had a profound influence on my intellectual development (an influence to which I paid an interim tribute in my *Democratic Rhondda: Politics and Society, 1885–1951* (University of Wales Press, 1996)) and whom I consider a close personal friend. Responding to his highly critical review is thus an uncomfortable if necessary task.

Dai Smith might have been well advised to subject himself to a self-denying ordinance on the subject of this volume, partly because his hostility to postcolonial discourse (in any form, it appears) had already been well trailed, but more importantly because the superficiality of his understanding of post-colonialism is here clearly revealed. Postcolonial theory is not only, perhaps not even mainly, about whether any given society (in this instance, Wales) can be seen as (historically or contemporaneously) a colony. It is thus much wider in its reach and relevance than the debates of the 1970s that surrounded Michael Hechter's *Internal Colonialism* (1975) and which Smith evidently is irritated by thinking he has to fight all over again. It is no good to protest that because (in my view, rightly) Wales cannot, in the modern period, be considered to have been a colony in any meaningful way, the ideas and insights of postcolonial theory are necessarily invalid. The ideas are in circulation and will be applied to Wales, like it or not. They have been extensively debated in Ireland (most recently, by Terrence McDonough (2005) and are now being considered in the Scottish context (see Liam Connell, 2004). My view is that it is preferable that they are debated and scrutinized, critiqued and moulded by those from a non- (or in my case, post-) national position, rather than the intellectual terrain simply being handed over to those whose preferred interpretation is less sophisticated and less attentive to the irreducibility of Wales's historical experience. Battles do have to be refought, for new conceptual weapons are forged over and again, and evidently the 'commonplace[s] of social historical scholarship across the globe since at least the 1960s and, arguably, earlier' have not been to everyone's taste, otherwise we would not be in the mess we are in now. Smith may well be right to argue that some of the theory is pretentious padding, obfuscation that serves no one other than the academics themselves, but postcolonialism is not the first theoretical discourse to be accused of this and it will not be the last.

Before they wrote their reviews, Mark Leslie Woods and Dai Smith would have done well to have consulted Kirsti Bohata's *Postcolonialism Revisited* (2004), where they would have found, in Bohata's first chapter, an excellent exploration, at somewhat greater length than was possible in my essay for *Postcolonial Wales*, of some of the issues concerning the nature of postcolonial theory and its applicability or otherwise to Wales. For Bohata, the 'wide appeal of postcolonialism' is due to its concern with 'shifting identity . . . and is of immediate relevance to and for a nation such as Wales' (p. 1). She acknowledges that standard progressions from coloniality to postcoloniality are problematic in the case of Wales 'whose history and literature in no way conform to the progressive-linear model of moving from colonization (and colonial literature) to decolonization (and postcolonial literature)' (pp. 2–3). But she believes 'there is most certainly space for the use and expression of postcolonial theory in the context of those countries not normally recognized as colonial or post-colonial' (p. 3) and that 'the case of Wales is an excellent example of how postcolonial paradigms may be employed . . . to reveal the ways in which the Welsh have been subjected to a form of imperialism over a long period of time, while also acknowledging the way in which the Welsh have been complicit in their own subjugation and in the colonization of others' (p. 3). It is precisely this blend of flexibility and discrimination that scholars need to bring to the postcolonial debate in Wales: it is just a shame they will not find very much of it in the pages of this volume of *Contemporary Wales*.

Response by Jane Aaron

Contemporary Wales has elicited two very different review articles on the essay collection *Postcolonial Wales*, which is all to the good, in terms of furthering discussion of the book's topic. I am glad of this opportunity to respond to them, and turn first to the more critical of the two.

Dai Smith sees the volume as a 'product of the underlying intellectual crisis' and 'cultural despair' which has afflicted Wales for the last twenty years, since the demise of the south Wales coalfield. *Postcolonial Wales* purports to dissect this crisis, he suggests, but instead it is in fact itself but a 'symptom' of it. At once 'bland' and 'grandiose', the book does not speak of – or to – an 'emerging Wales' which, according to Professor Smith, will in due course be seen to have its origins not in '1997 or even 1984 but the relationship between the end of one social dynamic and the still evolving institutional riposte that was half-heartedly substituted, as a salve to the bewilderment caused by disappearing certitudes'. If I understand this sentence correctly, the half-hearted substitute would appear to refer to the Welsh National Assembly, and the 'social dynamic' with its 'disappearing certitudes' to that version of Welshness forged by the nation's pre-1984 role in British industry. Dai Smith criticizes *Postcolonial Wales* for not addressing the reality of the tension between the lost 'certitudes' and the current miasma, and yet his own review makes it evident that the book has in fact addressed it, though not in terms of which he can approve.

For example, the review pays due attention to Richard Wyn Jones's chapter on 'the colonial legacy in Welsh politics', but criticizes it as 'considerably less controversial' than it claims to be without referring to the most controversial, or at any rate original, aspect of its analysis. Dr Jones not only argues that Wales's non-diversified industrial past (that is, its role as a producer of primary materials only, rather than as manufacturer of goods) was in itself a symptom of the country's subordinated relation to an imperial England, but that the specific nature of capitalist development within the British Empire also worked to marginalize and further disempower the Welsh. In nineteenth-century Britain, relatively few Welsh people gained entry to the 'city'; to deal in stocks and shares seemed so alien and anglicized an activity for a Welshman that it was represented in popular Welsh-language culture as a sign of betrayal akin to denying knowledge of the Welsh language (as I point out in another of *Postcolonial Wales*'s chapters). Stateless nations commonly develop an incomplete class structure, in which a limited upper class identifies with the ruling nation-state, and leaves the construction of indigenous identities to the peasant or working class (see Jones, *Barn*, 498/9, August 2004, p. 10). Wales has been no exception: that social dynamic with its lost certitudes constructed Welshness according to the experience and aspirations of white working-class males from certain specific regions of Wales. Which is not to say that the Wales thus created was not admirable, just as the Nonconformist Wales which preceded it was in many ways admirable: for one thing, of major significance to some of us, both produced literatures of intensity and lasting value, and both forged strong communities that sacrificed in order to provide for the education and maintenance of (male) leaders chosen by them from amongst their own ranks, in defiance of their more powerful neighbour's hierarchical organizations. The need to proclaim a Welsh identity which could differ, proudly, from that of the ruling nation-state led to such insistent equations as 'Methodist Calvinism = Wales' or, later, 'South Wales Miners Federation = Wales'. It is the identification of such traditions with Welshness, rendering all other influences or ideas alien and non-Welsh, which is problematic, transparently so when they lose power, but postcolonial theory understands those identifications as indirect attempts to resist the homogenizing force of the nation-state, and to survive as a distinct people within it.

In effect *Postcolonial Wales* (or at any rate some of its chapters) turns the tables on Dai Smith's argument: in it a post-imperial or postcolonial view of Wales is not a symptom of the malaise in which Wales has been floundering since 1985, but rather aspects of the pre-1985 Welsh industrial past are seen as in themselves symptomatic of the country's subordinance. Professor Smith argues that the economic and cultural conditions under which the Welsh laboured cannot be termed colonial because those who lived under them in twentieth-century Wales saw the solution to them in a British interventionist state, and voted socialist accordingly, as opposed to voting for greater independence from the British state. He might as well have argued that no socialist interpretation of mid-nineteenth century Welsh life is possible because the mass of the population opted for intensive chapel-going during that period. Of course people's choices are formed by the prevailing hegemonies of their localities and epochs, but that is not to say there is no other way of understanding their condition. At any rate, whichever interpretation is accepted, it is not a matter of fact that Dr Jones's paper and others like it in this volume are wallowing in some alien miasma and failing to address the current situation in Wales.

According to Professor Smith, however, the only 'real, unashamed thing' (who is ashamed, and of what, he does not explain) in this whole debate is the 'original core' of postcolonialism, which he defines as 'analysis leading to action and change when any undeniable colony sloughs off – in every sense – the colonizer'. From his point of view Wales is inapplicable on two counts: first, in that it has not been an 'undeniable colony' since the Middle Ages, if then; secondly, because it has not 'sloughed off' English influence 'in every sense'. Here the two prongs of his attack would appear to cross one another, for if Wales cannot really be considered ever to have been a colony how come it is so ineradicably steeped in Englishness? Further, his definition of postcolonialism is by no means current, as exemplified by Mark Woods's review. Quoting from Christopher Gittings, Woods defines postcolonialism as 'a critical practice dedicated to addressing the types of cultural marginalization propagated by imperialism'. According to the terms of this definition it is immaterial to what extent the influence of the imperial culture has been 'sloughed off'; on the contrary, the assumption is that such influence can never be entirely eradicated but will always remain part of the history and make-up of both the dominated and dominating cultures (which is where the shame comes in, presumably, but on what grounds is it more shameful to be amongst the defenders rather than the aggressors?). Such a concept of postcolonialism has been utilized for nearly two decades by now within literary theory in the analysis of diverse cultures, some with histories similar to that of Wales, with Ireland's case providing, perhaps, the most obvious parallel.

Informed as it is by this understanding of the term, Mark Woods's response to *Postcolonial Wales* differs markedly from that of Professor Smith, and is generally favourable. His main critique, however, is that the book adds nothing new to postcolonial theory; that it should do so was never its editors' intention. If it had been, the book's scope would have been limited to the cultural sphere, in which the theory has been most extensively developed, and more theoretically focused essays would have been commissioned. Rather, the book's aim was to collect together essays by a multi-disciplinary array of contributors exploring the pertinence to the Welsh situation of the concept of postcoloniality as currently understood within their particular discipline and research field. That such diversity should lead to many differing approaches to both postcoloniality and Wales was to be expected, and was indeed welcomed. It is curious that Dai Smith condemns as too inconclusive the multiplicity of opinion expressed in *Postcolonial Wales*, yet closes his review with a plea for 'a plural Welsh existence', for indicating the plurality of existences in contemporary Wales is what the book as a whole aims to do. Accepting difference without imposing any hierarchical structure upon it, understanding it not as a quality belonging to any 'other' but as part and parcel of the hybrid nation and hybrid self – that is the 'real, unashamed thing' at the 'original core' of postcolonial theory.

When Dai Smith refers to the importance of recognizing the reality of a plural Welsh existence he is in fact quoting from *Postcolonial Wales* itself, from the one essay in the volume which he unreservedly praises, Glenn Jordan's 'Post-colonialist reflections on immigrants and minorities in Wales' with its final questions, 'Can we reimagine Wales as consisting of a plurality of experiences, cultures and identities? Can we rethink Welshness as heterogeneous, as inclusive of difference?' Mark Woods rightly praises this essay too, and he also praises other chapters in the book – for example, Paul Chaney's chapter on post-colonialism as it relates to Welsh women's lack of political representation under the old pre-devolution regime and the startlingly sweeping change for the better which the Assembly has wrought, and Dylan Phillips's positive account of the fortunes of the Welsh language and its speakers under devolution. These experiences too are part of the realities of post-1997 Wales, as it looks with renewed hope towards the future, and they are analysed, for the most part, from hopeful perspectives in *Postcolonial Wales*. This is not cultural despair but a potentially more all-inclusive and open-ended understanding of Wales and Welshness, one which, to be sure, was not invented as a theory in Wales, but then neither were Marxism or Calvinism Welsh inventions.

In *The Wretched of the Earth* (2005), Frantz Fanon describes newly independent, postcolonial nations as in danger of breaking apart and following tribal rather than national loyalties because their sense of their own history has been disfigured by the colonizing process, leaving national consciousness an empty shell without the capacity to draw the tribes into relation with one another and acceptance of their differences. *Postcolonial Wales* was constructed as a deliberate, if modest enough, attempt to bring the Welsh 'tribes' into discussion with one another, sharing a platform as they did during those months of the 1997 devolution campaign. That it contains internal disagreement, and that it has aroused strongly differing responses, such as the two published here, is but to be expected.

NOTES

1 *New Welsh Review*, 2005
2 With every contributor to *Postcolonial Wales*, as mentioned above with Knight, the articles by each contributor in *Postcolonial Wales* have added-value, in that they offer an introduction of more expanded writing on the topics by the writer in each field of specialty. This is true with contributor Steve Blandford with his collection *Wales on Screen*, and with David M. Barlow, Philip Mitchell and Tom O'Malley's recent *The Media in Wales: Voices of a Small Nation.*
3 For a thorough discussion of nation, nationalism, etc., I recommend *Theorizing Nationalism* by Grahame Day and Andrew Thompson (2004). For a discussion of neo-nationalism and neo-federalism in Europe, I recommend *The Necessary Nation* by Gregory Jusdanis (2001).
4 With apologies to Gwyn A. Williams, *When was Wales?* (1982), p. 200.
5 Kirsti Bohata (2005) ' "Psycho-colonialism" revisited', *New Welsh Review*, 69.
6 Daniel Williams, 'Back to a national future?', *Planet: The Welsh Internationalist*, (2006).
7 Routledge, 2nd edn 2005.

REFERENCES

Aaron, J. and Williams, C. (2005). *Postcolonial Wales*, Cardiff: University of Wales Press.
Adamson, David L. (1991). *Class, Ideology and the Nation: A Theory of Welsh Nationalism*, Cardiff: University of Wales Press.
Adamson, David L. (1996). *Living on the Edge: Poverty and Deprivation in Wales*, Llandysul: Gomer.
Ashcroft, B., Griffiths, G. and Helen Tiffin (2000). *Post-colonial Studies: the Key Concepts*, London and New York: Routledge.
Barlow, D. M., Mitchell, P. and O'Malley, T. (2005). *The Media in Wales: Voices of a Small Nation*, Cardiff: University of Wales Press.
Blandford, S. (2000). *Wales on Screen*, Bridgend: Poetry Wales Press Ltd.
Bohata, K. (2004). *Postcolonialism Revisited*, Cardiff: University of Wales Press.
Bohata, K. (2005) ' "Psycho-colonialism" revisited', *New Welsh Review*, 69, 52–9.
Campbell, J. (1972). *Myths to Live By*, New York: Penguin Compass.
Connell, L. (2004). 'Scottish nationalism and the colonial vision of Scotland',

Interventions, 6, 17–21.

Day, G. and Thompson, A. (2004). *Theorizing Nationalism*, Hampshire and New York: Palgrave Macmillan.

Fanon, F. (2005). *The Wretched of the Earth*, London: Grove Press.

Gittings, C. E. (1996). *Imperialism and Gender: Constructions of Masculinity*, New Lambton, New South Wales: Dangaroo Press.

Hechter, M. (1975). *Internal Colonialism: The Celtic Fringe in British National Development, 1536–1966*, London: Routledge and Kegan Paul

Humphreys, E. (2000). *The Taliesin Tradition*, Bridgend: Seren.

Jones, J. B. and Balsom, D. (2000). *The Road to the National Assembly for Wales*, Cardiff: University of Wales Press.

Jones, R. W. (2004). 'Barn ar Gymru', *Barn*, 498/9, p. 10.

Jusdanis, G. (2001). *The Necessary Nation*, Princeton and Oxford: Princeton University Press.

Knight, S. (2004). *One Hundred Years of Fiction: Writing Wales in English*, Cardiff: University of Wales Press.

Loomba, A. (1998 (2nd edn, 2005)). *Colonialism/Postcolonialism*, London and New York: Routledge.

McDonough, T. (ed.) (2004). *Was Ireland a Colony?*, Dublin: Irish Academic Press.

McLeod, J. (2000). *Beginning Postcolonialism*, Manchester and New York: Manchester University Press.

Morgan, K. O. (1981). *Rebirth of a Nation: A History of Modern Wales*, Oxford: Oxford University Press.

Williams, C. (1996) *Democratic Rhondda: Politics and Society, 1885–1951*, Cardiff: University of Wales Press.

Williams, D. (2006) 'Back to a national future?', *Planet: The Welsh Internationalist*, pp. 64–72.

Williams, G. A. (1982). *When was Wales? The Welsh and their History*, London: Croom Helm.

17. BOOK REVIEWS

Paul Chambers, *Religion, Secularization and Social Change in Wales*, Cardiff: University of Wales Press, 2005, 246pp. £16.99 (pb). ISBN 0–7083–1884–3.

In the early 1970s, when the general decline of Christianity in the UK was becoming obvious, it was possible to identify one major form of resistance. The national peripheries of Northern Ireland, Scotland and Wales stood out as being more religious than the English core and this was not just because the secularizing influences of the metropolitan core were slow to reach the edges, though that was indeed the case. There was also an element of self-conscious 'cultural defence'. In contrasting themselves with the (especially southern) English, many people of the minority nations took pride in being better Christians. That difference has now gone.

Paul Chambers has produced an excellent study of the decline of religion in Swansea. On the model of the classic community studies that were the adornment of British sociology and anthropology in the 1950s and 1960s but have sadly since gone out of fashion, Chambers sets his detailed accounts of congregations in Swansea against a rich description of changes to the economy and society of the city and surrounding area. He is particularly fortunate to have Rosser and Harris's 1965 Swansea study as a baseline and inspiration.

Weaknesses first: although a chapter is devoted to the relative merits of competing explanations of secularization and is well written, Chambers has little to add to the arguments. And there is something missing from the conclusion. He rightly argues that you cannot understand the fate of congregations unless you look at their links with their environment but his discussion of circumstances barely mentions belief. Participation in churches is, in the end, a function of the plausibility of the Christian faith: what we need to explain is why social structural change undermines the ideological core of religion. Chambers is right to stress the importance of geographical mobility as the proximate cause of church decline. Changes in the economy (in particular the decline of particular industries and upward social mobility) cause people to move. This breaks their ties to their former local congregation. That church declines and closes. But in societies with a strong religious culture, people form new congregations and open new churches. In Belfast, the churches in declining inner city areas have closed but new ones are being built on the fringes and the new commuter suburbs. Identifying the local causes of decline does not complete the story: we need to explain why there is so little desire to create new congregations and that requires the general secularization approach which Chambers somewhat side-steps.

But as with all good community studies the strengths outweigh the weaknesses and these rich accounts provide ample material with which others can theorize. Typical of the text is the interesting cautionary tale of one Anglican parish. Two evangelicals in succession managed to hasten the decline. They neglected the wider social functions of the church (for example, allowing church halls that were widely used by non-church people to decay) and replaced the predictability of the conventional Prayer Book service with evangelical spontaneity and services that over-ran so that Sunday roasts were spoiled. They attracted large audience for special services but failed to turn these itinerant listeners into congregants and killed off the traditional congregation. The small recovery of membership after the disappearance of the enthusiasts suggests a viable strategy for a ritualistic church: keep up the familiar rituals; offer religious offices such as baptism, weddings and funerals to local people irrespective of their personal piety; visit the elderly; and provide premises and leadership for secular good works (such as a youth club).

In his conclusion Chambers divides congregations into 'communal' and 'associational' types. The former see themselves as having a mission to the surrounding people; the latter are gatherings of the saved members. He makes interesting points about differences in the circumstances of these two types: for example, communal churches such as the parishes of the Episcopalian Church of Wales or the Roman Catholic Church are less reliant on their own congregants because they are part of large bodies that believe in cross-subsidy. But there is a major theological difference between the communal and associational types of Christian body that underpins their structural differences. The Episcopalian and the Catholic Churches are better able to manage decline because they have a theory of religious activity (offices are pleasing to God even if performed by one professional with no congregation) that makes it sensible to plod on even when very few believe. The problem for the dissenting denominations and sects is that they need the believing congregation. If, as Protestants do, you strip your religion of all magic and ritual and reduce it to correct doctrine and ethical behaviour, then without a body of committed believers you have nothing. With few congregants a Catholic church is still a place of worship; without an audience to sing the great hymns and hear the preaching of the Word of God, the Baptist and Methodist churches are just empty halls.

Steve Bruce
University of Aberdeen

Diarmuid Ó'Neill (ed.), *Rebuilding the Celtic Languages: Reversing Language Shift in the Celtic Countries*, **Talybont:** Y Lolfa, 2005, 460pp. £19.95. ISBN 0–86243–723–7.

This book is more reminiscent of philology than the sociology of language. It seeks to apply Fishman's model for 'reversing language shift' to the six Celtic languages in different locations. I must admit that before taking on the task of reviewing the book I had not read Fishman's work on this topic which consists of an attempt to construct eight different stages for what he calls 'language revitalisation'. The reader should be aware that knowledge of his work is assumed. It is couched in Fishman's customary structural functionalist approach, involving an understanding of social change as a series of stages rather than a process, hence the emphasis on shift and change. He seeks to construct different contexts for language production and reproduction, resulting in a typology based on the relevance of the different social institutions and the use of language for the various language groups he studies. From this, Fishman claims to be able to define what needs to happen in order to reverse the ongoing process of socio-cultural change. As a typology it is descriptive rather than analytical.

The essays are on the Brythonic languages and the Gaelic languages. Half of the contents are written by the editor, and almost a further 20 per cent in a very long, previously published essay on Welsh by Colin Williams. The other four authors account for the remaining 30 per cent. Apart from the autochthonous language groups, the Welsh in Patagonia and the Scottish-Gaelic in Nova Scotia are included. All these essays consist of a very long historical account, followed by an exploration of how the contemporary context fits with Fishman's typology. Treating the entire territory where the language is spoken, and the social groups that use the language, as uniform, ignores the dynamics of change and the territorial and social group variation. This is what makes language planning difficult if not nigh on impossible.

Why choose the Celtic languages for comparison? This categorization derives from the philological tradition, having little to do with the sociology of language which Fishman has been so important in promoting. It carries considerable ideological baggage deriving from the early nineteenth century. A pronounced Eurocentrism led to the construction of a kinship of languages, and implicitly of speakers, who constituted the new citizenry of Europe. It welded the new European states into a kinship collective constructed out of a linguistic affinity that related to the construction and standardization of 'languages'. Within this discourse the Celtic languages were an expression of an emerging nationalism which completed the linguistic, if not the political, map of Europe. That which is compared would appear to have little in common beyond the syntactic and the 'lexical', while the diverse range of demographic and socio-political contexts is prohibitive. A linguistic construct, it is hardly appropriate for a sociological analysis. Whoever dreamt up the theme of the volume is no social scientist.

Two institutions are given priority in Fishman's model – the family and the community. Considerable mileage is made of this in the respective essays. Community has tended to be conceptualized by reference to overlapping institutions, involving the same members, living within a restricted space. For these social actors, community consisted of institutionalized social behaviour structured by location and institutions. Language use was a feature of this institutionalization[1]. This kind of community is now rare in the different societies considered here, and what is referred to as community tends to resemble a series of social networks that focus upon a much larger spatial radius, and involving a more diverse range of members. In this sense perhaps Fishman's reference to neighbourhoods rather than communities is closer to the mark. The institutionalization of language use in social networks tends to be quite different from that in communities. Perhaps it is not surprising that there is a constant interchange of the concepts of network and community in these essays. It is characteristic of the lack of rigour.

The current concern in Wales is with how to transform competence into use as institutionalized behaviour. Research indicates that once language density falls below 80–90 per cent the probability of social networks consisting of sufficient number of Welsh speakers to allow interaction to be predominantly through the medium of Welsh is unlikely. Furthermore, when the language density falls to between 60 and 80 per cent there is a tendency for interaction to involve distinctive language groups, and when it falls to less than 50 per cent English becomes almost the exclusive language used among young Welsh people. Failing to grasp the importance of language use perhaps accounts for some strange omissions among the authors. The chapter on Welsh ignores the only large scale survey of Welsh language use undertaken as part of the Euromosaic project, perhaps because this source also includes a critique of the neo-liberal political philosophy of the Welsh Language Board. Similarly, the work on Irish ignores the work of O'Riagain and Tovey, among the most vocal and theoretically sophisticated work on the failures of the Irish language planning initiative.

There is a claim that it is possible to create new communities. This would appear to be difficult, if not impossible. Individuals and social groups would have to forgo established social practices as institutionalized behaviour, in favour of new behaviour which would become institutionalized through imposition. It would be much more profitable to focus on striving to change the language use of established communities.

There is a strong faith that language revitalization is possible and this is exemplified by the positive and, at times, romantic conception of the respective language groups, and their presentation as victims of change rather than as voluntary accomplices. There is a tendency to emphasize every small achievement as seminal, and to ignore the fact that what they are trying to do is to reverse social processes which the population has voluntarily embraced. That is, they begin from the assumption that their own objective is somehow 'superior' to that of the people whom they are studying. This colours how they read the historical record, incorporating a false consciousness that is not theorized. In this respect the essays are a long way removed from the sociology of language, and involve very little sociological analysis. An exception is the essay by Colin Williams, but even here the analysis is largely asociological on account of the centrality of neo-liberalism as the defining discourse in his essay.

Overall, faith is placed in nationalism and activists, as if language becomes the exclusive prerogative of specific political positions. I would argue that this is the worst possible scenario for success.

Glyn Williams
Facultat de Ciencias de la Communicacio
Universidad Ramon Llull
Barcelona

NOTE

[1]   The various authors irritatingly persist in referring to this notion as 'normalization', a slogan rather than a concept. Whereas most sociologists refer to institutionalization as a tacit process wherein the individual does not reflect on his/her behaviour, those involved in language planning treat it as a rational process involving the conscious selection of one language rather than another.

CONTEMPORARY WALES
GUIDELINES FOR CONTRIBUTORS
OF ARTICLES

General policy:
Contemporary Wales is an annual review of economic and social developments and trends in Wales. It provides an authoritative analysis drawing upon the most up-to-date research, and represents the only comprehensive source of analysis across the range of economic and social research about Wales. It is a Board of Celtic Studies journal published once a year, and contains articles selected for their quality and significance to contemporary society in Wales. Submissions are refereed and are accepted for publication on the assumption that they have not been previously published and are not currently being submitted to any other journal. The normal maximum length for articles is about 5,000 words. An abstract of up to 200 words is required.

Copyright:
Copyright in the articles in printed and electronic forms will be retained by the University of Wales, but the right to reproduce their own articles by photocopying is granted to the contributors provided that the copies are not offered for sale. Contributors should obtain the necessary permission to use material already protected by copyright.

Preparation of typescripts:
If possible, please e-mail papers as Word attachments to one of the editors:
Paul Chaney (*chaneyp@cardiff.ac.uk*)
Elin Royles (*ear@aber.ac.uk*)
Andrew Thompson (*athompso@glam.ac.uk*)

If e-mail is not possible, please post 3 copies on single-sided A4 to:

either Paul Chaney
Cardiff School of Social Sciences
The Glamorgan Building
King Edward VII Avenue
Cardiff
CF10 3WT

or Elin Royles
Department of International Politics
University of Wales
Aberystwyth
Ceredigion
SY23 3DA

or Andrew Thompson
School of Humanities and Social Sciences
University of Glamorgan
Pontypridd
CF37 1DL

The editors can provide further guidance as to the form and style in which contributions should be submitted, but the following gives a brief guide for potential contributors. Additional general information is available on the UWP website, *www.wales.ac.uk/press* under the heading 'Guidelines for presentation of texts for publication'.

Articles submitted should be typed using double spacing with wide margins, unjustified on the right. Pages should be numbered throughout consecutively.

Preparation of typescripts on disk:
Once a paper has been accepted for publication, it should be sent to the editor in disk form, provided that a hard copy/printout of the full up-to-date text has also been submitted. Authors should retain a back-up copy of both disk and printout of their papers. PC disks using Word are preferred, but other softwares may be acceptable.

Notes and references

Notes and references should be supplied at the end of the article, also in double spacing. Notes should be numbered consecutively. References should be in alphabetical order of author (see below for style).

Tables, maps and diagrams

These will eventually appear within the printed page but should be provided on separate pages in the typescript and their position indicated by a marginal note in the text. Tables and figures should be provided in separate Excel/Tiff files, not embedded in Word. Some other kinds of software may be acceptable – please contact UWP for further information. All figures, diagrams, maps, charts, etc. must be saved in **black only**, not full colour, and should be saved at 1200 pixels per inch.

Diagrams and maps may be submitted in best possible condition on paper if the contributor is unable to supply a disk version. References in the text to illustrative material should take the form 'Table 1' etc. for tables and 'Figure 1' etc. for other illustrations including maps, not 'in the following diagram' since there is no guarantee that pagination will allow this precise positioning. The tables and figures will eventually be labelled 'Table 1.1', 'Figure 2.1', etc. according to the number of the chapter in which they appear.

Style of text:

Quotations within running text should be in single quote marks (double for quotes within quotes). Quotations of more than forty-five words should be indented without quotation marks and with a line space before and after.

Underline or type in italic any words which are to appear in italic. In English-language articles, single words or short phrases in any language other than English should be in italic, but longer quotations in another language should be in roman within single quotation marks.

Dates should be expressed as 1 January 1999; the 1990s; the twentieth century (but 'a twentieth-century record'); 1988–9; 1914–18 (not 1914–8). Numbers up to ninety-nine should be spelt out in full except in a list of statistics or in percentages (e.g. 25 per cent).

Use -ize endings when given as an alternative to -ise, for example, realize, privatize, organize; but note analyse, franchise, advertise.

Capitalization should be kept to a minimum in the text; for titles, initial capitals should be used only when attached to a personal name (thus 'President Clinton', but 'the president of the United States').

Journal style is that 'south' in 'south Wales' should take lower case (also 'north', 'east', 'west' Wales/England, etc.), since this is not a specific political, administrative or geographical region. South America or South Africa would take upper case since the term refers to the name of a continent or political entity respectively. When referring to a specific area for economic assessment, e.g. the South West of England, upper case may be used for clarity.

References
References in the text should be given in the Harvard system in the following format: (Dower, 1977), (Welsh Office, 1986), (White and Higgs, 1997), (Gripaios et al., 1995a).

The form of references listed under the heading 'References' at the end of the text should be as follows:

Ambrose, P. (1974). *The Quiet Revolution*, London: Chatto & Windus.
Buller, H. and Hoggart, K. (1994b). 'The social integration of British home owners into French rural communities', *Journal of Rural Studies*, 10, 2, 197–210.
Dower, M. (1977). 'Planning aspects of second homes', in J. T. Coppock (ed.), *Second Homes: Curse or Blessing?*, Oxford: Pergamon Press, pp. 17–45.

Note the use of lower case for all initial letters except the first in an article or unpublished thesis title, and capitals for initial letters of all significant words in book and journal titles.

Publications by the same author in the same year should be differentiated by means of a, b, or c, etc. after the year of publication, both in the text reference and in the list of references.

Proofs and complimentary copies:
Checking of proofs will be done by editors, with contributors expected to reply promptly to queries. Upon publication, contributors will receive one complimentary copy of the issue of the journal in which their article appears.